FAMILY

OF

STRANGERS

Molly Cone / Howard Droker / Jacqueline Williams

Washington State Jewish Historical Society, Seattle

in association with University of Washington Press, Seattle & London

FAMILY

OF

STRANGERS

Building a Jewish Community

in Washington State

Library of Congress Cataloging-in-Publication Data

Cone, Molly.

Family of strangers : building a Jewish community in Washington State /

Molly Cone, Howard Droker, and Jacqueline Williams.

    p. cm.

    Includes index.

    ISBN 0-295-98297-7

    1. Jews—Washington (State)History. 2. Immigrants—Washington (State)—History. 3. Washington (State)—Ethnic relations. I. Droker, Howard. II. Williams, Jacqueline. III. Title.

F900.J5 C66 2003

979.7'004924—DC21   2002038852

The paper used in this publication is acid-free and recycled from 10 percent post-consumer and at least 50 percent pre-consumer waste. It meets the minimum requirements of American National Standard for Information Sciences—Permanence of Paper for Printed Library Materials, ANSI z39.48-1984.

Abbreviations used in illustration credits:

MSCUA/UWL: Manuscripts, Special Collections, University Archives Division, University of Washington Libraries

WSJHS: Washington State Jewish Historical Society

MAGAZINE

SEATTLE'S JEWISH COMMUNITY

It took root and grew in a raw Northwest

Drawing of Seattle's early Jewish community. Courtesy of Irwin Caplan.

CONTENTS

Preface

M ORE THAN TWO DECADES AGO, AN OLD WOMAN SAT down to reflect on the more than eight decades of her life that stretched from the villages of Eastern Europe to the wooded frontier of western Washington. Esther Friedman remembered describing to a neighbor how her family got to America, and, eventually, Seattle. The old man who heard her was entranced. "Someone," he said, "should take down your life. It would make a terrific book."

Friedman, like so many pioneers and early settlers, never did put her stories down on paper. The closest she ever came to doing that was sitting down in front of a tape recorder for several hours to reminisce about her life and family for her grandchildren. For two hours she spun stories about fleeing Europe with her family, of being frightened by exploding firecrackers on her first Fourth of July in America, and of life on Puget Sound in the early days of the twentieth century.

The history of the Jewish community of Washington State is filled with the faint memories of hundreds of people who came from countless shtetls, villages, towns, and cities of Eastern and Central Europe and the Mediterranean Basin. These immigrants came in a small trickle during the middle of the nineteenth century and then in larger numbers during the great waves of immigration to the United States during the open-door era that stretched to 1924. It is a history later repeated by European Jews fleeing in the wake of the Holocaust and from a life of persecution in the Soviet Union, as well as by American Jews who were part of the great westward migration in the post–World War II era.

The narrative that follows is by no means all-inclusive. It would be impossible to envelop all who in some way helped create, build, and nurture Washington State's Jewish community. It also would be impossible to present the full histories of the congregations and organizations throughout the state. We worked, for the most part, with documents and interviews collected by the Washington State Jewish Historical Society in Seattle and by Jewish communities in Spokane, Tacoma, Bellingham, and other cities. The collections are housed in the Manuscripts, Special Collections, University Archives Division (MSCUA) of the University of Washington Libraries and in the Eastern Washington State Historical Society in Spokane. They include transcribed interviews; tapes; organizational, congregational, and personal papers; reports and minutes; clippings; scrapbooks; family memoirs; and thesis manuscripts. We also delved into local historical writings and items of Jewish interest in the newspapers of Seattle, Spokane, Tacoma, and Bellingham, and in issues of *The Jewish Voice* and *The Jewish Transcript*. Consultations with individuals in Jewish communities throughout the state added many important facts.

Some of the interview material is anecdotal, blurred by the passage of time. In putting the story together, we took these biases into account. We retained the original language in quotations, and used both maiden and married names of women whenever available. Although the book is written for a general audience, we hope its documented information will be useful to scholars.

This story presents a spectrum of representative individuals, some who were among the earliest pioneers, some who were illustrative of their group (or were not), some who were typical or characteristic of their time, and others who had special effects on the religious, economic, or cultural growth of our state. We are aware of major gaps in our history, gaps that future historians will fill. For instance, how people made their livings is not covered after the pioneer generation. We know that the general financial success of the community made possible much of what we write about. The large topic of the Jewish Federation of Greater Seattle is also left for future historians to research and interpret.

A diverse group of immigrants formed the nucleus of what we know today as Washington Jewry and the institutions they created. We have tried to present a concise but faithful picture of their first 125 years. Our narrative is a history, not of individual Jews, but of Jewish life in our state—when it began and how it grew. It is the kind of marvelous story that Esther Friedman and other Jewish pioneers, new and old, have left for us to tell.

Acknowledgments

WHEN THE WASHINGTON STATE JEWISH HISTORICAL Society invited us to write the history of the Jewish people in Washington State, we responded with enthusiasm. Even though we saw the work to be done as prodigious, the absence of such a history in our libraries was an impelling factor in our decision to proceed.

The wealth of resources of the Jewish Archives at the University of Washington Libraries, a joint project with the Washington State Jewish Historical Society, forms the foundation of this history. In the 1960s, the university archivist, Richard Berner, invited volunteers from the Jewish community, along with other ethnic groups, to preserve documents of their congregational and organizational life, to conduct interviews of pioneers, and to deposit that material in the library's collection. In 1968, Elsa Levinson, president of the Women's Division of the Jewish Federation, created an Archive Committee as part of the Women's Division to begin documenting the history of the Jewish community in Washington State. In 1970, the Jewish Archives project, under the direction of Jeanette Schrieber, became part of the Manuscripts, Special Collections, University Archives of the University of Washington Libraries. Karyl Winn, curator of manuscripts since 1970, has played a crucial role in the development of the project for over three decades, working with volunteers and providing a secure and professionally staffed home for the Jewish Archives. We are grateful to members of her staff who have catalogued the material and members of the Special Collections staff under Carla Rickerson who have shown us so many courtesies.

The Washington State Jewish Historical Society grew out of the Jewish Archives project in 1980 at the urging of Professor Joseph Cohen, who had long been committed to the National Jewish Historical Society. Howard Droker became the Society's first archivist, thanks to a grant from the National Endowment for the Humanities. We are indebted to all of the volunteers from the Washington State Jewish Historical Society who conducted interviews and collected papers and photographs over the past thirty years. Olga Butler, long-time chairperson of the Archive Committee, Meta Buttnick, Lily DeJaen, Rabbi Edward Ellenbogen, Ann Nieder, Dr. Eric Offenbacher, Mildred Rosenbaum, Adina Russack, Jeanette Schrieber, and Reba Twersky were among those who gave the project continuity; others followed.

We owe a special thanks to Meta Buttnick, Washington State Jewish Historical Society historian, who for so many years has diligently collected and written the history of Washington State's Jewish people and places; Lorraine Sidell, for her carefully researched articles written for the Washington State Jewish Historical Society Newsletter; Julia Niebuhr Eulenberg, whose Ph.D. dissertation on Jewish enterprise in the Northwest from 1853 to 1909 has been an invaluable resource; Tim Baker, who has tracked down every date and person connected with Bellingham Jewry; Deborah Freedman, whose ongoing research and writings have helped us document the lives of Jewish pioneers in Tacoma; and Nathan Grossman, who spearheaded the collecting of Spokane's Jewish historical records preserved by the Eastern Washington State Historical Society, now housed at Cheney Cowles Museum. We acknowledge with appreciation the help of Susan Levine and Mona Green, who were the Washington State Jewish Historical Society archive coordinators at the University of Washington Libraries while the work of this book was in progress. The beginning of our archival research was further facilitated by Ann Nieder and Isabelle Stusser, Jewish Historical Society volunteers.

We are indebted to Euguen Huppin (Spokane), Alan Barer (Walla Walla), Josephine Kleiner Heiman (Tacoma), Rhoda Sussman Lewis (Richland), Patricia Spaeth (Port Townsend), and the many Seattle and Tacoma residents who answered our questions and added bits and pieces to our research. They have been generous with their time and knowledge in tracking down obscure references and finding the people who contributed to Washington State's Jewish history.

The authors thank Meta Buttnick, Albert and Toby Franco, Albert Maimon, Erika Michael, and Jeanette Schrieber for their readings of the first draft of the manuscript and for their comments and suggestions.

Our appreciation also goes to Erika Michael, Washington State Jewish Historical Society advisor to this project, whose desire to see the significance of the state's Jewish presence recorded inspired this book. We are grateful as well to Professor Joan Ullman, a University of Washington specialist in the history of the Jews of Spain, for her early interest and advice; and to Arny Robbins, who helped us navigate the final course of our work. We are also indebted to University of Washington Press Associate Director and Editor-in-Chief Naomi B. Pascal for her continued support and assistance in the development of this book, and to Mary Ribesky, for her fine copyediting of the manuscript.

We add a special note of thanks to spouses Gerald Cone, Barbara Droker, and Walter Williams for their support, understanding, patience, and innumerable instances of help throughout our more than four years of research and writing.

The authors join with the Washington State Jewish Historical Society in thanking the Alfred and Tillie Shemanski Charitable Trust, Ernest and Erika Michael Fund, Jewish Federation of Greater Seattle, King County Landmarks and Heritage Commission,† Marsha and Jay Glazer Foundation, Maurice Amado Foundation, and the Samuel and Althea Stroum Foundation/JF (in memory of Samuel Stroum) for funding given to this endeavor. We thank all the individuals who contributed support and encouragement to this project. We are deeply grateful.

Molly Cone, Howard Droker, and Jacqueline Williams
Seattle, Washington, 2003

†

FAMILY
OF
STRANGERS

Central European Pioneers

LONG BEFORE WASHINGTON BECAME A STATE, JEWISH settlers lived in Olympia, Steilacoom, Tacoma, Port Townsend, Walla Walla, Seattle, Ellensburg, and Spokane. In the mid-1800s, when the first Jews began arriving in the far northwest corner of the United States, Jewish communities already existed in San Francisco, Portland, and Victoria, British Columbia, as well as in larger cities across the country. By 1889, when Washington Territory became the forty-second state, Jewish businesses had been contributing to the vitality of its economy and Jewish American citizens to its growth for four decades.

The history of Jewish Americans goes back to September 1654, when New York was still the Dutch colony of New Amsterdam. The first Jews in America were a group of twenty-three families, refugees from Dutch Brazil, driven out by the Portuguese Inquisition. When the Declaration of Independence was signed in 1776, as many as two thousand Jews lived in the thirteen colonies, and within a few years, synagogues had been established in New York, Newport, Savannah, Philadelphia, and Charleston. By 1830, about six thousand Jews lived in the United States. In 1880 their numbers had risen to 250,000, some of whom had spread westward to California, and from there to the territories of Oregon and Washington. By 1920, the number of Jewish Americans reached 4 million, the largest Jewish population in the world—although only a tiny proportion of the American population.[1]

While Jews in Washington numbered only a fraction of one percent of the area's population, their impact on the commercial and civic life of the territory and early years of the state was significant.[2] Early Jewish Washington history includes a territorial governor in Olympia; a graduating student from the University of Washington's first law school class; state legislators in Tacoma and Spokane;

3

and mayors of Port Townsend, Olympia, Ellensburg, and Seattle.[3] Two Seattle schools, Bailey Gatzert Elementary and Nathan Eckstein Middle School (originally Nathan Eckstein Junior High School), were named for pioneer Jews.

Jewish life in the state of Washington began with a single adventurer, a twenty-four-year-old Latvian native, Adolph Friedman, believed to be the first Jew to settle in the new territory.[4] He could be counted among the handful of explorers, fur traders, missionaries, and adventurers who made their way to the region before 1850. After Friedman, three distinct waves of Jewish immigration came to the Northwest. The first began in the 1850s, bringing German-speaking Jews from Central Europe. The second, from 1880 to 1924, were Yiddish-speaking Jews from Eastern Europe. The third, starting in 1902, brought Sephardic Jews from Turkey and Rhodes speaking Judeo-Spanish (Ladino). By 1920, just over ten thousand Jews made up only seven-tenths of one percent of the state's total population.[5]

In a general description, they might have been called "a community of Jews," but, in fact, they were not a community at all. Although bound together by their religion, Washington's Jews were separated by the diversity of their origins, customs, and languages. What made this region's Jews different from other Jewish populations was not only that they were dispersed over a wide domain at the remote end of America or that they were far from established Jewish communities, but also that they included the largest group of Sephardim (Judeo-Spanish-speaking Jews) outside of New York.[6]

These three immigrant Jewish groups shared with each other the need to create a livelihood and the problem of maintaining their separate Jewish identities while at the same time becoming Americans. In an area where all were newcomers, it was easy for some Jewish settlers in the small, sparsely settled towns of Washington to simply meld into the general society, and some did. Others formed organizations and congregations that connected them to Jewish life as towns grew—adapting in varying degrees to American life. Still others solved the problem by eventually moving their growing families and businesses into the larger Jewish populations of Seattle or Spokane.

From its earliest beginnings, Jewish life in Washington State was varied and unpredictable. Although in many ways it mirrored Jewish life in cities and towns throughout the country, in certain ways Washington Jewry was unique.

Early Jews in Olympia

Among the first of the German-speaking Jews arriving in Washington Territory, Louis Bettman settled in Olympia in 1853. Bettman's general merchandise store, which he later ran with his brothers Mose and Sig, was the third business established in the tiny town lying on the shores of Puget Sound.[7] In spite of its small size, Olympia was nevertheless the only metropolis in the area. With a population of 250 in 1852, Olympia consisted of ninety "houses, sheds, and shanties," and boasted a hotel and its own newspaper. Historian Murray Morgan has suggested that the newspaper and the hotel resulted in Olympia being pegged as the territorial capital, even though the newspaper could only be described as "thin" and the hotel as "rudimentary."[8]

One year later, Bettman & Brothers, offering dry goods, groceries, and clothing, both retail and wholesale, was one of three Jewish-owned stores at Second and Main. (Bettman soon opened a branch in Seattle.) Goldman and Rosenblatt, which became the People's Emporium, touted its fancy goods—"ladies' embroideries and dress trimmings imported straight from New York."[9] The third store, M. Louisson and Co., advertised goods specially selected by its San Francisco partner, including an 1856 shipment of violins.[10]

The Olympia entrepreneurs were typical of the Jews in early territorial times who settled first in California or other U.S. locations, then came to the Pacific Northwest for the opportunities offered by an undeveloped frontier. They were among the many Central Europeans arriving in the United States in the wave of immigration from 1830 to 1860, which brought approximately 144,000 German Jews as part of an emigration of millions of ethnic Germans, as well as Bohemians, Hungarians, and Austrians.[11] Although all came to America seeking economic betterment, German Jews harbored additional incentives. The civic and economic freedom that had been granted to Jews as Napoleon's armies conquered Europe was brief. Napoleon's final defeat in 1815 restored the old order, and governmental policy toward Jews became even harsher. Restrictions were placed on the number of Jewish families in an area, and limits were put on the number of marriages in a family (only the eldest son could acquire the proper papers to marry and settle in the community). As reported in a German Jewish newspaper in 1839, "The Jewish emigration appears to be less due to greed from gain than to consciousness of being unable in any other way to achieve independence or to found a family."[12] Escaping the political turmoil and worsening economic conditions in post-Napoleonic Europe, young German Jews came to a rapidly expanding America which had opened its doors to needed populations.[13]

Unlike many other pioneers, few of the earlier-arriving Jews came to farm or mine. Rather, these adventurers were urban pioneers, part of what one historian called "the central story of the nineteenth century West," that of an expanding economy linking cities to the small towns of the countryside.[14] Jewish entrepre-

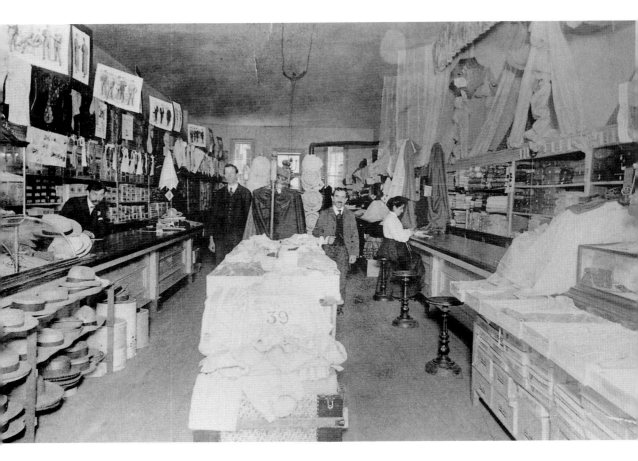

Jewish pioneers Gustave Rosenthal and his wife, Bertha, were among Olympia's early merchants. Pictured here is their store in Olympia in 1902; the Rosenthals are on the right. MSCUA/UWL, *neg.* 2096.

neurs played a large role in connecting the vast rural areas of Washington Territory to its growing towns as well as to San Francisco, the Midwest, and the world beyond.

They arrived in the newly formed Washington Territory in small numbers, some with family financial ties that enabled them to innovate, take business risks, and thus profit from the growth of the Territory. In the territorial years, most who came to the Northwest were unmarried and without families. These early settlers began as small merchants, and married and started families later. Of the married men, many left their families in California, on the East Coast, or in Europe, and sent for them after they were settled.

Generally, the objective of the German Jewish immigrant to America "was to become an American while remaining a Jew."[15] Influenced by the new liberal

My father in the early days had a pack train in Victoria. He used to go up to Hudson Bay [Company] and trade with the Indians. Victoria was a bigger city than Seattle at that time. He would bring rifles that the Indians would buy from him. They would take a shotgun, the height of it, and pile up furs until they got to the top. That's the way the Indians paid for the shotguns.

—Jennie Davis Schermer, MSCUA/UWL, 1534-001

consciousness that took root in their native lands during the late 1840s, these immigrants desired to be Jews in their homes and synagogues, and Americans everywhere else. To accomplish this in as short a time as possible, it is perhaps not surprising that many of Washington Territory's Jewish pioneer businessmen put their secular lives foremost and their religious lives on hold. As noted in 1897 about some of Spokane's early Jewish settlers, they "followed their business avocations and left religious matters to take care of itself [*sic*]."[16]

When Edward S. Salomon, a German Jew who served as Brevet Brigadier General during the Civil War, arrived in Olympia in 1870 to take up his position as ninth Territorial governor of Washington, a number of other German Jews had also migrated north to Olympia from San Francisco or Portland. Gustave and Bertha Rosenthal dealt in a variety of enterprises, including buying and shipping barrels of wool, coal, and oysters. The Kaufman Brothers sold clothing, and Isaac Harris operated one of the Territory's largest dry goods stores.[17] (Mitchell Harris, seven years old when he arrived with his parents, grew up in Olympia under the merchandising tutelage of his father. Elected mayor of Olympia in 1910, he held the office for three terms.)

Celebrating his arrival in the territory named for George Washington by adopting

Edward S. Salomon was thirty-two years old when he became Washington's territorial governor in 1870 and a leader in Olympia's small Jewish community. A Civil War hero and controversial governor, he submitted his resignation after serving two years. WSJHS, 19.

Speaking with a thick German accent and described as "short, plump and sport-
ing a magnificent spiked German moustache and goatee," Edward S. Salomon,
Olympia's ninth territorial governor, often incited hilarity. Disembarking from
the steamboat at Yesler's wharf, he climbed Mill Street (Yesler Way), made of
slabwood covered with partly rotted sawdust from Yesler's mill well-mixed with
horse droppings, and plunged into his speech to the waiting crowd. Suddenly he
paused, stooped down and gathered up a handful of the odorous street covering.
"Mein Gott!" he exclaimed, "Vot a splendid soil for cabbages!"
—Gordon Newell, *Rogues, Buffoons and Statesmen*

the first president's name, George Jacob Wolff arrived in Olympia in the 1880s to work for the Kaufman Brothers.[18] "I don't think there ever was a man who felt more genuinely patriotic than my father," said Sylvia Wolff Epstein, "or more thankful at being in the United States. He absolutely loved everything—the countryside, the flag, the government. It was a life he had never known, this kind of freedom."[19] Wolff, who had come from the Kaufmans' German hometown, found that very few of the forty other Jews living in Olympia shared his religious commitment or his strong sense of Jewish identity. Although they had established Washington's first Jewish cemetery, no attempt to establish a house of worship had been made or would be made for many years.[20]

Like other young immigrants who gained business training working for rela-
tives, in-laws, or friends before moving on, Wolff opened a branch of the Kaufman clothing business in the coastal lumber town of Aberdeen in 1897, and soon bought out his employers.[21]

Merchant Partners in Steilacoom and Tacoma

Many early Jewish businessmen in Washington Territory had received a commer-
cial education in German cities, and some had commercial experience on the frontiers of western Russia and Poland as well as in other parts of the United States. One of them was Isaac Pincus, son of a Polish timber merchant, who clerked in a store in Nashville, Tennessee, before moving on to San Francisco, Nevada City, British Columbia, and, finally, Washington Territory. He landed in Steilacoom on August 10, 1858, intending to go on to San Francisco. "Steilacoom was a great port in the early days. I have seen as many as five warships anchored in the harbor at one time," he said in an interview printed in the *Tacoma Daily Ledger* on the

The Pincus family at their hop farm in Ohop, Washington. Isaac Pincus, son of a Polish timber merchant, arrived in 1858 in Steilacoom, Washington Territory, then the busiest port in the area. Eventually he owned one of the largest hop businesses on the West Coast. Courtesy of Josephine Kleiner Heiman, Tacoma.

fiftieth anniversary of his arrival in the Northwest. "Cattle and sheep were driven there from the interior for shipment to Victoria . . . I thought Steilacoom was a pretty good place and I anchored there."[22]

Pincus opened a little store and married Seraphina Packscher, sister of his former Nevada partner, Adolph Packscher, who later joined Pincus in partnership in Steilacoom. "In time we had the biggest store on Puget Sound," said Pincus. Pincus and Packscher stocked their store with goods brought mainly from San Francisco, and with an additional partner, E. A. Light, they invested in a fleet of three vessels to transport their merchandise. Pincus, Packscher, and Light operated a sawmill, built a wharf, and successfully engaged in the coastal carrying trade before the partnership dissolved. Pincus entered prominently into county politics and served as county coroner. Later, he moved his family to the fast-growing town of Tacoma, joined Temple Beth Israel, helped form Tacoma's Chamber of Commerce, and became a member of Tacoma's City Council. Pincus lived a long and active life in Tacoma. Perhaps his biggest business venture was the growing of hops, and he was noted as "one of the greatest hop merchants in the world." He fathered seven children. The first four, born when Washington was still a territory, were probably the first Jewish children born in Pierce County.[23]

Port Townsend's Entrepreneurs

In the same year that Pincus set up shop in Steilacoom, David C. H. Rothschild, a Bavarian emigrant, settled in Port Townsend. He had worked in Kentucky and California, spent time in the East Indies, and sailed in the China trade. In the 1870s, Rothschild and his sons, Louis and Henry, established a shipping business at the strategically located entrance to Puget Sound at Port Townsend, performing stevedoring, customs, and brokerage activities.[24]

Called "the Baron" by Port Townsend residents, Rothschild easily acknowledged his relationship to the European banking family as "close enough to get the name, but not the money." In 1868, Rothschild and his wife, Dorette, built a home high on the bluff overlooking Admiralty Inlet. The stately house remained in the family until 1958, when their son deeded the house and grounds to Washington State Parks.[25]

The success of many early Jewish businessmen in Washington Territory rested to a significant degree on their family connections. The Port Townsend firm of Waterman & Katz received financing and obtained goods from E. L. Goldstein of San Francisco, Katz's uncle and Waterman's brother-in-law.[26] After clerking in California and failing in a sawmill venture at Port Orchard on Puget Sound, Solomon Katz and Sigmund Waterman, both German Jews, set up business in Port Townsend in the 1860s, selling merchandise such as carpets, furniture, liquor, and Indian goods. In its territorial days, Port Townsend, at the tip of Washington's Olympic Peninsula, challenged both Seattle and Tacoma for leadership in Northwest shipping. Its population jumped from three families and fifteen bache-

The Rothschild family home in Port Townsend, which is today open to the public, was deeded to Washington State by the Rothchild family's youngest son, Eugene. Preserved by Emilie Rothchild, the unmarried youngest daughter who lived in the house all her life, the house remained virtually unchanged from its construction in 1868. Most of the family furniture is still in the house, and the original carpet covers the guest bedroom and both upstairs and downstairs halls. Washington State Parks and Recreation, Olympia, Washington, E-75-05.

lors in May 1852 to about 590 residents in 1870. The partners' "Solomon's Temple," the third largest firm in the territory, came into the hands of Solomon Katz's son Israel in 1868. By 1890, Port Townsend had turned into a wild, prosperous lumber-boom port. Israel Katz served on the Port Townsend City Council and twice won election as mayor, ending his second term in 1917. (Another Jewish citizen of Port Townsend, Max Gerson, a clothing store proprietor, was elected mayor in 1908.)[27]

Although Port Townsend's Jews were a prominent part of the city's early history, few, if any, called attention to their Jewish identity. Mayor Israel Katz went so far as to protest when identified by the local newspaper as being Jewish. A man's religion was his own private affair, Katz wrote in a letter to the editor, and the newspaper had no right to print such information.[28]

Considering the discrimination Jews had faced in the Central European towns of their origin, Katz's attitude was not unique. Early Jews were among the

At 3:20 a.m., Sunday, January 14, 1917, twelve days after he had completed his second term as mayor of Port Townsend, Israel Katz rose early to say goodbye to his son Edwin, who was catching a 4 a.m. steamer to Friday Harbor. Having pleasantly dined at home with an old friend the night before, the former mayor was in good spirits when he returned to his bed after Edwin's departure. At 7:00 a.m. a maid heard the family bulldog barking in Katz's room. On investigating she found his bed empty, but his glasses, watch, topcoat, and derby were still in their accustomed places. A search was launched, but Katz was not found. His disappearance remained a mystery; no trace of Israel Katz was ever discovered.
—Pete Simpson, *City of Dreams: A Guide to Port Townsend*

founders and builders of the state. Downplaying their Jewish connections "for business reasons" or even simply for convenience in getting ahead in this new world was a choice some early Jewish immigrants made. Despite their concerns, Jews experienced little anti-Semitism in those early years in the Northwest. Much more intense discrimination was aimed at Chinese, black, and Japanese immigrants.

Enterprisers in Eastern Washington

Many enterprising young Jewish newcomers who came to America in the 1830–60 migration from Germany were initially drawn westward by the 1849 California gold rush. They then headed north, attracted by gold strikes in Oregon, eastern Washington, Idaho, Montana, and British Columbia.

News of the gold strikes on the Columbia River brought Marcus Oppenheimer directly to Fort Colville in eastern Washington. Marcus Oppenheimer was the only early Jewish settler in Washington Territory who at his death left a town bearing his name. He had first settled in Kentucky where his brothers were in business, and a few years later, moved with them to Missouri. In May 1862, he crossed the continent in a forty-caravan wagon train with his brother, Joseph, Joseph's wife, and two small children. After homesteading a site on the banks of the Columbia River about twenty-five miles south of the Canadian border, Marcus established a store with Joseph and another brother, Samuel. The town at the crossroads became the town of Marcus.[29]

The Oppenheimers participated in a variety of enterprises, including a freight line, a flour mill, and steamboats on the Upper Columbia. Forty years after the death of Marcus Oppenheimer, the original town of Marcus disappeared under

Marcus Oppenheimer crossed the country in a wagon train in 1862 and was the only Jewish immigrant in the state of Washington to live in a town named for him. MSCUA/ UWL, *neg. 3471.*

the waters rising behind Grand Coulee Dam. Its population of almost four hundred residents moved their town to a site a mile and a half farther north, taking with them its name and history. Holding to its past, Marcus remains the oldest town in Stevens County.

Generally, the wide distances in the Northwest wilderness and the lack of roads prevented the kind of peddling that Jews in the southern and midwestern United States engaged in at midcentury. Instead, most Jewish businessmen in Washington Territory established partnerships, mostly with other Jews, which enabled them to cover more than one Washington town and to deal directly with suppliers in Portland, San Francisco, St. Louis, and New York. The Wertheimer family, for instance, who eventually settled in Longview and made their fortune in the timber industry, had branches in eastern Washington and St. Louis, Missouri. Jewish-owned Brown Brothers and Company, based in Walla Walla in the 1860s and 1870s, sold goods and commodities on both sides of the Cascade Mountains. Each of the three Brown brothers worked different parts of Washington Territory, enabling them to make the most of their limited resources. They also formed partnerships with Jewish businessmen in other towns.[30]

Among the first to form partnerships in Washington Territory were the Schwabacher brothers. In 1860, Abraham, Louis and Sigmund Schwabacher established their warehouse in Walla Walla, the Territory's most important city, where at least three other Jewish-owned stores were located. The city was strategically sited on the route to gold fields at Colville, and in what now is Idaho and western Montana. Abraham and Louis, who arrived in California in the early 1850s, were initially financed by their father in San Francisco. They began with a store at The Dalles, near the end of the Oregon Trail, before establishing their

The Schwabacher Brothers store in Walla Walla, established in 1860, stands replicated in the Washington State Historical Museum in Tacoma. Pictured here in the 1870s (from left): Babette Schwabacher Gatzert and Bailey Gatzert; Bella and Abraham Schwabacher, Sara and Louis Schwabacher, and Sigmund and Rose Schwabacher. MSCUA/UWL, *neg. 1383.*

Walla Walla store. Each brother took responsibility for different counties as they sought to meet the needs of miners and farmers in the eastern half of the Territory. Younger brother Sigmund came later, after clerking in Portland and The Dalles with Jewish firms, and was given his own sales region.[31] "As the size of their enterprise increased," wrote historian Julia Eulenberg, "they brought one or two cousins into the partnership, but their ultimate coup lay in the marital choices of their sister Babette and Abraham's daughter Mina. Their husbands, Bailey Gatzert and Nathan Eckstein, respectively, were crucial in the firm's extension into Western Washington and into the twentieth century."[32] Conversely, "All the Schwabacher brothers married women who were strong personalities and had definite ideas of what they wanted," said Abraham's granddaughter Joanna Eckstein, "and what they wanted were great big Victorian houses in San Francisco."[33]

By the 1870s, Jewish merchants such as Pincus and Packscher, D. C. H.

Rothschild, and the Schwabachers were providing the region's lumber mills with credit and supplies that figured in the building of the Northwest lumber industry. In addition, they took lumber and agricultural products in trade, thus becoming brokers of commodities.[34]

The Merchant Who Became Mayor

In 1869 in Seattle, Schwabacher Brothers opened a wholesale grocery and hardware store, a division of the growing Schwabacher business empire, and placed their brother-in-law, Bailey Gatzert, in charge. Hardly more than a village at the time, with wooden houses, streets of mud, and Henry Yesler's first steam sawmill dominating Mill Street (later Yesler Way), Seattle counted 1,107 residents in 1870.[35] At least three Jewish families, all of German origin, were among them. They were Bailey and Babette Gatzert, the David Kaufmans, whose daughter, Sara Kaufman Rucker, was the first Jewish child born in Seattle, and the Samuel Frauenthals.[36]

Gatzert made Schwabacher's the leading wholesaler in Seattle, doing $120,000 worth of business during his first year.[37] Under Gatzert's management, Schwabacher Brothers built a brick building that boasted hydraulic elevators and electric lights.[38] Abraham Schwabacher spent most of his time in San Francisco purchasing goods for the operation in Washington. The family dominated grain purchasing in eastern Washington, processed the wheat in its own flour mills in Walla Walla and Seattle, and moved the flour through

David and Hulda Kaufman's daughter, Sara, born February 27, 1869, was the first Jewish child born in Seattle. MSCUA/ UWL, neg. 8580.

1885. *Happy New Year.* 1886

OUR FIFTEENTH ANNUAL CALL.

Bailey Gatzert.
H. L. Yesler. *M. R. Maddocks.*

Beauty Unadorned.

Beginning in 1871, Seattle's civic leaders sent New Year's greetings to friends and citizens. Bailey Gatzert (center), who married Babette Schwabacher, joined the Schwabacher family business and headed its Seattle branch in 1869. In 1875 he became mayor of Seattle. MSCUA/UWL, *neg. 7223.*

its own warehouse to ships at Schwabacher Wharf on the Seattle waterfront. The Schwabachers entered into partnerships outside the family to operate branches in the Washington towns of Colfax and Dayton and in Idaho Falls, Idaho. Before statehood in 1889, the then San Francisco–based family operation was the leading wholesaler in Washington.[39] Early Seattle historian Clarence Bagley wrote that "the advent of [the Schwabacher] firm was the starting point of Seattle's wholesale trade."[40]

Seattle citizens elected Bailey Gatzert, head of Seattle's Schwabacher firm, their sixth mayor in 1875. At Gatzert's death in 1893, the *Seattle Post-Intelligencer* began his obituary with these words: "The history of Seattle can never be told without telling much of the life of Bailey Gatzert." A Seattle public elementary

The Bailey Gatzert *paddle steamer, named for Seattle's Jewish mayor elected in 1875, appeared on a stamp issued by the U.S. Postal Service on August 22, 1996. The* Bailey Gatzert *plied the Columbia River and Puget Sound from 1890 to 1923 and sailed between Seattle, Tacoma, and Olympia. She was called "one of the finest sternwheel steamers afloat" by E. W. Wright, editor of* Lewis & Dryden Marine History of the Pacific Northwest.

school and the first passenger/cargo steamboat to operate in Puget Sound waters were named for him. Looking back ninety years later, one historian named Gatzert "a representative man of the city and the state."[41]

An immigrant to America from Germany in 1849, Bailey Gatzert got his first job as a clerk in a general merchandise store in Natchez, Mississippi, where he learned to speak English with a Southern accent. The accent remained with him all his life. Three years later, smitten with the gold fever spreading from coast to coast, Gatzert headed west to California. But for him the fever ended almost as soon as it began. He went back to clerking for a while, then established a grocery business. In San Francisco in 1861, Gatzert married Babette Schwabacher, clearly a good match for his enterprise and enthusiasm.

After a stint in Portland, Oregon, where Gatzert joined the wholesale grocery firm of Meerhox & Company, the Gatzerts moved on to eastern Washington. Here Gatzert established a general merchandise store in Wallula, at the junction of the Columbia and Snake Rivers, a natural supply point on the route to the Idaho and Montana mines.

From there in 1869, his Schwabacher brothers-in-law plucked him into their own world of wholesale and retail general merchandise, hardware, and agricultural implements. Even before the railroad crossed the Cascades in 1883, Gatzert began to make a name for himself in the young city of Seattle. Besides being the general manager of Seattle's Schwabacher enterprise, Gatzert helped many of the city's enterprises take their first steps. He was instrumental in the opening of the Newcastle Coal Mines in 1870, when coal was Seattle's major export; in the incorporation of Puget Sound National Bank and People's Savings Bank (serving as president of both); in the founding of banks in Snohomish, Yakima, and Bellingham; and in the creation of Seattle's cable car system. When Rutherford B. Hayes, the first president of the United States to venture west of the Rocky Mountains, came to town, the Gatzerts entertained him in their home.

A city councilman for several terms, Gatzert was a founder of the Seattle Chamber of Commerce in 1889 and its second president. He was also a founding member of the state's first Jewish house of worship, Ohaveth Sholum. Its ornate Torah curtains were a gift from the Gatzerts.

"Seattle's Most Useful Citizen"

Bailey Gatzert, like other Jewish immigrants in the first wave of immigration to the Northwest in the second half of the 1800s, encountered little of the discrimination that would bloom in America in the first half of the twentieth century. The promi-

Named "Seattle's Most Useful Citizen" in 1926 by ten social and cultural organizations, Bavarian-born Nathan Eckstein, who arrived in Seattle in 1898, was remembered by many in his adopted city long after he died at the age of seventy-two. Nathan Eckstein Middle School (originally a junior high school) carries his name. WSJHS, 23.

nence of Jews in the early history of Washington State is illustrated not only by Bailey Gatzert, but by Nathan Eckstein, another Seattle Jewish civic and business leader. Proclaimed "Seattle's Most Useful Citizen" in 1926 by a consensus of ten leading service clubs and social and cultural agencies, Eckstein was honored five years after his death in 1945 at the age of seventy-two by the naming of Nathan Eckstein Junior High School (later changed to Nathan Eckstein Middle School), built in 1950.[42]

Following in the wake of three older brothers, fifteen-year-old Eckstein arrived in New York in 1888 to live with an uncle's family. Ten years later, he came with his wife, Mina Schwabacher, daughter of Abraham Schwabacher, to the growing city on Puget Sound, succeeding Bailey Gatzert as head of Schwabacher Brothers. Eckstein customarily broke the Yom Kippur day fast with herring and boiled potatoes, a habit echoing back to his family in Bavaria, Germany.

One of the early members of Temple De Hirsch, and its second president, Eckstein had management skills and abilities that were quickly recognized by leaders in the affairs of the city. He persistently pursued causes and backed civic programs that he thought were good for Seattle, and just as persistently rejected what he considered detrimental. When, for example, many of his business associates favored the establishment of a city manager system and Seattle newspapers urged adoption of the idea, Eckstein strongly opposed. He fervently spoke out against the plan, debating the issue at public meetings and on the radio, and helped defeat the proposal by a substantial majority vote.

Eckstein's formal education didn't go beyond his studies at the Munich Gymnasium, the equivalent of a high school education. Yet, "he was one of the most cultured and truly educated men I have known," said Raphael L. Levine, rabbi of Temple De Hirsch, toward the end of Eckstein's tenure on the temple board. The first time Levine came to see Eckstein in the Schwabacher Building on First Avenue South at Jackson Street, he expected to be ushered into an elaborate private office. Instead, the woman at the front desk pointed to the back of the large room filled with numerous desks and people working at them. He followed the pointed finger and saw Eckstein sitting at an old oak rolltop desk. No partitions separated the president of the company from the other people in the office. Rabbi Levine considered this a small clue to the character of this Jew who, during his forty-six years in Seattle, was an active member of the Seattle Chamber of Commerce, twice president of the school board, a supporter of the symphony and the Seattle Art Museum, and a leader in local and national Jewish organizations.

Like the Schwabacher brothers, other early Jewish entrepreneurs also established their own sources of credit and goods from other Jewish business associates and suppliers. Washington merchants looked to San Francisco Jews to serve this role. They even featured their San Francisco–based partners in advertising their wares and their "San Francisco prices."

First Department Store and Leading Bank

By 1880, Seattle's Jewish population had jumped to nearly one hundred.[43] It included Paul Singerman, who arrived in 1874 via San Francisco, having crossed the country on his way to California by covered wagon six years earlier.[44] Auerbach, Toklas and Singerman, opening in Seattle in 1875, became one of the state's first department store, the first firm in the city to use electric lighting (1886), and the first to install a telephone (1883).[45] Singerman was the progenitor of at least six generations of prominent leaders in the Jewish community. His partner, Ferdinand Toklas, was the father of Alice B. Toklas, the famed friend of the equally famous Gertrude Stein.

Jacob Furth, who was sixteen years old when he set out for America from Bohemia, was forty-two when he discovered the growing little town of Seattle in 1882. He had learned all about business clerking in Nevada City and by running a clothing and dry goods store in Colusa, California. Marriage and the birth of three daughters encouraged him to expand his horizons. Described as a man of majestic appearance with a long pointed beard, Furth, it was widely reported, came to Seattle with $50,000 in hand and founded the Puget Sound National Bank. Since nobody had much collateral in this young community, Furth loaned money using only his own judgment of the character of the would-be borrower. Within ten years, Furth's bank was the biggest in town, and his skills translated into management of such ventures as wheat farms and pasturelands, electric utilities, and street railway facilities. When the state of Massachusetts raised a million dollars by public subscription to alleviate the disaster of the great earthquake and fire which devastated the city of San Francisco in 1906, it called on Jacob Furth, the banker, thousands of miles away in Seattle, to handle the money and organize the relief work.[46]

Furth belonged to the exclusive Rainier Club and the equally exclusive Seattle Golf Club. He also belonged to Seattle's first congregation, Ohaveth Sholum, and later to Temple De Hirsch. His wife, however, who was not Jewish, and their daughters, who were prominent in Seattle's society circles, had almost no ties to the Jewish community. Furth's Jewish connections were reflected mostly in his philanthropy, which included aid to Russian Jewish immigrants brought to him for help by Herman "Pop" Kessler, an early Orthodox leader. When this German-Jewish immigrant died in 1914, the *Seattle Post-Intelligencer* marked Jacob Furth not only as a "molder of great enterprises," but also as a kindly, generous gentleman. "It's an irony there's no street, statue or park named after him," wrote local historian William C. Speidel in his 1967 book *Sons of the Profits*.[47]

The first account in Jacob Furth's Puget Sound Bank was opened by Meyer A. Gottstein, a native of Poland, who arrived in Seattle in May 1883 and established a wholesale liquor business three months later. Almost the whole town lay along the street later known as First Avenue South, flanked by three rickety wharves. "The streets were not even planked," said Gottstein, "and yet somehow I knew this city was going to be a winner."[48] When Gottstein's cousin, Kassel Gottstein, joined him in business, the firm took the name of M. & K. Gottstein. Even before Seattle's great fire of June 6, 1889, died out, an optimistic sign appeared over the smoky wreck of the Gottstein store: "Will rebuild at once. Seattle will rise from the ashes, [signed] M. Gottstein."[49]

The "City of Destiny"

At the time Seattle was just beginning to grow, its neighboring city of Tacoma was a step ahead. In 1873, Tacoma was designated the western terminus for the Northern Pacific Railroad. Proclaimed the "Lumber Capital of the World" and touted as the "City of Destiny," Tacoma from the 1870s to the 1890s was a magnet for a number of Jews of Central European origin. Some, like David Levin, born in Kolmar, Germany (now Colmar, France), who came to Commencement Bay in 1874 at twenty-one years of age, built their lives in Tacoma. Levin remained a resident for thirty-one years, winning election to the lower house of the Washington State Legislature in 1897.[50] The Gross brothers, David and Ellis, born and raised in Rypin, Poland, arrived in the city of New Tacoma, Washington Territory, in 1878. Joined by younger brothers Morris and Abe, the brothers opened a department store at C and Ninth Streets on March 20, 1890, which, the *Tacoma Daily Ledger* reported, was the largest dry goods store on the Pacific Coast.[51]

A full-page article in *The Tacoma Sunday Ledger* described the opening of the new store:

Headed by a brass band, a procession of twenty carriages loaded with the firm's employees, paraded through the streets from the old store to the new. The men wore silk hats, the young women new spring bonnets and it was an altogether happy crowd. The formal opening was attended by thousands. A flag with twelve stars, one for each of the twelve years since the firm opened its first store in Tacoma, waved from the top of the building.[52]

Five stories in height on the C Street front, Gross Brothers Department Store contained twelve separate departments of merchandise and a baby-care facility with a nurse in charge for shopping mothers. Sixty-five clerks waited on customers, and an elaborate overhead system of baskets and wires carried parcels from the sales floor, through a wrapping room, to the cashier's box, and back to the sales floor. A footman greeted ladies at the door, and a line of cabs or hacks stood available to customers free of charge.[53]

The City of Destiny enticed more than a few ambitious entrepreneurial Jews. Charles Reichenbach closed a successful mercantile business he had established in Chicago, packed up his family, moved to Tacoma, and opened the London & Liverpool Clothing House in 1884.[54] Featured some years later on the front page of the *Tacoma Daily Ledger*, he was described as "a Prominent Tacoman" whose "liberality in charitable enterprises is known to everybody."[55] Albert Weinberg engaged in the wholesale liquor business in the city from 1882, then joined his brother-in-

In the fall of 1891, fifty Tacoma mothers registered their five-year-olds in a free kindergarten school established through the philanthropy of the Gross Brothers Department Store. "I believe in free kindergartens," said Morris Gross, speaking at the end of the first school year. "I believe that it is my duty to maintain this kindergarten. I think that the rich should help the poor, the learned, the ignorant."
—"Gross Bros. Kindergarten," Tacoma Daily Ledger, *17 June 1892*

When President Benjamin Harrison visited Tacoma on May 6, 1891, the Gross family cleared the entire Gross Brothers Department Store's first floor of merchandise and turned the second story balcony into a reviewing stand to accommodate the crowds of people that gathered to greet him. Courtesy of Tacoma Public Library.

law, S. Loeb, to operate the Milwaukee Brewing Company beginning in 1889.[56] When Theodore Roosevelt visited Tacoma in 1903, it was Loeb who escorted him around the town.[57]

Among others who succumbed to the lure of the City of Destiny was German-born Joseph Bachrach, who initially operated his dry goods trade in Cincinnati, then teamed up with Theophil Feist in the successful Tacoma merchandising venture of Feist & Bachrach.[58] Feist left Alsace-Lorraine in 1889, first stopped in San Francisco, and went on to Tacoma, which many believed would be the most important city in the new state of Washington. "We never forgave him for not staying in San Francisco," his daughter, Lucille Feist Hurst, a leader among Tacoma's Reform Jews throughout her life, lamented many years later.[59] Feist and Bachrach conducted a thriving dry goods and men's furnishing house and remained lifelong Tacoma residents.[60]

In 1891, the Tacoma City Directory listed more than a hundred Jewish residents, and Jewish stores peppered Pacific Avenue, one of the four major streets with planked sidewalks, for several blocks on both sides of the street. These transplanted Central Europeans played a prominent part in Tacoma's early civic and business affairs, and their social events were covered in detail in the columns of the *Tacoma News*.[61] But few of them remained beyond the early 1900s. The Gross Brothers Department Store closed following the economic depression of 1893 and the suicide of the youngest Gross brother, Abe. (The Gross Building, acquired by William Jones in 1916, was later demolished to make room for the building of the Pantages Theater.) By the turn of the century, the City of Destiny was languishing in the shadow of Seattle.[62]

"The most famous person to ever come from here was Herman Klaber," commented a Tacoma resident.[63] Herman Klaber was a passenger on the White Star Line's RMS *Titanic* when it struck an iceberg off Newfoundland and sank on Sunday, April 14, 1912. He was forty-one years old. Legendary because he went down with the *Titanic*, Klaber was once known as the "hops king" of Washington State. His two-hundred-acre hops field in Lewis County was the biggest single hops field in the world. Klaber lived in Tacoma in a large house on a North End bluff overlooking Commencement Bay and had offices and houses in Portland and San Francisco. His company town of "Klaber" in Lewis County (which no longer exists) housed as many as two thousand workers in the harvest season. Born of German-Jewish parents in San Francisco, Herman Klaber came to Puyallup in 1893, moved to Tacoma in 1897, and expanded his hops business to Lewis County in 1906. After a business trip to London selling Klaber's Chehalis Hops to European brewers, Klaber boarded the ill-fated ship in Southampton, England, to return home to his young wife, Gertrude, and their infant daughter. His body was never recovered. Among his bequests were awards to Tacoma's Beth Israel Congregation and to his niece Elsa Kaufman. (Elsa Kaufman married Seattle lawyer Sam Levinson. She helped establish the University of Washington's Jewish Archives and was a founder of the Washington State Jewish Historical Society.)[64]

Spokane's Early Merchants

The first permanent Jewish settler in Spokane Falls (later known as Spokane) was German immigrant Simon Berg, who arrived in 1879. When he discovered that merchants had been in and out, trading with the Indians in the area for some time, and that among these merchants were "egg eaters" (so called because they would not eat meat away from home and dined only on hard-boiled eggs, raw fruit, and vegetables), he knew that Jewish traders had been there before him.[65]

The town was hardly more than "a little cluster of houses, some fifty or more, upon the south side of the river near the falls" when Berg established a general merchandise store at what would become the corner of Howard Street and Main Avenue. His street-front colleagues consisted of a missionary, a miller, a district clerk, a blacksmith, and a tavern keeper. Like the smith who transported iron for his shop, Berg brought supplies for his store from Walla Walla, then the great supply center of the inland Northwest.[66]

After the linkup of the Northern Pacific Railroad to the East Coast in the mid 1880s, settlers flocked to the hamlet on the banks of the Spokane River, which soon became the commercial hub for the exploitation of the Inland Empire's timber, agricultural, and mining resources. Among the newcomers were a number of enterprising German Jews who were counted among the prominent figures in Spokane's pioneer history.

The first Jewish women to settle in Spokane Falls, Tillie Oppenheimer (later Mrs. Isaac Baum) and her sister, Mrs. Ben Scheeline, arrived in the autumn of 1883. In the next six months, the population of Spokane Falls grew from fifteen hundred to five thousand. Simon Auerbach held the first High Holiday services celebrated in Spokane in his home in 1885. The Rosenhaupts celebrated the birth of their daughter, May, the first Jewish child born in Spokane Falls, in 1888.[67]

By 1889, the year Washington Territory became a state, the flourishing town of Spokane Falls included ten banks, fifty-one saloons, and ninety real estate offices. The transportation and commercial hub of the area, it had grown to a population of nearly twenty thousand. But like other towns in the growing state of Washington, its wooden structures invited disaster.[68] On Sunday, August 4, 1889, a fire swept through the city. The young daughter of Joseph Kellner watched as flames destroyed almost every store in the downtown area. Nothing remained of "Joseph Kellner's Dry Goods—Ladies' and Children's Fine Shoes, Cloaks and Muslin Underwear A Specialty." For a time after the fire, Nettie Kellner Langert recalled, Spokane Falls's business area was a "city of tents." She witnessed the new city rising from the ashes, with brick and mortar replacing the rough wooden planks of the early frontier boomtown. Two years after the fire, Falls was dropped from the name.[69]

Social activities of members of the Jewish community increased in the fast-growing city as rapidly as their business enterprises. The January 28, 1892, *Spokane Review* gave almost a whole column to "The Hebrew Society Ball" held at the

Concordia Hall. More than two hundred guests attended the masquerade dance, which culminated in a grand march and prizes awarded for the best costumes.

Albert Heller, who arrived in Spokane with his family from California in 1888, erected the first brick building. Named the "Heller," it later became the Peyton Building. In 1895, Simon Oppenheimer earned the title of "Biggest Man in Spokane" when he secured a $300,000 investment for the city from Holland. Out of his financial wizardry came a sawmill, a large flouring mill, and a franchise to set poles and string electric power wires in the city streets. One of the incorporators of the Traders National Bank, he also established the Holland Bank.[70]

Early Spokane abounded with entrepreneurs. Foremost firms included the Jewish business houses of I.X.L. and Chicago Clothing Company; M. & S. Schulien Shoes; L. Bernheimer, tailor; D. Holzman & Co. and Harry L. Jackson, wholesale liquor dealers; M. Seller & Co., a branch of a Portland concern that sold hotel and restaurant supplies; J. Kellner's Dry Goods; and A. W. Siegal whose cigar store was the most prominent in Spokane.[71] Although not quite one-and-a-half percent of the total population of Spokane, Spokane's early Jews emerged as a formidable group of people, both enterprising and industrious, and they contributed in remarkable measure to the development of the city commercially, philanthropically, and politically.[72] The Galland brothers, Adolph, Julius, and Sam, incorporated Traders National Bank, which later became the Spokane and Eastern and then merged with Seafirst Bank. They also owned a brewery, which eventually was sold to Emile Sick, and became Rainier Brewery under yet another ownership. The Galland brothers' philanthropic activities provided a scholarship fund for Washington State College, the Galland Home of the Washington Children's Home Society, and construction and improvements for both the early Reform and the later Orthodox congregations. Harry Rosenhaupt, elected to the Washington State Legislature in 1889, served for twelve years. In 1893, Judge Adolph Munter became the leader of the Law and Order League, a referee in bankruptcy cases, and a justice of the peace. Jacob A. Schiller was elected to the city council in 1895 and served two terms. In 1904 Harry L. Cohn became assistant district attorney for Alaska, and the next year Max Newman won election to the legislature.[73]

Jewish Enterprise, an Integral Part of the Economy

Between 1860 and 1890, Jewish partnerships thrived as Seattle, Tacoma, and Spokane grew in size: branch stores opened in several locations, the variety of enterprises expanded, and prime markets developed. The enlarged firms created jobs for the increasing number of newly arrived Jewish relatives and friends. By the turn

Janet Fasten Levy, Marian Fasten Grinstein, and Natalie Fasten Rosenwald, the three granddaughters of Albert Mayer and Leah Phillips, grew up hearing stories of the Mayer Brothers clocks. The tales invariably began with their great-grandmother's journey to the West Coast to wed Albert Mayer's father in the mid-1800s. Eighteen-year-old Rebecca Phillips left Philadelphia on a sailing ship bound for the Isthmus of Panama. Disembarking on the Atlantic side and crossing the stretch of jungle on donkey back to continue by ship on the Pacific side, she was carried off by a band of marauding Indians. Rescued, Rebecca finally reached San Francisco, wed her cousin, Alexander Phillips, and in time bore eleven children, two of whom were Leah and Clara, the wives of early Seattle clockmakers Albert and Joseph Mayer.

—From the transcript of Janet Fasten Levy, MSCUA/UWL, 1824

of the century, Jewish-owned stores also flourished in Aberdeen, Kalama, Colville, Bellingham, Fairhaven, and other small towns, in addition to those in the larger cities. In a cash-poor economy, and in the absence of many banks, Jewish storekeepers extended much needed credit to prospectors and homesteaders, thus financing small-scale mining and agricultural growth. When customers defaulted on their debts, the merchants often were forced into bankruptcy themselves. Newspapers frequently carried advertisements pleading for repayment of debt. Rothschild & Co., for instance, published a notice in Port Townsend's *The Democratic Press* of March 23, 1878, threatening to refer all past-due accounts to an attorney for collection: "No distinction of persons will be made, as these accounts have been standing so long that patience has ceased to be a virtue." Creditors occasionally received land, crops, cattle, or timber through foreclosures, the same commodities that Jews brokered on the Russian frontier. As a consequence, they bartered into brokerage and wholesaling of commodities in Washington Territory.[74]

Ellensberg's Samuel and Henry Kleinberg, sons of a Bavarian hay merchant, were the first to ship Kittitas Valley hay to the Puget Sound region west of the mountains. They bought clover, alfalfa, and timothy hay from Kittitas farmers and ranchers, stored it in warehouses, and then sent it west by railroad. Eventually, the Kleinbergs owned as many as eight warehouses and between fifteen hundred and two thousand acres of choice irrigated land near Ellensburg. Samuel opened a Seattle office in 1898. Customers included racetracks, fire stations, and stables. Kleinberg Brothers became the dominant hay business in the Pacific Northwest. The Kleinberg Block, built in 1889 on the west side of Pearl Street between Third

The Kleinberg family in Ellensburg, ca. 1911. Standing in the rear are Henry Kleinberg and his son Alfred; in front from left to right are Lester Kleinberg, Lena Kleinberg, Amelia Senders Kleinberg, and Edward Kleinberg. MSCUA/UWL, *neg. 1206.*

and Fourth Streets in Ellensberg, is on the National Register of Historic Places. Only two Jewish families resided in Ellensburg during the time that Henry Kleinberg's family lived here. The other was the family of Samuel Kriedel, who became mayor of Ellensburg in 1915. Henry moved his family to Seattle in 1918 and added considerable real estate to his holdings there. He also established a dairy business in western Washington.[75]

Jews were not involved in the financing of major investments in the West such as deep pit mining and railroads, yet Jewish enterprise lay at the heart of much of the early commercial growth of Washington Territory. Jews in Washington were "conducting types of business activities far broader—and on a much larger scale—than the traditional mercantile enterprise" usually attributed to the Jews of the West.[76] Although most historians of American Jewry have focused on retail

> *Lena Kleinberg Holzman, who grew up in Ellensberg, recalled that the only thing she had known about being Jewish was "You don't sew on the Sabbath." On Jewish holidays the family went to the home of the other Jewish family in town, the Kreidels. "There were no services, just Jewish company. . . . The reason my parents moved to Seattle was so that we children would have [Jewish contacts]," said Lena. The Kleinbergs moved to Seattle in 1918.*
>
> —From transcript of Lena Kleinberg Holzman, MSCUA/UWL, 3199

trade in the West, historian Julia Eulenberg found that Jews filled several important economic niches in the development of the Territory.

By the time of statehood in 1889, the most successful of Jewish businessmen had enlarged their endeavors to include various aspects of real estate development, coal mining, the hotel industry, banking, insurance, the development of water services for growing cities and irrigation, manufacturing, and the transportation business. Pincus and Packscher's *Clara Light* hauled lumber and mail from Puget Sound to San Francisco, and returned north with goods and mail. In eastern Washington, Jewish-operated pack trains and wagons delivered goods from suppliers to mining camps and small towns. Rothschild's Port Townsend shipping business grew and prospered, as did the firm of Waterman & Katz, which handled ships' chandlery. Bailey Gatzert and Jacob Furth developed a dozen transportation companies, most of which were part of Seattle's expanding urban railway system, including the Madison Street Cable Railway Company; the Seattle, Lake Shore, and Eastern Railway Company; and the Seattle and Walla Walla Railroad and Transportation Company.[77] Furth consolidated Seattle's streetcar lines for the Boston-based Stone and Webster Company. Gatzert formed the Yakima Farm and Water Company in 1883, the system that served the consumption needs of Yakima and provided irrigation to the local farmers. Seattle's Spring Hill Water Company, founded in 1881 by Gatzert, Furth, and others, formed the beginning of Seattle's municipal water system.[78] Furth, founder of the Puget Sound National Bank, was also closely identified with the People's Savings Bank and Seattle National Bank. Clothing retailer Charles Reichenbach of Tacoma helped organize that city's Washington National Bank and Union Home Building and Loan Association.[79] These activities were more than financial investments. They were investments in infrastructure that set the stage for the next step of local and regional development. Jews thus connected Washington to the wider world through their own commercial networks and contributed to town and city building.

Of course, not all Jewish entrepreneurs succeeded in Washington, and many who eventually made good struggled in the early years. National depressions in the 1870s and 1890s impacted Washington Territory. And not all Jews were honest, civic-minded citizens. M. L. Hefron, an Olympia saloon keeper from 1859 to 1861, was convicted in territorial court of assault and battery in 1860 and tried on a gambling charge in 1862.[80] Port Townsend's notorious Max Levy ran a seamen's boardinghouse, a place where sailors could stay between voyages. Sailors and, sometimes, hapless soldiers, lumberjacks, and Indians gained a bed, food, tobacco, and liquor—"all on the cuff," as it were. When a ship needed a crew, Levy would fill the master's needs with indebted boarders. Although it was never verified, old-timers reported the existence of "shanghai" tunnels underlying the town, which were used to smuggle kidnapped sailors and others to ships.[81] Also infamous in this frontier seaport town was another pioneer Jew, Judge Morris B. Sachs, who presided over the Superior Court for Jefferson, Clallam, Island, San Juan, and Kitsap counties. Sachs was charged by the Port Townsend Bar Association with "misbehavior, malfeasance and delinquency in office" for gambling, prejudging cases, and sitting in cases in which he had conflicts of interest. Although the State Legislature acquitted Sachs of all charges in 1891, demands for his resignation did not abate.[82]

Family Networks

Consolidation or extension of business through marriage is an old custom and one certainly not limited to Jews. Among the Jews in the American West, the marriage of one partner to the sister or daughter of the other was not uncommon. Isaac Pincus married Seraphina Packscher, the sister of his partner, Adolph, in 1864, sailing to Victoria, British Columbia, to be wed at Congregation Emanu-El.[83] Tacoma dry goods merchant Joseph Bachrach married Lucy Feist, sister of his business partner Theophil Feist.[84] And, as noted, Bailey Gatzert and Nathan Eckstein, two of Seattle's most prominent citizens, married into the Schwabacher family and became Seattle partners in the family's business empire. Washington's Jewish businessmen sometimes met their prospective brides through business or family contacts in San Francisco, on the East Coast, or in Europe. Such marriages further solidified the Jewish business network in the West, linking isolated merchants to the larger cities. Olympia businessman Louis Bettman was introduced to his future wife, Amelia Coblentz of Los Angeles, while on a buying trip in San Francisco. The Coblentz family had business ties with the Schwabachers of San Francisco. Although a few, like Jacob Furth, married outside the faith, most of Washington's Central European Jewish pioneers managed to find Jewish mates.

While most Jewish women of the time were hausfraus, some played active social and communal roles in their towns and cities. Few were employed in business. But several of the wives of early Jewish pioneers, including Caroline Kline Galland and Babette Schwabacher Gatzert, brought property to their marriages, continued to hold it in their own names, and managed their own money after their husbands died. Some Jewish women worked alongside their husbands, some were virtual partners, and a few ran businesses of their own. In 1866, for example, Mrs. S. S. Kline of Vancouver, Washington Territory, billed herself as a "practical milliner and dressmaker." In 1873, Mrs. C. A. Silverman operated the millinery section of her husband's clothing store for men in the Columbia River settlement of Kalama, advertising "The latest styles of HATS, CAPS & BONNETS."[85]

Seattle Becomes the Center of State Jewry

The second half of the nineteenth century witnessed the growth of Washington from a territory to a state, the expansion of Spokane into the commercial hub of the Inland Empire, and the emerging success of Seattle over Tacoma as the major metropolis on Puget Sound. By the early 1890s, Seattle, the state's largest and most dynamic city, had the unmistakable beginnings of a Jewish community. With the presence of a colony of Central European Jews, a growing number of Eastern European Jewish immigrants starting in the 1880s, and the founding of Jewish organizations and two congregations as discussed in later chapters, Seattle was fast becoming the major focus of Jewish settlement in Washington State.

The discovery of gold in the Canadian Yukon and in Alaska in 1897 put Seattle on the world map and set off two decades of unprecedented economic growth. It was the biggest gold rush since the Forty-Niners invaded California, exciting worldwide interest and bringing tens of thousands of people to the Pacific Northwest. When the steamer *Portland* landed at Schwabacher Wharf in Seattle on July 17, 1897, with its legendary "ton of gold," the city experienced a frenzy of activity. Local businessmen created a flurry of publicity that convinced most of the would-be prospectors that Seattle was "the gateway to the Klondike."[86] The presence and excitement of thousands of people on their way north on the first available boats stimulated business. Ironically, many who outfitted the prospectors profited the most.

> "My grandfather was a very dapper man with a high hat and silver cane, and he was quite a scholar. He knew eight languages fluently.... Seattle had lots of Indians in those days... they could speak to him in their own dialects. Chief Seattle's daughter Princess Angelina came into the City of Paris frequently.... [She] could take anything [she] wanted, just take it, because he wanted to show friendship." Henry Grunbaum came to Seattle in 1889 immediately after the big fire and established the City of Paris, a dry goods store, with his brother Maurice.
> —Quotation from Helen Grunbaum Rosen, MSCUA/UWL, 3884–001

Supplies for prospectors bound for the Yukon overflow onto the street in front of the Cooper-Levy store at First Avenue South and Yesler Way, Seattle, ca. 1897. WSJHS, 130.

The Canadian Mounties required all prospectors entering Yukon Territory to carry a year's supply of goods and equipment. Those traveling to Alaska were advised to bring the same. At a price of almost $1,000, the obligatory outfits stood to make their suppliers rich. Three firms did the most business: Schwabacher Brothers, Schwabacher Hardware, and another Jewish-owned company, Cooper-Levy.

To attract the miner trade, Cooper-Levy began running advertisements on page one of the *Seattle Post-Intelligencer* two days before the *Portland* landed. Unlike other merchants who offered a few of the items required, Cooper-Levy sold total outfits packed for shipment. "GOLD SEEKERS are invited to call at our store and procure an accurate list comprising 'supplies for one man for one year,'" their July 22, 1897, ad stated. "The list has been made up with great care, and is just what every one going to Alaska ought to have."

Cooper-Levy's store at Commercial Avenue (First Avenue South) and Yesler, with its goods stacked up on the sidewalk in front, stayed open twenty-four hours a day to keep up with the demand. Their ad in the *Post-Intelligencer* of July 24 read:

NIGHT AND DAY . . . for . . . Clondyke

We are better prepared than ever to supply miners and prospectors for the Clondyke. We have two large forces—one works all day, the other all night. Bring in your orders and see how quickly and how well we fill them.

A *Post-Intelligencer* reporter covering the phenomenal events interviewed Isaac Cooper in his store. "With one hand filled with orders and the other engaged in checking off articles on bills of lading," a harried Cooper told the reporter, "'They're coming swifter all the time. I haven't much time to talk.'"[87]

During the month after the *Portland*'s landing, Seattle's merchants sold $325,000 worth of goods. Those heading for the gold fields of the north continued to stimulate business in Seattle for several years to come, and newcomers poured into towns and cities all over Washington State.[88]

Coinciding with the unheralded rush of gold seekers to Washington State came increasing numbers of Jewish immigrants from Eastern Europe, and the third wave of Jews—Sephardim from regions around the Mediterranean. These Jews brought religious and commercial cultures that contrasted sharply with those of the first wave of Jewish immigrants. Seattle suddenly and explosively grew to be the largest city in the Pacific Northwest, the gateway to the Alaska gold fields, and the center of Jewish and other ethnic settlements in the region.

All Seattle told time by the great street clocks made by the Joseph Mayer Company, manufacturing jewelers, headed by Jewish pioneer Joseph Mayer. This one on First Avenue between Cherry and Columbia, ca. 1905, was one of the many early clocks weighing a thousand pounds or more seen on the streets of Seattle, San Francisco, and other West Coast cities beginning in 1900. Seattle Museum of History and Industry, 10609.

Eastern European Pioneers

THE SECOND WAVE OF JEWS TO WASHINGTON, BEGINNING in the 1880s, came from Eastern Europe. These immigrants quickly outnumbered their German predecessors. Their number coming through the gateway of New York between 1880 and 1920 mounted to 3.5 million.[1] Many came, in author Irving Howe's phrase, "to ease lives that had become intolerable and release ambitions long suppressed."[2]

These Jews left behind them economic, social, and political turmoil, which had made them scapegoats in Russia and the victims of hundreds of pogroms costing thousands of lives. In the general economic upheaval, Jews who had worked as traditional merchants, peddlers, and artisans were pushed out by the modernization of agriculture and the beginnings of industrialization. At the same time that the Polish and Russian governments imposed high taxes on Jewish families, Russia drafted a disproportionate number of Jewish youth into its army in an effort to convert and assimilate them. Under the May laws of 1882, a half million Jews were expelled from rural areas of Russia, and by 1891 another 700,000 were removed from Moscow and other cities to the Pale of Settlement. They came to America by the hundreds of thousands seeking freedom and opportunity.[3]

Illustrative of the joy many felt upon arrival was Jack Radinsky's family. Jack and his mother, Celia, and two other members of his family had left an agricultural village in Russia, where "if you don't have rain, you starve." "We got into Colman Dock on November 22, 1916," recalled Jack, where his father, Benzion, anxiously awaited them. "And it was a typical November day in Seattle, dark and grey and rainy. . . . So my mother looks at the Seattle rain and almost with rapture, she says, "We've landed in a *mazeldiche shaw* (a lucky hour). My father says, "Don't worry, every hour in Seattle is a *mazeldiche shaw*."[4]

To the many Eastern European Jewish immigrants, America was, in their Yiddish idiom, a *goldena medina*, a golden land, full of hope—a new chance at life. Approximately one third left their homelands in the thirty-three years between the assassination of Czar Alexander II in 1881 and the outbreak of the First World War in 1914.[5] Some found their way to the Northwest and the rapidly growing Washington Territory.

Coming to America

For many Eastern European Jews, escape from the "old country" more often than not was fraught with difficulties. Endless red tape involving the threat of refusal or even imprisonment terrified the travelers. Jews who chose to bypass the capricious tyranny of passports and bureaucrats by crossing the border surreptitiously at night faced other ordeals.[6]

The Rickles family, arriving in Seattle in 1887, came from the town of Koshinchiv in the Russian province of Bessarabia, near the Romanian border.

Grandpa would sit at the head of the table drinking his coffee out of his saucer through a lump of sugar that he held in his front teeth. I used to think he did this for the benefit of his grandchildren, but since [then] I've learned this was the common way coffee [and tea] was drunk in the European countries. I remember Grandpa's favorite treat: goose grease and raw onions on rye bread. . . . Every Easter, although my Grandpa Jake was an Orthodox Jew, he and Grandma held an Easter Egg hunt for their grandchildren. It wasn't until years later that I questioned the logic of this.

—Caroline Blumenthal Danz, MSCUA/UWL, 3895

"We couldn't talk their language, they couldn't talk our language," recalled Esther Borish Friedman, who arrived in Seattle in 1909 from Russia at age seven. "We came here and everybody was so excited about getting here . . . but nobody showed up to meet us at the station. . . . Here's my mother and my aunt and five little kids sitting and waiting." They waited all night, sleeping on the King Street station benches before Esther's father located them.

—From transcript of Esther Borish Friedman, MSCUA/UWL, 2273

Crossing at night with six children, Rose Rickles clasped the youngest, an infant, tightly to her breast to stifle his cries. It wasn't until she, her husband Gershon, and the five other children had reached safety that she discovered the child she had held so closely had been smothered to death.[7]

The ocean trip to New York from the ports of Hamburg or Bremen, to which many traveled from their home towns, often took three weeks or longer. Most Jewish immigrants traveled at the cheapest rate in generally grim steerage accommodations below the ship's water level. They slept in separated male and female compartments on mattresses that were hardly more than sacks of straw. Washing and toilet facilities were inadequate.[8] Sol Esfeld, traveling in steerage as a child with his mother, remembered being given herring and bread to eat and not much else. Some families practically starved, noted a member of the Rickles family, because they ate only kosher food.[9]

By far the greatest number of immigrants landed in New York. The American immigration station, whether Castle Garden (opened in 1855) or Ellis Island (opened after 1892), held its own terrors.[10] Many new arrivals who failed to pass medical examinations were refused entry into the United States.[11] Shmuel Thal, who came to Ellis Island with his wife, Sarah, did not pass the eye exam, and so the Thals had to make the sad and difficult voyage back to Russia. Sarah made the trip again after her husband's death, this time entering, as many others chose to do, through Canada, and traveling from there into the United States.[12]

Especially bewildering to the Yiddish-speaking immigrants were the officials who received them. Many "lacked the imagination to respect cultural styles radically different from their own."[13] Faced with the hordes of anxiety-ridden applicants who passed before them, officials dealt with them as quickly as possible, ignoring questions and often putting their

Young Sol Esfeld selling newspapers on Seattle's streets, ca. 1912. He grew up to become one of Seattle's prominent Jewish leaders and philanthropists. WSJHS, 3.

The wedding portrait of Frank Antell and his bride, Ann Ornstein, wearing a gown she made herself, ca. 1886. By arriving in Seattle when Washington was still a territory, Orthodox Frank Antell was automatically a citizen of the United States when Washington achieved statehood. Yet no one could keep him from attending citizenship classes at Yesler Library, said his daughter Celia "Babe" Antell Burnett: "He was so proud of the little symbolic flag that he got at the ceremony." MSCUA/UWL, *neg. 994.*

own spellings on names they could not pronounce. Names were often changed, sometimes inadvertently. When asked by an Ellis Island official how to spell his name, Lithuanian Yechiel Boon, the first of the Boon family to settle in the Far West, haltingly replied: "Mit a B und an N"—and Yechiel Boon became Eli Bean.[14] However, perhaps the greatest number of name changes were made by the immigrants themselves, who enthusiastically adopted their New World of America and "Americanized" their names as quickly as they could.

A few of the hordes of newcomers arriving in New York came to the Northwest at the direction of the Industrial Removal Office of New York, part of the Jewish Agricultural and Industrial Aid Society, whose job it was to settle immigrants outside of New York. Many were directed to settlements outside of New York by the Hebrew Immigrant Aid Society (HIAS), one of the first such organizations established by the Eastern European Jews themselves rather than by their German-Jewish predecessors.[15]

To some, land itself was the lure to settle in the Northwest. Under the czars, Jews had been denied the right to own real estate. Longing to work the soil, grow food, and live their own lives, some came to homestead areas like Republic or other agricultural colonies. A group of Orthodox Jews who eventually settled in Washington first attempted to homestead in the Garske area, fifteen miles from Devils Lake, North Dakota. They were sponsored by the Hebrew Emigrant Aid

Society, which began in New York in 1881 and dissolved two years later. The experimental colony proved unsuccessful, and many left. The last to leave, the family of Sara Kahn Siegel, came to Seattle in 1891.[16]

Many of the Orthodox Jews arriving in Washington State in this wave of settlement may well have thought they had come to the very ends of the earth. Far from the cosmopolitan cities of Europe and a long way from the thriving, bustling Jewish community of New York, this distant state in the Pacific Northwest seemed a world far different from the shtetl villages of Lithuania, Poland, and Russia. There were no synagogues, no kosher food, and no Yiddish newspapers. They spoke Yiddish, a language generally disdained by the assimilated Jews from Germany. Most had little secular education and few connections.

For many, their arrival in America meant a departure from old-country customs, which up to then had directed their lives. Few talked about the life they had left behind them. "I don't think my mother ever saw my father until it was time to get married," said Esther Rickles King, daughter of one of the first Orthodox Jewish families to settle in Washington. The marriage of her parents, Gershon and Rose Rickles, had taken place in Russia after being arranged through a matchmaker. Max Katz believed

The Rickles family, who often provided beds to newly arrived immigrants, came to Seattle in 1887. Pictured here are the five sisters among the nine Rickles children. Seated: Sophie (Mrs. Steiner Kline) and Goldie (Mrs. Samuel Cone); standing: Simmie (Mrs. Herman Mosler), Esther (Mrs. Weiss King), and Bertha (Mrs. Sam Mosler). MSCUA/UWL, neg. 18970.

Rabbi Hirsch Genss, a member of Seattle's Bikur Cholim (although not its rabbi), helped eastern European immigrants cope with legal and other requirements of an unfamiliar society, and aided Seattle's first Sephardic immigrants in finding housing and work. MSCUA/UWL, *neg. 1097.*

that it was this old-country marriage custom that had brought his father to Seattle. Although Isaac Jacob Katz said he had fled Russia to evade the Russian draft, Max suspected that his father escaped not only the Russian draft, but also his wife by an arranged marriage. In Seattle, Rabbi Hirsch Genss granted Katz a divorce, freeing him to marry the young Russian immigrant who became Max's mother. Rabbi Genss was a wise as well as a conscientious man. Before marrying any young Jewish immigrant to the girl of his choice, Genss insisted that a letter be written back to the old country first to make sure that the prospective groom was not already married.[17]

The established German-Jewish community in America did not heartily welcome the growing numbers of Eastern Europeans. "American Jewry [in 1881], a quarter of a million strong, was at first indifferent, apathetic and unfriendly, to say the least, toward hordes of immigrants from Eastern Europe," reported Irving Howe in his book *World of Our Fathers.* The large-scale arrival of mostly Russian Jews generally dismayed the German Jews, although the reaction was perhaps less intense in the sparsely populated Northwest than elsewhere. The flow of immigrants speaking Yiddish was threatening, "even terrifying," to the assimilated German Jews who had been living equally among the general population for several decades. They may have been motivated less by snobbism than by anxiety, since Jews had been inconspicuous until large numbers of new immigrants began to arrive in the 1880s. They feared that the discrimination Jews had historically faced, but not felt to much extent in this new land of America, would now begin.[18]

The pattern of relative following relative and friend following friend occurred among Eastern European Jewish immigrants to Washington State, as it did generally in immigrant ethnic groups throughout the country. Other Friedmans came to Tacoma in the wake of the first Friedman; almost the whole town of Skapiskis in Northern Lithuania followed their earlier landsmen to Bellingham; and kin followed kin to Everett.

In Washington State, as in other parts of the country, as the Eastern European immigrants earned money, they sent funds home to finance passage for members of their families, who in turn brought over other family members. Harry Pruzan, whose father arrived in Seattle from Latvia in 1900, observed in 1932, "My father figured out that there are more than 100 persons in Seattle now who would not be here had he not come."[19]

From Latvia to Tacoma

The families of Friedmans, who became a prominent part of Tacoma's Jewish community through the first half of the 1900s, were the relatives of Adolph Friedman, who had settled in Tacoma fifty years before. Following the example set by their great uncle Adolph, six grandsons and one granddaughter of Adolph Friedman's brother, Zalman, left Latvia to settle in Tacoma beginning in 1896. "At one time," observed Judge Leonard Friedman, born in Tacoma in 1915, "I counted fifty first cousins."[20]

Although little is known about Adolph Friedman, believed to be the first Jew to settle in Washington Territory, family records reveal that he left Kurland, Latvia, at age nineteen.

Adolph Friedman, an adventurer from Latvia, is believed to have reached the deep-water port of present-day Tacoma (then British territory) in about 1845. He died in Tacoma in 1911 at the age of ninety. Courtesy of Lorraine Sussman Braverman, Tacoma.

We always celebrated the holidays with special foods—challah on Friday night for our Sabbath dinner, matzo ball soup on Pasach, latkes for Chanukah, hamentashen for Purim. . . . On Purim when I and my sister were little girls, one of us would get to wear the Queen Esther crown that my grandfather, Louis Benson, had made over one hundred years ago for my mother when she was a child in Michigan. It is cast of gold pot metal, set with colorful stones. Dressed as Queen Esther, my mother wore it every Purim. After her, I and my sister wore it, and after us, my daughters.

—Rhoda Sussman Lewis, daughter of Joe and Minnie Sussman, Tacoma

Five years later, as a crewman on a Scandinavian ship, Friedman arrived in the strangely isolated and beautiful setting of Puget Sound. After a few years of supplying goods to pioneer fishermen, he joined the gold rush to California, returning to Tacoma a number of years later. He ran a general merchandising store in the part of Tacoma that was called Old Town, and later a real estate business on south Tacoma Avenue. At some time during his business dealings in Tacoma, he acquired a large property in the Steilacoom area and named it the "Friedman Addition." Friedman married a very much younger relative, Masha Stusser, of Victoria, British Columbia, and died childless in 1911. In 1917, the Friedman Addition became part of the acreage on which the U.S. government built Camp Lewis.[21]

When Rebecca Sussman Olswang left the little town of Sassmachen in the eastern part of Latvia to make a home first in Bellingham, then in Tacoma, with her husband, Pete, she started an almost total Sussman family emigration. Her fifteen-year-old brother Frank followed in 1895, and other members of her family came after him. Frank's future wife, Ida Yudelson, came to Tacoma in 1902 at the age of ten with her mother and three little sisters to join her father and older sister.[22] As relatives and friends of the Friedmans, Sussmans, and other Yiddish-speaking Jews came to Tacoma, the number of Tacoma's Eastern Europeans soon equaled the established Central Europeans.

What these transplanted Jews from the small towns and villages of Eastern Europe liked about Tacoma was that all its Jews knew one another even though each family lived surrounded by non-Jewish neighbors. All knew Phil Brodsky, with his crackly voice and ever-present cigar; Anna Brodsky, with her strong Russian accent persisting throughout the years of her life; Lena Rotman, whose strudel and *teiglach* graced every Bar Mitzvah buffet; Louie Lamken, with his wide grin and stock of scatological stories; and the superb cook, Lizzie Lamken, who never revealed a recipe.[23]

From Skapiski to Bellingham

The roots of Bellingham's Jewish community stretch back to the little town of Skopishok in northeast Lithuania. (Skopishok is Yiddish for the town of Skapiskis.) The Glazers, one of the early families of the community, came in 1904. Frances Glazer Garmo's mother followed her sister (Mrs. Eli Schuman) and her two brothers, Sam and Louis, after receiving a letter from her sister. In Yiddish, it said, "It is hard to be a Jew in a small city, but it is clean and pretty, and a man can make a living."[24]

The little sawmill town on the shore of Bellingham Bay was indeed pretty and offered a ready livelihood. The outlying forests supplied virgin-growth Douglas fir, Sitka spruce, hemlock, and cedar, and the offshore waters offered up salmon in abundance. The rumor in 1858 of a gold strike nearby had swelled the

little town of New Whatcom (later called Bellingham) into a city of ten thousand almost overnight. But the excitement, as local historian William Speidel pointed out, proved to be only excitement.[25]

In the mid-1850s, the Lithuanian town of Skopishok consisted of about 330 people, wrote the historian of Bellingham's Jewish community, Tim Baker. Eighty-five percent of them were Jews—half Hasidim and half Mitnaggedim, who, for the most part, kept separate from each other and did

Four daughters of Bellingham pioneers pose for a picture, ca. 1920. From left: Sarah Schuman, Ethel Schuman, Margaret Hurwitz, and Eve Glazer. Courtesy of Temple Beth Israel Archives, Bellingham.

*Operated by Eli Bean and Louis Thal, the San Francisco Store in New Whatcom
(Bellingham) sold everything from secondhand baby carriages to guns. Thal (at center,
wearing cap) worked there for several years following his arrival in late 1904. Courtesy
of Temple Beth Israel Archives, Bellingham.*

not intermarry. The Hasidim, who worshipped with ecstatic joy and dance, followed a tzaddik, or charismatic leader; the Mitnaggedim took their authority from
more conventional Torah studies. "As far as we know," said Baker, "the Jews who
traveled from Skopishok to Bellingham were all Mitnaggedim." Hasidim preferred
to stay near their tzaddik.

It was no secret why so many Jews left Skopishok. Even though pogroms were
rare in Lithuania, Skopishok Jewish families in the late 1800s led a hard life. They
lived in extreme poverty, and anti-Semitism was high. The first three Jewish families in Bellingham were Eli Schuman and his family from Skopishok; Esther and

Lazarus Jacobs, from either Poland or Germany; and Leon Lobe, who arrived in the United States from France in the 1860s and had lived for a time in California. Yechiel Boon, who had served in the czar's army playing a brass horn in the band, had married Ruchel Leah Schuman. Boon followed his brother-in-law, Eli, to America, and arrived in Bellingham in 1902. As noted above, Boon's name was changed by Ellis Island officials to Eli Bean.[26] Later the Bean family moved on to Olympia. Other Skopishok immigrants settling in Bellingham in the early 1900s included the Thal, Horowitz, and Pearlstein families.

By 1906 some forty Jewish families—enough to start a little shul, Beth Israel, on F Street—had become Bellingham citizens. Some had come from Rokishok, just nine or ten miles to the east of Skopishok. This group revolved around the household of David and Marita Shure, and included the Grieff, Poplack, Levin, and Jaffe families. Each group had its own landsman society, both of which collected clothing for shipment back to friends and relatives in their towns. Frances Glazer remembered her father bundling up the clothing in their living room, using burlap cloth, rope, and string. Her brother, Edward, born in Bellingham in 1908, estimated a maximum of fifty Jewish families at Bellingham's peak in the early decades. "We all knew everybody," Glazer said. Because of marriages between individuals of Skopishok and Rokishok, "everyone was more or less related to each other directly or indirectly."[27]

Everett's First Jewish Settlers

Following a brother and a married sister who had immigrated to Everett a few years earlier, nineteen-year-old Abe Kosher left his home and his future wife in Kiev for America in 1913. Although neither his brother nor his sister remained in Everett, Kosher found the town exactly to his liking. A year of working and saving

> Helen Ellenbogen, who grew up in Everett, recalled that a schochet (ritual slaughterer) came from Seattle every Friday and went from one Jewish house to another to kill chickens for the Sabbath dinner. "At our house he would slaughter the chickens in the backyard under a tree." Her father, who came to America from Redutta, Lithuania, settled in Everett in 1907, and moved his family to Seattle in the early 1930s.
>
> —Meta Buttnick and Julia Niebuhr Eulenberg, "Jewish Settlement in the Small Towns of Washington State: Republic," WSJHS Newsletter, March 1984

*Moe Michelson and his mother in the secondhand store Michelson's father opened in
Everett in 1906. Following his Sussman cousins from Tacoma, the Latvian-born elder
Abe Michelson chose to settle with his Canadian bride in Everett and remained there
the length of his life.* MSCUA/UWL, neg. 1916.

brought his bride to Everett. The newly married couple celebrated their wedding
with a traditional "shivaree"—the banging of pots and pans outside the windows, a
custom transported from their Russian villages. Mary Kosher Brown's mother told
her that their celebration was so successful that "some of the Gentile neighbors
joined in."[28]

Latvian-born Abe Michelson first followed his relatives to Tacoma, then
moved with his wife to Everett in 1906. Abe and a young brother, Sam, started
out peddling junk with a horse and wagon, and progressed to opening a secondhand store on Hewitt Avenue. By the 1920s, they established the Riverside Junk
Company, and later a large wiping-rag business. The eldest of Michelsons' six children, Moe, born in Everett in 1908, became a private railroad owner in the state of
Washington and an active participant in Everett politics. An independent thinker

and a sometimes feisty member of the Everett City Council, on which he served for sixteen years, he won election to public office five times.[29]

The Surge to Seattle

While Tacoma, Olympia, Bellingham, Everett, and Spokane each had its coterie of Jewish settlers in the wave of Eastern European emigration from the late 1880s through the early 1900s, it was to Seattle that the greatest number came. Once gold was discovered in Alaska, Seattle's dominance as the Jewish center of the state grew. "Seattle was a magic word because of the gold rush in 1898," noted William Rosen. To his father, Morris Rosen, as it was to many others, Seattle was synonymous with Alaska. Morris Rosen called the small shop he rented at the foot of King Street the Alaskan Copper Works.[30]

Rosen, a journeyman coppersmith, learned his trade in the Baltic port of Libau before arriving in Philadelphia at the age of eighteen. He married an acquaintance from Europe, worked on the Panama Canal in 1908, and came to Bremerton, Washington, in 1914 to work at the Navy shipyard. Within two years, he established Alaska Copper Works, and two years later moved the company to Spokane Street and Railroad Avenue. His customers came from shipyards, dairies, and candy manufacturers. Beginning in 1924, Alaska Copper Works supplied Puget Sound's new pulp mills with copper pipes and fittings. Later, as the Alaskan Copper and Brass Company, the Rosen family engaged in the purchase and distribution of raw materials rather than in fabrication.

Like Rosen, many Eastern European Jewish immigrants started their new life in Washington State with skills they had brought with them. Some worked as tinsmiths, tailors, and bakers. Others opened stores selling secondhand merchandise,

On May 29, 1901, the first graduating class of the University of Washington's new law school included Bella Weretnikow, of Russian Jewish immigrant parents. "There was only one other Jewish student in the class, a young man named Aubrey Levey," wrote Bella in her memoirs. Bella and her parents first went to Winnipeg, Manitoba, in the spring of 1882, when Bella was an infant. She and her mother, Eliza Marks (who had divorced and remarried), resettled in Seattle in 1893.

—Judith W. Rosenthal, "My Maternal Grandparents: Bella Weretnikow and Lewis Newman ("L.N.") Rosenbaum," WSJHS Newsletter, winter 2001

Morris Rosen founded Alaska Copper Works during World War I. His descendants contin-ued to own and operate the business into the twenty-first century. MSCUA/UWL, *neg. 1353.*

clothing, and household furnishings. Many would spend years establishing eco-nomic footholds and managed only to "make a living," and others would develop substantial firms from humble beginnings.

Alfred Shemanski began his career in Seattle peddling from door to door in a wagon drawn by a horse named "Challenge." He later became a president of the Board of Regents of the University of Washington, a director of Seattle's First National Bank, and a city leader. "What a wonderful country America is that an immigrant Jewish boy from Poland with no formal education could become presi-dent of the Board of Regents of a great University," he once observed.[31]

Alfred Shemanski left his Orthodox home in his native land for the United States in 1897, one day before he would have been inducted into the army. Over six feet tall, this lanky twenty-six-year-old arrived in Seattle with $300 advanced by his brother in San Francisco. He began his career selling curtains and other household goods house-to-house. The Eastern Outfitting Company, a chain of de-

*The Eastern Outfitting Company were pioneers of [retail] credit. Credit in the
early days was considered living beyond your means. Our little account books
never had the name of the company. Because anyone looking at that could say,
"See, he had to buy on credit." Today if you don't have credit you're considered
there must be something wrong with you. Just the opposite.*

—Herbert Lipman, MSCUA/UWL, 2301

partment stores in Seattle, Tacoma, and Spokane, sprang from this first enterprise
of Shemanski's and was developed in partnership with his two brothers.

"Shemanski became a prominent force in the community shortly after he
arrived here," said Ross Cunningham in a *Seattle Times* article in August 1966.
Shemanski remained influential until his death at the age of ninety-two. "For
more than six decades he was a giant in this community. The important thing
about this greatly and widely beloved civic leader was not the extent of his influence, which was vast, but how he used that influence." Shemanski was a leader in
numerous agencies and organizations, many of which were concerned with the
welfare of people, young and old, no matter their race, nationality, or religion. He
was appointed to the Board of Regents of the University of Washington in 1933,
served for twenty-two years, and won election twice as board president.[32]

Although Eastern European immigrants who came to Washington comprised
only a trickle compared with the stream of those who settled in the eastern and
midwestern cities of the United States, Seattle's Jewish population grew large
enough by 1910 to sustain kosher restaurants, butcher shops, and bakeries. Rabbi
Hirsch Genss, who performed ritual slaughter of animals for Seattle Jews in the
1890s, operated a meat market at the turn of the century. In 1909, Joshua Pinch's
and Moses Kopstein's butcher shop at 1220 Main Street sold kosher products.

Samuel Mosler opened a bakery near Pike Place Market in 1898 and called it
the New York Bakery. By 1909, the New York Bakery had moved to 661 Weller Street
in the heart of Seattle's Chinatown (now International District), where it continued for fifteen years. Harry and Herman Mosler, Sam's brothers, also established a
bakery business, first on Jackson Street and then on Yesler, and like their brother,

*The Eastern Outfitting Company started under the entrepreneurship of Alfred Shemanski,
who sold goods from door to door on a wagon drawn by his horse "Challenge."*
MSCUA/UWL, *neg. 1401.*

> *My father was in partnership with his two brothers running a hardware store busi-*
> *ness closing on Saturday, the Sabbath, in accordance with Jewish law. My uncles*
> *decided they were losing a lot of business. They wanted to open up Saturday. My*
> *mother told my father that if they open that store on Saturday she'd divorce him.*
> *So the partnership split up.*
> —Sam Aronin, MSCUA/UWL, 2660-001

endowed it with a "back East" flavor by naming it the Brooklyn Bakery. However, neither the New York Bakery nor the Brooklyn Bakery endured under the Mosler entrepreneurship. Harry moved on to Portland, and in 1925, Sam Mosler left the bakery business to set up what was perhaps the first health foods store in the state. "Sam, he was just crazy about all that stuff," said Henry Ralkowski, who, with his father, took over the New York Bakery. "He opened a little place on Union Street . . . he made dry cereal before Kellogg did. He used to toast bran . . . sprinkle it with malt and oat, no sugar, and that was a health food, and a very good laxative." What Sam Mosler pursued for personal interest and satisfaction, others like Kellogg and Post developed to immense profit. Henry Ralkowski pointed out that "around Skid Road [Yesler Way], there were quite a few famous people, like Mr. Campbell. . . . He was cooking down there. He went East, and everyone said, 'that crazy cook is going to put soup in cans.' It was a joke."[33]

Unfortunately, the kind of joke produced by Mr. Campbell of Campbell Soups was not reproduced by any of the start-up businesses of Seattle's Jewish immigrant butchers, bakers, and grocers. Nevertheless, many of them built their businesses and prospered, some to a greater degree than others. For example, Abe Brenner started his first bakery near the King Street railroad station (ca. 1903), but later moved it to 1803 Yesler Way. Other kosher shops followed on Yesler Way, Cherry Street, and streets in between, such as Louis Hoffman's kosher grocery on Yesler between Seventeenth and Eighteenth (1918).

The bakery that Abe Brenner started early in the 1900s provided bagels, pumpernickel, rye bread, and challah, and it remained an institution in Seattle and its environs for almost a century. Consistently turning out hard-crusted bread, Brenner's Bakery was one of the few Jewish bakeries to sustain Old World tastes through the years when soft white breads such as Wonder and Langendorf were the norm. A number of bakeries were established by men who had worked with Sam Mosler or Abe Brenner and who later left to open their own firms. These included Lippman's Bakery and Eger Brothers Bakery.

How Abe Brenner came to Seattle in 1902 after working a year or two in a bakery owned by a relative in Newport News, Virginia, was a story he often told. Constantly in trouble with his disapproving uncle, Brenner went to the train station and asked for a ticket that would take him "as far away as I can get." The ticket brought him to Seattle.[34]

After Brenner opened his first bakery near the King Street Station, he peddled his bread door-to-door with a horse and wagon. He never really approved of the delivery truck that eventually replaced the horse-drawn wagon because it "wouldn't follow you door-to-door like a horse."

"Once our reputation spread, people from all over town came to buy our bread," said his son Joe. Brenner's family grew as steadily as did his bakery business. Itsy, Charlie, and Joe grew up measuring and stirring flour, firing ovens, and delivering bread. Five sons were followed by a daughter, Yetta, and a sixth son, Joe. A seventh son, Mark, was born after the death of Brenner's wife, Bessie Rosenthal, and a second marriage to Ruth Kutoff.

Charles Aronson at the reins of his express wagon, outside his hardware business at 111 First Avenue South, ca. 1905–10. Like Aronson, many immigrant Jews who began peddling goods house-to-house eventually became store owners. WSJHS, 98.

Owners and employees of Pacific Coast Casing Company, a sausage manufacturer, at Twentieth and Columbia, 1923: Hugo Jassny (far left), Max Rind (sixth from right), and Max Munchein (far right). MSCUA/UWL, neg. 1342.

Russian-born Julius Shafer's secondhand clothing store at Second and Jackson greatly profited from the Alaska-Yukon gold rush. Shafer arrived in the United States at age twelve, worked for uncles in Kansas and Texas, and made his way to Seattle in 1890 at age eighteen, attracted by opportunities created by the Great Fire. In 1906, with his brother Izzie, Shafer purchased the Arcade Building at Second and Union, north of the business district on what was known as "Denny's cow pasture." There, having anticipated the shift of commerce northward, they opened Shafer Brothers, the city's largest retail clothing and men's furnishings store. After retiring from the clothing business in 1921, Shafer made a fortune in real estate.[35]

In the first decade following the gold rush, some Jews came to Seattle to try their luck simply because Seattle was the most important city in Washington. But it was more than luck that worked for Moses Genauer. He arrived in Seattle in 1909 after leaving his wife and two children in Galicia and traveling through Montreal to get to New York. In Seattle, he walked the city's neighborhoods, buying used clothing door-to-door and selling it to the secondhand stores on First Avenue downtown. Within three years, Genauer sent for his family. His son, Ben, recalled that his father found a wedding ring in the pocket of a suit he purchased at a home and returned it the next day. The ring belonged to an officer of the National Bank of Commerce. Genauer's integrity had made a valuable friend. From then on, he was always able to get credit from the bank, even during the Great Depression. M. Genauer and Company opened a used clothing store at Second and Jackson in

The Miller family's Seattle Quilt Manufacturing Company struck a bonanza with their sleeping bag designed for the Alaska trade. The Seattle Quilt building still stands in Pioneer Square. MSCUA/UWL, *neg. 11559.*

about 1920, and then dealt only in new clothing. The company became a jobber, buying from New York manufacturers, and eventually manufactured its own line of suits in the east and in Seattle.[36]

Seattle's early expanding era of business provided a jump start for mechanically minded Louis Diamond, the oldest of three sons of Russian-born parents. In 1922, after leaving high school, Louis Diamond began servicing cars for the doctors and dentists in the Medical Dental Building. So convenient was his service that customers began leaving their cars in his working lot across from the Bon Marche. Hoping to gain a little more work space, Louis began to charge ten cents a day for the parking—thereby creating the first pay-for-parking lot in the country. In 1945, after serving in World War II, his brother Joe, an attorney, with the help of youngest brother Leon, expanded the business into a pay-for-parking empire. Today Diamond Parking reigns throughout the United States and Canada.[37]

As Seattle grew, many pawnshops that had been opened by Eastern European Jewish immigrants evolved into jewelry stores, and secondhand clothing stores became first-class establishments. Max Weisfield, a role model in the pawn-to-jewelry business, created the motto, "If Max Weisfield can't fix your watch, throw it away." He and the Friedlanders, Burnetts, Bridges, and Rivkins were some of Seattle's most prominent Jewish-owned jewelers.

To Seattle for Jewish Life

The growth of Seattle's Jewish population influenced many other Jewish families who had first settled in Washington's smaller towns. Among them were Morris Schneider and his wife, Henrietta, who arrived in Woolley, Skagit County, in 1892, with a daughter, Rebecca, born in Los Angeles, and a son, Benjamin, born in Anacortes. Along with its twin town, Sedro, Wooley lay at the junction of two railroad lines—one connecting Seattle with Vancouver, British Columbia, and the other running eastward from Anacortes across the Cascade crest to join the Northern Pacific at Spokane. Although there were no other Jews in either Wooley or Sedro, Schneider, an Orthodox Jew, unpacked his bags, settled down with his wife and children, established a general store, and added another daughter, Jochabed (Jean). In 1899, the year Jean was born, the two towns combined and became Sedro-Wooley.[38]

Born as Moishe Nicianski in the Russian Pale of Settlement, just east of the present border between Poland and Germany, Nicianski immigrated to New York in 1880 at age twenty-three and changed his name to Schneider. In New York City, he went to work as a tailor, and five years later married a seventeen-year-old New

Yorker, Yetta Berkowitz, who gave her age on the marriage certificate as twenty-one and her name as Henrietta.

The Schneider family lived in Sedro-Wooley until 1909. The Schneider Department Store grew into a major firm in the county. The store dealt in merchandise ranging from wool yarn bought by Coast Salish Indian women living in the area for knitting socks (which Schneider bought and sold to the loggers) to silks and brocades purchased by the town's prostitutes. Small daughter Jean once received a gift of a large decorated hat from one of the ladies, in which she paraded happily around town until corralled by her anxious parents.[39]

As the only Jewish family in the community, Schneider found it next to impossible to keep Orthodox Jewish observances. The kosher meat he ordered from San Francisco usually arrived spoiled, and teaching Hebrew to his small son, Bennie, was an effort he soon abandoned. When Rebecca and Ben graduated from Sedro-Wooley High School, Henrietta saw a need to remove her family from the non-Jewish atmosphere of Sedro-Wooley. The Schneiders moved to the thriving city of Seattle in 1909.

Jewish families living in other far-off corners of Washington State also gravitated to the more Jewish-populated Seattle. Among them were almost all of the twenty-five Jewish families who had originally homesteaded in Republic. In 1900 this small town, with a population of ten to twelve thousand, ranked as the sixth-largest city in eastern Washington. The discovery of gold lured some to settle there; others came to homestead land advertised as "free." But neither the gold mining nor the farming panned out in the mountainous area of Republic. The heyday of the gold rush ended by 1906, and the difficulties of working the rocky and arid soil diminished the promise of free farmland.[40]

Charles Abraham Greenberg, a Russian immigrant from Bessarabia, became the third Jew to settle in Republic, and when his wife and seven children joined him a few years later, the Greenbergs became Republic's first Jewish family. Three more children were added to the brood in the large five-bedroom house that Greenberg built. Selling supplies to miners, Greenberg was the last Jewish settler to leave. He transferred his family to Spokane; others moved to Seattle.

Ownership of land in Republic required five years of working the land. Eager to settle on farming land of his own, neither Harry Kossen, a Russian immigrant, nor others who came with equally high hopes, foresaw the difficulties that lay ahead. Rose Kossen Abrams remembered that her father "nearly killed himself digging for water." She remembered her mother carrying water from a neighbor's well to bathe the children and saying, "With bloody tears I carry this water." Added to the hardship of wresting a living from the land was the isolation. The Kossen

"We observed all the Jewish holidays," said Jenny Krajewski Shafran, born on a homestead of 365 acres on the outskirts of Republic in 1911. "I have never seen a more beautiful Pesach conducted to this day than in our little log cabin four miles from any neighbor."

—Helen Ellenbogen, MSCUA/UWL, 1849

family left their homestead, giving up the land and everything they had put into it, and moved to Seattle in 1909 "where there were shuls and Hebrew schools." A second group of Jewish settlers came to Republic in 1914 from Glace Bay, Nova Scotia, and brought with them a rabbi, Hebrew teachers, and loan money from various agricultural aid societies. Most of its members lived on the land, sharing property, improvements, livestock, and equipment in common. "My father helped them out with milk and eggs and cheese and potatoes and onions, everything he could give them," said Jenny Krajewski. "But they couldn't make a living, and they didn't stay." Louis Krajewski had worked as a baker in Chicago until he could afford to bring his wife and three children over from Poland. When Krajewski died in 1919, his family had to give up the free land that had brought them to the area. They, too, eventually moved to Seattle.

A Search for Utopia

Although, in general, Jews from both central and Eastern Europe who settled in Washington established and maintained Jewish connections, some came with the purpose of abandoning them. Such were the Jewish pioneers who settled in the western Washington town of Home Colony.

Home Colony, a place for "free thinkers," was settled by a group of intellectuals, many of whom were Jews who had come to America from Eastern Europe. They established Home Colony on the shores of Puget Sound on Joe's Bay, off Carr Inlet, thirteen miles west of Tacoma, in February 1896. No roads linked the bay to civilization. One of a half dozen or so early communal settlements in western Washington commonly called utopian or socialist colonies, Home Colony guaranteed settlers an opportunity to live as they pleased. In the words of journalist Stewart H. Holbrook, "Home was a place where two-acre farmers were as conversant with Marx as with poultry." Residents numbered 120 in 1905 and 213 five years later. [41]

The Chicago home of Michael and Ida Rubenstein had been "a favorite anarchist gathering place where traditional Jewish foods offset less Orthodox guests, stories and songs."[42] When the Rubensteins heard about the tiny commune far off in the Northwest, they traveled by train to Tacoma, and from there to Home Colony by boat. As soon as Ben Alt arrived at Home, he wrote back to tell his friends in Chicago about the commune. Jacob Ilitowitz, born in Vilna, Lithuania, who came to work the land at Home, was one of those friends. Among other early Jewish settlers at Home were the Haiman brothers: Louis, a barber, and Joe, the first storekeeper for the community.[43]

Publicized as an ideal community, Home Colony had no laws, rules, or regulations, except for the prohibition of tobacco and intoxicants. Each family, expected to build and maintain its own home, purchased one or two acres of land from the association. A library, a literary society, and a philosophy discussion group existed at Home, but no church or synagogue. The many Jews who settled at Home appeared to have put their religious traditions behind them. Members organized lectures, musical events, and summer art classes for children. A Home baseball team competed with other teams in the area. Home residents maintained a peaceful community, opposing physical force, violence, and many of the restrictions imposed by government and society in general.

A famous Jewish visitor, Emma Goldman, the most noted woman anarchist in the nation, visited Home during her first western tour in 1898. When Seattle and Tacoma cancelled her speaking arrangements, she lectured for three successive evenings in Home on "The Woman Question," "Authority vs. Liberty," and "Patriotism." But she did not find Home Colony memorable. "The people seemed more interested in vegetables and chickens than in propaganda," she was reported to have said.

Neighboring communities, however, did not view Home Colony with similar equanimity. "Shall anarchy and free love live in Pierce County?" blazed a banner headline in 1908 in Tacoma's *Evening News*. Other papers in the area and as far away as Bellingham joined in angry denunciations of Home Colony. In 1911, after the arrest of four Home residents for swimming in the nude, an article in the Home Colony's publication, *The Agitator*, defended the right of colonists to swim with or without bathing suits. Newspapers in the surrounding communities termed the writer and editor, Jay Fox, a radical who promoted the idea of free love. With such harassments increasing, the shine on the idyllic community gradually wore off. Residents began to leave, and commonly owned land began to fall into disrepair. Of the Jews who lived at Home Colony:

Many stayed for a number of years and then left. They did not find it the heaven they had been looking for. . . . Anita Rubenstein Snyder lived at Home off and on from the time she was six months old. Her father, Michael, couldn't make a living off the land and like many other residents found it necessary to work in Tacoma or Seattle. The men would come out to be with their families at Home as often as possible. Anita and her sister went to a two-room school at Home. . . . After the Rubenstein family moved to Seattle permanently, Anita finished high school and went on to attend the University of Washington. . . . Ernest Falkoff [another Home-grown child] entered the University of Washington at the age of 13, graduated with honors and practiced law.[44]

The association of Home Colony dissolved in May 1921. Much of the land passed into private ownership, and many members sold or rented their property to busi-

Picnicking at Ault Farm, Home Colony, became a favored weekend pastime for many Seattle Jewish families in the early 1900s. WSJHS, 96.

nesses. After World War I, when Home Colony became a conventional rural community, former member Ben Alt built a large hotel across the bay as a resort for summer visitors who were largely Jewish.

Home Colony had been "a strong little magnet in the remote Northwest," wrote Charles LeWarne in his book *Utopias on Puget Sound*. "A large number of celebrated persons, mostly noncomformists of one shade or another, came to this small backwater community. . . . It was a remarkable place to live, populated with fascinating, colorful, provocative and highly intelligent people. . . . Its residents talked and read and wrote about topics and ideas that conventional society preferred to leave unchallenged . . . issues that society later would be forced to confront."[45]

Unlike the large Jewish populations of New York, Philadelphia, Chicago, and other big eastern and midwestern U.S. cities, the Eastern European Jews who came to Washington were mainly merchants rather than laborers. Many who started as junk peddlers became prominent dealers in scrap metal. These firms included the Michelsons in Everett, Sussman's Steel in Tacoma, Sidell's Iron and Metal, and Glant's Pacific Iron and Metal in Seattle. In this, Washington was typical of the entire country. As historian Henry Feingold has noted, Eastern European Jewish immigrants owned 90 percent of the scrap metal business in the United States by the 1930s.[46]

Most Eastern European immigrants to Washington State, however, did not realize great success in the business world during their lifetimes. Their great achievement was to make the leap of immigration that gave their children the freedom and opportunities that America offered. In the next generation, many would attain prosperity in business and in the professions, and more than a few would achieve great financial success.

Sephardic Pioneers

T HE FIRST SEPHARDIM TO COME TO SEATTLE, THE inadvertent founders of Seattle's astonishingly large Sephardic community, were two young men who arrived almost by chance in June 1902. They accompanied a Greek friend who was returning to Seattle after a visit to his Mediterranean family. Solomon Calvo and Jacob Policar arrived from the Turkish island of Marmara, wearing *tsizis* (a fringed garment) under their shirts and carrying their prayer books, their *tefillin*, and one change of underwear.[1]

Calvo and Policar were the first of the third wave of Jews to Washington State, arriving in Seattle from Turkey and the island of Rhodes. Unable to speak English, and eager to find other Jews, they stood on the waterfront street near a second-hand store saying "Yahudi, Yahudi" ("Jew, Jew"). When a curious crowd gathered around them, thirteen-year-old Jacob Kaplan, who was working in the store, came out to tell them that he, too, was a Jew. He took them to Rabbi Hirsch Genss, who introduced them to members of the Orthodox *shul*.[2]

Both young men were delighted to find other Jews in Seattle. However, Calvo and Policar were not like any Jews the Seattle Jews had known. Their language sounded strange. While the Jews who had previously settled in Seattle spoke German or Yiddish, the Sephardim spoke Ladino, or more precisely, Judeo-Spanish.[3] When, in an effort to prove themselves Jewish, Calvo and Policar read aloud from their prayer books, their pronunciation of Hebrew words was unfamiliar. The puzzled members of Seattle's Ashkenazic community were not entirely convinced that these newcomers were indeed Jews.

Orthodox Gershon Rickles set about to solve the mystery. He wrote to the Jewish community in New York to inquire about these new arrivals, and the reply set everyone's mind at ease.[4] The two young men were Sephardim, descendants

The first Sephardic Jews to Washington State found little in common with the earlier arriving Ashkenazic Jews. For many years, each group regarded the other as strangers, and intermarriage was frowned upon. Standing: Mushon (Patatel) Eskanazi, Jacob Policar, Moshon Adatto; seated: Solomon Calvo and unidentified individual. MSCUA/UWL, neg. 1084.

of Jews who had been expelled from Spain in 1492. Sephardim were among the first settlers to America in the seventeenth century. The Sephardim coming to America at the beginning of the twentieth century, like Calvo and Policar, came from the lands of the Ottoman Empire, where Jews had been severely affected by rising Turkish and other nationalism in the Balkans and precarious economic circumstances. They came to the United States seeking political and religious freedom as well as economic opportunities.[5]

Satisfied that the two young men from Marmara were as Jewish as himself, Rabbi Hirsch Genss found a place for Calvo and Policar to live, and work for them to do. Late in the fall of 1903, David Levy, another Sephardic Jew from Marmara, arrived. The first thing he did was go to the waterfront and take a deep breath of the salty Puget Sound air which, he said, "was just like Marmara."[6]

The three Sephardic young men, uncomfortable because their lack of Yiddish cut them off from many of their Jewish neighbors, spent much of their spare time at a Greek coffee house, chatting with Greek acquaintances, eating Greek food, and drinking Turkish coffee. It was at this coffee house, in 1904, that Calvo, Policar, and Levy met Nessim Alhadeff, the first immigrant to Seattle from the

Nessim Alhadeff, the first Jew from the island of Rhodes to settle in Seattle, and his wife, Rosa, also from Rhodes. Nessim established a large retail and wholesale fish business, which provided employment for his brothers and other immigrants who followed him. WSJHS, 191.

Greek island of Rhodes. By 1906 there were eighteen Sephardim in Seattle—seventeen bachelors and Dorah Levy, the first young Sephardic woman to arrive.[7]

The arrival of eighteen-year-old Dora Levy bewildered Rabbi Hirsch Genss. Muttering in Yiddish to his wife, he wondered what they were going to do with a young Sephardic girl among all those Sephardic men. Speaking in Yiddish that was as clear as Genss's, Levy interrupted. She wanted to get a job, she said. She had no intention of depending on other Sephardim, and she planned to live in a hotel until she could find a permanent residence.[8] The rabbi and his wife listened to the flood of Yiddish in astonishment. "Here is a Yidenah!" the rabbi said

Harry Policar (front row, center) was the first Sephardic boy born in Washington State. His father and mother, Isaac and Calo Policar, are seated behind him, and his siblings, Sultana and Morris, are on either side of him. Sol and Ralph Policar are in top row. MSCUA/UWL, neg. 10432.

in delight. Levy's knowledge of Yiddish was certainly unusual for a Sephardic Jew. Born in Istanbul, Levy received her education at the Scotch Missionary School, where she learned English, French, German, history, mathematics, geography, and literature. She knew Spanish because it was spoken at home, and Turkish since it was the native language. The Yiddish she picked up from her family's Ashkenazic neighbors.[9]

In Seattle, the Sephardic "Yidenah" soon proved her worth. She had no trouble finding work, and when other Sephardic women came to Seattle, she was their lifeline, acting as an interpreter because none of them could speak either English or Yiddish. In 1910, Dorah Levy became Mrs. Asher Cohen.[10]

The Newcomers

This young group of Seattle immigrants, which included such surnames as Alhadeff, Calvo, Policar, Peha, Hazan, Israel, Eskenazy, and Benezra, became the nucleus of Seattle's Sephardim. Among them were Sephardi from Istanbul and Rodosto, as well as from Rhodes and Marmara.

Esther Adatto, the first Sephardic bride, married David Levy in 1907 in a ceremony performed by Rabbi Hirsch Genss in his home. The first Seattle-born Sephardi was Aaron Policar (1908). Fortuna Calvo, the first Sephardic girl born in Seattle, remembered her father standing with her on the shore of Lake Washington when she was a small child and pointing to Mercer Island. "See across there?" he said. "That's Marmara!"[11]

It was the Alhadeffs who soon constituted the largest family unit in the Sephardic community. Nessim Alhadeff worked for a while for his Greek friends in their small fruit, vegetable, and fish stalls, then created a delivery business, delivering fresh fish to restaurants from Everett to Renton, riding on the Interurban railway. He opened the Palace Market in about 1907. One by one he brought his seven brothers, a sister, and his mother and father to Seattle, and brought Rosa Israel from Rhodes to Seattle as his bride. "He helped finance the bringing over of many, many of the Sephardic community of Rhodes," said his son Charles.

My father was seventeen when he arrived in Seattle [1904]. When he left the island of Rhodes, all he came with was a shopping bag of food and a big huge quilt that all the mothers would sew for their children. Each child got a quilt.
—Leni Peha LaMarche, MSCUA/UWL, 3452

*My father and Mr. Nhimas left Turkey because they didn't want to go into the
Turkish Army. They hid in a boat in the coal bins. After the ship departed from
Istanbul, they paid the purser for their passage and arrived in New York in
January of 1907. Knowing that there were some Sephardic men here in Seattle,
they took the train and came to Seattle. We arrived, my mother, my uncle Joe
Cohen, and myself as a baby, six months later. I was nine months of age, the first
Sephardic girl brought over from the old country to Seattle.*

—Rebecca Moshcatel, MSCUA/UWL, 2137-001

Developing his fish business (which eventually became the Palace Fish and Oyster
Company), Nessim provided work for everyone he helped bring to Seattle, including two brothers-in-law. "He was a bit of a philosopher," recalled Charles. "He
often used to say to us that if he never left us anything in life except a good name
. . . we could get along."[12]

Within a few years after the first arrivals, about forty Sephardic families
had settled in Seattle.[13] (Only a few Sephardim first settled outside of Seattle.
Centralia's early Jewish community included Sephardim who sold fish, fruits, and
vegetables. After a time, they forsook their businesses in Centralia to settle with
their families in Seattle.)

The early Sephardim in Seattle were augmented in 1909 when Bechor
Chiprut, living in the village of Tekirdag (Turkish for Rodosto) in mainland
Turkey, arrived with seventy young Sephardim fleeing conscription into the
Turkish army.[14] But not all immigrants heading for Washington State had a clear
picture of their exact destination. Jacob Aroghetti, living in Rhodes, campaigned
for emigration and made plans for himself and for a group of companions to follow
his fellow Sephardim to Seattle. Arriving in New York, he carefully bought tickets

*Many of Washington's immigrants arrived not only without money, but "often
with personal belongings consisting only of the clothes they wore," said Jack
Caston, who reached Seattle in 1911 from Turkey with his parents and two
brothers. "It was the accepted custom among our small Sephardic community
that no home was ever too small to accommodate new arrivals."*

—Jack Caston, "Pioneers Made Needed Sacrifices," *The Seattle Times*, undated
clipping in Moshcatel papers, MSCUA/UWL, 2137-001

and boarded the train—to Washington, D.C. Searching in vain for his Seattle friends, he finally discovered his mistake. Not willing to risk any more travel, Aroghetti settled in New York.[15]

The Ashkenazim in Seattle didn't know what to make of this fast growing group of Jews who smoked water pipes, drank Turkish coffee, and were so different from them. "My father," David Genss said, "often remarked that these Turks were more religious and devout than the Ashkenazim—he called them 'Turkishe Yiden.'"[16]

By 1913, six hundred Sephardim constituted Seattle's Judeo-Spanish colony, the largest number of Sephardim in any U.S. city outside of New York. (San Francisco and Atlanta each had a hundred.)[17] During immigration, a number of Turkish Sephardim came to Seattle through the office of the Jewish Agricultural and Industrial Aid Society. The overthrow of Turkish Sultan Abdul Hamid and

Ashkenazic Seattle Jews didn't know what to make of the fast-growing group of Sephardim who smoked water pipes, drank Turkish coffee, and made buñuelos *(a sort of donut without a hole, dipped in oil, fried and served with sugar and honey) instead of potato latkes on Hanukkah.* MSCUA/UWL, neg. 15643.

It was June 6, 1909, the year of the Alaska-Yukon-Pacific Exposition when David Mossafer, a native of the island of Rhodes, arrived in Seattle. After going from New York to relatives in Alabama, nineteen-year-old Mossafer had traveled across the country on the train and saw, for the first time, a Chinese person, and the wonder of falling snow. With a new feeling of worldliness, Mossafer demanded nickels instead of dimes in the change received from his first purchase in Seattle. The nickels were larger, therefore he surmised, they were worth more.
—From transcript of David Mossafer, MSCUA/UWL, 1742

the end of World War I brought hundreds more to Seattle—until the change in U.S. immigration rules in 1924 cut off all immigration from Southern and Eastern Europe. By the time the post–World War I immigration laws of the United States went into effect, the Seattle Sephardic community numbered over three thousand. They were among the twenty to twenty-five thousand Sephardic Jews settling in America coming primarily from Turkey, Greece, and Syria.[18]

Working Toward Prosperity

Like Nessim Alhadeff, Seattle's Sephardim quickly gravitated to the fish and produce trade, although there is little evidence that any of them had experience in these fields in Turkey or Rhodes. Solomon Calvo peddled fish from a cart for several years before opening Waterfront Fish and Oyster Company. Morris Hanan and others worked in the Pike Place Public Market, opening produce stalls, fish markets, and restaurants. Marco Franco operated produce stands in the Market from about 1911 to 1938, first with Herman Kronfeld, and then with his brother-in-law David Mossafer. (A few Sephardic-owned Public Market businesses remain today.) Israel Fis came to Seattle from Rhodes in 1914, worked in the Market for other Sephardic merchants, and opened the Palace Grocery at Fourteenth Avenue and East Spruce Street in 1922.[19] Many worked as bootblacks, shoe repairmen, and barbers. A few bootblacks, such as Sabitai Naon, saved enough to open shoe stores. Generally, this immigrant generation of Sephardim labored long hours for little pay, and many families lived in poverty through the Great Depression.

One of the exceptional Sephardic entrepreneurs was Sam Israel, who arrived in Seattle in 1919 at age twenty, never married, and accumulated a fortune by putting his earnings into buying buildings and land. Described as short, stout, excitable, and intolerant of anything bureaucratic, Israel bought his first building in the 1930s with savings earned from making and repairing shoes. After World War II, with profits made on a boot-repair contract with the U.S. Army, he started to buy real estate. During the next fifty years, this immigrant shoemaker from the island of Rhodes accumulated more than five hundred properties. They ranged over the entire state and included commercial buildings, home sites, wheat fields, orchards, ranches, and timber stands. He owned more than forty properties in Seattle, fourteen of them in Pioneer Square, and great stretches of land in eastern Washington.[20]

After World War II, he moved into a house on ranch property he owned overlooking Soap Lake. It included a vinyl sofa, a plastic table, and a few kitchen chairs. Although Israel could afford to live in luxurious style, he saw little need to augment his furnishings. Twenty years later he was still living in the house and still buying land, renting out the buildings he owned, and seldom selling anything. Often called a miserly landlord who never put any money into maintaining the building space he rented out, Sam Israel first made headlines in 1942 with a donation to

Sephardic immigrants first worked as bootblacks and did other manual labor. Many later went into shoe repair and the retail and wholesale shoe trade. Top row: Sam Amon and unidentified individual; first row: unidentified individual, Raliamin Calderon, Edward Tarica, Ralph Policar, Alvert Ovadia, and Isaac Eskenazi. MSCUA/UWL, neg. 143.

Solomon Calvo, Solti Levy, and a Greek friend in front of the Waterfront Fish and Oyster Company, ca. 1912. MSCUA/UWL, *neg. 1092.*

a wartime rubber drive of six tons of heels collected through his repair business. He made headlines again at his death in 1994 at age ninety-five, bequeathing the greater part of his $100 million estate to causes that had to do with ecology, Jewish life, and Jewish education.[21]

Like many of the Ashkenazim who preceded them, the Sephardim brought few resources other than their Jewish traditions, their sense of adventure, their capacity for long hours of hard work, and their hopes. David Behar described his Seattle antecedents this way: "That first generation of Sephardim in Seattle came from a Mediterranean culture, dominated by Islam yet scrupulously Jewish, a society whose form was not unlike the Spanish communities of their ancestors."[22] This description concurs with the reflection of community historian Albert Adatto, who suggested in a thesis written in 1939: "If Columbus were to return to life and live among the Seattle Sephardim he would be able to talk with them in an intelligible manner." Despite their four-century stopover in Turkey and Greece, "Columbus would find there existed a greater temperamental affinity with these Sephardim than any group of modern Spaniards."[23]

Foundation for a New Generation

The timing of arrival of the three waves of immigrants—German-speaking Central European, Yiddish-speaking Eastern European, and Ladino-speaking Sephardim—profoundly affected their respective economic development. The earliest to arrive in Washington Territory had a wide-open frontier economy to work in, with great opportunity for gain and an equal opportunity for failure. By the time of statehood in 1889, many had been in Washington for more than three decades and in the United States for even longer. Several of their business enterprises evolved from small beginnings to large, complex concerns over a period of many years.

The Eastern European Jews, who began coming to Washington in significant numbers after the completion of the transcontinental railroad in 1883, found a more developed, but still young, economy. The Alaska-Yukon gold rush and World War I boosted the state's economy, allowing some of these pioneers to establish firm beginnings for their enterprises. But it took decades for most to achieve economic stability.

The Sephardim who came after the turn of the century, and most after World War I, shared the same economic difficulties as the Eastern European immigrants. While a few of the Sephardic immigrants achieved business success relatively early, within ten or fifteen years of settling in Seattle, most of the immigrant generation of Sephardim lacked the skills or resources to achieve more than a bare subsistence. It was the children of the Sephardic immigrants, sustained by the sacrifices of their parents, who would gain economic success in Washington. By the 1990s, Sephardic Jews were included among Seattle's wealthiest families. When the city's new symphony hall was opened in 1998, it was named in honor of its largest benefactor, the Benaroya family.

Unity, Diversity, and Friction

T HE THREE WAVES OF WASHINGTON IMMIGRANTS FROM Central Europe, Eastern Europe, and the Mediterranean areas, part of the worldwide family of Jews, were a family of strangers in Washington State. Although diversity existed in Jewish communities throughout America, in Washington State, with its small Jewish population remote from established Jewish centers, the frictions arising from diversity were acute. Religious, cultural, and social divisions continued to separate the Central European from the Eastern European Jews, and both of them from the Mediterranean Jews, through more than half of the twentieth century.

In Seattle, for example, the longer-established, prosperous German-speaking Jews found it hard not to look down their noses at the Yiddish-speaking Eastern Europeans. "I would be much more blunt and frank and say there was a wall between the German Jews and others," admitted Morton Schwabacher.[1] The Eastern European Jews, in turn, viewed the Central Europeans from a cautious distance. They called them the *"Daitschen,"* Yiddish for Germans, not so much out of respect (although there was that, too) as from suspicion. On the other hand, they didn't hesitate to look down their own noses at the Ladino-speaking Sephardim.[2] And although Leni Peha LaMarche recalled that her mother "always felt kindly" towards the Ashkenazim, she said, "We knew we couldn't get along together. . . . They had a different type of a culture, so different."[3]

Divisions within Ashkenazim

In Washington State, as in Oregon, California, or almost every other region, the differences between German-speaking and Yiddish-speaking immigrant Jews went beyond language. Central Europeans, after decades in the United States, practiced Reform Judaism, and the Eastern Europeans were mainly Orthodox in the immigrant generation. Yet both were part of the Ashkenazic culture.

In Tacoma, where no Sephardim settled, the Jewish community was divided between those Jews who had come from the various German states and established a house of worship they referred to as temple, and those from the Russian areas, who formed their own house of worship which they called *shul*. Despite this separation, Morris Kleiner, a leader among Tacoma's Jews, recalled that everyone in the Jewish community "mingled." A kindly and caring man, Kleiner, who arrived in Tacoma in 1914 and established the beginnings of a three-generation lumber business, joined both temple and shul and participated in fund-raising and activities of both. Much of the mingling he referred to occurred among the lodge members of the B'nai B'rith, which drew from both houses of worship. However, not many of the *shul*-going, Russian-background group were "close" to the *Daitschen* or German-background temple group—even though a few, like Morris Kleiner, were reluctant to see any separation at all. Each "kept to themselves" in some degree in their social lives as well as in their religious lives. In those early years, most Jewish Tacomans simply accepted such divisions as inevitable.[4]

Like Tacoma, Spokane in its early years also found itself with two distinct Jewish communities. Betty Meyersberg, daughter of Harry Rosenhaupt, described the feeling "between the temple kids and the synagogue kids" as "very bristly." "The synagogue people didn't consider us as knowledgeable Jews and they let us know it."[5] Pearl Duitch Singer, whose mother was brought to Fargo, North Dakota, at age sixteen by the Hebrew Immigrant Aid Society with part of her family in 1909, and who moved from there to Spokane, agreed. "Usually there was a big distinction between people at the shul and at the temple. In later years, some families were members of both. . . ." As in Tacoma, the "meeting ground" was the B'nai B'rith.[6]

Divisions between Ashkenazim and Sephardim

Differences between the two mainstream Jewish cultures, Ashkenazim (which included both Central and Eastern European Jews) and Sephardim (those from the Mediterranean regions) went beyond both language and religious practices. While the content of the religion was the same for Ashkenazim and Sephardim, their liturgies and sacred tunes, as well as their pronunciation of Hebrew, were not. In addition, their customs differed, as did their cuisine. Ashkenazim cooked in the style of Germany, Poland, or Russia, and the Sephardim in the style of Mediterranean

The heart of every temple and synagogue, whether Ashkenazic or Sephardic, is the Torah, the first five books of Moses hand-printed in Hebrew on a parchment scroll. In contrast to the silk or velvet covering of a Torah scroll in an Ashkenazic sanctuary, a Torah in a Sephardic synagogue is traditionally cradled within a decorated shell of wood. This one in the Bikur Holim Synagogue was a gift from the Funes children in the name of their parents and pioneer grandparents, Jack and Julia Funes. Museum of History and Industry, Seattle.

countries. While such foods as gefilte fish, tzimmes, or kreplach were "Jewish" to the Ashkenazim, such foods as *borekas, bolemas*, and *huevos haminados* were "Jewish" to the Sephardim. Under the law which prohibited cooking on the Sabbath, Orthodox Jews developed certain dishes which could be precooked and kept warm. Ashkenazim prepared *cholent* (a combination of beans, barley, and meat) for the next day's Sabbath meal, and the Sephardim made *haminero* (a vegetable stew with whole eggs roasted inside).[7]

Ashkenazic women gasped when they glimpsed Sephardic men on the Sabbath smoking "those things with the water underneath, and the wives sitting on the floor."[8] For prayer, Ashkenazim went to temple or to *shul*, while Sephardim went to *kehila* or *kal*. Ashkenazim named their newborn infants after a deceased grandparent or relative, and the Sephardim, after a living grandparent or relative. When an Ashkenazic grandmother rocked a cradle, she crooned about raisins and almonds. When a Sephardic grandmother sang, she gave voice to romance bal-

lads, the preserved songs of her ancestors. Such differences didn't make for easy relationships. "They're Jews and we're Jews, we just didn't get along," recalled Esther
Borish Friedman, a turn-of-the-century Seattle resident of Russian origin.[9]

In Seattle, where Washington Sephardim were concentrated, many young
Sephardic Jews grew up in an essentially Ashkenazic environment while remaining totally Sephardic at home and in their synagogues. Many simply accepted and
took for granted the differences they encountered everyday in their neighborhood
and among their classmates.

Marc D. Angel described growing up Sephardic in Seattle this way:

The Sephardim formed an island within the general Jewish community with only a
few bridges linking them with the Ashkenazim. In those early days, the two communities developed along their own lines, almost oblivious of the other's existence, except
for some minor taunting.

Angel's mother remembered Ashkenazic kids yelling "Mazola" at the Sephardim
who cooked with olive or other vegetable oils. In response, Sephardic kids would
shout back "schmaltz," chicken fat, a staple in Ashkenazic cooking.[10]

Angel's grandparents, originally from the island of Rhodes and towns near
Istanbul in Turkey, came to the United States in the first decade of the 1900s. His
parents, both of whom were born in Seattle, spoke and sang in Judeo-Spanish.
"They might just as well have spent their childhoods in Turkey or Rhodes," said
Angel. "My mother Rachel, the daughter of Marco and Sultana Romey, did not
learn English until she entered public school. My father Victor, who began violin
lessons as a young boy, was ultimately forced to give up the violin because he was
not learning to play 'our' music."

Angel, who grew up to become Rabbi Marc D. Angel of Congregation
Shearith Israel Synagogue in New York, the oldest still-existent synagogue in the
United States, summed up his early years in Seattle by stating, "It is not easy for
a Sephardic Jew to maintain his identity. Being a Jew, he is a minority among
Americans. Being a Sephardi, he is a minority among Jews."[11]

"For many, many years I felt a little estranged from the other Jewish community," recalled Charles Alhadeff. "My mother and father were not socially involved
with anybody outside of the Sephardic community or my family. . . ." Of his childhood living on the fringe of the Ashkenazic Jewish neighborhood, Alhadeff said,
"We were not integrated and then there was an underlying feeling as between
the Sephardic Jews, the Ashkenazic Jews, and the so called German Jews. . . . I
didn't know them and they didn't know me." Within a few weeks after Alhadeff
and his friend John Franco joined the German-Jewish dominated Zeta Beta Tau

fraternity at the University of Washington in 1926, each was visited by the fraternity president and de-pledged. "The feeling being that we, being Sephardics, were not welcome," observed Alhadeff.[12]

Dating between a Sephardi and an Ashkenazi was forbidden in many Seattle families during Alhadeff's and Franco's college years and for some time beyond. Marriage between the two groups was frowned upon by both sides. In the 1930s, Charles Alhadeff's marriage to Doris Kessler, an Ashkenazic Jew, was one of the very first "intermarriages" in the Jewish faith in the Seattle area. "It was a rather traumatic time for my family at that time . . . they didn't know about the other side of the fence except that they were Jews," observed Alhadeff.[13]

Divisions within Sephardim

Cultural prejudices persisted not only between Ashkenazim and Sephardim, but also within the Sephardic community. Like the two differing groups of Ashkenazim, Sephardim from the Marmara group and those from Rhodes remained divided when they arrived in Seattle. A union between a Sephardic Jew from Rhodes and a Sephardic Jew from Marmara was considered intermarriage. Such attitudes were not at all unusual, said Rabbi Marc D. Angel. His father's family was from the island of Rhodes, his mother's from Rodosto, on the shores of the Sea of Marmara. Long after his parents married, some of the older Rhodes immigrants continued to refer to his mother as *ajena*, which means foreigner.[14]

The Sephardim from Marmara and those from Rhodes represented two patterns of culture, differing to some degree in liturgical practices, language, and customs. Until they met in Seattle, the Sephardim from Rhodes had almost no contact with the Marmara Sephardim. In Seattle they continued to maintain their differences, each group feeling "more comfortable" with their own people.[15]

The Invisible Bond

Despite the marked differences between the two mainstream Jewish cultures and the separations within both the Ashkenazim and the Sephardim, the tradition of "Klal Yisrael" (peoplehood), the spiritual connection of every Jew to every other Jew, created an invisible bond that could not be ignored. Although they were divided by religious, cultural, and social differences, the Jews of Washington, as Jews did in other parts of the country, came to each other's aid when aid was needed. For example, predominantly Reform volunteers from the National Council of Jewish Women Seattle Section's Settlement House helped the Orthodox "greenhorns" learn English and become more Americanized. They continued to help even when it was occasionally whispered that some did so more to preserve their own image among the gentiles than out of the goodness of their hearts.

During the Klondike gold rush of 1898, Jewish prospectors who returned to Seattle penniless and ill received help from their co-religionists in making a new start. Jewish immigrants fleeing Eastern Europe through Harbin, China, and landing in Seattle found hospitable Jews waiting. When a ship sailed into Seattle carrying immigrants from Russia, Julius Shafer could be seen standing on the dock to pay the landing fee required of disembarking Jewish families.[16] Herman "Pop" Kessler, another early Orthodox leader, aided Russian newcomers by taking them to the German Jew Jacob Furth, who owned Puget Sound National Bank, to borrow needed money to start a business, often with little collateral of any kind. Jacob Buttnick, an early Ashkenazic pioneer, often acted in the role of counselor to Sephardim who didn't trust banks, holding their money for them.[17] When the Sephardic community began to scramble for funds to build their Orthodox Ezra Bessaroth Synagogue, Temple De Hirsch Jews stepped forward to help. Their support enabled the fledgling congregation to raise enough funds to build its first sanctuary at Fifteenth and Fir Street. Noted Albert Franco, Seattle attorney and community activist, "Socially and economically they were so far above us," yet they helped, and they helped generously.[18]

Sephardic Jews also encountered financial difficulty while constructing their new synagogue, Bikur Holim, at the beginning of the Great Depression, and stood in danger of losing the property. A committee of temple Jews, Nathan Eckstein, J. R. Hiller, and Alfred Shemanski (a member of both temple and synagogue), investigated the matter and sent an urgent appeal to "a certain group of men with foresight":

[T]hey well deserve and must have the whole-hearted interest and support of the Jewish Community. To aid them in their sad situation it is imperative that the sum of $2000.00 be raised immediately. . . . These people, whose purpose in erecting this synagogue was so noble, who are so bravely struggling in the world for better life, must not find us lacking in their need now.[19]

Aubrey Levy (of the Cooper-Levy family), one of the "hatless Jews," as the Sephardim often called Reform Jews, became in effect the Sephardim's mentor. A lawyer, and fluent in the Spanish language, he helped them to negotiate the purchase of the Orthodox Ashkenazic Bikur Cholim synagogue building for their Sephardic Bikur Holim, and drew up their Spanish-written constitution. Levy, one of the rare non-Sephardim considered an honorary member of Seattle's Sephardic community, helped many to obtain citizenship papers and performed pro bono much of the legal work in the early Sephardic community.[20]

The practice of Jews helping newly arrived Jews, regardless of their dissimilarity, has continued from the early waves of immigration to the present day in towns and cities throughout Washington State.

The three early waves of Jewish immigrants to Washington State brought with them their unique strengths and identities. In preserving their differences, they did not easily form a cohesive community. Differences arising from geographical, environmental, and historical processes were not easily dissolved. More than two generations would pass before some of the old divisions would fade.

First Organizations

OR THOUSANDS OF YEARS, JEWS HAVE OBSERVED THE obligation of *pikua'nefesh*, coming to the aid of others through acts of loving kindness. From almsgiving to systematic and careful "'relief,'" which might win the approval of charity organizations, these fundamental practices, cited often in the Torah and promulgated by rabbis, are an important aspect of the Jewish religion.[1] Like Jews everywhere, Washington's secular and traditional Jewish pioneers retained *tzedakah*, an age-old tradition of obligation to people in need. Although they might have complained that "we have our hands full" when helping undesirable transient men San Francisco had sent north, they adhered to the idea of social justice, which provided assistance to those in need regardless of origins.[2]

Tzedakah, however, was not the only factor that created a myriad of benevolent societies, Free Loan Societies, and groups such as B'nai B'rith and National Council of Jewish Women in Washington. Political ideas, such as the emerging Reform theology and changing roles for women, as well as the basic needs of a fledgling immigrant community to meet the challenges posed by new ideologies and economic patterns shaped the first Jewish institutions and organizations in Washington.

Although the experience of Jews coming from Europe varied widely, most had probably been influenced by the political changes and economic modernization that had been occurring in that continent since the nineteenth century. "Without exception Jews of western and central Europe and the United States publicly accepted emancipation and welcomed the possibilities it offered, including opportunities for acculturation and social integration," wrote Jewish historian Paula Hyman.[3] The Jews who immigrated to Washington were no exception. They embraced the idea that in order to be a part of the modern state, they would have to adapt their organizational patterns and way of life to the world around them.[4] Given their circumstances and guided by these worldwide events, it is not surprising that the first Jewish organizations in Washington were benevolent societies rather than temples or synagogues.[5]

The first families did not, however, abandon Judaism. On the contrary, the early Jewish families seemingly had what Nathan Glazer calls a "simple unreflecting attachment to the Jewish people, a subconscious insistence that the Jews be maintained as a people."[6] Despite the smallness of the Jewish population and the fact that many Western and Central European Jews generally had abandoned traditional rituals, most Jews settling in towns throughout Washington maintained their Jewishness. They purchased land for cemeteries, instituted social clubs as places to meet other Jews and so discourage intermarriage, which even the most Reform of rabbis opposed, and set up organizations to provide help to the newly arrived Eastern Europeans and their brethren in Europe.

Olympia

Jewish families in Olympia, Washington Territory, were the first to organize a permanent Jewish institution. Their desire for a Jewish cemetery led them to establish the Hebrew Benevolent Society of Puget Sound in 1873, an act that might have been motivated by the death of a Rosenthal son who had to be taken to Portland for a Jewish burial.[7] (Prior to this time in the Pacific Northwest, only Victoria on Vancouver Island, British Columbia, and Portland and Jacksonville in Oregon had Jewish cemeteries.)

Founding members of the Society, which as the name suggests would serve not just Olympia but the other small towns along Puget Sound, were Louis Bettman, Benjamin Blumauer, Gustav Rosenthal, and Ben Bettman. In keeping with the Jewish notion of providing aid to the needy, the articles of incorporation stated that the members would "aid and assist poor and distressed co-religionists as far as the means of the association permit."[8]

The Hebrew Benevolent Society of Puget Sound purchased about three acres of land for the cemetery from Olympia Lodge No. 1, Free and Accepted Masons. The land, in the southwest corner of the Masons' cemetery, cost fifty dollars. As owners, the Society agreed to "keep in repair the necessary gate or gates in the enclosed grounds."[9] Edward S. Salomon, Worshipful Master of Olympia Lodge No. 1 and former Territorial Governor of Washington State, signed for the Masons on January 30, 1874. Ben Bettman, one of the Society's founders, was also a member of the Masonic Lodge. In 1922 the Society returned all but a small portion of the land to the Olympia Lodge No. 1, which agreed to maintain the Jewish cemetery in good condition. Thirty-three years later, that remaining land came under the jurisdiction of Olympia's Temple Beth Hatfiloh.[10]

A Jewish cemetery is important to Jews whether they are Reform, Conservative, or Orthodox. As soon as they had funds and enough interested people, Jews in other Washington cities set up organizations responsible for maintaining cemeteries. Some would follow the example in Olympia and do this through a benevolent society; others placed the cemetery under the auspices of a temple or synagogue, or set up a separate *chevrah kaddishah* (burial society).

Tacoma

In 1889 Jewish families in Tacoma began the process of obtaining a cemetery. A year later at the annual meeting of the Hebrew Benevolent Association of Tacoma, the trustees, prominent businessmen Meyer Kaufman, Isaac Pincus, and Isaac Harris, "were empowered to have the society incorporated." On April 24, 1891, the Benevolent Association purchased 8.1 acres of land for a cemetery at the corner of Steilacoom Boulevard Southwest and Lakewood Drive in Tacoma.[11]

Members, "any co-religionist elected by the association," owned the cemetery, Givos Olom, and received first choice of lots. But nonmembers could be buried if they agreed to pay the requisite amount of money. Like the Hebrew Benevolent Society of Puget Sound, the Tacoma group established rules to minister relief to the distressed.[12]

The society changed the cemetery's name to Home of Peace cemetery in 1922, and businessman Meyer Jacob became president. When Jacob left for California, S. Nathan Witenberg began his long term as president. Unlike other cemeteries, which sell plots, Home of Peace remains an association of dues-paying members.

The cemetery association was not the only organization created by this active, prosperous Jewish community. In 1890, perhaps inspired by non-Jewish elite social clubs such as the Aloha Club, Jews formed the Harmony Club. Reports of club functions between 1890 and 1896, when it seemed to disband, assert that the club held balls (a common name for any dance in the nineteenth and early twentieth centuries), with guests coming from Seattle and other Puget Sound cities. The club owned rooms, first at 1137 Railroad Avenue, then at 1149 1/2 South "C", and held dances and other entertainments there.[13] The formation of the club may have marked the desire of upwardly mobile Jews to imitate Protestant society, but it also suggests that isolated Jews were cognizant of the importance of maintaining Jewish connections. At that time there did not seem to be evidence of anti-Semitism in

Tacoma. In fact, the names of prominent Jews appeared in Tacoma Society Blue Books.[14]

The same year that they formed the Harmony Club, early Tacoma Jews also formed the Tacoma Lodge of the Independent Order of B'nai B'rith. And like the Harmony Club, that first B'nai B'rith lasted only until 1896. Both organizations lost members most probably after the 1893 depression brought about a decrease of business in the Tacoma area. Also, some of the more well-to-do families left for Seattle or San Francisco when their children came of marriageable age.[15]

In 1843, B'nai B'rith, a Jewish organization created "not in the religious but in the social sphere," was founded in New York by German Jews.[16] Based on mutual aid and solidarity, it quickly became a major middle-class organization in the Jewish community.

In Washington, Jews in small and large towns launched B'nai B'rith lodges. It gave them a nucleus around which to crystallize, "to have some kind of group . . . keep in touch with your people there. It was partly social and partly, maybe, for fear of anti-Semitism," said Roy Rosenthal, a former president of Grays Harbor B'nai B'rith, founded in 1914.[17] In the late nineteenth and early twentieth centuries, joining B'nai B'rith conveyed status to its members. This was an era of acculturation, when Jews emulated their Christian neighbors, for whom belonging to a certain club let others know one's social standing.

In 1913, under the leadership of Theophil Feist, Jewish men in Tacoma, which by now had a temple and synagogue, installed officers in B'nai B'rith Lodge No. 741. "Membership was made up of all the religious denominations," recalled Morris Kleiner.[18]

Besides acting as a social club where men could come for cigars and conversation, Tacoma Lodge raised its voice against acts of anti-Semitism. For example, when the Empress Theatre showed *Levinsky at the Wedding*, the lodge organized a protest accusing the theatre of ridiculing and offending the Jew. To accomplish this, they asked for support from lodges in Seattle and Portland, the Anti-Defamation League, and *The Jewish Tribune* of Portland.[19] The lodge also protested to the Tacoma Board of Education the introduction of the Bible in the city's public schools, a courageous move in an era when conservative Christians stressed Biblical truths over intellectual developments.[20]

During World War I, Tacoma B'nai B'rith, with assistance from lodges in San Francisco, Portland, and Seattle, opened a nonsectarian clubhouse complete with dormitories, lounging, and music rooms for soldiers at Camp Lewis. "Whatever we do for the soldiers and sailors will be done as a privilege at all times. All of the Jewish faith will join in making the club house a great success," said Seattle's

Nathan Eckstein in his opening remarks at the club's dedication.[21] The clubhouse, at Sixth and Broadway, also served as Tacoma's Jewish Community Center.[22]

Although men organized and headed most of Tacoma's Jewish organizations, women also participated in Jewish activities. Tacoma's Lady Judith Montefiore Society, founded May 1, 1890, serves as an example of how isolated pioneer Jewish women found a means of expressing their Jewish identity. Before the community formed a Reform temple, the women of the Lady Judith Montefiore Society, led by its president, Mrs. William Wolff, started a Sunday school and organized a community Hanukkah festival. Some years later, in February 1903, Tacoma women organized the Tacoma section, National Council of Jewish Women. Mrs. D. M. Hoffman served as president. The council disbanded in 1906 and turned its funds over to the Montefiore society.[23]

In 1917, young men in Tacoma formed a Young Men's Hebrew Association, with Aaron Friedman as president. Their purpose, according to *The Jewish Transcript* of August 3, 1917, was "to further Jewish ideals, and to provide a place where the younger Jews may spend their time."[24]

Seattle

Unlike in Olympia and Tacoma, Seattle's Jewish community did not develop an early Jewish cemetery. No definitive information suggests why this occurred. Did the small Jewish community feel it did not have enough funds to support a cemetery? Were people content to journey to Victoria or Olympia when a death occurred? Did the early Seattle Jews feel comfortable with a burial in cemeteries such as Lake View, which to this day still has the occasional Jewish funeral? Were there Jewish burials of which we have no record? Or was the Seattle community young enough to think of socializing rather than funerals?

Whatever the reasons may be, Seattle formed a B'nai B'rith rather than a cemetery as its first Jewish institution. On October 28, 1883, Jewish men in Seattle established the International Order of B'nai B'rith #342 to pursue the organization's guiding principles of benevolence, brotherhood, and harmony.[25] The following year, an elegant Seattle ball to honor the one-hundredth birthday of the influential English Jew, Sir Moses Montefiore, attracted forty Jewish couples to the decorated dancing hall of the Arlington Hotel.[26] Surely the act of organizing a Jewish club and celebrating the birthday of a well-known Jew indicates that in Seattle, Jews were comfortable being Jews. Names listed in a *Seattle Daily Post-Intelligencer* article describing the dance included people that would soon be a part of Seattle's Reform temple.

Picnics sponsored by various Jewish groups brought young people together. Dressed for a swim at Luna Park in June 1912 are Esther Klein, Eva Esfeld Deutsch, and others. MSCUA/ UWL, *neg. 1123.*

Seattle's first B'nai B'rith remained an active lodge through the early 1900s. However, there were growing pains. In 1901 Leo Kohn, in his annual presidential report to Temple De Hirsch, chastised the young men for not participating in Jewish affairs, citing as evidence the inability to form a quorum of eight out of a B'nai B'rith membership of seventy-five.[27]

In the early 1900s B'nai B'rith may have had competition from the Concordia Club. This elite social club first appeared in 1890 in *Polk's Seattle City Directory* and was still listed in the *Jewish Voice*, a Seattle newspaper, in 1916. A check of the presidents listed in *Polk's Seattle City Directory* and reports of people attending Concordia's social events suggest that Reform men predominated. If so, the club would have had a membership similar to ones in Portland and San Francisco. It was another example of men seeking status through their organization affiliation.[28]

As the number of Eastern European Jews increased in Seattle, men formed new lodges, sorting out members by their connections with synagogues. Sometime

Every Sunday we would go out to the cemetery. There was a cable car that went up the hill and a turntable at the top of Queen Anne hill. It was quite a distance from the cemetery. From there, the man would come from the cemetery with his horse and buggy and take us across. It was a wilderness out there.

—Jennie Davis Schermer, whose father, Jacob Davis, was one of the first to be
    buried in the Hills of Eternity Cemetery in 1891. MSCUA/UWL, 1534-001

in 1900, Herman "Pop" Kessler, a respected lay leader, gathered together a group of Orthodox men and formalized Hildesheimer Lodge. It officially merged with the International Order of B'nai B'rith #342 in 1906 and became Hildesheimer #503. Several years later, business leader Emanuel Rosenberg interested Reform men in joining Rainier Lodge.

At lodge meetings men called each other "Brother" and the lodge rooms buzzed with the voices of card players, speakers, and businessmen, whose talk enlightened established Jews as well as newcomers.[29] During Seattle's warm summer days, picnics at Fortuna Park on Mercer Island cemented friendships. Baseball games that pitted the Rainier Kosher Kelleys against the Hildesheimer Lockshen Fressers forged links among Jews. Harry Tall, a young businessman, came all the way from Wenatchee to "enjoy the good things" at Fortuna Park and declared that "it was well worth coming such a long way."[30] A women's auxiliary, Emma Lazarus, was chartered in 1916 and brought women into the B'nai B'rith organization. The Hildesheimer #503 merged with Rainier Lodge in 1921.[31]

The Seattle Hebrew Benevolent Society, another organization led by Reform men such as Gustave Winehill, Leo Kohn, Elkan Morgenstern, and Paul Singerman, organized in 1895. Its purpose was to "provide for the worthy helpless poor of the Jewish Faith who by reason of misfortune are subjects of charity . . . and proper burial services and interment in a Jewish Cemetery."[32]

In 1895, when the state's first Jewish house of worship, Ohaveth Sholum, dissolved, the Seattle Hebrew Benevolent Association assumed responsibility for its cemetery, "Giboth Olum" (Hills of Eternity). In 1910 the Benevolent Society ceded control of the cemetery and its land to Temple De Hirsch. Virtually all of the members now belonged there.

Besides managing the cemetery, the organization concentrated on helping needy men. Sometime in 1914, the society opened a temporary home where men could receive room and board for three days.[33] Seattle's growth, the large sums of money involved, and a need to centralize aid to the needy may have brought about the merger of Seattle Hebrew Benevolent Association with the Ladies' Hebrew Benevolent Society in 1917.[34]

Orthodox men also organized to provide aid to the poor. To help transient men coming through the city, Joseph Hurwitz and N. Gersonowitz in 1907 urged men from Bikur Cholim, the Orthodox synagogue, to form the Hebrew Relief Society, or Seattle Hachnosas Orchim. It stood "in the same relation to the Seattle Hebrew Benevolent Association as the Ladies' Montefiore Aid Society . . . does to the Ladies' Hebrew Benevolent Society," said Roy Rosenthal in his short 1914 "History of the Jews of Seattle." "Both are careful not to duplicate one another's work."[35] Yet, when national disasters threatened world Jewry, Reform and Orthodox Jews joined together to provide money and support. The variety of both Reform and Orthodox religious institutions that organized a dance in Seattle in 1916 to raise money for the relief of war sufferers in Europe is an example of this kind of mutual cooperation.[36]

Young Men's Hebrew Association

In 1910, Seattle Jewish men, some formerly members of a social group called the Cosmos Club, founded the Young Men's Hebrew Association. A year later, under the presidency of Adolph Rosenthal, the club acquired rooms in the Silver Building and offered members and guests Jewish literature and historical materials, pool and billiard tables, and a place to just hang out with friends. Many considered the "Y" to be a training ground for future civic leaders.[37]

Within three years, the successful organization, which now had a ladies' auxiliary, demanded larger facilities. The Young Men's Hebrew Association acquired a permanent home at Seventeenth Avenue and Jefferson Street. There some of its members learned boxing skills from Barney Lustig, an amateur fighter. Other members fondly remembered theatrical performances organized by Phil Gross, who later became a New York City promoter. The Association sponsored Yom Kippur dances at the conclusion of services and social clubs such as the Beth Hai Sorority, an organization of young Jewish girls. During World War I, the Association served as a place for Jewish soldiers on leave from Camp Lewis to meet other Jews. Temporary beds installed during the war made it possible for the men to sleep over.

With the curtailment of activities at Camp Lewis, activities at the Association diminished. They picked up in 1924 when the Young Men's Hebrew Association and the Ancient Order of the Sphinx, a men's club, joined forces and made plans for new services, such as employment and housing referrals.[38]

Menorah Society

In the first decades of the twentieth century, fraternities and sororities at the University of Washington barred Jewish men and women. This restriction inspired Jewish students Max A. Silver, Eimon Wiener, and Charlotte Kolmitz to organize a local Menorah Society in 1913.[39] It was one of fifty or more similar organizations centralized by the Intercollegiate Menorah Association, started at Harvard in 1907. Such Menorah Societies were found on college campuses throughout America and Canada.

The restriction also transformed unaffiliated Jewish young people into active volunteers, recalled Viola Gutmann Silver:

When I was a senior in high school I was invited to join a very desirable sorority at the University of Washington . . . I told them that I would have to ask my father. I asked my father and he said, "You have to tell them that you are Jewish before you say yes." So I came back to her and I said, "My father said that I must tell you that I'm Jewish before I accept." "Oh," she says, "I'll have to ask the committee." "No, if you have to take it up with the committee the answer is No." And from that time on I felt that I ought to try and affiliate with a Jewish group and of course it was easy."[40]

Through lectures, study groups, dramatic presentations, and Menorah Nights in temples and synagogues, the Menorah Society "urged an understanding and devotion to American institutions and at the same time a hearty interest and love in the traditions and ideals of our Jewish heritage," said Max A. Silver.[41] In 1917 the society received the coveted Irving Lehmann Trophy as the most outstanding Menorah group in the United States.

The Menorah Society became so popular that young people who had already graduated from other colleges joined when they returned to Seattle. A number of Seattle marriages trace their beginnings to Menorah Society activities. During the First World War, the society lost members. A reorganization in 1928 rekindled new enthusiasm, but the emergence of Jewish fraternities and sororities coupled with the Great Depression finally caused its demise.

Young Men's Sephardic Association

The Sephardim and the Ashkenazim did not mix socially, and in 1914, the highly insular Sephardim community made plans for its own social organizations. Since those from Rhodes, Marmara, and Rodosto maintained independent identities, this small community formed two groups, the Young Hebrew's Prosperity Club and the Young Men's Sephardic Association (YMSA). According to Gordon DeLeon, single men from Constantinople joined the Prosperity Club, and the Young Men's Sephardic Association attracted those from "Rhodes and those that came from Turkey proper."[42]

Realizing they could accomplish more with a combined membership, the two Sephardic groups joined in 1917 under the YMSA name and elected Harry Tarica president. They purchased a house on Fourteenth Avenue between Washington Street and Yesler Way and set up a clubhouse with pool tables, card rooms, a library, and a coffee shop. The YMSA became a popular meeting place for many Sephardic men who primarily lived within a mile of the clubhouse. "On Sunday we'd go to the YMSA. Upstairs they had a little gymnasium room for the kids to play with," recalled DeLeon.[43] The camaraderie, however, did not last. After an intense election in 1918, the club split along geographical lines. The Rhodes men withdrew support, and within a few years the group disbanded.[44]

Sons of Israel

Before the days of health insurance, organizations frequently offered financial assistance for those who were ill. In Seattle, the fraternal order Sons of Israel became

Members of the Sephardic Young Men's Hebrew Association on a hike in the mountains. Left to right, first row: Jud DeLeon and Sam Caston; second row: David Alhadeff, Albert DeLeon, Ralph Israel, and Tom Cordova; back row: Isaac Ovadia, Gordon DeLeon, Albert Levy, Sam Alhadeff, Max Bensal, unidentified individual, and Ralph Eskenazi. MSCUA/UWL, neg. 10158.

Passover dinner to raise money for Sephardic organizations. Left to right: Mercada Oziel, Judah Oziel, Dudu Caston, Joseph Caston, Rabbi Chaim Nahum, Sam Barokas, Louise Kadun Barokas, Albert Barokas, Isaac Barokas, Grace Caston Israel, Nissim Sam Benezra, Sultana Funis, Joseph Haleva, Esther Haleva, Louise Caston Benezra, and Bolisa Caston. MSCUA/UWL, neg. 18968.

a leading advocate of guaranteeing sick benefits to its members. Some even called it the Benefit Lodge. At the initial meeting in 1916, speeches in English by Eimon Wiener and in Yiddish by Rabbi Gedaliah Halpern stressed that the benefits would "fill the place of insurance, both sickness and accident at minimum cost. The weekly check from the lodge will help considerably in buying groceries and paying the rent when the breadwinner is laid up."[45] A sick committee approved the requests. During the Depression the Sons of Israel also provided medical services.

Woman Unite

Between 1890 and 1920, Seattle's Jewish community faced a plethora of problems brought about by a growing community and an increasingly large immigrant

Sons of Israel picnic at Fortuna Park on Mercer Island, ca. 1916. The park was named after the steamer Fortuna, *built in 1906 for the Anderson Steamboat Company, which operated excursion boats and ferries on Lake Washington for many years.* MSCUA/UWL, *neg. 7003.*

population. This period of time overlapped with the Progressive Era, roughly from the turn of the century to America's entrance into World War I, when reformers across the country confidently grappled with a broad range of issues associated with urbanization and industrialization. Also within this time frame, American innovation transformed traditional, informal women's groups into self-governing, voluntary, philanthropic women's organizations.[46]

For middle-class and upper-class Jewish women, joining a women's benevolent society concerned with urban social problems provided a way to fulfill ambitions for achievement outside the home, as it did for the Protestant women among whom they lived.[47] Planning fund-raising events for charitable organizations and distributing gifts to the poor allowed women to respond to communal needs in the late nineteenth and early twentieth centuries as well as to confirm their social standing.

My mother went to night school at the Yesler Library. It was a special program
for older immigrants. The library was just a block away. The Jewish Welfare and
the Loan Society women used to come to the homes. "Mrs. Policar, why don't you
go to school? It'd be good for you. You're living in this country. You should learn."
The whole bunch, the [Sephardic] friends, went [with her]. They used to make
it like a party. This was a relief from the kids. It was like playing Mah Jong, they
loved it. They'd go twice a week [in the evening].
—Sema Calvo, MSCUA/UWL, 1938-002

Like Helen Berkman Blumenthal, these women also worked within the larger community. Blumenthal, a Seattle native who grew up on Yesler Way, was one of the original members of the Community Services for the Blind. She had become involved in the organization after hearing a blind rabbi tell about the work that some of the women in the east were doing with Braille. She and a few of her fellow Temple De Hirsch sisterhood members, among them Minnie Bernhard, Rose Jordan, Lila Stone, and Golda Robbins, began translating books and articles for blind students at the University of Washington. In 1981, the Broadway High School Alumnae Association elected Helen Berkman Blumenthal, then eighty-nine years old, to their Hall of Fame.[48]

Reform Jewish women, beneficiaries of economic affluence and increased free

Esther Newman Levy and her husband,
Aaron Levy, came to Seattle six weeks after
the Seattle fire of 1889. Three years later,
Esther Levy and her daughter Elizabeth
(Lizzy) Cooper founded the Seattle Ladies'
Hebrew Benevolent Society. Photograph by
Edward Curtis, then Seattle's leading society
photographer and famous today for his por-
traits of Native Americans. WSJHS, 128.

time, began expanding their social and civic options in the 1890s. Well-educated, they were no longer content with limiting themselves to such activities as preparation of the dead for burials or visiting the sick. Desiring to emulate the secular socio-cultural associations of middle-class Anglo-American women, they began the "transformation of Jewish women's traditional mitzvah of tzedaka into independent and self-governing voluntary associations with multiple purposes."[49] It was a trend that would be emulated by Eastern European Orthodox women when they, too, achieved economic prosperity and leisure time. They were both part of an effort by middle-class women to expand their options, demonstrate their skills, and embrace the larger society.

In Seattle, the Ladies' Hebrew Benevolent Society, the Ladies' Montefiore Aid Society, and the National Council of Jewish Women, Seattle Section, would follow these trends and create the institutional foundations for many contemporary organizations that now serve a rapidly growing Jewish community.

Seattle Ladies' Hebrew Benevolent Society. Esther Levy and her daughter Elizabeth (Lizzy) Cooper founded the Seattle Ladies' Hebrew Benevolent Society in 1892. From the beginning the members decided to support only those whom the society felt worthy, a decision which implied that giving without questioning the applicant's needs would no longer be acceptable.[50]

Although the Ladies' Hebrew Benevolent Society extended an invitation to all Jewish women, those who preferred Reform Judaism predominated. Many Orthodox women who spoke only Yiddish or a European language such as Russian or Polish, and often had to work to support the family, did not mix socially with the Reform women in the early years.

Ladies' Hebrew Benevolent Society members, called "friendly visitors," trudged up and down hills with baskets of food on their arms and clothing from their own homes to bring comfort to Jews in need. When money instead of services seemed more appropriate, events such as dances and card games raised funds for a variety of charitable causes both inside and outside the Jewish community. One

> *My mother accepted a family as her responsibility. This is the way they did it*
> *[in the Ladies' Hebrew Benevolent Society]. She used to take me with her when*
> *she would take baskets. Whenever there was a problem that this woman had she*
> *would phone my mother. My mother would take care of it.*
> —Lena Kleinberg Holzman, MSCUA/UWL, 3199

event enabled the society to send $167.25 to survivors of a mine explosion in the central Washington town of Roslyn.[51]

Some construed the "friendly visitors" as merely playing at "lady bountiful," saying that the women "would complain if the homes weren't kept as their homes were." But most members really wanted to help, said Bernice Degginger Greengard, the society's first long-term, paid staff person. "It was a question of money mostly. . . . After all, you can't teach a person traditions or anything else when their tummies are empty. They had to have jobs and they had to have money first."[52] With an experienced organization in place, members of the Ladies' Hebrew Benevolent Society eventually applied their knowledge and resources to deal with problems brought on by the Great Depression. The Ladies' Hebrew Benevolent Society later became the Jewish Welfare Society (1929), Jewish Family and Child Service (1947), and, finally, Jewish Family Service (1978).

Ladies' Montefiore Aid Society. Desiring to work within their own organization, eighteen Orthodox women led by Goldie Shucklin and Mrs. Dave Taylor organized the Ladies' Montefiore Aid Society sometime between 1895 and 1899.[53] Shucklin served as president until her death, as members consistently nominated her, and she always accepted. The only other known president was Mrs. Julius Wigodsky, elected in 1937.[54]

Shucklin, described by an admirer as "a little fat old lady with a black outfit, little pudgy hands and a big smile, not too much hair, and kind of a round face, just a real doll," received widespread praise and respect. A relentless fundraiser, nobody turned her down. "Some people you can't say no to. That was Mrs. Shucklin," commented Abe Hoffman, who operated a grocery on Yesler Way and frequently contributed to Shucklin's causes.[55]

Members of the Ladies' Montefiore Aid Society honored Goldie Shucklin for her thirty-second term as president with the gift of a purse. Shucklin commented that it was the ideal gift because it showed that her friends still had confidence in her as a collector of moneys for the poor. WSJHS, 32.

Goldie Shucklin knew how to say "no" to unscrupulous persons. At a public meeting, a group of traveling shnorrers [beggars] seeing a little Yiddish-speaking lady, pleaded, "If you will help our cause . . . there will be a place for you in Heaven with the seven rabbis." To which Shucklin replied, "I have a man waiting for me in Heaven. How is it going to look for me to walk in with seven men?"
—Gerald Shucklin, MSCUA/UWL, 2331

The society furnished food, fuel, clothing, and funds to needy families. In contrast to the Ladies' Hebrew Benevolent Society, which might question a recipient's real need, the Ladies' Montefiore Aid Society operated under the principal that "they would rather that an unworthy person should receive of their bounty, than that the needy should be allowed to suffer."[56] Whereas the Ladies' Hebrew Benevolent Society might view transient men as "agency tramps" seeking handouts and taking funds that could go to "truly needy" persons, the Ladies' Montefiore Aid Society didn't ask questions.

Since so many organizations, Jewish and non-Jewish, faced similar problems regarding how to determine who was truly needy, Seattle in 1892 organized the Bureau of Associated Charities (later changed to Charity Organization Society) to help distinguish between the "worthy" and "unworthy" poor and to "assure that services [among the various relief agencies] were not duplicated."[57]

A few years after Shucklin's death, the Ladies' Montefiore Aid Society became part of the Jewish Welfare Society (the new name for the Ladies' Hebrew Benevolent Society). In 1940, to perpetuate her memory and to use funds left in her will, the Jewish Welfare Society set up the Goldie Shucklin Memorial Fund to provide funds to bury the poor.[58]

National Council of Jewish Women, Seattle Section. The National Council of Jewish Women (NCJW) started in Chicago in 1893 to prove that Jewish women working together could achieve results.[59] Its members were committed to "social justice, the preservation of Judaism and the Jewish community in the United States and a vision of religion that combined the two."[60] The founding leadership overwhelmingly identified with Reform Judaism. Furthermore, NCJW, unlike Christian women organizations, did not see poor immigrant girls as "fallen" and in need of saving. Rather, they felt their clients just needed help to overcome unfortunate circumstances.

In Seattle, Babette Schwabacher Gatzert suggested to some of her friends that Seattle form a local section of the National Council of Jewish Women. The first group met at the home of Eva Morgenstern Aronson and called for an organizational meeting on November 19, 1900, at Morris Hall. At that meeting place, thirty-four women, led by temporary chairwomen Mrs. Albert Fortlouis and Aronson, elected Merle (Dolly) Degginger president.[61] The members, for the most part, represented Reform Jewish women who were first-generation Americans or who had lived in the United States for several decades.

The Seattle Section's philanthropic committee played a major role in extending aid to the needy. At first members visited hospitals and sent flowers to funerals, traditional "friendly visitor activities." Soon they established a sewing school, opened a class in religious instruction, and began an ongoing effort to support progressive social legislation.

The women decided to organize a Settlement House, a place where poor immigrants would learn how to be productive members of society, after being chastised for not doing so by Blanche Blumauer, a prominent member of Portland's

Sewing classes at Settlement House were considered a necessary part of every girl's education. In Settlement House's first report the chairman noted that "torn buttons and ripped seams are getting more scarce." MSCUA/UWL, neg. 1614.

NCJW.[62] Before the rise of professional social workers and organized charitable agencies, the Settlement House movement, which proliferated between 1900 and 1915, was enthusiastically seen as the main vehicle to bring about social reform.

With money raised through rummage sales, luncheons, vaudeville performances, card parties, and dances, NCJW, Seattle Section, opened a home in the lower part of a rented house on the corner of Twelfth and Washington in 1906. "It aims to be a civic center," Mrs. Emar Goldberg, chairman of the Philanthropic Committee, wrote in her first report. "Whatever the Settlement attempts to do, it must do in answer to a real need of the neighborhood . . . earnest study of the family groups and an endeavor to improve these is the real settlement work."[63]

Initial projects, a religious school and sewing school, had a slow start but soon attracted so many new immigrants that in a year Settlement House moved to larger quarters.[64] At the sewing school, Sara Efron recalled, they "were taught every single seam and every single stitch and . . . everything was done by hand, no sewing machine—we had to make a pair of bloomers which incorporated every stitch . . . it took two years."[65]

Within two years of the founding of Settlement House, the NCJW hired Hannah Schwartz, who had experience in working with immigrant families, and again moved to a bigger building at Seventeenth Avenue and Main Street. Schwartz remained for fourteen years. A "very, very small but very, very pleasant woman—always ready to help," Gordon DeLeon remembered.[66]

Settlement House, through its free religious school, sewing school, night school for English instruction, branch library, citizenship classes, free baths (the first in Seattle), funding of a district nurse to visit homes, and social clubs for young people, had widespread respect among Jewish immigrants. Recalling her attendance at the religious school, Sara Efron told an interviewer:

Thinking back on it, it amazes me that my parents [let me go] . . . being so Orthodox . . . but it was innocuous. The stories were bible, and I believe they felt that they should in every way try to [help me] become Americanized and take on American ways.[67]

Many of the people who joined in the activities at Settlement House considered it the place to compare how things were done in America to the ways they were done at home. In fact, instilling middle-class aspirations was a key element of the Settlement House movement. Although some suspected that volunteers looked upon their work in the NCJW Settlement House as a way to "uplift" newcomers so they would be less embarrassing to the established Jews of Seattle, the interactions usually depended on the immigrant's expectations, the personality of the

I remember going to the Education Center. I remember the ladies of the Ezra Bessaroth having a meeting there, and I walked down the halls and smelled the coffee. Even now when I smell coffee perking, I always think of the Education Center. It's a very warm feeling.

—Leni Peha LaMarche, MSCUA/UWL, 3452

settlement workers, and the quality of the programs.[68] Whatever anyone believed, Seattle's hardworking, dedicated NCJW members made Settlement House a popular, active locale for young and old.[69]

Realizing the need for a larger site to serve immigrants fleeing anti-Semitism in Europe and the devastating destruction of World War I, the Seattle Section raised funds to finance a new and larger facility. Called the "Educational Center," the new building opened in 1916 at 304 Eighteenth Avenue South with six classrooms, a library, a clubroom with kitchenette, two emergency bedrooms, a clinic, and a ballroom with a stage and motion picture gallery.[70] To manage and supervise its programs, the NCJW Seattle Section hired social worker Anna Bragman, from Syracuse, New York, in 1920. She was the first of many such workers, all Jewish, who would guide Jewish immigrants as they learned how to be Americans.[71]

The entire Jewish community supported the Educational Center. Often committees representing several organizations, such as the Ladies' Hebrew Benevolent Society and B'nai B'rith lodges, joined together to raise money. Reviewing one fund-raising event, Samuel Ostrow, president of B'nai B'rith Rainier Lodge, wrote: "The one best result of this affair was that every person in the community felt that he had a part in it, and the spirit of united action . . . was greatly strengthened."[72]

Free Loan Societies

In the Jewish tradition, lending money without profit constituted a "loving kindness," not a business transaction, and repaying such loans became a moral obligation. Free loan associations abounded in the shtetls of Eastern Europe. Seattle had two, one led by women, one by men.

Jennie Friedman understood the need for such an association in Seattle when, in 1909, she suggested to her whist and sewing club that members use accumulated treasury dues to give free loans to impoverished Jews. These women from Congregation Bikur Cholim had first wanted to purchase needed articles for the synagogue, but the rabbi refused to take money raised from card playing.

Incorporated as a nonprofit organization in 1913, the Hebrew Ladies' Free Loan Society initially made $5 and $10 loans, allowing the borrower to repay at the rate of twenty-five cents a month. The loans paid for clothes and food for the holidays, especially Rosh Hashanah and Passover. On other occasions the money might buy a widow a new coat and her children shoes so that she could remarry as a proper bride, explained Dora Zeeve, who headed the volunteer staff for thirty-six years starting in 1916.[73]

The men's Hebrew Education and Free Loan Association began its work in 1913. In addition to giving loans, it provided "for the mutual protection and aid of the members," spread knowledge of Jewish law and history, and paid sick and death benefits to its members. Nonmembers would receive loans if "deemed advisable by the board of directors."[74] Myer Goodglick served as president.

In 1921 the association officially reorganized and became the Hebrew Free Loan Association. At that time it mainly concerned itself with granting loans, and left education and mutual aid to other organizations.[75]

Hebrew Immigrant Aid Society

Worried about the mass arrival of poor Eastern European Jews who could undermine their decades-long drive for social acceptance, in 1881 rich German Jews in New York set up the Hebrew Emigrant Aid Society (HEAS). It was a good idea poorly implemented by people unprepared for the ensuing flood of immigrants, and in 1883 HEAS dissolved.

Nine years later, another group in New York City formed the Hebrew Immigrant Aid Society (HIAS). As their first task, they stationed a representative who could mediate between immigration officials and immigrants on Ellis Island. On shore they began the job of placing immigrants with relatives and provided detailed information and advice concerning life in America.

By 1914 HIAS had grown from a modest New York welfare agency to a nationwide organization with affiliations throughout the world. Although started and managed by Eastern European Jews, the HIAS leadership understood the benefits to be gained by forming an alliance with German Jews.[76]

That type of cooperation characterized the Seattle branch of HIAS, which opened in 1915. Men representing Orthodox and Reform congregations attended an organizational meeting and elected Leo Schwabacher president and Isaac Cooper, Herman "Pop" Kessler, and Sam Bloom vice-presidents.[77] Because submarine warfare had made traveling across the Atlantic Ocean dangerous, the Seattle area was swamped with the arrival of refugees coming by way of Vladivostok, Harbin, and

*New immigrants celebrated Passover by reciting the story of the exodus from Egypt,
asking the four questions, and opening the door for Elijah at the Hebrew Sheltering
and Immigrant Aid Society's 1916 Shelter House seder.* MSCUA/UWL, *neg. 7530*

Yokohama. Although the society befriended mostly Jewish immigrants, the group
adopted a nonsectarian policy. HIAS members helped immigrants locate relatives
and friends throughout the country, and operated a shelter house for those who
had no sponsors and could not leave Seattle within a few days.

The shelter or feeding station, sometimes called by its Russian name "Stolofa,"
first occupied a building at 811 Yesler Way, but HIAS soon opened a larger, better-
equipped house at 512 Eighteenth Avenue. Under the management of Abe Spring,
the home provided beds, baths, and meals. A garden and poultry yard supplied vegetables and enough eggs so that women and children each had one daily.[78] Those
who came in the spring of 1916 had the good fortune of sitting down to a Passover
meal served on a white tablecloth set with a symbolic plate of matzo, shank bone,
roasted egg, and horseradish.[79]

Sara Efron recalled that her mother "and many of the women [Orthodox and
Reform] were involved in getting blankets, sheets, pillows, clothing, and especially
cooking. . . . Ladies did laundry in their own homes . . . we had washboards and

the clothes were boiled on the stove and then hung out to dry."[80] Men who owned grocery stores and restaurants delivered food. The employment committee found work for immigrants who remained in Seattle. "All are anxious to obtain work of some kind, any kind, even street cleaning or similar day labor is not tabooed," reported the *Jewish Voice* on October 31, 1915. Some men went to Wenatchee and worked in Nathan Neubauer's Wenatchee Department Store. A number of Jewish immigrants picked apples in the Wenatchee orchards,[81] an activity that caused *The Spokesman-Review* to announce:

Jewish refugees from Russia, many of them deserters from the army and who had seen active service against the Germans, are employed by the Clark Orchard company. . . . Confronted with a labor shortage, it was forced to resort to hiring those immigrants, unfamiliar with apple harvesting and not knowing a word of English. . . . Their work has been so satisfactory that a second lot of 16 will arrive tomorrow. . . . The Russians are intelligent and many are well educated . . . they were shown how to pick apples and they fell to work without the usual murmurs and objections. They are being paid $2.75 a day.[82]

All the Jewish organizations supported the Hebrew Immigrant Aid Society. The Ladies' Montefiore Aid Society; temple and synagogue sisterhoods; benevolent societies; the National Council of Jewish Women, Seattle Section; B'nai B'rith; and the free loan associations raised funds, brought food, and found jobs for the new arrivals. Before HIAS opened rooms, a group of individuals that included merchants Harry Silver and M. K. Gottstein gave space in a building on Second Avenue and Columbia Street to HIAS's Immigrant Relief Committee.[83] A benefit dance, given by the Seattle Jewish War Relief Committee, an ad hoc group set up by Seattle Jews and headed by Samuel Ostrow, Dave Limman, and Miss S. Kadushin, and comprised of representatives from all the Jewish organizations, raised funds for the relief of war sufferers in Europe.

HIAS also sent fund-raisers to the smaller Jewish communities. The Rev. Dr. B. Kornblith, district secretary, visited Temple Emanu-El in Spokane in 1916 and raised $850. Several years later social workers, ministers, and others planned a campaign in Yakima and surrounding small towns. They raised $17,500 for the American Jewish Relief Committee, which helped the poor in war-torn Europe.[84]

Spokane

Although Jews came to Spokane in the early 1880s, it was not until the 1890s that the community began to think about organizing a temple and Jewish organizations. Unlike Tacoma and Seattle, which began with voluntary organizations, in Spokane the temple came first, albeit by one year.[85]

The Temple Emanu-El was Reform, as was the Spokane Hebrew Ladies' Benevolent Society, organized by Rabbi Rudolph Farber. In fact, in addition to providing help to destitute families, the women acted as a sisterhood within the temple. Temple Emanu-El minutes, dated December 18, 1892, thank the ladies "for their indefatigable efforts to make the [Harvest] festival a success . . . financially and otherwise."[86]

Led by its president, Mrs. B. Solomon, "The Hebrew Ladies' Benevolent Society not only gave families temporary relief, they tried to fix whatever caused the distress."[87] The fact that the help attracted undesirables caused one disgruntled person to write to *The American Israelite*, a Jewish weekly newspaper written in English, that the Society "is doing some effective work here, and as soon as it became known . . . beggars arrived from all quarters."[88] Funds for this organization came from generous individuals such as businessman Moe Oppenheimer.[89]

With the establishment of the temple, Spokane Jewish men, just like those in Tacoma and Seattle, announced the formation of a B'nai B'rith. On March 22, 1892, a notice printed in Spokane's newspaper, *The Spokesman Review*, called "all Israelites from the age of 18 upward to come to a meeting at the Unitarian Church to organize a B'nai B'rith." Almost a year later, on January 22, 1893, B'nai B'rith members elected Leopold Stern president and named themselves Abraham Geiger Lodge.

The Daughters of the Covenant, the women's auxiliary of the Abraham Geiger Lodge, began in 1912 with Mrs. Hyman Cohn as president. The name later changed to the Ida Bluen Strauss Auxiliary to honor Ida Bluen Strauss, a resident of Spokane who chose to remain with her husband aboard the ill-fated *Titanic*.[90]

To help the thousands of Jews who came to America during and after World War I, Orthodox men in Spokane in 1917 organized the Spokane Hebrew Free Loan Society. The society, which by 1926 had 115 members, lent individuals up to $150 each in interest-free loans. Another organization, the Jewish Welfare Society, or Tzdoko Gdolo (Great Charity), which included both men and women, also cared for distressed individuals and families. Samuel Edelstein was its first president, and Mrs. S. Hanuer was its first vice-president.[91]

Spokane women joined the National Council of Jewish Women in 1917 at the urging of Rabbi Jerome Rosen of Temple Emanu-El. As one of its first projects, the Spokane Section of the NCJW used money received from the Adelaide Galland Memorial Fund to establish a children's library at Edgecliff, a tuberculosis sanitarium.[92] They also learned to transcribe *The Braille News*, an activity NCJW women

Jeanette Weinstein, Bessie Copeland, Alice Barkan, Agnes Hersholt, and Ann Weinstein continued even after the Spokane Section of the NCJW disbanded.[93]

To have fun and meet unmarried persons, Spokane's young men and women joined the Bilou Club. In 1919 at the Davenport Hotel, with the help of Rabbi Julius A. Leibert from Temple Emanu-El, the group formed a "permanent society that shall have as its prime purpose the promoting of good fellowship, the spreading of Jewish knowledge and lore and the fostering of general culture." At the second meeting they voted to hold a "dance once every month when possible."[94] This was the beginning of a shift away from a total emphasis on religious practices and a move toward a more social environment. "Almost every Jewish youth of both sexes belongs to it," wrote Moses Janton in 1926.

New Directions

By 1920, as Jewish organization members in Washington pointed with pride at their efforts to provide *tzedakah*, they also recognized the complexity of community problems. The continuing influx of European immigrants, the national agitation against immigration (which would culminate in a few years in very restrictive policies), and the growth of secular Zionist sentiment called for new directions. Most organizations needed more funds and professional staffs.

As new groups such as Hadassah, Jewish Consumptive Relief Society, Mizrachi, and Seattle Sephardic Brotherhood joined the roster of philanthropic and social groups, a way had to be found to consolidate and coordinate charitable events and fund-raising. So many people belonged to so many organizations that the overall effort often seemed confused. "The outstanding difficulties . . . were the over-organization of Jewish Women's groups and the consequent difficulty of increasing membership, the collection of dues, the problems of finance and the matter of program," reported Elsie Weil when the National Council of Jewish Women, Seattle Section, tried to bring all the Jewish women's groups together to discuss their mutual concerns.[95]

Although this group, made up of two representatives from each organization and called the Federation of Jewish Women's Organizations, did not last, the large number of philanthropic and social groups spurred the creation of the Seattle Jewish Federated Fund, and eventually the Jewish Federation of Greater Seattle and the Jewish Community Council in Spokane. As the rules of the game changed, the Jewish community, which had always looked to community members for funds, would have to face up to the challenge of finding broader funding sources and meeting demands for a wider variety of services.

First Congregations

IN 1889, THE YEAR THE U.S. CONGRESS ESTABLISHED Washington as the forty-second state, Jewish people began to make plans to build religious institutions and to administer to the spiritual needs of their diverse community. It was a trend followed by other religious denominations as Washington's rural frontier society moved toward urbanization. By this time, Jewish families from Eastern Europe had joined the earlier settlers who came from Central and Western Europe. This was forty years after Jews began settling in Washington Territory and sixteen years after consecrating the Territory's first Jewish cemetery.

During the formative years of Jewish settlement, however, few Jews refrained from celebrating Jewish holidays, even if it was only on the High Holy Days of Rosh Hashanah and Yom Kippur. Jewish men and women who founded new communities may have departed from the Orthodox European model, but they did not reject all tradition. As early as 1871, *The Washington Standard*, an Olympia newspaper, announced: "Tuesday and several succeeding days have been observed by our Jewish citizens as religious holidays attended by the ceremonies peculiar to their celebration of the New Year."[1]

Throughout the territory in cities and towns without temples or synagogues, rituals were repeated even with only a handful of Jewish settlers. Men familiar with the prayers conducted services in either a rented hall or home. For example, in Spokane in 1885, Samuel Auerbach conducted services at his home, acting as a stand-in cantor and rabbi.[2] As noted by Hasia Diner in *A Time For Gathering*, "Jews who spent the whole calendar year seemingly living like all other Americans, on these days, at least, demonstrated their distinctiveness."[3]

The first Jewish houses of worship in Washington State chose Reform (sometimes modified to contain elements of an Orthodox service). The majority of their members came from German-speaking states and had been in this country twenty to thirty years. In Europe they most likely had experienced what scholars call an "encounter with emancipation," witnessed the "origins of the modern Jew," and moved "out of the ghetto" and into confrontation with the "ordeal of civility."[4] Along the way they encountered the beginnings of Reform Judaism, which grew from the Emancipation era. This period began in the early nineteenth century with Napoleon's invasion of the Germanic states and continued until 1871, when Otto Von Bismarck united the German states.

Emancipation had both benefited and weakened Judaism. Before emancipation, a country's rulers and administrative officials decided where Jews lived and worked and what kind of taxes they paid. After emancipation, which granted Jews in central and western Europe fuller rights and greater civic equality, Jews were required to become "German," shedding much that was Jewish and considered odious by non-Jews. In certain places they had to learn German, could not use Yiddish, and had to take German surnames. In some synagogues Yiddish was banned.[5] In many areas this caused a defection from Judaism and a move toward Christianity.

To forestall the increase in conversions, especially among women, where it had skyrocketed, and to weaken the church's appeal, some of the German rabbis instituted reforms that eventually became a part of Reform Judaism. They embraced modern European aesthetic standards that were typical of churches, introduced congregational singing, preached inspiring sermons, encouraged quiet decorum in the synagogues, and built lofty buildings to reflect their congregations' affluence. Most importantly, they "asserted the right of Jews to mold the law to fit their environment."[6]

When German rabbis who had played a part in the Reform movement immigrated to America, they brought their ideas with them, and eventually worked out a position for American Reform Judaism. Debate centered on the thorny question of whether the Jews were still a *people*, required to consider themselves strangers in the land in which they settled and expecting to return to Palestine (Israel), or were they a religion like all other religions with a set of beliefs? In 1885 at a Reform conference in Pittsburgh, this radical concept culminated in a statement asserting that "Judaism was a 'progressive religion, ever striving to be in accord with the postulates of reason . . . [and] the rejection of all Mosaic laws which are not adapted to the views and habits of modern civilization.'"[7] On a more practical level, this assertion meant that congregations had permission to adopt the social atmosphere of a Protestant church rather than the disarray found in traditional Jewish synagogues.

Influenced by these changes, the Jews from Germany who settled in Washington used Reform ideology to justify the changes needed to solve the problem of preserving Jewish identity within the non-Jewish world. The idea of men and women sitting together, observing only the first day of major holidays instead of the traditional two-day celebration, and being able to eat forbidden foods appealed to people who had been living secular lives with only casual attachment to religious observance. Moreover, in the closing years of the nineteenth century, successful immigrant merchants wanted to be accepted—to be American. By this time, many Jews were prominent members of the larger business community. Being able to announce that they, too, had an organized religious institution, an important part of life in the late nineteenth and early twentieth centuries, added to their prestige. Engaging in programs with churches such as Seattle's St. Marks Cathedral or Westminster Presbyterian, or participating in a fund-raising fair for St. James Cathedral, made them a part of the greater Seattle community.

The Eastern European immigrants who came to Washington State between 1880 and 1924 brought their traditions with them. Arriving with families or linked through marriages to earlier settlers, these Jews were tied to the Orthodox culture in which they were raised. For this group, religion was one of the ways in which they could transfer the values of the old country to their new environment. Among them were men with knowledge of traditional law and the text of prayers. In Seattle, as well as in smaller towns like Tacoma, Spokane, Bellingham, and Everett, within ten to fifteen years after the first Eastern European arrivals, one could find an Orthodox synagogue. In towns without a rabbi, men educated in Hebrew conducted services, or the people recruited rabbis from Seattle, Vancouver, British Columbia, or even Portland.

Seattle's First Congregations

Ohaveth Sholum

In 1889, David Kaufman, who had been a resident of Seattle for about twenty years, gathered together other well-intentioned Jews and created the nucleus for Washington's first Jewish congregation, Ohaveth Sholum, a quasi-Reform temple. Most likely Kaufman understood that religious services in rented halls made it difficult to establish an effective Jewish community. Articles of Incorporation, signed November 4, 1889, indicate that any person of the Jewish faith, including women, had full rights of membership. It also stated that the congregation would "establish a burial place or cemetery for the sepulture of the dead of the Jewish faith."[8] To accomplish that, Ohaveth Sholum members purchased 2.6 acres of cemetery land on Queen Anne Hill for one thousand dollars.

The group elected Sigismund Aronson, a Schwabacher Brothers executive, president. Early trustees in addition to Aronson included Seattle businessmen Kassel Gottstein and Paul Singerman. By 1891 the energetic membership had acquired property for a synagogue on the northwest corner of Eighth Avenue and Seneca Street, had made plans to build a house of worship, and had hired Aaron Brown as rabbi. With help from Fanny Degginger and the Ladies' Auxiliary, the temple started a religious school.[9]

The dedication of Ohaveth Sholum at Eighth and Seneca in September 1892 celebrated the opening of Seattle's first Jewish house of worship. Incorporated three years earlier, Ohaveth Sholum was the first Jewish congregation established in Washington State. WSJHS, 42.

Having women teaching Sunday school and being involved in temple matters stemmed from the influence of the American church. This innovation, supported by Reform rabbis, gave women an active participation in synagogue affairs and "contributed to the preservation of Jewish tradition." As noted in the Reform movement's Pittsburgh Platform (1885), women would become "the saviors of Jewish religion."[10]

On September 18, 1892, an overflow crowd of Jews and Seattle dignitaries entered the sanctuary and dedicated Ohaveth Sholum. With so many of Seattle's Jewish businesses connected to families in San Francisco, it is no wonder that the Gothic-style building at Eighth and Seneca resembled San Francisco's temples.[11] The temple had 125 members and a seating capacity of about 800.

Minutes from August 18, 1889, show that the organizing group decided to conduct services "according with Minuich [Minhag] America," a Hebrew-German-English prayer book co-authored by Isaac Mayer Wise.[12] Reports of dedication events show that the temple used an organ and that men and women sat together.

It is unclear, however, whether Ohaveth Sholum was a Reform temple. A newspaper article in the *Seattle Press Times* of August 1, 1891, stated that the mode of worship was "according to the Orthodox faith." And several years later, Rabbi Theodore F. Joseph, first rabbi of Temple De Hirsch, recalled that "the ritual used at the time was orthodox. The majority of the members [were] orthodox . . . they wore the prayer shawl.[13] This latter fact was verified by Julius Rickles, a member of a pioneer Jewish family, who said, "The men sat with yarmulkes [skullcap, also called *kepot*] on and a little *tallit* [prayer shawl]."[14] A transitional temple might be the best description of this temple that chose a variegated pattern of worship rather than full-blown Reform.

Ohaveth Sholum survived for several years. Rabbi Aaron Brown and then Rabbi Reuben Abrahamson conducted Friday evening and Saturday morning services. Children studied twice-weekly at a Hebrew school, and the Young Ladies' Auxiliary presented entertaining programs. However, caught between the national depression of 1893 and the lack of broad support from Seattle's Jewish community, by 1896 Ohaveth Sholum faced financial ruin. Unable to pay its rabbi and honor other obligations, its doors closed. "Its People Were Indifferent," proclaimed *The Seattle Times* on July 17, 1896.

But were they? The evidence suggests otherwise. Most likely, organizational problems and/or factional disputes about liturgy and the proper way to conduct services, problems common among all denominations trying to establish religious institutions among persons from diverse backgrounds, caused the temple's ignominious end. Also, by this time Orthodox Jews had established Chevra Bikur Cholim,

The cornerstone for Temple De Hirsch's first sanctuary on Boylston Avenue and Marion Street was laid on June 9, 1901. Esther Levy, Samuel Frauenthal, Henry Grunbaum, I. E. Moses, Emil Lobe, and Leo Kohn were among the Jewish leaders who took part in the ceremony. WSJHS, 148.

so it is likely that Jews who wanted more traditional services may have left.

Within a few years of the demise of Ohaveth Sholum, many of its members became charter members and stalwart supporters of Temple De Hirsh, a thoroughly Reform temple. Would "indifferent" persons become entangled in the politics of establishing another congregation?

Temple De Hirsch

On May 29, 1899, at Morris Hall, Seattle's Reform-minded Jewish people organized Temple De Hirsch, named for Baron Maurice de Hirsch, a nineteenth-century French Jewish philanthropist. Inspired by a committee that included Emanuel Rosenberg, F. Bories, N. N. Grunbaum, Sol Friedenthal, and Leo Kohn, seventy supporters gave money toward establishing a Jewish congregation "in keeping with the times and on thoroughly American lines."[15]

The trustees elected Leo Kohn president, and within a few months hired Rabbi Theodore F. Joseph. Holiday services that first year were at Jefferson Hall, but thereafter the congregation rented Morris Hall for all temple events, including Friday evening services. They used the *Hebrew Union Prayer Book*, recently endorsed by Reform rabbis. At the end of a busy, productive year, the temple board purchased property for a house of worship on the northwest corner of Boylston Avenue and Marion Street for $4,050.[16]

Two years later, on June 9, 1901, De Hirsch members laid the cornerstone for their temple building. In his address to the one thousand people attending the ceremony, Rabbi Joseph said, "We have made a start . . . I feel confident that the start has been made with such a will that we cannot stop, but must continue."[17] By September, members attended Rosh Hashanah services in their own building. But because the temple leaders had resolved "to build according to the funds subscribed for and on hand," only the basement was finished.[18]

The pioneer founders, among them Leo Kohn, Emanuel Rosenberg, Sol Friedenthal, Leo S. Schwabacher, S. Degginger, I. E. Moses, and Max Bornstein, firmly stated in the Articles of Incorporation that the form of worship would be "what is known as Reform American Service."[19] However, they did vote that "the privilege of wearing skull-caps of uniform description be accorded anyone attending service who may desire to worship with covered head."[20]

A Sunday school with teachers Merle (Dolly) Degginger and Ida Gottstein opened in October 1899.[21] The Bar Mitzvah ceremony, frequently dismissed in Reform temples, remained along with the Confirmation ceremony, as did teaching Hebrew in the religious school and allowing women to be part of a minyan (the ten adults necessary for public prayers). "Reverend," not "rabbi," designated the spiritual leader, although after the first few years, "rabbi" prevailed. Board members voted to charge for High Holiday seats in addition to dues, but set aside free seats for those who could not pay.[22]

Mrs. L. Gottstein's Matzo Cake from One Thousand Favorite Recipes *produced under the auspices of the Ladies' Auxiliary to Temple De Hirsh, 1908: 10 eggs, 1 cup sugar, 1 cup chopped walnuts, 3 tablespoons of chocolate, 1 teaspoon of allspice, 1 teaspoon of cinnamon, 1 scant cup of matzo meal browned and soaked in white wine to moisten well. Beat yolks of eggs and sugar till very light, then add chocolate and spices, then the meal and nuts; lastly the well-beaten whites. Bake in a spring form and put a chocolate icing on top.*

Under the leadership of Fannie Degginger, women from the Young Ladies' Auxiliary at Ohaveth Sholum, who had kept on meeting after that temple's demise, established a Ladies' Auxiliary, and planned events to increase the congregation's treasury.[23] A volunteer Jewish choir, featuring soloist Rose Morganstern (Mrs. M. A.) Gottstein under the direction of Alfred Lueben, enhanced the services until 1905, when the board made the decision to engage professionals.[24]

The congregation soon outgrew its building, and rather than enlarge and re-model, the members decided to start again at a new site. Exactly nine years after its first organizational meeting, Temple De Hirsch dedicated its completed, new building at Fifteenth Avenue and Union Street. Rabbi Samuel Koch, who in 1906 started his thirty-seven-year tenure as spiritual leader of Temple De Hirsch, offici-ated at the opening ceremony.

Over the next thirty-five years, Rabbi Koch would establish himself both locally and nationally as a spiritual leader, teacher, innovator, and committed re-former. He devoted a significant part of his time to education, particularly toward the religious education of the temple's young people.

Equally close to Rabbi Koch's heart were his social justice activities. By 1914 he was on the board of nearly every social welfare organization and worthy civic cause in Seattle. Working with Rev. Sydney Strong and Seattle Mayor George

The [De Hirsch] temple board met in homes of board members whose wives outdid one another in providing a sumptuous feast. It [all] began on a cold night [when the temple] heating system was not working. Julius Lang moved [the] meeting to his house and advised his butler by phone to set up a meeting for seven people. When he [and others] got there the poker table with cards and chips were ready. At the conclusion [of the meeting] someone raided the ice box and from then on every meeting had food.
—Melville Monheimer, MSCUA/UWL, 1992-001

The one thing I remember about Rabbi Koch is that he had a habit of coming up to a youngster and putting his face real close, and reaching out and pinching his cheeks.
—Martin Rind, MSCUA/UWL, 3603-001

Active head of Temple De Hirsch until his retirement in 1942 and Rabbi Emeritus for the two years that remained of his life, Rabbi Samuel Koch, spiritual leader, teacher, innovator, and committed reformer, laid the groundwork for the inspired tenure of his successor, Rabbi Raphael Levine. MSCUA/UWL, neg. 1583.

Cotterill in 1913, he helped unite all of Seattle's nearly fifty social agencies into a central council, Seattle Community Chest, a predecessor of United Way.

When Temple De Hirsch's board in 1914 asked Koch to "refrain from participation in political affairs in a public manner," he turned increasingly to the needs of the local and national Jewish communities.[25] He was one of the fifteen original members of the executive committee of the Central Conference of Reform American Rabbis' Commission on Social Justice. Like many other Reform rabbis of the time, he shied away from ardent support of a Jewish homeland. He strongly supported the classical Reform, anti-Zionism position, which stated that Jews were no longer a nation but a religious community.

During his tenure, Koch stressed that "every religion that is alive must evolve, develop, progress."[26] The temple grew in size and stature under Koch, one of Seattle's most visible Jews.

Chevra Bikur Cholim Synagogue

Eastern European Jews lived in an Orthodox culture that enveloped their lives and dictated their behavior. Most of the men had some knowledge of traditional law, read Hebrew, and knew the prayers well enough to lead services. In Seattle they created a flourishing religious life.

One group of men, among them Bernhardt Myers, M.D., Aaron Garfinkel, and Jacob Berkman, regularly met in Jacob Alpern's store on Front Street, and rented a hall for High Holy Day services. In 1889, during a Simchas Torah holiday service, the men decided they needed a more permanent organization and made plans to establish Chevra Bikur Cholim (Society to Visit the Sick). They elected Dr. Bernhardt Myers president.[27]

The Articles of Incorporation signed November 17, 1891, by Myers, Aaron Garfinkle, Philip Rottenstein, Jacob Alpern, Harry Lasky, Benjamin Levy, Phil A. Silverstone, and Joseph Abramowitz describe Chevra Bikur Cholim as a "benefit and benevolent society for the care of the sick and to furnish medicine, nurses and physicians as required, and to furnish a cemetery and suitably bury the dead."[28]

Iron gates with an 1890 date suggest Bikur Cholim acquired the cemetery at that time, but the gate may not have been installed until 1917. Congregational minutes from June 3, 1917, state: "Brother H. Ross of the Iron Gate Committee reported that an iron gate can be gotten very reasonable now."[29] In 1895, the date of the earliest identifiable grave, the cemetery at Oak Lake, 115th North, just east of Aurora Avenue, first appears in *Polk's Seattle City Directory.*[30] Before automobiles, attending a funeral meant a day's journey, as many miles separated the cemetery from the Jewish neighborhoods around Cherry and Yesler. "When there was a funeral, I closed my store and harnessed my horse and wagon and drove to the cemetery. It took a whole day to get there," recalled Frank Antel, a member of Chevra Bikur Cholim.[31]

Within a decade, Chevra Bikur Cholim evolved into an Orthodox religious congregation. In 1900 members amended the Articles of Incorporation and legally established "a benevolent, benefit and religious society for the dissemination of religious instruction and for the purpose of maintaining a house of worship."[32]

Herman "Pop" Kessler, who later became president of the congregation, inaugurated his lengthy career in providing services to the Jewish community when he offered to collect monthly dues. A Hebrew Relief Society, Seattle Hachnosas Orchin, continued the Chevra's interest in caring for the poor.

Julius Rickles, son of Orthodox pioneers, noted that for several years Chevra Bikur Cholim held services in the old Hinckley Block on Second Avenue and Columbia Street. In 1893 the Chevra rented a building at Fifth Avenue and Washington Street known as Seattle Central, and established a permanent *shul* and *heder* (Hebrew school) at one location.[33] In 1896, the Chevra held Rosh Hashanah services in rented quarters at the corner of Eleventh Avenue and Yesler Way. Mr. Abramowitz led the services.[34]

In 1898, Zalman Grozinsky, who came to Seattle around 1892, encouraged Bikur Cholim to acquire property and erect its own building. According to his granddaughter, Esther Gross, Grozinsky and other religious men were upset because on their walk to services they had to pass a bordello and were often shouted at by the women.[35]

Seattle's Orthodox Jews celebrated the opening of their first synagogue, Bikur Cholim at Thirteenth and Washington, in a dedication ceremony on October 2, 1898. The celebration concluded with the placing of the Torah in the new Ark, a privilege auctioned and accepted by several members of the congregation. MSCUA/UWL, *neg. 28.*

Grozinsky was not the only one upset with the area south of Yesler Way. Although historian Roger Sale asserted it "was not as wild and dangerous as many who lived elsewhere in the city thought," it did house more illegal activities than any other Seattle neighborhood. It was the sort of area that a growing city, bent on becoming a metropolitan area, singled out and denounced.[36]

To encourage and persuade the members, Grozinsky proposed to the Chevra that if they paid the $1,000 loan on a parcel of land he had purchased between Twelfth and Fourteenth Avenues on South Washington Street, he would donate the $200 he had paid as deposit, and give the members the deed.[37] Grozinsky also installed Seattle's first *mikvah* (ritual bath) in his home at 1217 South Washington Street, and purchased additional lots to be used for a Talmud Torah. The *mikvah* was later moved to Eighteenth Avenue and Spruce Street.[38]

On October 2, 1898, Chevra Bikur Cholim dedicated a building which seated 120 persons downstairs and 80 upstairs. Members paid 75 cents per month for dues and $2.50 per year for holiday tickets; nonmembers paid $5. A day after the dedication, the *Seattle Post-Intelligencer* described the new building:

This new temple of worship, while small, is prettily arranged, the Ark of the covenant, in white and gold, being located in the east end of the building and overhung with elaborate tapestry curtains. On top of this are the Ten Commandments in Hebrew, the whole surmounted by the crown of Judaism. One of the odd features of the arrangements, which is in accordance with an ancient custom [is that] the lower floor is devoted to the men and the galleries to the ladies.[39]

Within a few years the small synagogue could not accommodate the crowds attending Rosh Hashanah and Yom Kippur services, and the congregation had to rent a hall for the High Holy Days. Interviews with pioneers attributed the decision to build a new and larger building to the difficulties experienced when a rented hall was double booked. The managers of the hall, not knowing about all-day Yom Kippur services, had billed a dance band that evening. When the band arrived and wanted to set up for the dance, congregation members Frank Antel and Herman "Pop" Kessler picked up the Torahs and, according to eyewitnesses, "ran out of there like from a fire."[40] The next day, members of the congregation, swayed by Kessler's plea for a new building, pledged $15,000 to build a new and larger synagogue.

This overbooking story is similar to one the Sephardim gave for the building of a larger Sephardic Bikur Holim and Ezra Bessaroth. Whether the rented hall story is true or apocryphal is unknown. But the image of a synagogue member racing from the rented hall holding up a Torah sums up, as myths sometimes do, the urgent need to explain the necessity of acquiring a place of worship.[41] This story, no matter how transformed, provides a shared sense of Jewish history in Washington.

On January 24, 1909, the congregation purchased a site at Seventeenth Avenue and Yesler Way. The pioneers "laid the foundation for us," wrote Sam Prottas, son of one of Bikur Cholim's early members, Solomon Prottas.[42] Walls for a syna-

People would visit, one synagogue to the other [on High Holy Days]. People from the Bikur Cholim synagogue would like to go to the temple and some people from the temple would want to see what's going on in the synagogue so there was this walking back and forth between synagogues. That was known as a sort of a [holiday] parade.

—Sol Esfeld, MSCUA/UWL, 2018-3

My poor mother never knew who my father was going to bring home after the [Bikur Cholim] services to make our kiddush to start the Sabbath. Sometimes it would be five; sometimes it would be ten. Mother was a great baker, so she was always prepared for everything. . . .

—Esther Borish Friedman, MSCUA/UWL, 2273

If it was a nice [Sabbath] day papa . . . used to say, "Come on, let's go." I know what he meant. We two walked downtown, and we'd go to the Hippodrome, and ahead of time I'd buy one bag of pink peppermints and one bag of white. We'd go to the show and papa would sit right in front where the girls were dancing. After they were through we'd sit in the back . . . and then we'd find a movie . . . [because] we [had] started out early so we couldn't ride home yet . . . and by that time it got dark so papa said, "Now we can take the cable car, and you'll go home, and I'll go to services." This was every Saturday.

—Esther Borish Friedman, MSCUA/UWL, 2273

gogue went up soon after, but financial difficulties and bad design delayed construction, and only a lower floor was completed. Between 1910 and 1915, services took place in the basement vestry. "I got Bar Mitzvah at 17th and Yesler, before the top got up," Abe Hoffman remembered.[43] Julius Rickles recalled that when they finally transferred the Torah to its permanent home, "we had like a parade. One man carried [the Torah] and a guard of honor went on each side in case he got tired."[44] Architect B. Marcus Priteca redesigned the plans in order to finish the shul.

In the early years, Rabbi Hirsch Genss, who came to Seattle in 1889, and Rabbi Ludwig Brooks, who came in 1895, participated in congregation services, but neither had official status as rabbi. In 1905 the congregation gave the honor to Rabbi Gedaliah Halpern, who stayed for five years. All of the congregation's early rabbis studied in yeshivas (rabbinical schools) in Eastern Europe and brought an old-world philosophy to the pulpit. In 1911 the synagogue board voted to "engage a rabbi who can deliver a lecture in English."[45] Rabbi Simon Glazer, a Hebrew scholar who came in 1918, met that criterion. To chant the prayers, the congregation hired Cantor Solomon Tovbin, who had received traditional and secular education in Russia. The board also tried to make the services more orderly by establishing fines for "any person disturbing the worship . . . by abusive language or loud talking or quarreling."[46]

Herzl Congregation

In 1906, Jake Kaplan, Frank Schwartz, and other men affiliated with Chevra Bikur Cholim decided they needed their own Jewish Orthodox congregation, which would "always be in favor of the principles of Zionism."[47] Meeting in a home at 1028 Main Street for the first few years, they created Herzl Congregation of Seattle. "They used to call it the *Tzionistiche Shul.* When I was a child I didn't know it was named Herzl," said early Seattle resident George Prottas.[48]

Whereas Jews in Germany had responded to the Emancipation era by transforming the Jewish religion, in Eastern Europe this trend led to Zionism and socialist movements, some of which had no place for religion, traditional or reformed. The Seattle Zionists who founded Herzl were religious men. They intended to make their Orthodox synagogue meet their needs for both religion and Zionism.

Assisted by a number of local dignitaries, Herzl members laid the cornerstone of the new synagogue at Sixteenth Avenue and East Fir Street on August 22, 1909. Rabbi Ludwig Brooks delivered the invocation. Fund-raising had begun under the leadership of President Ezra Fislerman.[49] Two years later, members heard the shofar in their partially completed building. A succession of rabbis, some who had led services at Bikur Cholim, and monetary problems made it difficult to retain members and complete the *shul.*

The same year it laid the cornerstone for a new synagogue, Herzl Congregation purchased cemetery land at 165th and Dayton Avenue North. It established a burial society in 1917 with Mr. W. Frankfurter as president, and made plans to "apply all money donated by the departed themselves or their relatives for the cemetery of Herzl Congregation."[50] The Herzl Memorial Park Cemetery Association incorporated on September 30, 1936, with Herman A. Horowitz as president.[51] A year later, Lewis N. Rosenbaum, a New York financier who began his successful career in Seattle, donated the money for the Fani Rosenbaum Memorial Chapel in Herzl Memorial Park Cemetery in memory of his mother. Lewis Rosenbaum was married to Bella Weretnikow, one of two women in the University of Washington's first law school class in 1901. B. Marcus Priteca designed the chapel.[52]

In 1923 the congregation convinced Rabbi Baruch Shapiro, a scholar known for his deeply held Orthodoxy, to become their spiritual leader. Shapiro, a persuasive leader who served during a robust economy, inspired the members to finish

Leaders of Herzl Congregation conduct a joyous procession transferring Torahs from the old Herzl to the new synagogue at Twentieth Avenue and East Spruce Street in 1925. Rabbi Baruch Shapiro is at center in a silk top hat. WSJHS, 43.

their synagogue. In 1925 Herzl Congregation finally moved into a completed building at Twentieth Avenue and East Spruce Street.

Shapiro, along with his wife, Hinda, brought a love of Jewish learning, leadership, and stability to the congregation. "Rabbi Shapiro got along well with the members. He visited the sick and answered the *shilahs* (questions on religious procedures)," recalled Barney Robbins, an early member. "The Rebbetzin could handle everybody and everything. She made everything work. She was a very brilliant woman. She knew how to handle people, she was wonderful with children," said Charles Jassen.[53] Shapiro would stay on until 1929, when Herzl Congregation began its move to become a Conservative shul.

Seattle's First Sephardic Congregations

Seattle's Sephardim launched their own religious institutions in the first decade of the 1900s. However, in the beginning, Jews from Marmara, Rhodes, Constantinople, and Rodosto attended religious services at Bikur Cholim, even though the liturgy and tunes of the Ashkenazic prayers sounded unfamiliar. As the number of Sephardic immigrants increased, the small community thought of forming its own religious congregation so they could retain their Judeo-Spanish traditions. In 1907, with a borrowed Sefer Torah, the Sephardim rented an empty house near Tenth Avenue and Yesler Way and prepared for Rosh Hashanah and Yom Kippur services. Rabbi Hirsch Genss, who often arranged services for both Ashkenazim and Sephardim, blew the shofar.

Although the rented quarters accommodated all the Sephardim, services tended to be confusing and chaotic. The different geographic groups had evolved distinct chants and customs. Within a year Sephardim from Rhodes and Marmara, recognizing divisions in liturgy and language, started thinking about separate congregations.[54] In a short time each group decided it needed its own synagogue, and the Sephardim split into Sephardic Bikur Holim, Avhavath Ahim, and Ezra Bessaroth congregations.

Bikur Holim

In 1916, members of the Rodosto group, which had been using three small rooms adjacent to the old Ashkenazic Bikur Cholim on South Washington Street, negotiated the purchase of the old *shul*. These Sephardim had first come together around 1910 as an "orphan and widows welfare society known as Yetomim Ve Almanot," wrote Rabbi Marc D. Angel, whose grandfather, Marco Romey, was one of the founders.[55] "[T]hey have a completely organized Jewry of their own . . . with a full complement of congregational activities," reported the *Jewish Voice* of March 3, 1916. Rabbi Shelomo Azose, who came to Seattle in 1910, conducted services, read the weekly Torah portion, chanted prayers, and officiated at special events. When he died in 1919, his brother Rabbi Isaac Azose took his place.[56]

> The funeral [for Rabbi Abraham Maimon] was something that was done very much in the custom of the old country. They had a casket, which was a wooden box, in the home. My dad had brought the children down from our Talmud Torah and he lined them up in the street. He gave them each a candle with a black ribbon on it. When the funeral was going to start the men came by and, like they did in the old country, they took the casket from the house, put it on their shoulders and they marched, singing certain psalms. The coffin was draped with the rabbi's tallit [prayer shawl].
>
> —Elazar Behar, MSCUA/UWL, 3209

But the synagogue lacked a strong leader, and in 1924, members who had known Haham Abraham Maimon in Tekirdag, Turkey, arranged to bring him to Seattle. Under his guidance, which lasted until his death in 1931, many Sephardim who had neglected going to services returned to the synagogue. In 1929, with the encouragement of men such as Nessim Adatto, Joseph Cordova, Marco Cordova, Shmuel Morheim, Joseph Caston, and Marco Romey, Sephardic Bikur Holim moved into a new building at Twentieth Avenue and East Fir Street. Much of the money came from a six-day bazaar that joined Ashkenazic and Sephardic organizations into a common effort. Temple De Hirsch members raised $5,000, said John Calderon, an active member and one-time president.

Ahavath Ahim Synagogue

Marmara Jews, including the first Sephardic pioneers Jacob Policar and Solomon Calvo, began meeting informally for prayers in 1906 and formed Congregation Ahavath Ahim (Brotherly Love) in 1909. Members called themselves "Los Balkanes" (the Balkans). Congregates David Levy and Yacovachi Eskenazi conducted services.[57] A similar group organized in Portland in 1912, and included Sephardic families from Seattle. It also chose the name Ahavath Ahim.[58]

In 1922, the Seattle group built a synagogue on Seventeenth Avenue and East Fir Street. The synagogue, with a Jewish Star visible on the front porch, had a special section (*azara*) for women. Rabbi Sabetai Israel, formerly rabbi and hazan with Ezra Bessaroth, became spiritual leader in 1925. He also acted as mohel and shohet. The membership purchased cemetery land from Congregation Bikur Cholim in 1929.

But dissatisfaction, characteristic of the individualistic Sephardim who suffered from disorganization and lack of communal direction, soon developed. Some people left and joined either Bikur Holim or Ezra Bessaroth.[59] The contingent that merged with Bikur Holim called itself the Bikur Holim Ahavath Ahim Congregation. "Merger of the two congregations exemplifies the spirit of brotherhood and the strength to be derived from unity," said the new president, Sam Baruch. Baruch represented the Sephardim trying to connect the disparate groups.[60]

Ezra Bessaroth Synagogue

In 1909, Sephardim from Rhodes under the leadership of Haim DeLeon formed the Koupa Ozer Dalim Anshe Rhodes (Fund for the Aid of Poor People in Rhodes).

Within a few years, differences divided the membership, but eventually the factious men united to form Koupa Ezra Bessaroth of Rhodes and elected Solomon Alhadeff president. Several years later, on June 19, 1914, under the presidency of Marco Franco, the congregation incorporated. An increase in membership prompted the congregation to purchase two houses and lots at Fifteenth Avenue and East Fir Street. Because the houses could not accommodate all the people on the High Holidays, the membership soon made plans to erect a larger sanctuary. The new Ezra Bessaroth, the first new Sephardic building to be constructed in Seattle, dedicated its building on Fifteenth and East Fir on June 9, 1918.[61]

With a new building, Ezra Bessaroth hired David J. Behar as *haham*, or wise man, which in Sephardic tradition implied spiritual leader and cantor. As *haham* he was "the superior and the final expert on anything regarding ethics or law."[62] Because Behar had come from Beirut, Lebanon, Haim DeLeon taught Behar the customs and traditions of Rhodes that Ezra Bessaroth congregates wanted in their

Morris and Gentil Israel, with members of their wedding party, pose for pictures on the steps of Ezra Bessaroth Synagogue at Fifteenth and East Fir in 1924. WSJHS, 107.

David J. Behar with his family. Back row, left to right: daughters Donnetta and Rachel standing behind their brother, Jacob, mother Leah, and Elazar and Alegra. Baby Julia is on her father's lap. Reverand Behar chanted prayers at Ezra Bessaroth for nearly six decades. MSCUA/UWL, *neg. 1010.*

service.[63] Initially Behar agreed to serve as a temporary spiritual leader. He stayed and cared for the congregation and community for half a century. He used Judeo-Spanish for sermons until the 1930s, when he switched to English.

In 1915, Seattle Sephardim made an attempt at unification. As a first step, they hired Aharon Benezra from New York City as rabbi and head of the Sephardic Talmud Torah. Alas, the spirit of unity between the congregations lasted only one year. Although Benezra tried to keep the different factions together, the discord among the congregations increased. Benezra soon headed back to New York.[64]

Spokane's First Congregations

In 1890, Jews in Spokane, who by this time were mostly "well-to-do" or "comfortable" businessmen with families, set in motion the process of planning a Reform temple. Many had migrated to Seattle from other American cities and had ties to people in Seattle and California. J. W. Toklas, chairman of the committee to organize a congregation, was brother to businessman Ferdinand Toklas, a member of Ohaveth Sholum in Seattle.

To inspire their potential members, Spokane's Jewish population invited Ray Frank, superintendent of the Hebrew Sabbath School in Oakland, California, to speak at Yom Kipper services. "The most prominent Hebrews of the city, with their wives and children," attended the services, according to the *Spokane Falls Review.* Frank, who had attended Hebrew Union College but grew up in an Orthodox family, urged Spokane Jewry:

[T]o decide whether you will effect a permanent organization or whether you will continue to go on and hold only one or two services a year . . . cling to the old orthodox style or take up the reform. . . . It would be well for you to throw aside all little disagreements. . . . Drop all dissension about whether you should take off your hats during services and other unimportant ceremonies and join hands in one glorious cause.[65]

Temple Emanu-El

Less than a month after that Yom Kippur service, J. W. Toklas, acting chairman, set up a meeting to draft a constitution and bylaws for Reform Temple Emanu-El. The following year, on September 16, 1891, Emanu-El trustees Joseph Kellner, Napthali Phillips, and Albert Heller signed the Articles of Incorporation and hired Emanuel Schreiber as its first rabbi. Arthur Benjamin and Hannah Munter organized the first religious school.[66] The temple congregation met in the Unitarian church on the corner of Sprague Avenue and Jefferson Street.[67] It was a classic Reform temple. At board meetings during the early years, members often used "church" when speaking of the temple.[68]

Due to the fund-raising abilities of Fanny Heller, Flora Munter, and Rosa Raphael, the board had enough money in 1892 to construct a building. "It will be 40 by 70 feet . . . a gallery will be constructed in the rear of the church. The building is to be frame with stone foundation and will cost about $3500," reported the *Spokane Review* on April 2, 1892. On September 14, 1892, four days before Seattle's Ohaveth Sholum's dedication ceremonies, Reform Temple Emanu-El opened its doors on Third and Madison Streets. Until 1896, the temple held religious services on Friday evenings and Sunday mornings.

Rabbi Emanuel Schreiber left after one year. "A beautiful temple stands silent and a menace to the religious training of our young, instead of being a haven of in-

Although incorporated two years after Seattle's Ohaveth Sholum, Spokane's Reform Temple Emanu-El rivaled Ohaveth Sholum as the first Jewish house of worship in the state: Emanu-El opened the doors of its first sanctuary, a frame building on Third and Madison, on September 14, 1892, four days before Seattle's Ohaveth Sholum's dedication ceremonies. Its replacement, the temple above at Eighth and Walnut, completed in 1928, served Spokane's Reform Jews for thirty-nine years. Courtesy of Temple Beth Shalom Archives, Spokane.

struction," complained a Spokane letter writer in 1894 to *The American Israelite*.[69] Evidently the congregation heeded the warning, for by 1895, they had paid off the mortgage and had hired Rabbi Rudolph Farber as spiritual leader.

Women gathered for a Sisterhood in 1902 under the guidance of Rabbi Jacob Block. First called the Judith Montefiore Society, then the Women's Auxiliary, the Sisterhood supported the religious school, entertained the children on Hanukkah and Purim, and assisted the choir. They also held "socials," card parties, and luncheons for the ladies as a way to attract new members and earn a little money.[70]

A deteriorating, antiquated wooden building made it necessary to begin thinking of a new temple. Board minutes of June 13, 1919, stated "that a committee of three be appointed to investigate sites for the new temple, and to ascertain what can be done for the use of another house of worship until the building of our new temple."[71] Under the inspiration of Rabbi Julius A. Leibert, and with the generous donation of Charles Lewis, who paid $5,000 to purchase the land, the congregation laid the cornerstone for a new temple on the corner of Eighth and Walnut Streets on July 5, 1920.[72] At that service, Samuel Edelstein, an active member of the congregation, emphasized that "while the new temple shall essentially be a place where the Jewish religion will be worshipped and the highest ethics of Judaism taught yet there shall be breathed within it a spirit of tolerance for all other religions."[73]

Dr. Stephen S. Wise, a leader in the Reform movement, officiated at the services. Soon classrooms opened, and community organizations such as the National Council of Jewish Women and B'nai B'rith used the rooms for meetings. A lack of funds delayed construction of the main sanctuary until 1928, when funds from the estates of Julius Galland and Mary Jaskulck made that a possibility.[74]

Orthodox Jewish settlers in Spokane built their two-story synagogue, Keneseth Israel, at Fourth and Adams in 1905. Their synagogue Hebrew school functioned four days a week, two hours a day, after public school. Courtesy of Temple Beth Shalom Archives, Spokane.

One of the Temple's most notable rabbis, Adolph Fink, who came to Spokane in 1930, was also active in the larger Spokane community. He had the distinction of being the first Reform rabbi to speak to Seattle's Talmud Torah. His topic, "The Importance of Talmud Torah in Jewish Life," stressed that it is impossible to learn Jewish history without weekday instruction.[75]

Keneseth Israel Synagogue

The Jewish population, like the rest of Spokane, grew after a fire in 1889 destroyed much of the city. Jews adhering to the Orthodox traditions were among the new residents. In 1901 they had enough interested people to obtain a charter for Congregation Keneseth Israel. Board minutes record that the members elected Joe Cohn president and paid fifty cents per month for dues and one dollar for holiday tickets. Two years later, the congregation formed a women's auxiliary, Daughters of Israel, which provided support for many synagogue activities.[76] It eventually became the Sisterhood.

On October 28, 1906, the congregation began making plans to build a synagogue, and made a $25 deposit on a lot at Fourth Avenue and Adams Street. The asking price was $1100.[77] The lot stood empty until the fall of 1908 because the congregation had decided to withhold building until they had $4000 in the bank.

But in the closing days of 1908, the Board announced that the Great Northern Railroad would pay $5500 for the right of way of the land that ran through a portion of Keneseth Israel's cemetery.[78] The congregation had purchased three acres of land for a cemetery in 1904 for $1500.[79] With money in the bank, the congregation commenced building. On March 7, 1909, the Board met for the first time in their new building at Fourth Avenue and Adams Street. Rabbi S. Reuben, who the Board had hired in 1908, conducted services at the first religious services held in the sanctuary.

Spokane's active *chevrah kaddishah* began with a ten-person, all-male committee appointed by the Keneseth Israel Board of Directors, which named the cemetery "Mount Nebo" at a meeting on February 3, 1908.[80] To help the burial society prepare and dress bodies for Jewish funerals, Spokane women in 1911 organized the Helping Hand Society. They also made shrouds, which were given gratis to those who could not pay. The Helping Hand Society, guided by Mrs. F. Silverstein for fourteen years, managed Mount Nebo cemetery, built a home for the cemetery caretaker, paid for paved roads into the cemetery, and made certain that all graves were marked and properly cared for.[81]

A fully paid mortgage in 1923 left the congregation debt-free. Money from

Part of the 1922 dedication ceremony for Tacoma's Reform Temple Beth Israel included a procession headed by the rabbi, who was followed by four little girls dressed in white (one with an embroidered cushion holding the key to the Ark) and officers of the congregation, who carried the Torah into the new building. Courtesy of Josephine Kleiner Heiman, Tacoma.

businessman Julius Galland made it possible to remodel the old synagogue and put in a *mikvah* in 1929.

Keneseth Israel made certain Jews in Spokane had kosher meat. In 1912 the Board agreed to "tell the new *shochet* to do the killing for anyone who was willing to pay for same . . . [and] a committee of three [was] appointed to investigate a complaint that the *shochet* refused to kill for certain people."[82] This became such an important function that the 1926 bylaws clearly stated that the congregation would provide a shochet "to butcher meat, according to the ritualistic custom . . . [and] shall at all times within reasonable hours *shecht* poultry or fowl for any member of the Congregation in good standing at a reasonable compensation."[83]

As in other small congregations in Washington State throughout the early years, Keneseth Israel's congregation enjoyed only temporary periods of rabbinical leadership. Rabbi S. Reuben and Rabbi Bernard H. Rosengard each served for a few years. Rabbi Joseph Krixtein became the congregation's first long-term rabbi in 1925.[84]

Ahaveth Israel Synagogue

Sometime in 1913, another group of Spokane Orthodox Jews came together as Congregation Ahavath Israel, and acquired burial ground. By 1917 they had a Ladies' Auxiliary, with Sarah Ida (Mrs. A.) Taitch as secretary. They did not have a building, and according to Spokane city directories, only gathered together on Saturdays and holidays.[85]

Tacoma's First Congregations

Notices of Jewish religious activities, such as announcements of "Hebrew New Year Services," began appearing in the *Tacoma News* in 1873. By the fall of 1889, the holidays appeared on the front page. The fact that the majority of the paper's prominent advertisers were Jewish merchants may have been a factor, observed local historian Deborah Freedman. At this time Tacoma did not have a rabbi, temple, or synagogue. Its Jewish community did, however, have a desire to keep their Jewish identity, and had already organized the Hebrew Benevolent Association of Tacoma. Temple Beth Israel and eventually Talmud Torah Synagogue would grow from those beginnings.

Temple Beth Israel

On February 15, 1892, William Wolf, Sol Jacoby, Elias Gross, and Archie S. Ash invited the Jewish community to attend a meeting for the "purpose of organizing a Hebrew congregation."[86] The men, all members of the Hebrew Benevolent Association, which just a year earlier had purchased cemetery land, were wealthy Tacoma merchants.

A month later, Tacoma had Temple Beth Israel, with Jacoby elected as president. At that date the Reform congregation was "seventy-five members and still growing," reported the *Tacoma Daily Ledger.* Women from the Lady Judith Montefiore Society agreed to "turn over [their] Sunday school to them [Beth Israel], thus increasing the attendance and prospect of success."[87]

With an enthusiastic membership, Temple Beth Israel acquired two lots at South Tenth and I Streets, considered spending $10,000 to build a temple, and requested that students from the Hebrew Union College of Cincinnati lead High Holy Day services. Women from the Temple Aid Society, headed by Florence Donau, solicited money for the building fund by hosting a three-day bazaar at the then-new Olympic Theater.[88] The description of the event in the December 15, 1892 *Tacoma Daily News* filled several columns. It read in part:

Promptly at 8 o'clock tonight Mayor Huson in an address from the stage will open the fair and the gaiety then begins and will continue unabated to its close Saturday night at midnight. At 11 o'clock each evening dancing will begin and will continue until midnight. Saturday afternoon will be Children's day and every child attending will be given a ticket entitling it to a chance upon a magnificent doll which will be raffled during the afternoon on the stage.

In 1893 a frame structure welcomed the congregation. The building accommodated the congregation's members for thirty-three years. The *Tacoma Daily Ledger* described the dedication ceremonies:

The services began at 10 o'clock . . . a procession composed of the rabbi, officers of the congregation and visiting rabbis assembled in the vestry room. When they arrived at the inner door they halted and asked for admission, the rabbi saying: "open unto me the gates of righteousness"—which was responded to by the chorus. Then the procession entered, the rabbi first, followed by four little girls dressed in white and bearing bouquets, one of whom carried an embroidered cushion on which lay the key to the holy shrine. . . . President Jacoby, who carried the holy scroll, opened the ark and deposited it within. . . . The lighting of the perpetual lamp was the most impressive of the ceremony . . . Mr. Jacoby lighted a taper and handed it to the rabbi who slowly climbed three steps. . . . The flame dimly shone through the colored glass and everybody knew that the light of Judah burned in Tacoma.[89]

Although the congregation had voted to become a Reform temple, members found themselves constantly negotiating a balance between Reform and Orthodox practices. Not until 1912 did members crystallize their Reform status by voting that "no hats be worn by the male members of this congregation." Even so, some must have continued to cover their heads, for Temple minutes dated December 21, 1924, mention the "the policy of hats off [should] be followed."[90]

Beth Israel hired Rabbi Montague N. A. Cohen 1903, but he left a year later. Though the Tacoma Jewish community discussed hiring a rabbi to serve both Reform and Orthodox, it did not happen. In 1919 Beth Israel hired Dr. Raphael

Goldenstein. He was replaced by Rabbi Montague N. A. Cohen, who was rehired in 1924.[91] Cohen took part in community affairs and served several terms on the executive committee of the General Counsel of Tacoma Social Agencies and the Community Chest.[92] A new temple on the corner of North Fourth and J Streets opened in 1922.

Hevra Talmud Torah Synagogue

Tacoma's Orthodox Jews, most of whom arrived in the early 1900s, first organized themselves into a small "Hevra" and began meeting on weekdays to recite the *yartzite* (a prayer to honor the dead). The gathering took place in the rear of Hugo Stusser's store. In 1907, under the leadership of Julius Friedman, the small group formed a minion and rented rooms for religious services and a Hebrew school at the Sampson Hotel. Two years later, Tacoma had the beginnings of an Orthodox synagogue, Congregation Hevra Talmud Torah. Julius Friedman served as the first president.

Tacoma Talmud Torah Sisterhood, 1930. Front row from left: Nura LeBid, Mary Friedman, Helen Klegman, Fanny Warnick, Lizzie Lamken, Fannie Lamken, and Lena Rotman; back row: Rebecca Olswang, Ida Sussman, Louis Benson (guest), Mrs. Herman Dobry, Emma Novikoff, Pauline Benson, Rosie Sussman, Bessie Meier, Anna Meier, Betty Friedman, and Bessie Warnick. Courtesy of Josephine Kleiner Heiman, Tacoma.

Tacoma's Talmud Torah Synagogue , located across the street from Wright's Park, harbored Orthodox and Conservative members of the community from 1925 to 1968. Courtesy of Josephine Kleiner Heiman, Tacoma.

In 1914, when an influx of immigrants swelled its membership, the congregation purchased a deserted church at 1529 South Tacoma Avenue and remodeled it into a synagogue. Affirming their commitment to Orthodoxy, the congregation's articles of incorporation stated "under no circumstances will any man or boy be allowed in the place of worship with head uncovered." [93]

That building served the members well, but by 1922, still more newcomers enticed Julius Friedman to investigate the possibility of building a new building. Generous financial pledges made it possible to purchase land and secure contractors for a building at the corner of Fourth and I Streets. The congregation also officially changed its name from Hevra Talmud Torah to Congregation Talmud Torah. Although members would lay the cornerstone for the new Talmud Torah in 1925, the synagogue would not be completed until March 30, 1930.

Like Spokane's Keneseth Israel, Tacoma's Talmud Torah suffered the on-again, off-again services of temporary rabbis. And, also like Spokane's Orthodox congregation, despite the deep-felt commitment to tradition, a dwindling population caused the congregation to gradually shift to Conservative practices. It joined the Conservative movement in 1938, when Baruch I. Treiger became rabbi, and eventually changed its name to Sinai Temple.

First Congregations in Bellingham, Everett, and Aberdeen

In the early twentieth century, Jews in small Washington towns such as Bellingham, Everett, and Aberdeen also organized religious institutions. Unlike most western Jewish communities, which usually chose Reform, Orthodox practices prevailed first in Bellingham and Everett. Even Aberdeen's community, which organized around a Reform temple, retained traditional elements, such as the inclusion of Hebrew prayers. Here in this far northwest corner of the United States, familiar Orthodox services would bind people together in a strange land. These small synagogues, often with only laypeople as leaders, became centerpieces of self-defined Jewish communities. In addition to providing a place to recite prayers, the synagogues and temples gave their members unambiguous places where they could be Jews, where explanations were unnecessary.[94]

Bellingham's Beth Israel Synagogue

"There are about 35 Hebrews on the Bay and it is expected that nearly all of them will participate in the festivities of the Jewish New Year," reported *The Blade*, a New Whatcom newspaper, on September 16, 1900. Bellingham Jews celebrated the holiday that year in a rented hall, as Jews in other small towns were doing all over the state. Jacob Olswang conducted the evening services, and Isaac Schuman and E. Jacobs read the morning prayers.

Olswang and Schuman had come to Bellingham with extended families and landsmen; details of Jacobs's history are unknown. Both Olswang and Schuman had been in the United States for about fifteen years and had become accustomed to maintaining a traditional Jewish lifestyle in the midst of Christian communities. Although the Olswang, Schuman, and Jacobs families left Bellingham soon after the synagogue opened, historian Tim Baker notes they had a significant influence on the town's Jewish community.[95]

Six years after that first service, the Jewish community in Bellingham bought the old Congregational church near the corner of F Street and Astor for $950 and established Congregation Beth Israel. Paint and other improvements applied over the summer made it possible for the synagogue to hold Rosh Hashanah services in September.

The congregation hired its first rabbi, Joseph Polakoff, in 1907. He stayed only one year. He not only conducted services, but acted as *shochet* and taught Hebrew to the children. "Like [in] every other little community they [the rabbis] would come and stay awhile. Then they were on their way," noted Edward Glazer, son of Benjamin David Glazer, an early member of Beth Israel.[96] One of the congregation's longer-lasting rabbis was Rabbi Benjamin Cohen, who was hired in 1913 and stayed four years.

"We were all active in the *shul*," Glazer said. "We didn't call it a synagogue. It was a *shul* at that time. . . . I can't remember when we didn't have it. I was born in 1908. I had my Bar Mitzvah there . . . it even had a Mikvah."[97]

Sometime in either 1914 or 1915, the members of Beth Israel organized a *chevrah kaddishah* to establish rules and regulations regarding burial in the Jewish-owned part of Bay View Cemetery. Members of the *chevrah* could choose the place in the cemetery they wished to be buried, but nonmembers had to accept the decisions of the *chevrah* committee.[98]

As Bellingham's Jewish population increased, the congregation decided to seek larger facilities. In 1925, a new building opened at 2200 Broadway. "It was a beautiful and memorable sight when the Jewish men . . . carrying the Holy Scrolls, walked from F Street to the new synagogue," recalled Edward Glazer's sister Frances Glazer Garmo, an active member of the synagogue and of the larger Bellingham community.[99] A canopy bearing Jewish religious insignia covered the Torahs. The ancient time-honored ceremony closed with the singing of Hatikva. "The religious edifice is a pride to the city and the Northwest," reported the *Bellingham American* on August 24, 1925.

Everett's Moses Montefiore Synagogue

In 1915, a calendar printed in the *Jewish Voice* reported that Congregation House of Israel and Congregation Moses Montefiore held services in Everett. Both met on the second Sunday of each month, the House of Israel at 2710 Broadway, and Moses Montefiore at 27th and Lombard. House of Israel, which left no records, is

Tallitot hanging on a door in Everett's Montefiore Synagogue display the traditional stripes and fringes mentioned in the Book of Numbers. MSCUA/UWL, *neg. 18967.*

listed in the calendar through 1919, but apparently did not survive.[100]

Congregants attending Moses Montefiore turned the house on Lombard Street into a synagogue, with men sitting on the right and women on the left, and inaugurated their Orthodox rituals. This northern enclave of Jews made certain that their children learned about Jewish prayers and holidays. H. Salhinger served as first president, and M. Shapiro as secretary. Moise Silverstone and Moe Michelson alternated as president in the 1920s, with help from Isaac John Sherman, Abe Kosher, and Dave Brenner. For many years Silverstone conducted the services, but the congregation usually hired a rabbi for High Holiday services.[101]

In recalling those early days, William (Billy) Sturman said, "Whenever a Jewish family moved into Everett, the first thing they did was to see if there was a Jewish shul. They all were eager to participate in the services . . . we took them in with open arms."[102] In the 1920s and 1930s, Everett's small but thriving Jewish community rose to nearly sixty families. They attended weekly Orthodox services at their synagogue and held religious school classes for the children. The attendance began to decline when the construction of Highway 99 north from Seattle made it easier for Everett families to drive to Seattle for Jewish activities.

Aberdeen's Congregations

In Aberdeen, Jewish families chose Reform, but "the services were always a sort of a compromise between the two [Orthodox and Reform]," said Sylvia Wolff Epstein, whose father, George Jacob Wolff, was one of the founders of Aberdeen's Beth Israel Congregation. "We were always Reform Jews. My mother hadn't been, but became so," added Epstein.[103]

By 1913, Grays Harbor Reform Hebrew Congregation, with forty-six members, met in a hall owned by the Fraternal Order of Eagles, and hired an out-of-town rabbi for the High Holidays. At other times its president, Joseph Jacobs, an educated Frenchman who ran a local shoe store, conducted services. "It fills me with pride to know that the children of Aberdeen and surrounding territory do no shirking from their religious services," said Jacobs. During the services the boys read "descriptive" passages, and the girls read from the prophets. A Miss Penn presided over the Sabbath School. The temple used the *Hebrew Union Prayer Book*.[104]

Sylvia Wolff Epstein described Joseph Jacobs as "a very unsuccessful businessman who only cared for learning," spoke eight languages (including Hebrew, but not Yiddish), and "sat at the back of his store and grumbled if anyone ever came in because he was always reading and always studying."[105] Unfortunately, congre-

Aberdeen's small Jewish community of both Orthodox and Reform worshipped together and maintained a happy compromise. When they built Beth Israel Synagogue in 1930, it was the only Jewish institution between Portland and Tacoma. MSCUA/UWL, neg. 1033.

gational records have not survived, so there is no way of knowing when the Grays Harbor Reform Hebrew Congregation dissolved.

In 1928, community members organized Reform Beth Israel Congregation. Israel Nudelman, who headed the building committee, designed and made the Ark for the synagogue. At the cornerstone ceremony in 1930, *The Jewish Transcript* noted that it was "the first to be built between Portland and Tacoma."[106]

Hoping to promote a spirit of Judaism, the congregation supplied matzoh to all Jews living in the district. They felt that this very Jewish symbol might link Jews, scattered in cities without religious institutions, to the larger Jewish community. In the era of the 1920s and 1930s, growing numbers of these Jews, as well as second-generation Jews in the larger cities, maintained only tenuous ties to religious institutions.

Whether redefining Judaism by choosing Reform thought or holding on to the orthodoxy that bound traditional Jews to their faith, Washington's pioneer Jews clearly preserved their links to Judaism. By the 1920s, they had not only established permanent religious institutions on both sides of the Cascade Mountains, but had created the foundation for Jewish life in Washington today. That most of those early congregations are still a part of Jewish Washington testifies to the long-term impact of these pioneers. This commitment to establishing a Jewish community or Jewish survival is what Jonathan Sarna characterizes as one of the four broad characteristic features that identify what Jewish life in America is all about.[107]

Seattle's Jewish Neighborhood

N O DEFINABLE "NEIGHBORHOODS" EXISTED IN THE TINY settlement on Elliott Bay when Bailey Gatzert built his home in the 1870s at Third and James. Seattle could boast only of scattered wood-framed houses and a small business district in what is today Pioneer Square. Seattle's first Jews lived scattered among their Gentile neighbors. Seattle's Jewish neighborhood began on Profanity Hill in the 1890s,[1] between Ninth and Fourteenth Avenues, and Yesler Way and King Street, where the growing number of Eastern European Jewish immigrants first made their homes. Rents were low, and access by cable car was convenient to the nearby business district, where many Jews had stores.

The immigrants sought continuity at the same time that they left their old society behind, creating a tension between tradition and change. As in other immigrant and minority communities, Jewish immigrants sought to live among people with similar backgrounds, people who spoke their language and followed their customs. Interestingly, the Sephardic Jews, who began arriving in about 1903, settled in the Seattle Jewish enclave even though they spoke a different native language than the Ashkenazim. The nascent Jewish neighborhood, though strange, drew the Sephardim.

In 1910, Seattle's Jewish population totaled about 4,500, not quite 2 percent of the city's 237,194 inhabitants. Eighty-five percent of Seattle's Jews lived in central Seattle, with almost half concentrated in six census tracts. Central Seattle included the area around Temple De Hirsch, at Fifteenth and Union, and the Yesler Way–Cherry Street neighborhood.[2]

Louis Ziegman and Louis Woron in front of the Union Market on Yesler Way, ca. 1930,
one of several kosher butcher shops in the Yesler Way–Cherry Street neighborhood.
MSCUA/UWL, *neg. 1447.*

Capitol Hill

By 1920, the wealthier Temple De Hirsch Jews lived in large homes on Capitol Hill
to the north of the temple, near Volunteer Park. The Ecksteins' red-brick Georgian
home on Fourteenth Avenue had "a music room paneled in lavender silk, a library lined with glass fronted shelves, and a third floor ballroom. . . ."[3] Sigismund
Aronson, of Schwabacher Brothers, and his wife, Eva Morgenstern Aronson, built
a large Federalist style house at Sixteenth and Aloha. "The entrance hall, 'large
enough to turn a coach and four,' had its own fireplace, an inlaid parquet floor of
quartered oak and walls covered with wine-red silk damask. The third floor contained a large oak-floored ballroom with a stage at one end."[4]

The density of Jews in this neighborhood was not nearly so great as in the
Yesler Way community to the south. Benjamin Asia, who lived in three different
houses to the east of Volunteer Park in the 1920s, remembered the area as a largely

The original cable car from Yesler Way is on display in the Smithsonian Institute
in Washington D.C. Bill and I have seen it. I've stood on it. I've told strangers,
"My mother used to ride on this very car!" They weren't impressed, but I was. . . .
The Yesler Way cable car was part of Mother's life as she grew up. She rode it to
Sunday School and to Broadway High School.
—Caroline Blumenthal Danz, daughter of Helen Berkman Blumenthal, born
   in Seattle September 15, 1892. MSCUA/UWL, 3895

"My mother loved going to school. She learned to read. She learned to write.
Yet she fiercely resisted losing her accent. She had a great ear for corrupting the
English language." Hearing his mother talk about a "Mrs. Moonshine," Max Katz
remembered feeling puzzled—"until I discovered she meant Mrs. Mondschein.
Then there was another lady she used to call Mrs. Chocolate. Mrs. Chocolate?
One day it finally came out there was a Mrs. Shucklin, who was a very prominent
charitable Jewish lady."
—Max Katz, MSCUA/UWL, 3247

Catholic neighborhood surrounding Holy Names Academy for girls and Saint
Joseph's Church and its school for boys. Asia recalled several Jewish neighbors:
Harry and Emma Rogers, Rabbi Samuel and Cora Koch, the Metzenbaums,
the Friedlanders, the Starins, the Danzes, the Langs, the Marks, the Levanskys,
and the Lindenbergers. "There were Jews all over the place, but it was mainly a
Catholic neighborhood."[5]

Elite Jewish society in Seattle enjoyed rounds of parties and entertainment at
the downtown Concordia Social Club, organized in 1890; at Glendale Country
Club, founded in 1922; and in their luxurious homes and summer houses. Jews
founded their own clubs in response to growing exclusion from the city's elite
clubs, such as the Seattle Golf Club and the Seattle Tennis Club, both of which
had Jewish founding members, and Broadmoor Golf Club. The Jewish clubs
served to separate the old established families from the more recent Jewish immigrants and also allowed their members "to demonstrate their own credentials to
America's WASP elite."[6]

The children of the elite believed themselves to be more democratic than
their parents in choosing friends. Joanna Eckstein, daughter of Nathan and Mina

Eckstein, commented on a high school club for Jewish girls, Sigma Theta Pi (a national group):

[W]e did do good work and we weren't that snobby because we took in a lot of people whose—let us say, whose parents were not friends of our parents who we had met in school or through Sunday School. . . .[7]

The "good work" included volunteering at the Educational Center in the Yesler Way neighborhood and at the Kline Galland Home, which served the Eastern European and Sephardic Jews. But Eckstein and others who *were* the children of their parents' friends—the Langs, Kreilsheimers, Schoenfelds, Pickards, and Plechners, to name a few—had a social life that revolved around the Glendale Country Club, parties, and horseback riding.[8]

As one historian observed, "Jews often knew who they were by where they lived."[9] Little social contact existed between the Capitol Hill Jews and the Eastern European and Sephardic immigrants who arrived later. The acculturated and financially comfortable temple Jews saw the need to aid their co-religionists and to quickly educate them to American ways, but not to include them in their social circles.

Not surprisingly, the Orthodox Jews of the Yesler Way–Cherry Street area regarded the temple Jews with a wariness that bordered on

Jewish members of Boy Scout Troup 45, ca. 1926. Left to right: Abe Condiotty, Al Caraco, unidentified individual, Henry Payley, Mel Abrams, Ralph Eskenazi, and Milton Shindell. MSCUA/UWL, *neg. 1251.*

suspicion.[10] The Americanized and Reform temple Jews in the Capitol Hill area lived in a different world. All the same, even though many Jews lived there, no one considered Capitol Hill a "Jewish neighborhood."

The Yesler Way–Cherry Street Neighborhood

Seattle's distinctive Jewish neighborhood lay between Twelfth and Twentieth Avenues, bounded on the south by Yesler Way and on the north by Cherry Street. The initial Jewish settlement on Profanity Hill had shifted to this neighborhood by the beginning of the First World War. One early commentator attributed the move to the influx of blacks and Asians, whose neighborhood had been disrupted by the Jackson Street regrade, a large engineering project which lowered the south slope of First Hill and washed the earth down to fill the Elliott Bay tideflats south of Pioneer Square.[11] Whatever the reason for the movement east, the old Profanity Hill neighborhood was transformed to fit its name. In 1940, eighteen brothels and some of the worst housing in the city were torn down to create Yesler Terrace, the Seattle Housing Authority's first urban renewal project.[12]

The Yesler Way–Cherry Street neighborhood contained a mixture of ethnic groups which included Jews, Scandinavians, African Americans, and Asians. No one census tract in the area ever had more than 41 percent of Jewish residents.[13] But

> [My mother] baked . . . challah every Friday. She would make little challah for every child in the family. She also made challah for the children in the neighborhood. I remember a little black girl coming to our door every Friday and saying, "Is my challah ready yet?"
> — Esther Rickles King, "Journal"; courtesy of Evelyn Brickman, San Francisco

> Every Sephardic [kitchen] had a little couch. My dad was very handy, and made one; we called it a canape. It's about large enough for two to three people to sit on very close together. It's made with wood, and you put a mattress there, and you put a fancy embroidered ruffle on the bottom and pillows behind it. Every Friday you'd take all the material out, take all the pins out, wash it and starch it, iron it and put it back on again.
> —Leni Peha LaMarche, MSCUA/UWL, 3452

Anchor of Seattle's Jewish neighborhood from 1914 to 1968 was the Bikur Cholim Synagogue at Seventeenth and Yesler, designed by B. Marcus Priteca. The building later became the Langston Hughes Cultural Arts Center. So close had the synagogue been to the heart of Ashkenazic Orthodoxy that even years later, some former members attending a Langston Hughes Center event whisked on their kepot as they came into the building. Miriam Suttermeister, WSJHS.

Seattle was not unique in this respect. "Jews were too small a part of most cities' populations to do more than set the tone through the establishment of organizations and businesses and by the presence of religious and cultural activities," a review of histories of Jews in several American cities outside of New York revealed. "They could dominate blocks but never whole neighborhoods."[14]

Synagogues, Stores, and Homes

Despite the fact that Jews never constituted a majority, the Yesler Way–Cherry Street neighborhood had a distinctively Jewish flavor. During the decade after

World War I, a visitor to Yesler Way would have encountered the impressive Bikur Cholim sanctuary looming at Seventeenth Avenue. Three more synagogues lay to the north within a block or two of Yesler Way: Herzl, Ezra Bessaroth, and Sephardic Bikur Holim. By 1930, Machzikay Hadath's little sanctuary appeared at Twenty-sixth Avenue and Spruce Street. Bikur Cholim overlooked the New York Restaurant, Hoffman's grocery store, and Ziegman's butcher shop across the street, all bearing the Hebrew letters for "kosher." The *tref* (nonkosher) meat market operated by Harry Rose, a Jew, attracted the irate oaths of Orthodox women: "ham seller" they shouted, shaking their fists.[15]

Until the late 1920s, the center of the Sephardic community occupied the area between Twelfth and Fourteenth Avenues and Jackson and Spruce Streets.

Posing in this 1934 photo of the Twenty-fourth Avenue Market are, from left to right, Frank Varon, Joseph Romey (who owned the butcher shop next door), Isaac Maimon, Jack Funes, and Solomon Maimon. Isaac Maimon was one of the owners of the store. Solomon Maimon went on to become the first Sephardic Jew trained as a rabbi in the United States. WSJHS, 121.

The Mosler Apartments, ca. 1910, between Twelfth and Fourteenth on Yesler was the first home for many new Eastern European Jewish families. The Moslers were bakers whose motto for their bread was "The life is in it." Sam Mosler established the first health-food store in Seattle. MSCUA/UWL, *neg. 5.*

Many Sephardic families, despite the small size of their dwellings, took in one or two boarders from the old country. Some of the boarders took their meals in a nearby Sephardic restaurant, where a backgammon game could also be found.[16]

Farther east, the visitor would have found more kosher butcher shops—Kaminoff's, Harris's, and Varon and Romey's—where the acrid smell of burnt chicken feathers often hovered over the counter and a Yiddish-speaking housewife bargained for a *bissel* more of beef liver. A good Yiddishe housewife was not above cajoling the butcher into throwing in a few extra chicken feet, prized by Jewish cooks for chicken soup. Salamis, corned beef, and pastrami (shipped from Chicago until Rev. Yehuda Slotnik, a *shochet* or ritual slaughterer, opened a factory at 1809 Yesler Way in 1932) were often subjected to experienced housewifery sniffs and pokes over the loud remonstrations of the shopkeeper. The butcher wore his splattered and stained apron proudly, often unceremoniously tossing scraps onto the sawdust-covered floor, and seldom bothered to wash the front windows of his shop. Everything in his shop was kosher and therefore "clean." Few butchers of those days believed in catering to their customers.

Intermingled with the butcher shops, the visitor would come upon Brenner's and Lippman's Jewish bakeries and the enticing smell of freshly-baked challah, pumpernickel, and rye breads. On a Sunday, people from both Capitol Hill and the Yesler Way–Cherry Street neighborhood often lined up in front of Brenner's Bakery for bagels. Brenner's baked only one kind of bagel in those days—plain, then considered a uniquely "Jewish" food.

In the early years, Moise Tacher's Eagle Grocery at Fourteenth and Yesler, and Hiam Fiss's fruit and grocery at Fourteenth and Fir provisioned the community. By the 1930s, a visitor walking farther east would discover two more Sephardic-owned grocery stores: Altaras's, between Eighteenth and Nineteenth Avenues, and Sam Maimon's and Jack Funes's Twenty-fourth Avenue market. Nearby, on East Fir Street, was the entrance to the Seattle Kosher Sausage Factory and Meat Market.

Dozens of other businesses, Jewish and Gentile, could be found scattered along or near Yesler Way. Favorites included Condiotty's candy shop and the Yesler Theater, where children paid a nickel for movies. Funes's and Oziel's Yesler Furniture Company, jewelers and watchmakers, laundries, barbershops, drug and hardware stores, plumbers, and shoe repair shops provided goods and services to a close-knit community.[17]

The people who frequented the stores lived nearby, in apartments, rented homes, or their own single-family homes. A few lived a block or two south of Yesler Way, but most lived to the north. The Mosler Apartments at Twelfth and Yesler, and, across the street, the apartments above Aroni's furniture store provided

When you had company in those days it was a custom to have a silver tray, and on the silver tray was a beautiful ornate container that was round, and the spoons hung around this ornate bowl. You'd take a spoon and you'd take a teaspoon of the sweet candy that was inside. Before you'd put the candy in your mouth, you'd bless the hostess and her children. If they have unmarried children, you hope that they be married with a lot of happiness. If the woman didn't have children, you'd ask she be blessed with children. It was a regular ritual. Then you'd eat the candy—it was just out of this world—and you'd put the spoon in the glass of water, and with the spoon in the water, you'd sip your water. Right now it's not proper to drink water with a spoon it. Then, it was okay.

—Leni Peha LaMarche, MSCUA/UWL, 3452

Guests at Harry Schwartz's B'rith (circumcision) in 1907 included Joseph Sussman of Tacoma (lower right), Samuel Mosler (fifth from lower right), and Louis Dulien (second row, with cap and necktie). Also included are Joseph Cohen, David Schuman with wife and baby, and Herman Keisler. On left with those on the porch is Frank Schwartz, the infant's father. MSCUA/UWL, neg. 1388.

temporary housing for "greenhorns," the newly arrived immigrants. Many single men and a few women lived as boarders with families. But Seattle had no tenement housing comparable to that of New York and other large eastern cities. Once established, all but the poorest Jews, and most Seattleites, purchased their own single-family houses.

Yiddish, Ladino, broken English, and American slang mingled as people conversed. Young men met at a Sephardic restaurant and coffee house, sipped Turkish coffee, and played backgammon. The stores, cafes, cardrooms, saloons, and billiard parlors stayed open late for the neighbors who crowded the sidewalks during the evening hours.[18]

Religious Life

On Shabbat, the Sabbath, the atmosphere in the Yesler Way–Cherry Street neighborhood was different from any other day of the week. Early Friday the streets bustled with housewives shopping for the makings of the Friday night dinner. Orthodox husbands and sons went to *shul* or *kal* (synagogue) while their wives laid the white tablecloth and set out the candlesticks. After the men returned and sun had set, families said blessings over the candles, challah, and wine. Saturday was a day of rest and prayer.

On Jewish holidays, people paraded on Yesler Way, greeting each other in Yiddish, Ladino, and English. "Our synagogue was on Fir Street," Elazar Behar of Ezra Bessaroth recalled:

You might have lived on 25th and Fir but you would not walk straight up Fir Street. You would go to Yesler Way and then you would walk up to 25th or 29th . . . and then you would walk back to your block. . . . Yesler Way was the parade route. . . . On Yom Kippur night it would be unbelievable. It looked like a never-ending procession for a good hour. . . . They'd walk three steps forward, stop and talk a little bit more, take a couple more steps and talk. As we said in Spanish, they would be *saludando* . . . greeting each other. You'd have to stop and wish everybody a happy holiday.[19]

Sol Esfeld recalled similar parading of the Ashkenazim on High Holidays and the Yom Tov (good day) greetings that flew up and down the neighborhood streets.[20] On Purim, the Sephardim bought *pepitas* (roasted pumpkin seeds) and pine nuts at Condiotty's candy store, and the children distributed *shalach manoth*, trays of baked goods and fruit, to friends and family throughout the neighborhood. The Ashkenazim celebrated with parties and the eating of *hamentashen* (fruit-filled, three-cornered cookies).

The religious life of the Yesler Way–Cherry Street neighborhood was outwardly Orthodox, at least until Herzl Congregation switched affiliation to the Conservative movement in 1932. However, the necessities of making a living often impinged on Sabbath observance. Closing their doors to business every Saturday was difficult for family heads barely making a living.[21]

As the children acculturated in public schools, many turned to the progressive practices of Judaism at Temple De Hirsch, which offered free religious school to

[Sephardic wedding] receptions were held at home. The whole week would be a celebration. In the family of the bride and bridegroom there would be, every night, different people at the house [for a] special dinner. . . . It was like a law to them that you're required to make the bride and the bridegroom happy. Every night there would be an entertainment in the home of the bride or bridegroom or one of their relatives. There would be singing and dancing and eating and drinking every night.

—Elazar Behar, MSCUA/UWL, 3209

all. This was a two-way street. Boys, such as Herbert Droker, had the opportunity to become Bar Mitzvah at Temple De Hirsch even if their families did not belong.[22] Benjamin Asia's family belonged to Temple De Hirsch, but his Bar Mitzvah was held at Bikur Cholim. "My father, I think, tended to be estranged from the rulers of Temple De Hirsch which was largely dominated by the German early settlers of the community and . . . their immediate descendants. And so there were doctrinal or social differences. . . ." Asia's father also served on the fund-raising committee for the Talmud Torah at Twenty-fifth and Columbia, a school which Asia never attended.[23]

Social Life

The social life of the adult community centered mainly around homes, synagogues, and the Workman's Circle, a secular self-help organization with branches across the nation. Most families were too poor to eat in restaurants or take long vacations. Men worked long hours to earn money. Women, lacking modern conveniences such as washing machines and refrigerators, had little leisure time. For many, the extended family served as the focus of social life. Grandparents, aunts, uncles, and cousins gathered together not only for religious celebrations but also for entertainment and mutual support.

Synagogue and Talmud Torah fund-raising events provided some of the most memorable festivities. Picnickers rode the cable car to the Leschi neighborhood, then the ferry to Fortuna Park on Mercer Island, a favored spot. There the various Jewish organizations held daylong events that included raffles, races, contests, games, and prizes. The days would end with dancing before everyone embarked back to Seattle.[24] Families from Tacoma, Everett, and Olympia often attended these festive gatherings, widening their social contacts with other Jews. The

Sephardim also held *nochadas*, social nights with dancing, eating, and drinking, to raise money for the synagogue or the Hebrew school.[25]

The more secular, socialist-leaning Jewish immigrants focused their social life on the Workman's Circle's Seattle Branch No. 304, organized in 1919. *The Jewish Transcript* carried a regular column concerning its activities throughout the 1920s, 1930s, and 1940s. Harry Glickman remembered:

The Workman's Circle provided a community of people with similar backgrounds, who had been in the United States a relatively short time, the much needed support and friendship of an extended family. . . . The social aspect of the Circle also provided entertainment in the form of musicals and plays in Yiddish, which were regularly performed on the tiny stage in the Workman's Circle Hall, which was located near 21st and Alder. . . . Other functions of the Club included medical coverage by Dr. Jerome Jacobs, and above all the Credit Union, where interest free loans could be obtained.[26]

The credit union, established in 1926 and one of the first in Washington State, enabled members to start small businesses or to keep them afloat. Most members operated small businesses. The Workman's Circle served largely as a Yiddish culture society, and the children learned Yiddish and Jewish history instead of the usual Talmud Torah education.[27] "The children . . . formed friendships that remained throughout their lives," Glickman recalled. "However, with only a few exceptions, they stopped or lost interest in the Circle at about high school age."[28]

First-generation Ashkenazim and Sephardim rarely mixed socially. Differences in language and custom were barriers that only the Americanization of the next generation would lower. "The Ashkenazic [sic] thought they were better than the Sephardim. The Sephardim knew they were better than us," one Seattle native recalled. The Ashkenazim "looked down on [the Sephardim] as any group looks down on the next wave. They were . . . greenhorns. They talked funny. They cooked different."[29] Young adults from the Ashkenazic community formed the Young Men's Hebrew Association in 1910 to meet their social needs, and the Sephardim had their own clubs (see chapter 5, "First Organizations").

Education

Seattle's Jewish children were Americanized in the public schools and on the playgrounds. Collins Field House at Fifteenth Avenue and Main Street was a recreational center frequented largely by Jewish and Japanese children.[30] Immigrant children started school in the lower grades until their English skills allowed them to move to age-appropriate levels. In the early years, most Jewish children attended

The 1917 eighth-grade class of Seattle's Pacific Elementary School, the first American school for many immigrant Jewish children. MSCUA/UWL, *neg. 18969.*

the Old South School at Twelfth and Weller (later named for Bailey Gatzert) and the Pacific Elementary School on Twelfth Avenue at Jefferson Street. In 1915, Pacific reported that 85 percent of its student body was Jewish.[31]

As families moved up the hill to the east after 1910, Washington School, at Nineteenth Avenue and Washington Street, absorbed the children of the immigrants. On the eve of the First World War, Jewish children made up 65 percent

The Jews at that time were the championship basketball players. They were tricky. Until it became a black sport, it was a Jewish sport. The wonder team of Garfield High School was mostly Jews at the time. That was in the late '20s. Marty Backer was an all-city player.
—Joseph Russak, MSCUA/UWL, 2669

Most of us had some kind of work to do [after school]. I used to sell newspapers, and others did other kinds of work, but in the evening we'd get together at the YMHA and go to dances and that was the main indoor sport in those days. They'd have these public dances, sponsored by the city and by groups. Down at Leschi Park they had a big pavilion. And we'd go on picnics together over in Fortuna Park [Mercer Island]. That was the favorite picnic grounds where you'd take the ferryboat from Leschi Park.
—Sol Esfeld, MSCUA/UWL, 2018-3

of the Washington School student body, with Sephardim heavily represented; by 1928, Jews constituted only about 35 to 40 percent.[32] By the 1920s, Japanese children comprised the largest minority at Washington, with a scattering of African American and Filipino students. "Of course," Max Katz recalled, "the teachers were all these old maid schoolteachers from Iowa and Wisconsin and Minnesota. The first principal was Mr. Stanton. If you'd ask what God looked like, we'd close our eyes and answer either Mr. Stanton or Rabbi Shapiro. . . ."[33]

Some Jewish children attended Rainier School, still farther east, on Jackson Street. In the 1930s, Horace Mann School at Twenty-fifth Avenue and Cherry Street had the largest number of Jewish students of any elementary in the city.[34]

Garfield High School was "a stock pot of ethnic diversity,"[35] drawing teenagers from Seattle's Jewish, African American, and Asian American neighborhoods as well as from the wealthy, elite neighborhoods of Broadmoor, Washington Park, and Madison Park. Jews excelled in academics and athletics at Garfield. Coach Leon Brigham successfully unified players from diverse origins to forge the Bulldog's championship football, basketball, and track teams. Among the star Jewish athletes were record-setting basketball scorer Ackie Kessler, Al Franco, Sam Zedick, Vic Calderon, and Moe Rose, two-time city tennis champion.

The important role played by the Educational Center in the life of the Jewish community is discussed in chapter 5, "First Organizations."

The Shift to Cherry Street

By the early 1930s, the center of the Jewish business district had shifted six blocks north, from Yesler Way to Cherry Street, although the synagogues remained nearer to Yesler. Kosher groceries, bakeries, and butcher shops followed the migration of the Jewish community as it fanned north and east from its anchor at

Seventeenth and Yesler. Many Jewish families purchased homes to the east of Garfield High School following the First World War. Jewish children now made up about 51 percent of the student body at Horace Mann Elementary School, and many attended Madrona School, farther east. The Seattle Talmud Torah moved into a new building across the street from Horace Mann in 1930, designed by the noted Jewish theater architect B. Marcus Priteca.[36]

The Legacy of Seattle's Jewish Neighborhood

In most ways, Seattle's Jewish neighborhood resembled those of several other cities of similar size in the United States. As in South Portland, Los Angeles's Boyle Heights, and Denver's West Colfax section, most families lived in detached, single-family houses because the city had a high proportion of this kind of dwelling.

The Louis Hoffman store in Seattle's Jewish neighborhood, with Al (the songwriter), David (the character actor), and Abe Hoffman in front of store on right, ca. 1915. WSJHS, 44.

Yetta Brenner, clerking in her father's bakery, delighted in handing out free cook-
ies to children coming in with their mothers. Youngsters were drawn to Yetta by
more than cookies. She wore glittery pins on her chest, flowers and ribbons in her
platinum blond hair, and red, red polish on her fingernails. Children loved her.
When the youngsters in a Sunday school class at Temple De Hirsch Sinai were
asked to come dressed as a famous person, a person they admired, one little girl
put on all her jewelry, all her bangles and beads—and came dressed as Yetta
Brenner, the lady at the bakery.
—"Yetta," *The Bellevue Journal-American,* 31 July 1989

This gave a sense of spaciousness and openness to the neighborhood, with lawns in front and in back of every house. Furthermore, "no single nationality group, including Jews, ever constituted a majority in any area as large as a half-mile square" outside the large eastern cities of the United States.[37] The presence of a large number of Sephardim relative to the whole Jewish population lent a richness and diversity to Seattle Jewry. The Sephardim formed a critical mass that allowed them to maintain their traditions, customs, and language to an extent not seen outside of New York.

The Jewish neighborhood began to break up after the Second World War (see chapter 13, "Postwar Growth"). While it lasted, the neighborhood produced a vibrant Jewish community. The legacy of the Yesler Way–Cherry Street neighborhood is still evident in many buildings and families. For instance, the Bikur Cholim sanctuary at Seventeenth Avenue and Yesler Way has been recycled as the Langston Hughes Cultural Arts Center, and the Seattle Talmud Torah building on Twenty-fifth Avenue, near Cherry Street, now houses the Islamic School of Seattle.

According to a prominent historian of American Jewry, Henry Feingold, "Most urbanized American-born Jews found their mates within a 20-block radius of their homes. . . ."[38] While there are no statistics to prove it, Seattle Jews who grew up in the old Yesler Way–Cherry Street neighborhood would concur with

On Saturday afternoons, children congregated in Cherry Street's Madrona Garden
Theater to see Hoot Gibson, Tom Mix, or Rin-Tin-Tin. The soda fountain in the Garden
Drug Store next door was the neighborhood source for pints and quarts of hand-packed
ice cream. MSCUA/UWL, *neg. 14648.*

Olive oil, that's all there was in Rhodes. Everybody [here] had corn oil, Mazola.
Everybody used to get oil in the five-gallon cans. There was an Ashkenazic man,
I don't remember his name, who lived about a half block from the old Herzl, and
everybody would go there and buy the five-gallon can of Mazola oil.
—Leni Peha LaMarche, MSCUA/UWL, 3452

Feingold's statement. Families started there, and enduring friendships were made there. Although most Jews living in the Seattle area today are not natives of the city, Seattle has a core group who grew up in the Yesler Way–Cherry Street neighborhood in the 1920s and 1930s. For those people, the old Jewish neighborhood provided a community vital to their continued identity as Jews.

Art, Music & Theater in the Early Years

I N 1 9 2 9 , T H E   S E A T T L E   A R T   I N S T I T U T E   (F O R M E R L Y   T H E
Seattle Fine Arts Society), an organization dedicated to promoting the fine
arts, exhibited the works of Boris Deutsch, a Jewish artist from a small village
near Riga, Latvia.[1] Deutsch, who lived in Seattle between 1916 and 1920, had been
a student of the Talmud in his youth and specialized in Jewish subjects. According
to critics, he "chose to characterize the Jewish race as a medium for the development of his artistic style."[2] The exhibition motivated the Menorah Alumni Society
to hold a symposium titled, "Is There a Distinctive Jewish Art?"[3]

Although the Menorah Society was addressing only the visual arts, this question could be asked about any of the other arts—writing, music, and the theater.
Records of what the Menorah Alumni Society concluded are not available, but the
question is still relevant. What is Jewish art, and what makes art Jewish?

Is Jewish art only art where both author and subject are Jewish, or does one
take a broader view and include books, paintings, musical scores, and dramatic
productions by artists who happen to be Jewish? An examination of the work and
history of Jewish Washington artists reveals many who created art with definable
Jewish themes, but few, except for those writing religious music, did so exclusively.
The narrow definition of Jewish art would not allow mention of artists such as songwriter Al Hoffman, or Rose Morganstern Gottstein, whose work with the Ladies
Musical Club furthered the careers of both Jewish and non-Jewish musicians. Yet
these Jewish artists and many like them enriched Jewish life in Washington.

The broader definition that defines the substance of this chapter and chapter
15, "Arts in the Postwar Years," considers contributions to the visual arts, literature,
music, and theater by Washington Jewish artists as well as the institutions that
provided venues for their presentations. Artists range from those who primarily

reached Jews, such as cantors in synagogues and the Yiddish theater, to those who pursued Washington State, American, and international audiences without regard to religious affiliation. It includes artists who today are known only by their families and friends, as well as more famous individuals.

Visual Art

Jewish art has existed since Biblical days. The Bible (Exodus 31:2) describes the artistry of the Tabernacle in the wilderness and gives the name of the first Jewish artist, Bezalel. Decorative elements on Torah curtains, candlesticks, spice boxes, prayer shawls, and other ritual items attest to the existence of Jewish artists in the Middle Ages. Even in Russia's Pale of Settlement, arts and crafts *chevras* (societies) gave artisans a place to develop their talents. In Europe, before Hitler's invasion, one could see paintings by Jewish artists such as Amedeo Modigliani and Camille Pissarro.

Art institutions began in Washington when Tacoma established the Tacoma Art League in 1891 and the Ferry Museum in 1893. Seattle soon followed by opening the Seattle Art School in 1894, and the Seattle Fine Arts Society in 1906. Whether Jews, many of whom were poor immigrants, attended these classes and museums, or even knew about them, is unknown.

Jewish artists do name the Cornish School, which Nellie Centennial Cornish opened in 1914, as a place where they received professional instruction in art, music, and the theater. They also attended art classes at the Settlement House of the National Council of Jewish Women, Seattle Section, and may have had instruction from Norma Lee Lasco, who in 1933 received permission from Temple De Hirsch to conduct classes in Jewish art.[4] Later, artists gained training at the University of Washington under such well-known teachers as Walter Isaacs and Ambrose Patterson. To pay for these classes, especially during the Depression, quite a few students applied for scholarships from the Vocational Scholarship Fund of the National Council of Jewish Women, Seattle Section. The Fund had so many requests from potential artists that its committee finally decided "not to take on any [additional] artist [or] musician."[5]

As the state's population grew, and as artists sought places to exhibit, gallery space increased. Many were additions to other businesses. Frederick and Nelson Department Store, Lowman and Hanford Company, and the Moore Theater all displayed and sold art. Some exhibition spaces, such as the Cherry Street Art Colony and Northwest Art Galleries, were artists' cooperatives where members paid an annual fee for the privilege of exhibiting their work. Local artists who were considered noteworthy may have had their works hung in the Henry Art Gallery on the University of Washington campus. That gallery opened in 1927, when Horace C. Henry gave his fine art collection to the people of the state under the auspices of the university. Others turned to The Northwest Printmakers annual exhibition, begun in 1928, and to summer fairs held in many cities throughout Washington.[6]

Except for Deutsch, who had exhibited Jewish art at the Seattle Art Institute, few Jewish artists painted Jewish themes. Outside of the occasional piece of ceremonial art, almost all the Jewish artists in Washington asserted their relation to art by working within the broader professional arts community. Washington had few Jewish artists. M. B. Appleton's book *Who's Who in Northwest Art*, which documents Washington artists achieving some fame before 1941, lists only three Jewish artists: Abe Blashko, Becky Blashko, and Irwin Caplan, all from Seattle.[7] All three were at the beginning of their careers; Abe Blashko and Caplan would continue working through the 1980s and 1990s. During the settlement years, most Jewish people struggled to make a living, and had neither the resources nor time to pursue painting and sculpturing, which were expensive. Not until the late 1940s and early 1950s, when an influx of newcomers, a rise in personal income, and increased exhibition venues made art a more lucrative profession, would the list of Jewish artists grow.

Abe and Becky Blashko and Caplan, the artists mentioned in Appleton's book, grew up in Seattle and had strong ties to the Jewish community. A self-taught artist, Abe Blashko dropped out of high school because of health problems. He did not,

Although Seattle-born Irwin Caplan regarded himself primarily as a commercial artist, he made a name for himself not only in graphic design but as a top-ten cartoonist and a fine artist whose paintings hung in major shows. Here Caplan paints on site at the Science Center in 1962. Courtesy of Irwin Caplan.

however, stop drawing or painting. Blashko's first known art, a mural of the Pike Place Public Market, decorated a wall of the nursery school at the Educational Center. According to its director, Sylvia Allper, Blashko was about sixteen years old when he asked to do the mural. The center provided materials, but did not pay him.[8]

Blashko spent much time at the Seattle Art Museum, where he met its director, Dr. Richard Fuller, who let Blashko use the museum's equipment to produce lithographs. In 1938, Blashko became the youngest artist to have a solo show at the newly opened Seattle Art Museum. He also exhibited at the Northwest Annual Art Show. In 1942 Blashko produced a series of drawings on the theme "Seeds of Aryan Kultur." In the drawings, which depict in graphic detail the horrors of the Holocaust, the Nazis are shown as "Ratman."[9]

Blashko moved to New York in 1942. His work is included in the permanent collections of the Henry Art Gallery, Seattle Art Museum, Library of Congress, and numerous public and private collections.[10]

Becky Blashko, Abe's older sister, specialized in handicraft art and taught art to children at the Educational Center, where she herself had played and received medical attention as a child. "By one of life's nice coincidences, the room where she taught her classes was the same room she had been in at the time she had her tonsils out," wrote Jean Devine in her history of the Educational Center.[11]

For many years, students at Seattle's Garfield High School have enjoyed Irwin Caplan's classroom mural of Paul Bunyan, painted in 1939. One of the top magazine cartoonists in the country during the 1940s and early 1950s, the familiar Irwin Caplan signature appeared on cartoons in *Look, Parade, Argosy, The Saturday Evening Post*, and *Collier's*. His cartoon "Full Speed Ahead" received first prize in the Seattle Art Museum's World War II war poster contest. Previously, in 1936, Caplan had received an award for his City of Seattle poster.[12] A fine arts graduate of the University of Washington, Caplan eventually turned to graphic design and taught graphic art at the University of Washington. He has exhibited at local galleries, such as Francine Seders, and has paintings in the Seattle Art Museum and Henry Art Gallery collections.

Although she was not included in Appleton's *Who's Who in Northwest Art*, Rose Silver received a mention in *Great Magazine Covers of the World* for her imaginative design on the cover of *The New Yorker* of October 24, 1931. Silver, who went by the professional name of Lisa Rhana Bornet, was a Seattle native who pursued her career in New York. Other sketches by Silver appeared in *Vanity Fair, Dance Magazine*, and *New York American*.[13] Silver had been the beneficiary of a scholarship from the National Council of Jewish Women, Seattle Section.

Appreciation for Music

Sporadic signs of a modern Jewish music movement that would include organized choral groups and musical compositions for piano, violin, and orchestra began in the nineteenth century, but it did not attract large numbers of followers until the early part of the twentieth century.[14] That is about the time synagogues and temples in Washington began hiring trained cantors and musical directors, including Solomon Tovbin at Bikur Cholim, David Behar at Ezra Bessaroth, and musical director Samuel E. Goldfarb at Temple De Hirsch. In the 1940s and 1950s, they would be joined by Cantor Frederick S. Gartner from Bellingham, and Nathan Grossman, choir director of Congregation Keneseth Israel in Spokane. In addition to singing traditional melodies, these men also participated in community concerts, trained young people, and stimulated an interest in Jewish liturgical music.

They were fortunate in being in an area where music, particularly Jewish music, flourished. Seattle, which had the state's largest concentration of Jews, temples, and synagogues as well as community organizations such as the Young Men's Hebrew Association, provided a stage for talented violinists, pianists, and vocalists. Jewish people could join a choral group singing Yiddish songs, sing in a choir, or perform with an orchestra. Additionally, they engaged in secular musical activities. Not long after Washington became a state, Jewish names appeared in discussions of Seattle's musical community.

Aubrey Levy and Rose Morganstern Gottstein were the first known Jews to enter the mainstream music scene in Seattle in the late nineteenth century. In addition to pursuing their professional careers, both Gottstein and Levy sang with Temple De Hirsch's choir, which in the beginning tried to function with Jewish volunteer members only.[15]

Levy, son of Esther and Aaron Levy, was an accomplished violinist. He formed the first orchestra at the University of Washington in 1898. Two years later, the *Tyee Yearbook* reported: "This year the orchestra has been an indispensable part of assembly exercises, and their willingness to play when called upon has been very much appreciated by the students."[16]

Levy's musical career received notice with the publication of his composition "Princess Angeline Two-Step," a march dedicated to the Seattle Athletic Club and named in honor of the daughter of Chief Seattle. First played at the opening of the Seattle Food Show in 1897, the song became an instant hit.[17] Although in later years Levy occasionally appeared with amateur musical groups, he abandoned a career in music for law.

Trained in San Francisco as an opera singer, Rose Morganstern Gottstein gave up a singing career when she married. In 1900, she became the unpaid executive secretary of Seattle's Ladies Musical Club, a position she held for over forty years. Started in 1891, the club supported the professional aspirations of its members and brought concerts and guest artists to Seattle. During her tenure, Gottstein, called the "silver-tongued financier," managed the "expenditure of $1,000,000 . . . and aided in putting aside a trust fund for the club."[18] Concert violinist Julius Friedman, who attended West Seattle High School before pursuing his career in New York and Europe, stands out as one of the promising Jewish musicians supported by the club.[19]

Other young Seattle Jews went beyond the obligatory piano and violin lessons to pursue musical careers. Among those receiving special mention in *The Jewish Transcript* were Coraine Frada Goldstein, who in 1913 gave her first piano recital at the age of seven; Minnie Hurwitz Bergman, who frequently played at special Jewish community events and became a popular violin instructor; Helen Schuman, winner of the Young Artists Contest held under the auspices of the National Federation of Music Clubs; Anita Lipp, who at eighteen received enthusiastic reviews following her violin concert in New York; and Judith Poska, who was invited to play her violin before Calvin Coolidge at the White House.[20]

Needless to say, not every Seattle Jewish musician was an accomplished classical soloist. Jean Singer Savan, who had an unusual, deep baritone voice, made a name for herself singing popular ballads in cabarets and music halls during the 1920s and 1930s. Recalling that time, Savan said her mother would say in Yiddish, "I never knew my daughter had such a sweet voice . . . and she gets paid?"[21] Like so many women of that era, Savan retired from the stage after she married.

Music thrived at the Educational Center of the National Council of Jewish Women, Seattle Section. Seattle NCJW members, like their counterparts around the country, saw the arts as a way to Americanize newly arriving Jewish immigrants. Attendees learned to play the piano or violin, act in a play or operetta, sing in one of three glee clubs, or perform in the Center orchestra under the baton of Leo Wiseman. They could also take advantage of music and dance classes offered by teachers from the Cornish School, or, between 1922 and 1924, attend a branch of the Cornish School at the center.[22]

A review of *The Jewish Transcript* indicates that local organizations regularly ended their meetings with a piano or violin solo, and sometimes even with a musical or theatrical performance. Presenting a program of song and dance not only provided entertainment, it also added funds to the club's treasury. Occasionally several organizations would join forces for one extravagant show. Hine Brown,

Louis Sherman, Minnie Hurwitz Bergman, Helen Schuman, Kathy Barokas, Leon Israel, Sophie Coyne, and Isaac Levy are just a few who entertained for Jewish organizations.[23] In Seattle, so many Jewish residents professed an interest in music that in 1928 a number of them, led by Edward Handlin, formed a Jewish Music-Art Society.[24]

"They've Brought Jewish Music to Seattle—Here's All About Them," announced *The Jewish Transcript* on May 4, 1928, in a story about Solomon Tovbin, cantor of Bikur Cholim; Eric Friedland, conductor of the B'nai B'rith Lodge No. 503 Glee Club; and Boris Dolgoff, leader of the Hazomir Choral Society. European trained, the men introduced Washington Jews to the modern Jewish music movement, which produced many piano, violin, vocal, and chamber music works and developed an appreciation for Jewish folk music.

Cantor Solomon Tovbin (top row, center) and Boris Dolgoff (bottom row, center), with an all-male choir enriched the services at Bikur Cholim; ca. 1917. Among the singers: first row, second from left, Meyer Aronin; fourth from left, Dave Hoffman; third from right, Dick Sadick; and far right, Adolph Warshall. Second row, far right, Billy Warshall; and second from right, Ben Flaks. WSJHS, 102.

8-3. *Boris Dolgoff (first row, center) led the Hazomir Choral Society, which introduced Washington Jews to modern Jewish music.* MSCUA/UWL, *neg. 7278.*

Solomon Tovbin learned his prayers in a Russian *heder* and *yeshivah*, and at the age of ten sang with other *hazanim* in the synagogue choir. To further his musical career, he studied at the Odessa Conservatory. He also received a secular education. Bikur Cholim engaged him as cantor in 1916. He stayed for seven years, left for Chicago, and finally returned to Seattle. Critics and lay people lavished praise whenever Tovbin chanted the age-old melodies.[25]

Professor Eric Friedland studied violin and music at the State Conservatory of Music in Warsaw and with private tutors. He taught violin and composition in Leipzig before coming to Seattle during World War I. In the late 1920s, Friedland aroused enthusiasm for Jewish music as conductor of the B'nai B'rith Glee Club. The Glee Club not only sang for local functions, but traveled throughout the Pacific Northwest, introducing people to Jewish music. Friedland also established a choir and taught music at Bikur Cholim, conducted the Young Men's Hebrew Association Orchestra, led the Arbeiter Ring Chorus, and organized a mixed choir among members of the Sephardic Progressive Fraternity. Asked "what is synagogue music," Friedland replied that the question was still being debated, but he believed "sooner or later . . . cantors will learn that opera and oratorios have no place in the synagogue ritual."[26]

Boris Dolgoff received an education in composition and conducting in European conservatories before coming to Seattle in 1916. He organized the Hazomir Choral Society, a mixed choir, in 1925. At their concerts the group mostly sang the plaintive melodies of Eastern European Yiddish folk songs. Writing about those Jewish melodies, *The Jewish Transcript* had this to say:

A lot of Jews who secretly enjoy these Yiddish melodies have until recently been ashamed to admit it publicly. . . . But of late years the goyim themselves have begun to appreciate them immensely—what a fuss they've been making over "Eli, Eli"—so we suppose its quite all-right now for Jews—or shall we rather say Jewesses? . . . to admit that they like that sort of stuff.[27]

Tovbin and Dolgoff, assisted by the congregational choir of Bikur Cholim and young boys with exceptional soprano voices, presented Rosh Hashanah and Yom Kippur songs on the first Jewish congregational radio broadcast in Seattle.[28] This, however, was not the first Jewish music broadcast. Two years earlier, in 1927, local station KJR initiated a series of international programs, including a Jewish concert. The second radio concert, directed by prominent and rising young violinist Edward Handlin, included popular tenor Louis Sherman and the Hazomir choir.[29] Approximately twenty years later, Cantor Chaim Gottlieb and the Bikur Cholim Male Choir, directed by Kurt Steinbrecher, gave the first concert in Seattle of authentic orthodox Jewish liturgical and folk music for the general public.[30]

In his book *Jews in Music*, Artur Holde wrote that Samuel E. Goldfarb was a significant American synagogue composer.[31] Before coming to Seattle in 1930, Mr. Goldfarb had been director of music for the Bureau of Jewish Education in New York. As an educator, Goldfarb taught "many thousands of youngsters . . . who later became members of Jewish choruses throughout the land."[32] Songs from his book *The Jewish Songster* inspired children all over America.

While visiting Seattle to attend a wedding, Goldfarb met Rabbi Samuel Koch, who offered him the job as musical director at Temple De Hirsch. Goldfarb not only accepted, he made Seattle his home for almost forty years. During his tenure he brought a more traditional tone to Temple De Hirsch's Friday and Saturday services, enhanced congregational participation, formed a children's choir, directed the Halevy Singers, composed "I See an America," and wrote the song "My Dreidel." In addition, he gave private Hebrew and singing lessons. "Almost at any time singing of Jewish songs in choruses can be heard at the Temple Center," wrote *The Jewish Transcript* four months after Goldfarb became musical director.[33]

Soon after his arrival, Goldfarb, with a group of eager young men and women, formed the Halevy Singers. Named in honor of the great Hebrew poet Judah Halevi, the amateur choral society included members from Reform, Conservative, and Orthodox congregations, both Ashkenazim and Sephardim. Leo A. Meltzer served as first president. For their first show they presented the operetta *Israel through the Ages.* Local singers Flossie Mendelssohn, Eva Finesilver, Celia Brenner, and Harold Bialock, with guest soprano Sophie Coyne, sang dramatic music that ranged from sacred and solemn melodies heard in the synagogues on holy days to twentieth-century Israeli folk music. Hadassah and B'nai B'rith, assisted by production managers Leslie Stusser and Harry Nieder, sponsored the event.[34] In the 1930s, the Halevy Singers familiarized Jew and non-Jew with the significance of Jewish music.

In 1936, Philip A. Langh, rabbi of Herzl Congregation, used his lecture series on Jewish culture to introduce people to the history and sounds of both liturgical and secular Jewish music. He began by asking concert pianist Susie Michael Friedman and her husband, baritone Maurice Friedman, to illustrate his talk with musical examples. "We accepted the invitation with great reluctance, even condescension. To us this was a step down from the Three

Concert pianist Susie Michael Friedman and her husband, baritone Maurice Friedman, educated as well as entertained hundreds of audiences in their "Cavalcade of Jewish Music" performances in Hebrew and Yiddish as well as English. MSCUA/UWL, neg. 18964.

Sephardic Bikur Holim's young men's choir, 1931. Among the singers are: David Romey, Leon Israel, Isaac Levy, Solomon Maimon, Joseph Benezra, Solomon Halfon, and Shaya Romey. WSJHS, 126.

B's, [Beethoven, Bach, Brahms]—an attitude unfortunately typical of our average American-Jewish musicians toward their own music," wrote Susie Michael Friedman.[35]

The evening not only changed their lives, it played a part in educating Jews about the rich heritage of their music. Inspired by audiences' response to the ancient Jewish melodies, the Friedmans became modern Jewish troubadours. Forming the Cavalcade of Jewish Music, originally billed as "Music of the Wandering Race," they traveled for nearly two decades to more than five hundred North American cities. Maurice Friedman sang the songs in Hebrew and Yiddish while Susie Friedman explained them with English narrative.

In the early years, the Friedmans' arranged their own bookings. Later they received aid from the National Jewish Musical Council. The Council, founded in 1944 and sponsored by the National Jewish Welfare Board, assisted communities sponsoring Jewish Music Festivals.[36]

Sephardic Music

If you went to the synagogue, a person could tell "just from listening from what he [the *hazan*] was singing . . . that somebody in there was going to get married, or somebody had a baby girl, or somebody had had a baby boy," explained Elazar Behar.[37] For almost sixty years, the voice which began early morning services at Ezra Bessaroth belonged to his father, David Behar, who came from Beirut,

Lebanon, in 1916. Unfamiliar with many of the tunes and melodies in this Seattle congregation, and because he fervently wished to give the people the service that they were used to in the old country, Behar learned the customs, natal traditions, and liturgy of the congregation. Haim DeLeon served as his tutor. The two developed a special friendship, as both believed that no substantive changes should be made in the rituals and customs.[38] Behar served the congregation for almost sixty years.

To preserve the old Sephardic melodies, Emma Adatto, with the assistance of University of Washington anthropologist Melville Jacobs, recorded Sephardic "romansas" (ballads), stories, and proverbs in 1935. "It seemed almost incredible that these same songs and stories have been handed down for the past few centuries," wrote Adatto.[39] In one recording, Louise Adatto sings in Ladino, "My dear parents, I shall sing for you now some of the songs you used to like so much. When you get lonesome, you can listen to this recording, so you can remember."[40] The ballads, according to David Romey, who continued and enlarged Adatto's collection in 1950, recall "memories of a happy youth.[41]

Popular Music

Al Hoffman began his musical career as a boy soprano singing in the Bikur Cholim Male Choir. Then his voice changed. Abe Hoffman knew his brother had musical talent, so he suggested that Al learn to write music. He agreed, and Abe hired a music teacher. Next, Abe bought an organ and encouraged his brother to learn to play it and "write a song like Irving Berlin." Because songwriters need lyrics, he hired a lyric writer. Although Abe and Al plugged the song at dance halls and nightclubs, they lost money. "You gotta go to New York, people told us," recalled Abe Hoffman.[42]

With his brother's financial help, young Al Hoffman boarded the train for New York. Life there was not easy, and within a year he came back to Seattle. In 1924, Bikur Cholim hired Hoffman to "drill and lead the choir to superintend the Sunday School and be its music teacher for $100 a month and his services be engaged from month to month."[43] In his spare time he played with local bands.

But New York beckoned, and, with the backing of Anna and John Holmes, active members of the Jewish community, Hoffman returned. This time, success followed. "My compensation until the present time has been in the satisfaction of having broken through what is generally accepted as a very difficult barrier," Hoffman wrote in a letter published in the March 3, 1929 edition of *The Jewish Transcript*. "Mairzy Doats," "If I Knew You Were Comin' I'da Baked a Cake,"

Al Goodhart and Al Hoffman. Hoffman wrote more than fifteen hundred songs during his thirty-year career and became famous with "Heartaches," a tune which he said was inspired by hardships he faced in his first three years in New York. MSCUA/UWL, *neg. 18961.*

"Heartaches," and "It's a Hundred to One You're from Washington," the official Golden Jubilee (1939) song, are among his hits. Hoffman received the American Song Writer Award in 1947.

Washington State and the world has hummed, sung, and whistled Arthur Freed's songs such as "Singing in the Rain" and "All I Do Is Dream of You." Although he wrote most of his songs with Nacio Herb Brown, Freed and Al Hoffman occasionally collaborated. "Fit As a Fiddle" and "Meet Me in the Gloaming" are two songs bearing the names of both Seattle men.[44] As head of the Freed Unit at MGM, he gained fame for the movies *The Broadway Melody, Singing in the Rain, That's Entertainment*, and *Gigi*.[45] *Gigi* and *An American in Paris* both won Best Picture honors at the Academy Awards.

Freed was born in 1894 in South Carolina, but his father's business moved the family around the United States. They came to Seattle from Vancouver, British Columbia, in 1909, and lived in the Capitol Hill area. Max and Rose Freed joined Temple De Hirsch and enrolled their children in the religious school.[46] Freed attended Broadway High School from 1909–12, but sometime during 1912 he transferred to Phillips Exeter Academy in New Hampshire.[47] After working as a piano player in a Chicago music publishing house and touring with the Marx Brothers, he returned to Seattle in 1920. During this brief period he had his own company, Wallace and Freed, Inc., which managed Musicland, a music store at 220 Pine Street. He left Seattle permanently in 1922.[48]

Goddard Lieberson, who became president of Columbia Records in 1955, spent most of his musical career in New York, but Seattle gave him a start. While a student at the University of Washington he received funding from the Vocational Scholarship Fund of the National Council of Jewish Women, Seattle Section. That money made it possible for him to continue his musical education at the Eastman School of Music in Rochester, New York. "Goddard is a musical genius who wishes to go to New York. . . . He would require his railroad fare and a monthly stipend. . . . It was decided to give him $50 per month for three months, $100 for railroad fare and $25 in his pocket and a little extra if necessary," stated 1932 Council minutes.[49] During his illustrious career at Columbia Records, Lieberson strengthened its classical catalog, pioneered in the recording of new music by contemporary composers, and recorded dramatic productions and musical comedies.[50]

Jewish Musicians from Washington's Smaller Cities

Because Washington's smaller cities did not have a Jewish newspaper that recorded events and accomplishments of local Jewish people, there is a sparse record of information about Jewish musicians outside of Seattle. If any went on to national fame, their achievements are not evident. The few we do know about only performed locally or were connected with temples and synagogues. Although cities such as Tacoma and Everett no doubt had Jews who sang or played musical instruments for Jewish organizational events, there is no written record. At the time of writing this book, only Spokane and Bellingham could supply documentation and names.

Marion Eugenie Bauer, born in Walla Walla in 1892, started her musical career with training from her sister Emilie, an accomplished pianist. She continued her career in New York, where she lived with her sister before pursuing studies in Europe. In 1926, Bauer joined the music faculty of New York University and soon earned a national reputation as a musicologist and composer.[51]

The Walker Orchestra, with Isadore, Herman, and Frances Walker, was one of the earliest and probably the smallest Jewish music group in Spokane. At nearly every entertainment sponsored by Jewish organizations in Spokane and in small neighboring communities, this group played music for the dances. The Walkers, who between them played six instruments, started their careers around 1925 by playing for dances given by the Bilou Club, a young adults social club.[52]

Around that time, musically talented Jews from Spokane's B'nai B'rith; the Spokane Section of the National Council of Jewish Women; the Bilou Club; and Temple Emanu-El's sisterhood joined together to raise money to complete the building of Temple Emanu-El. "The program was made up of amateurs, but was received enthusiastically by the audience," reported *The Spokesman-Review*. The cast, which presented a variety of songs and dance, included Dr. W. Copeland appearing as a comic toreador impersonating Al Jolson; Sara Soss, Mrs. B. Freede, and Frances Walker as pianists; and Jean Starr as dancer. Henry Callin and Waine Hetzka staged the productions.[53]

Violinist Arthur Thal and his brother Harry, an accomplished pianist, taught many would-be virtuosos in Bellingham. A concert presented by their youthful students in 1932 was the first for Jewish children in Bellingham.[54] A year later, Arthur Thal opened a Seattle studio and taught violin to children three to six years old.[55]

Theatrical Productions

Theatrical productions that were written, produced, directed, and acted by Jews can be traced back to at least the thirteenth century, when itinerant professional jesters (*leitzim*) and singers, relying on improvisation, traveled the countryside. Known later as "merry Jews," they performed before a public whose tastes would today be considered "low-brow."[56]

Spokane's B'nai B'rith Girls provide entertainment for a 1937 card party. From left: pianist Pearl Duitch Singer, dancers Esther Shank, Gertrude Soss, Goldeen Simon, Mary Ann Weinstein, Hannah Rashkov, and Beverly Soss Jaffe, and director Ethel Simon. Courtesy of Temple Beth Shalom Archives, Spokane.

Hundreds of years later in 1876, Abraham Goldfaden, an Eastern European writer of Yiddish songs like "Rozhinkes mit Mandlen" (raisins and almonds), added dialog to the performances and initiated the Yiddish theater. In 1882 a New York troop of six men and two women dramatized Goldfaden's operetta *The Sorceress*. It was the first Yiddish stage production in New York. The musical play, with its mixture of historical pageantry, family melodrama, and musical comedy, formed the backbone of the repertoire in the early Yiddish theater. Occasionally the companies adapted famous playwrights such as Shakespeare, Schiller, and Goethe, albeit in hopeless translations.[57]

Washington Jewry began acting in plays in about 1910. By this time the Yiddish theater featured more drama than song, and it aspired to be a highbrow culture. The traditional fare, which playwright Jacob Gordin labeled *shund* (trash), worked less well. New playwrights, gifted actors, and ambitious repertory companies all intent on doing plays of merit infused a new spirit into the Yiddish theater. According to Henry Feingold, "not only did American Jewry far outpace other ethnic communities in this area, it more than matched the legitimate American stage."[58]

Jewish youth in Washington may have first acquired the desire to become thespians within the temple and synagogue Sunday schools, where mothers dressed their sons as Mordecai and daughters as Queen Esther, and at the Educational Center (known as the Settlement House prior to 1917). At the Educational Center they could participate in one of the four dramatic clubs supervised by the Cornish School or in productions by the Neighborhood Players (also known as the Neighborhood Dramatic Club), directed by Maurice Browne, who headed the drama department at the Cornish School.[59] Settlement workers saw festive occasions like Hanukkah and Purim, based on stories from the Bible, as a place to socialize the newly arriving immigrants into the mainstream culture. The plays were given in English because until the mid-1920s, the Yiddish theater was considered uncouth melodrama.[60]

As teenagers they may have learned about drama from David Romey, who guided the productions at the Sephardic Youth Club. Those who attended the University of Washington, among them Leslie Stusser, Roy Rosenthal, and Harriet Calkins from Seattle, and Sadie Michaels from Chehalis, received coaching from drama coach Frank Price Giles for roles in Seattle's Menorah Club productions at the Moore Theater. Calkins subsequently became director for the Young Men's Hebrew Association Players.[61]

A few, including dancers Ida Levin, Sylvia Bernhard, and actress Helen Gyle Bornstein, bypassed the amateur groups and went directly to New York or to other large cities. Levin danced with the Albertina Rasch Dancers and was a featured dancer in the Ziegfeld Follies, Bernhard joined the Chicago Civic Opera, and Bornstein had roles with the Duffy Players, a traveling professional theater group based in New York.[62]

Dramatic Groups

Seattle gave Jewish actors many opportunities to appear before the footlights. During the period from 1910 to 1940, organizations such as the Menorah Society, a University of Washington social club, or B'nai B'rith would hire a hall and dramatic coach and present a play complete with costumes and appropriate props. For example, in 1924, B'nai B'rith Lodge No. 503 staged *Disraeli* by Louis Parker at the Orpheum (Moore) Theater with a large cast that included Selma Friedlander, Sarah Schuman, Harriet Calkins, Sonia Krasnova, and Leslie Stusser.[63] Schuman, a talented University of Washington student from Bellingham, had the leading female role. In her honor, her father, David Schuman, each year donated a trophy to the Jewish student at the University of Washington who did the best work in scholarship and dramatics. A board of judges from the Menorah Society selected the applicant.[64]

In addition, many Jews organized dramatic societies. Before the rise of companies such as the Seattle Repertory Playhouse, with its better-trained and more professional actors, these amateur societies gave ordinary people a place to perform as well. A few of the notable ones included The Temple Players, Sephardic Drama Group, Jewish Dramatic Club, and the "Y" Players. The Temple Players, directed by Frank Price Giles, usually presented performances at Temple De Hirsch's Temple Center, an all-purpose facility with a large auditorium that adjoined the temple.[65] Leon Behar directed the Sephardic Drama Group, Mrs. David Schlosberg lent assistance to the Jewish Dramatic Club, and Harriet Calkins coached the "Y" Players.[66] On occasion, the Cornish School of the Theater, directed by Ellen Van Volkenburg (Mrs. Maurice Browne) presented plays by Jewish writers. *The Devil's Sabbath* by S. Ansky and starring Daniel Rosenburg had its American premiere in English in Seattle, reported *The Jewish Transcript*.[67]

In Tacoma, Mrs. G. Farber took the age-old motif of the Jewish daughter loving a Gentile and in 1925 wrote *The Stranger*. Performed by local talent at Tacoma's Talmud Torah Synagogue, the play featured actors Ethel Farber and Moe Elyn, and musicians Isadore Epstein, Max Shain, and Phillip Sussman.[68] A few years later, Dorothy Rashbaum, Milton Klegman, and Sigfried Friedman performed in the Young Hebrew Moderates' vaudeville productions.[69] And although we don't know much about it, a Jewish Dramatic Club was organized in Everett in 1915 with A. Glassberg as president.[70]

Sephardic Theater

Leon Behar produced many plays in Judeo-Spanish for the Sephardic Drama Group at Washington Hall, located at Fourteenth Avenue and East Fir Street. He came to Seattle in 1920 from Istanbul, where he had been active in the theater. Ezra Bessaroth sponsored *Dreyfus*, his first Seattle play, which opened on March 19, 1922, but the profits benefited the Sephardic Talmud Torah. The play's success before an enthusiastic audience launched the Sephardic theater.

Behar paid particular attention to costumes, renting them rather than having actors appear in unprofessional, homemade outfits. He also seemed to favor multiple-act plays. In one, *Joseph Sold by His Brothers*, the curtain rose and fell between eleven acts. Usually the plays featured a Jewish theme, but a few, such as *Genoveva* and *Love and Religion*, left out the Jewish content and depicted ordinary scenes of

Leon Behar staged a number of plays in Judeo-Spanish at Washington Hall. WSJHS, 30.

Sol Krems founded Seattle's first Jewish newspaper, The Jewish Voice, *which was printed on a handpress with the help of his wife, Sara. Krems began publishing in October 1915 and discontinued in October 1919. His son Nathan later wrote for* The Jewish Transcript, *which began publishing in 1924. Nathan recalled, "I remember very well troops of Yiddish players coming to Seattle . . . and they would come to [my father's] printing plant, some, I recall, in the traditional actors' garb of fur-trimmed coats and top hats . . . for him to set up the posters, advance posters, because he had the [Hebrew] type."*
—From transcript of Nathan Krems, MSCUA/UWL, 2145

love, violence, and passion. Menashe Israel, Jack Almeleh, Morris Israel, Phinhas Almeleh, Morris Alhadeff, Joseph Souriano, Joseph Capelluto, Morris ("Mushon") Eskenazy, and Rebecca Morhaime are just a few of the actors who delighted audiences. Eskenazy also entertained audiences with his original impromptu verse. "[H]e was a first-rank wit, able to compose humorous verse impromptu to the amazement and entertainment of his audiences," recalled Rabbi Marc D. Angel.[71]

The Great Depression ended Behar's career in the theater, but not before he directed a play that would foretell the importance of maintaining Jewish unity. The production, *The Massacre of the Jews in Russia,* used Jewish people speaking Judeo-Spanish in a drama about Russian Yiddish-speaking Jews. The theater, maintained Angel, "helped to bring Sephardim of different origins together. . . . They provided cultural and educational opportunities. They gave the Levantine Sephardim of Seattle reason for pride in their language and their heritage."[72]

Yiddish Theater

In 1924, The Yiddish Theatrical Academy, directed by Sam Bendel, presented the popular *Yiddish King Lear* by Jacob Gordin at the newly remodeled Oak Theater on Madison Street between First and Second Avenues.[73] A few years later, Sam Morris, an actor with the Jewish theater in New York, came to Seattle in an effort to raise money for Seattle's Yiddish players and played the role of "Poppus the Avenger" in *Bar Kochba.* The production, a Yiddish Biblical operetta written by Abraham Goldfaden, starred tenor Louis Sherman and a Yiddish chorus directed by Wolf Dolgoff (Boris Dolgoff's father). To help those who could not understand Yiddish, *The Jewish Transcript* described the plot in a news release before the opening.[74]

In 1928, Albert Youngman directed the Yiddish Dramatic Society in *The Devil's Sabbath* by noted Jewish playwright S. Ansky. "Some of the actors were splendid," wrote *The Jewish Transcript*, but the paper also noted that "the Mademoiselle who acted as Miriam should learn to pronounce her "r's" like a Yiddish-speaking Jew, not like a Protestant Nordic Yankee."[75]

Unfortunately, according to Youngman, the exodus from the Cherry Street neighborhood eventually caused the Yiddish theater to disband. Also, many second-generation Jews neither spoke Yiddish nor identified with many of the themes prevalent in traditional Yiddish theater. They preferred to satisfy their cultural appetites with more modern tales performed in English.

Youngman, who had studied at the Dramatic Academy in Warsaw, first came to Seattle with his family in 1921. But he soon left for California and a job promoting traveling New York Yiddish theater companies. When that activity declined, he returned to Seattle in the late 1920s. It was then he became involved with the Yiddish Dramatic Society and the Habima Players, a non-Yiddish drama club promoting Jewish culture and dramatic talent among young men and women. The Habima members, among them Mary Klatzker Brown, Ruth Krakovsky, Sid Jaffe, Lou Laventhal, and Barney Shain, were just graduating from Garfield High School when Sylvia Perlman persuaded Youngman to be their director. Saul Krakovsky (Steve Hill), who went on to fame on television's *Mission Impossible* and *Law and Order*, was one of his students.[76] His sister, Ruth Krakovsky, who also shortened her name to Hill, toured with the U.S.O. during World War II.

One of the Habima Players' best shows, *Awake and Sing*, a drama of Jewish family life, played to a sold-out audience at the Seattle Repertory Playhouse in 1936. Admission was one dollar. The Seattle Habima Players Orchestra provided a musical backdrop for the plays. Of the Habima Players, "I would say in nine years, over 100 Jewish kids came through," said Youngman. Besides presenting live theater, the Players could be heard reading one-act plays about Jewish life on Seattle radio stations KOL and KXA.

Jewish Professional Actors

Dave Hoffman, brother of songwriter Al Hoffman, first dreamed of the stage when he played William Tell in the fourth grade. Like his brother, he left Seattle to pursue a professional life, but unlike Al, who went to New York, Dave set out for Hollywood.[77] A notable career in the movies (*Kismet*), on Broadway (*Uncle Vanya*), and in television attests to his success.

When Florence and Burton James opened the Seattle Repertory Playhouse in 1928, Jewish actors Sophie Rosenstein and Albert Ottenheimer appeared on stage, and Mrs. A. M. Goldstein, a founding member of The Temple Players, had a seat on the theater's Board of Trustees. Rosenstein became an instructor of drama at the University of Washington and eventually went to Hollywood, where she worked with stars Van Johnson, Jeff Chandler, and Tony Curtis.[78] Ottenheimer stayed with the group for more than twenty years.

The son of German-Jewish immigrants Solomon and Ida Ottenheimer, who had come to Tacoma in the 1880s, Albert Ottenheimer's stage career spanned half a century. In addition to his work with the Playhouse, Ottenheimer managed a radio station in Tacoma in 1922, wrote scripts for MGM during the 1930s, appeared in *West Side Story* for over three years and in other Broadway shows, and won an Obie in 1955 for his role in *Juno and the Paycock.*[79]

Philburn Friedman started his acting career at the age of seven in *Alice in Wonderland.* Every Tacoma theater group presenting a juvenile show picked this accomplished performer to play a role. Some years later he turned from acting to directing, and in 1938 began a four-year run at Tacoma's Theater Guild. A move to New York brought him acclaim as a stage manager for several of Broadway's big hits, such as *How to Succeed in Business Without Really Trying* and *Kismet.*[80]

Maxine Bennigson Mandles was born in Spokane but later moved to Tacoma. Along the way she acted in the University of Washington drama department, where she received coaching from Sophie Rosenstein. She appeared often in the Tacoma Little Theater. After a move to California in 1965, she became a prominent actress in radio, television, and movies.[81]

Motion Pictures and Vaudeville

In the early twentieth century, Jewish men, excluded from a network of fashionable clubs and certain businesses, such as banking and corporate bureaucracies, often turned to managing and owning theaters as a way to make a living. In Washington, as in other American cities, many started their movie companies as small storefront business ventures, not unlike owning a bakery or butcher shop. Others acquired an interest in established companies or managed local theaters frequently controlled by eastern syndicates.

One of the best-known Seattle landmarks, the Coliseum Theater, had the backing of Jacob L. Gottstein, the organizer and vice-president of the Greater Theater Company, which promoted several theaters between 1915 and 1926. The Greater Theater Company later merged with Jensen and Von Herberg, owners of several other Seattle theaters, and Jacob Gottstein remained as vice-president.

When the Coliseum opened on January 8, 1916, *The Seattle Times* called it "Seattle's most impressive photoplay . . . [it] is a triumph in three gasps—Oh! Um!! Ah!!"[82]

Other Jewish men connected with the early movies included Peter Gevurtz, Fred Rothchild, S. Schoenfeld, S. Metzger, and M. F. Winstock, all investors in the Peoples' Amusement Company, which in 1911 controlled twenty-five picture houses in Oregon and Washington. Mike and Al Rosenberg were managing owners of the De Luxe Feature Film Company, a large feature film releasing company. In their building at 2014 Third Avenue, the Rosenbergs provided their clients with a fireproof viewing room, vaults to safeguard film, and a library containing promotional material such as billboard papers.[83]

The De Luxe Feature Film Company and the Peoples' Amusement Company did not last, but Sterling Recreation Company, which also had an early beginning, went on to become a major motion picture chain. It began in 1913 when, in order to increase foot traffic by his haberdashery business, John Danz installed a nickelodeon, an early motion picture theater showing a film or a variety show, in a vacant space next door. With admission at five cents, the movie house soon became more profitable than his store. Realizing that the movies meant profits, Danz purchased other theaters, including the Star Theater, which was operated by the Peoples' Amusement Company. He named his company Sterling Recreation after his first business, Sterling Men's Wear. Recognizing the need for deluxe suburban theaters, Danz eventually opened movie houses in West Seattle, Magnolia, and the Northgate shopping center. Zollie Volchok, who became one of Seattle's leading theater impresarios, came to Seattle in 1946 to manage the Sterling Theaters. In gratitude for their good fortune, John and Jessie Danz endowed a prestigious lecture series at the University of Washington.[84]

To improve the West Coast's fledgling moving picture industry, Eugene Levy purchased a controlling interest in the Consolidated Film Company of New York in 1912. This enabled him to offer Seattle-area movie houses a first-choice selection.[85] Several years later, a large advertisement in *The Seattle Times* announced Eugene Levy's Road Show at the Grand Opera House would feature pictures that "will appeal to the family trade."[86]

As manager of the New Orpheum Theater at Third Avenue and Madison Street, Levy presented vaudeville road shows—five acts at each performance. According to Levy, the million-dollar theater was one of the largest and finest in America. It even had a ventilating system that cooled air in the summertime. Other "improvements" included "twenty red-haired girl ushers in smart uniforms, and maids who will be in constant attendance for the purpose of checking babies and attending to the wants and comforts of women and children."[87] Levy also became part of a thirty-three-city vaudeville circuit, a venture that allowed traveling shows to play a complete chain of affiliated houses.[88] Unfortunately the influenza epidemic hit in 1918, and all theaters had to close. When the New Orpheum Theater reopened in 1919, vaudeville was dying, and Levy switched to musical comedies and drama.

Carl Reiter, who managed the Orpheum Circuit Theater (no connection to Levy's New Orpheum Theater) in Seattle from 1908 until his retirement in 1929, made a point of operating his theaters as a business. "System, is the key note of our affairs," explained Reiter when he first came to Seattle.[89] The theater originated in San Francisco as part of a national chain. When it opened in Seattle, newspaper advertisements dubbed it "the big time, all seats reserved, ten, twenty-five, fifty, and seventy-five cents; season tickets for patrons who wanted the same location week after week."[90]

Reiter, who grew up in San Francisco, played in honky-tonks and saloon theaters from the Barbary Coast of San Francisco to Seattle before joining the Orpheum Circuit in Omaha. By the time he retired, he had become one of the most popular theater men in the city. "He has not been a mere manager, but he has been the perfect host throughout his long career in the theatre business," wrote Stella Sameth in *The Jewish Transcript*.[91]

Joe Rosenfield, known affectionately as "Joe of Spokane," came west in 1935 to manage the Evergreen Theaters in Spokane. Before his move, Rosenfield had been in charge of publicity and promotion for the Paramount-Publix chain in Minnesota, and general manager of the John Hamrick theaters in Seattle.[92] As manager of Evergreen Theaters, Rosenfield successfully handled numerous road-show attractions and booked all movies for the Evergreen Theaters.[93] He left in 1940 to manage the Sterling Theaters (later SRO) in Seattle, but by 1945 he was back in Spokane opening drive-ins and starting his own company, the Favorite Theaters, a chain of nine movie theaters and drive-ins. The move launched the beginning of a five-decade career in regional theater management.

Although the musical stage and the theater attracted a large number of Jewish people, outside of professionals such as Hoffman and paid cantors and musical directors, most of those who sang in choirs, played in small community orchestras, and acted in the many drama groups received no pay. Only applause and possibly a notice in the local paper were their reward. With the end of World War II and a rising economy, this would change. Meanwhile, Jewish people had positioned themselves to be a part of the arts in Washington.

An Obligation to Study

I N   W A S H I N G T O N   S T A T E ,   A S   I N   J E W I S H   C O M M U N I T I E S   A L L over America, the content and methods of Jewish education became a divisive issue between traditional teachers associated with the European *heder* (Hebrew School) system and educators who favored the teaching of Hebrew language and Jewish history through progressive methods. About the only thing they agreed on was that learning Hebrew was important.

This conflict occurred during a time when Jewish education in America faced many obstacles. A 1909 survey executed by Mordecai Kaplan and Bernard Cronson, leaders in a movement to bring progressive ideas to Jewish education, not only found little demand for Jewish education, when there was demand "there is a lack either of system or content."[1] Although some teachers ardently believed the European *heder* curriculum provided effective education, most educators in both Reform and Orthodox movements realized the need to find better ways to teach. The establishment of the Jewish Board of Education in New York in 1910 started the process to rectify the dismal education programs.

Samson Benderly, who abandoned a career in medicine to further Jewish education, was one of the first to take a more "modern" approach. He developed his ideas at the Hebrew Free School for Poor and Orphaned Children in Baltimore between 1902 and 1908. Assisted by influential thinkers such as Mordecai Kaplan and Alexander Dushkin, Benderly preached that the future of American Judaism depended on a sound program of Jewish education rooted in Jewish values and sensitive to the needs of young people living in America. Furthermore, he stressed that "a total community effort must be exerted in support of the Jewish school."[2] To pursue those goals, he experimented with new methods of language instruction, hired well-trained young men and women, and integrated extracurricular

*I can still vividly recall as a child attending the Seattle Talmud Torah and listen-
ing with mouth agape and fired imagination as our teacher spun the legend of the
Lamed Vov Tsadikim, the thirty-six unknown unheralded obscure humble just
men, upon whom rests the fate of the world. And I still remember turning to a
bosom pal to disclose the fact that I knew the identity of one of these tsadikim—
my father.*

    —Rabbi Irwin Isaacson of New York, son of Joseph Isaacson, who came to
      Seattle from Russia at the turn of the century and raised five children,
      WSJHS *Newsletter*, July 1991

activities into the educational program.

As is so often the case, implementing the goals turned out to be a difficult problem. In some communities that were torn between secularists and religionists, finding a communal structure to pay for and develop an acceptable curriculum seemed at times impossible. Although more and more temples and synagogues taught Hebrew and offered Jewish education, what and how to teach varied from school to school.

Similar problems arose in Washington State, as Jewish people from Bellingham to Walla Walla followed predictable educational patterns established in Europe and on the East Coast. Reform congregations opened congregational Sunday morning religious schools, usually with untrained volunteer teachers who lacked a set curriculum or books geared to the age levels of the children. They usually taught what children could most easily learn about Jewish history and holidays. Whether students learned Hebrew depended upon the individual teacher.

Orthodox congregations reverted to the old forms of instruction such as *heders*, private tutors, and Talmud Torahs, prevalent in the Jewish villages and towns of Eastern Europe. Congregational leaders and rabbis wanted to make students conversant in Hebrew so they could participate in services. Students learned to read enough Biblical Hebrew to get through their Bar Mitzvahs and say Kaddish (prayer for the dead), but they received ineffective schooling in history and religion from untrained instructors who received little if any pay.

Seattle's First Religious Schools

Young Jews in Seattle first attended Hebrew classes in 1893 and 1894 at Seattle's first congregations, Ohaveth Sholum and Bikur Cholim. Ohaveth Sholum had

Hebrew classes at 4 P.M. on Tuesday and Thursday afternoons; Bikur Cholim's Hebrew Free School met everyday from 3 to 7 P.M.[3] Ohaveth Sholum's congregation and school did not last, but Bikur Cholim never wavered in its mission to teach Hebrew to Seattle's youth.

Recognizing the importance of Hebrew instruction, Bikur Cholim members, among them Zalman Grozinsky, Herman "Pop" Kessler, Samuel Shapiro, and J. H. Shucklin, engaged teachers in 1898 and set up a separate Talmud Torah corporation in rooms behind the newly acquired synagogue. Articles of Incorporation filed February 9, 1899, describe the Talmud Torah as an "educational institution for the promotion of the study of the Talmud; and the dissemination of religious and educational instruction, and to establish and maintain a library and Hebrew School."[4] A year later Bikur Cholim deeded land to the Talmud Torah for as long as it "shall maintain a Hebrew School."[5] "Liberal donations by the Jewish people of this city provided the funds. . . . instruction in the school is free to all Jewish children," reported the *Seattle Post-Intelligencer* on June 23, 1900, at the dedication of a new building at Fourteenth and South Washington Street.

The pioneers did not stop with organizing. They made certain that the children attended school. Many fondly recall Zalman Grozinsky carrying children in his arms across muddy streets so they would not miss Hebrew lessons, and Mendel Aronin going to the playgrounds, taking children by the hand, and gently saying, "Kinderlach, Kumt in Cheder Lernen" (Come children, you will learn in Hebrew School).[6]

The instructors, who knew little about teaching, seemed to believe "each child must receive his regular beating in order to learn his Jewishness," wrote P. Allen Rickles, who had attended the school as a boy. He admitted "most of these teachers suffered at our hands as much as we suffered at theirs. . . . The city still had its boy 'gangs' and our bunch was up to as many pranks as any group of boys in those days." He went on to say:

I look back upon those old Cheder days with conflicting emotions. On the one hand I recall them with much pleasure. . . . Every boy came to Cheder with his lunch. And what a time we had when lunch time came and we got together with our lunch partners to divide up! There was a great deal of play mixed with the learning, but learn we did. I also vividly recall the close of the Cheder day in the winter and fall months when each student would light his lantern and wend his way homeward. . . . a traditional feature of heder attendance.[7]

"Teachers were very strict," said Sol Esfeld. "They believed in corporal punishment and they weren't pedagogues in the sense that we have today. They were old time Talmudists and they were learned in Hebrew and their religion but they didn't have any special teaching abilities like we have today."[8] Others also complained about the teachers, but admitted they learned because of Jewish backgrounds at home. That is, while the schools taught only the rudiments of the Hebrew language, children became familiar with the prayers and rituals because they grew up in religious homes and regularly attended synagogue services.

In addition to attending Hebrew school, some young people received instruction from family members or private tutors. "Even parallel with my attendance at the Talmud Torah, on weekends I was also taught at home," said George Prottas.[9] "My *zayde* [grandfather] taught me my *aleph-baiz* [ABCs], and he was the one who started me with my Hebrew education," recalled Sarah Efron. "And, of course, I remember the important thing to incite a child from play to come into a home and study was to give him something sweet and many times he would say, 'Look up there.' And I would look and there would be a penny on the table. It was a reward, you know, the Melech, the One above, threw down a penny because I was a good student."[10]

Seattle Sunday School

Families who did not want an extensive Hebrew education usually sent their children to Temple De Hirsch's religious school. The school opened in 1899, and its board agreed that "the privileges of our Sunday School [should] be extended to all Jewish children."[11] Unfortunately the decision had to be changed in a few years to avoid overcrowded classrooms. Those who truly could not pay received free tuition.[12] Interviews with pioneer Jews, especially the Sephardim, indicate many Orthodox families chose to send their children to Temple De Hirsch's Sunday School in addition to the Sephardic Talmud Torah. "She [Bolissa Rozula Franco (Mrs. Marco Franco)] suggested to my mother that she should send us to Temple De Hirsch where we could get a little bit of a better background on the Jewish history. So my mother enrolled us," said Tillie DeLeon.[13] Although for a brief time Herzl Congregation had a religious school which followed Orthodox doctrine, Temple De Hirsch's school seems to have been the only congregational one in Seattle.[14]

Rabbi Samuel Koch, an advocate of the importance of a Jewish education, kept the Bar Mitzvah ceremony (frequently eliminated in Reform temples), insisted that the students learn some Hebrew, and extended the religious school to include high school and college freshmen. Students attended mid-week classes as well as Sunday School.

Temple De Hirsch's 1918 confirmation class. Top row, from left: Harry Sigman, unidentified individual, Rabbi Samuel Koch, Joanna Eckstein, Dorothy Shuback, Jack Schermer, and Morton Schwabacher. Middle row: Jeanette Rosenfeld, Alfred Pleckner, Olga Dover, and three unidentified individuals. First row: Molly Esfeld, Carolyn Stern, Helen Bornstein (Rucker), and an individual with the last name of Adler (Hochberg). WSJHS, 106.

The Modern Hebrew School

When, in 1913, the Talmud Torah knew it had to vacate its quarters because Bikur Cholim sold its building to the Sephardic congregation, its leaders invited all the Jewish people in Seattle to a meeting to establish a community Hebrew school. Called The Modern Hebrew School, its board and officers included influential Orthodox Jewish men such as Myer Goodglick, Herman "Pop" Kessler, and Solomon Prottas.[15] The board hired Dr. L. Jacobs, formerly rabbi of B'nai Joseph in Chicago, as principal.[16] Within a year, The Modern Hebrew School at Eighteenth and East Fir had 125 students. In 1915, thanks to the fund-raising ability of Goldie Shucklin and Jennie Friedman, the school paid off its mortgage.[17]

The faculty consisted of students from the newly formed Menorah Society at the University of Washington and young Russian immigrants. The university students were from both Orthodox and Reform backgrounds and included Sol

There was on outstanding exception in this group of early [heder] teachers and that was the late Mr. Sol Prottas. . . . He was a scholarly man. . . . When in his classes, we learned a great deal. In all probability what most of the boys of my class still remember is what they were taught in Mr. Prottas's classes.
—P. Allen Rickles, "I Remember When," *The Jewish Transcript,* 8 September 1933

Herzog, Max A. Silver, Charlotte Kolmitz, Ann Hurwitz, Abe Rickles, and Eimon Wiener. They saw the school as a worthy community project needing assistance.[18] The Russians, grounded in Jewish learning and acquainted with modern Hebrew authors, brought vitality and enthusiasm for Hebrew to their teaching, noted Joseph Cohen.[19] Men like Solomon Prottas, "a prominent member of Bikur Cholim, labored to make the word 'modern' of real meaning," wrote *The Jewish Transcript* in 1924.[20] For the first time, Seattle students learned about contemporary Jewish history and the expressiveness of modern Hebrew rather than merely translating a sacred text.

Unfortunately, "all was not serene—for several of 'the old guard' dominating the affairs of the Modern Hebrew School were vigorously opposed [to the new teaching methods]," Eimon Wiener wrote in *The Jewish Transcript.*[21] Many years later, Max A. Silver concurred with Wiener's assessment:

I organized a group of teachers just to teach on Sundays . . . books were in English and some of the books not only had references to Judaism but also other religions . . . Velvel Rabinovitch caught a glimpse of one of these books in my room and he let out an oath. . . . We quit that day.[22]

School records are not available, but a comparison of two newspaper accounts supports Wiener's and Silver's statements. In 1913 at the dedication ceremony, Reform Rabbi Samuel Koch, the main speaker, emphasized that study "will be laid on planning character for good citizenship" with the Hebrew language part of the curriculum. At the mortgage burning ceremony several years later, Herman "Pop" Kessler, who was from the Orthodox community, spoke. He announced that the school had hired H. Greenberg, a well-known and more traditional Hebrew teacher.[23]

Because the two factions could not compromise and the school lacked strong supporters, it closed in early 1917. A few months later, Herman "Pop" Kessler and Solomon Prottas called interested people together for the purpose of organizing and building another city-wide Talmud Torah.[24]

This, too, had management and financial problems, and in November 1917, Bikur Cholim announced that "for the sake of Judaism . . . [the synagogue] found itself compelled to assume management of the Talmud Torah."[25] Bikur Cholim used the Eighteenth and Fir building, vacated by the defunct Modern Hebrew School.[26]

A City-Wide Talmud Torah Begins

Despite concerted efforts, Hebrew education floundered. For a short time Herzl Congregation also opened its own Talmud Torah, but one synagogue did not have the funds to support a school. In 1920, Bikur Cholim's Rabbi Simon Glazer again

Ben Flaks, age twelve (third from left in first row), and his classmates pose in front of their Seattle Talmud Torah at Seventeenth and East Fir, 1915. WSJHS, 101.

proposed a city-wide Talmud Torah supported by all the Jewish organizations. Recognizing it as a "proper organization," Bikur Cholim's board on June 17, 1920, voted to deed land at Seventeenth Avenue and East Alder Street to the Talmud Torah.[27]

Hired as director for the Seattle Talmud Torah, Abe Spring resolved to never go back to the old ways and to retain well-qualified teachers.[28] Spring had help from Leo Greenfield, formerly headmaster of the Jewish Public School at Tientsin, China, and then a teacher at the Seattle Talmud Torah. By teaching the history, literature, legends, and music of the Jews as well as Hebrew, Greenfield believed "the children will get the true Jewish spirit and be able to better appreciate and feel their religion."[29]

The reorganized Talmud Torah eventually occupied wooden buildings on lots at Seventeenth Avenue and East Alder Street. One building had four large, well-ventilated classrooms; the other housed an assembly hall. About 175 children ranging from ages five to fourteen attended school from 3:30 to 8:30 P.M. and from 9 to 12 noon on Sundays. The teachers, supervised by a Board of Education and Rabbi Simon Winograd from Bikur Cholim Synagogue, received small salaries.[30] Sarah Efron, who attended the school, recalled "our classes were upstairs. We had to climb the stairs those years that I went to school from five to seven and we had a break and so I would run home sometimes to get a bite to eat because we lived a block away or else I would take a sandwich."[31]

Disagreements and dissentions did not disappear at the Talmud Torah. When professional educators challenged outmoded educational ideas, they confronted differences between the various religious factions. Moreover, both factions had groups within them that disagreed on what to teach.[32] "The mere mention of the Talmud Torah at Jewish meetings or gatherings aroused hostilities and the unfavorable comment," said Fred H. Bergman, an early president of Seattle Talmud Torah.[33] Expressing frustration over the constant bickering, *The Jewish Transcript* called for unification:

Everybody knows [the importance of a Jewish education] and everybody agrees that we ought to try to make every effort to save the young American Jew. . . . but how do we go about this. . . . We talk a lot, we quarrel even more, and then we wonder why such a small percentage of American Jewish children are getting a Jewish education. . . . Are the Orthodox Jews of this city, who squabble among themselves and thus waste so much of the precious energy that is needed to save their children for Judaism, really sane?"[34]

The Talmud Torah, however, persevered, and in 1928, when the wooden buildings showed signs of deterioration, the Board began rallying the community to support a new building. A year later, under the leadership of Jacob Kaplan, Michael Berch, and Sam Prottas, the school's board announced plans for one intensive week of fund raising. In supporting this project, *The Jewish Transcript* wrote that the Talmud Torah's "educational system is conducted on a thoroughly modern basis. . . .

On a cold February morning in 1930, Sam Asia, Goldie Shucklin, Rosa Steinfeld, and Laura Berch began the ground breaking for a new Seattle Talmud Torah. MSCUA/UWL, neg. 19032.

the best pedagogic methods are employed. . . . [but] over two hundred and fifty pupils are compelled to crowd daily into the unhealthy and unsanitary conditions of those dilapidated shacks."[35]

A year and a half later, on February 23, 1930, the Jewish community celebrated a ground-breaking ceremony for a city-wide Talmud Torah. The new building, designed by B. Marcus Priteca, was located at Twenty-fifth Avenue and Columbia Street. A year after the stock market crash, $47,000 of a $75,000 goal had been pledged. Several months later, on July 20, the cornerstone was laid, and on October 26 Seattle youth had a chance to learn and speak Hebrew in a modern building. To show support, Herzl Congregation closed its Talmud Torah on Sixteenth Avenue and East Fir Street and urged its members to attend the Seattle Talmud Torah.[36] Fund-raising events, including a week-long bazaar started in 1931 under the leadership of chairman Joseph Vinikow, had the support of all local Jewish organizations and involved the entire community.

Financial problems and too few pupils, however, continually plagued the school. In 1939, President G. Rubin stated that "it was absolutely necessary to get children to the Talmud Torah and [to find] funds to pay our deficits and keep our budget up."[37] In a move to save money, Seattle Talmud Torah eliminated its Sunday School in 1943, causing the Board of Directors of Bikur Cholim to protest "we cannot discriminate and close the doors of the Talmud Torah to those of our children who cannot attend the daily classes thereby diverting them into channels and atmosphere[s] foreign to traditional Judaism."[38]

A few months later, the Board of Directors reinstated the Sunday School against the wishes of the director, Rabbi Jacob Cohn, who thought a Sunday School would cause a decrease in the daily enrollment. The Talmud Torah also opened branch schools in Madrona and Montlake, a decision calculated to appeal to families moving away from the Jewish neighborhood.

During this same period of the late 1940s and 1950s, when a new generation brought in ideas for new functions, other temples and synagogues began to offer mid-afternoon Hebrew classes. At Herzl Ner Tamid, Joseph Frankel established and became principal of a three-day, six-hour-per-week school, which offered a compromise between the Talmud Torah and Sunday School.[39] Most of the religious schools in Washington would follow this format, with the Reform offering only two-day-per-week classes.

The problem of whether to teach students solely according to traditional Judaism or to include Conservative and Reform concerns as well continually affected the curriculum and fund-raising ability of the Seattle Talmud Torah. In 1940, Herman Keisler, a member of Temple De Hirsch and president of Seattle

Talmud Torah, addressed the problem in his annual report:

Do our Leaders agree that this Talmud Torah should be operated strictly in line with, and in adherence to, Traditional Judaism without deviation? If so let Traditional Jewry come forward and . . . assume full responsibility . . . as an example of unselfish devotion to Traditional Judaism. If such program can be carried out, it will not be necessary to try and prove to the community that this is a City-wide Institution. On the other hand—should Traditional Jewry fail—you will have to learn more about tolerance as well as compromise.[40]

Day School Begins

In 1945, Rabbi Solomon Wohlgelernter of Bikur Cholim and Rabbi Solomon Maimon, newly installed spiritual head of Sephardic Bikur Holim, planted the idea for an independent day school where all Seattle Jewish youth, both Ashkenazim and Sephardim, could study together in Hebrew and secular classes. Both rabbis understood the deficiencies in Seattle's Jewish educational system and worried that few students had the training to attend advanced classes at eastern *yeshivas*. By combining resources and compromising on matters such as whether to use Sephardic or Ashkenazic pronunciations, Maimon and Wohlgelernter aimed to reinstate quality education. "We didn't want to make too much of a fuss about it because problems there's plenty, but solutions there's not," said Maimon.[41]

Interestingly, *The Jewish Transcript* in 1928 had raised the question of whether Hebrew with the Ashkenazic or Sephardic accent should be taught in a united Seattle Talmud Torah. They came out for the Sephardic accent because that is what was being spoken in Palestine, and said that "Seattle should be glad that we have a large number of Sephardim to teach us."[42]

In the beginning, many in Seattle and throughout the United States opposed the day school option. The opposition held that synagogues and temples should be the sole support of Jewish religious education, and that secular education belonged in the public schools. Recalling that time, Maimon told *The Seattle Times*, "I told my people . . . we're going to be called all kinds of names. We're going to be called parochial. We're going to be called non-comformist. We're going to be called un-American. I don't care what we're going to be called. We're going to get our kids educated. And we did it."[43]

A Jewish day school established by Rabbi Wohlgelernter and Rabbi Maimon opened in 1947 with a first grade providing half a day of secular education and half a day of Hebrew studies. Thereafter the school added a class a year. Rabbi Samuel

Graudenz, the first principal, guided the school for sixteen years. During the early years, both the day school and the Talmud Torah continued to meet in the Talmud Torah building and together were known as the Seattle Hebrew Day School. Ben Genauer, who throughout his lifetime worked to advance Jewish education, served as first president of the new organization.

Eventually the Seattle Hebrew Day School absorbed the students attending afternoon classes at the Talmud Torah. With a declining enrollment, the Talmud Torah disbanded in 1962. The little *heder* that had first met in rented rooms in 1898 became The Seattle Hebrew Academy in 1969. The school offered standard secular curriculum as well as the traditional study of Torah in accordance with Halacha, the Jewish code of living.

Improving Jewish Education

Meanwhile, in 1949, the Seattle Talmud Torah along with all Jewish education programs in Seattle received unfavorable criticism from "The Survey on Local Jewish Education" written by Samuel Dinin, executive director of the Bureau of Jewish Education in Los Angeles, in collaboration with Jacob Kartzinel, regional director of the Western States Region of the American Association for Jewish Education. This report, requested by the Seattle Jewish Federated Fund, was subsequently known as the Levy Report after Dr. Ruth Levy, chairman of Federated Fund's education committee. Levy, a nationally known clinical psychologist, was a graduate of the Teachers Institute of the Jewish Theological Seminary. The report found problems with costs, deteriorating structures, size of classes, and inadequate teachers in Seattle's Sunday schools, after-school Hebrew classes, the Talmud Torah, and the newly opened Seattle Hebrew Day School.[44]

As expected, people criticized the report and its recommendations, and the report was never published. Rabbi Samuel Graudenz, principal and educational director of the Seattle Hebrew Day School, challenged "The Survey," or the Levy Report, "to prove lack of qualification or of license of any of the faculty members of the Seattle Hebrew Day School during the year 1949."[45] To help reconcile differences, in 1951 Seattle's Jewish Community Council appointed an education committee to study the problem.

The committee included community leaders who tried to discover the best way to provide quality Jewish education in Seattle. Temple De Hirsch's Religion Committee and the Seattle Hebrew Day School Board of Directors declined a place on the Jewish Community Council's education committee. De Hirsch "felt it can independently achieve any desired end in the way of raising standards and the like"; the Seattle Hebrew Day School, which desired financial assistance from the Jewish Federated Fund, announced "it would like to make its appeal directly and not through an intermediary organization."[46]

Although the Jewish Community Council education committee realized that the Seattle Jewish Federated Fund did not have the financial means to act on all of its recommendations, it emphasized that a start must be made. To implement its ideas, committee members urged, as had Dinin's report, the formation of a Jewish Education Committee. The Jewish Education Committee, representing all educational agencies and the community at large, would set standards and administer funds. A minority report issued by Edward Starin of Temple De Hirsh held that the "function of Jewish religious education is a matter which is within the sole jurisdiction of the respective synagogues."[47] In spite of the fact that the Federated Fund's Board of Directors approved the committee's recommendation, in view of the dissenting attitudes of Temple De Hirsch and the Seattle Hebrew Day School, the recommendations had to be tabled.[48] Nevertheless, the Jewish Community Council education committee report "motivated people to look into the Jewish education situation and improve it. . . . Some of the people even got to the stage where in the late 60s we formed the equivalent of the Bureau of Jewish Education. Actually, it was Benjamin [Bud] and Hilda Asia who were the motivating force behind doing that," said Harry Ash.[49] The Jewish Education Committee (JEC), formed in 1970 and made up of representatives of all Jewish organizations plus interested lay persons, established an Institute of Jewish Studies under the direction of Kay Pomeranz and opened a community-wide high school.[50]

High School and Beyond

Students who desired more advanced Jewish education studied in a *yeshiva* (an Orthodox school of higher learning). Mendel Aronin and Herman "Pop" Kessler established the first one in 1925 at Bikur Cholim Synagogue. In 1930 the Seattle Talmud Torah absorbed the *yeshiva* program. When the Talmud Torah had to cancel the classes in 1938, Rabbi Solomon Wohlgelernter continued the instruction of Talmud, Torah, and prophets in his study.

Supported by Bikur Cholim, Rabbi Wohlgelernter's students made up the first class of Yeshiva Rabeninu Hayim Ozer, which opened under the leadership of Rabbi Jacob Levine, the first *rosh yeshiva* (principal). A report in *The Synagogue Tribune* described the school as a place where "young high school students learn the Talmud, and Bible with commentaries, and may prepare for entrance into Yeshivoth and Seminaries in the East."[51]

In 1974, when Rabbi Daniel Rosenthal, headmaster of The Seattle Hebrew Academy, established classes for high school boys, Yeshiva Rabeninu Hayim Ozer closed its doors. Rosenthal assumed that by providing intensive Hebrew studies the school would retain students who would otherwise enroll in East Coast schools. Three years later, the *yeshiva* incorporated as Yeshivat Or Hazafon, an independent school. Girls were admitted in 1979.[52]

Seattle's Sephardic Hebrew Schools

In the early years, each of Seattle's Sephardic congregations had its own school where older men taught a smattering of Hebrew so children could participate in the service. "I used to go to the Ezra Bessaroth Talmud Torah," recalled Gordon DeLeon. "We'd get out of grammar school at about 2:45, run down to 15th Avenue from 18th Avenue, go to classes from 3:00 until 5:30, then go home. . . . We got used to it . . . they taught us how to read Hebrew fluently but we didn't understand what we were reading."[53] Albert Adatto wrote: "When any student created an unnecessary disturbance he would get slapped on the back of his hands with a ruler. . . . On a rare occasion the teacher would grab the 'problem child,' take his shoes off and beat the bottom of his feet with a ruler. They called this punishment, *falaka*."[54]

In 1915, Seattle Sephardim invited Rabbi Aharon Benezra to be chief rabbi and head of a community Talmud Torah.[55] But that first attempt at amalgamation did not prove successful, and Benezra left the following year. Each synagogue continued to operate its own school until 1931.

Ezra Bessaroth's school, under the direction of brother-in-laws Revs. David Behar and Morris Scharhon, was the largest. Scharhon, like so many teachers, also taught private students in rooms behind his house.[56] When Rabbi Abraham Maimon arrived in Seattle in 1924 he stimulated a renewed interest in studying Hebrew at Bikur Holim. Three sons of Maimon, Isaac, Jack, and Sam Bension, taught the classes in the little rooms adjacent to the synagogue, but it was difficult for the brothers to keep discipline. "These were American born children who were used to the ways of America," recalled their younger brother, Solomon Maimon, who would eventually become Sephardic Bikur Holim's rabbi.[57]

In 1931, realizing the urgent need of a modern religious education, representatives from Bikur Holim and Ezra Bessaroth again tried to consolidate their Talmud Torahs. The school, Sephardic Talmud Torah, led by chairman Dr. Harry Tarica, had its own organization independent of any congregation. To improve the curriculum, the members brought Albert David Levy in as educational director. Levy, an experienced Hebrew teacher in New York and editor of *La Vara*, a Ladino news-paper published in New York, greatly improved Hebrew teaching in the Sephardic community by offering a curriculum of Hebrew language, history, Bible study, and Sephardic liturgy. In 1933 about 120 pupils attended the Sephardic Talmud Torah located at Ezra Bessaroth.[58] The school met every day except Friday nights and Saturdays.

With the rise of unemployment during the Great Depression, financial sup-port for the school lagged. Morris Scharhon withdrew his students, and the school faced a crisis. Dr. Tarica set up a committee to reorganize, but it does not appear to have been successful.[59] Finally, disagreements between Albert David Levy and Ezra Bessaroth caused Levy to return to New York, and once again Sephardim studied Hebrew in two synagogue schools plus Scharhon's private academy. When Levy returned to Seattle in 1938, he accepted a position at Bikur Holim. There he offered free night classes and taught Judeo-Spanish along with Hebrew.

Testimony from those who attended the Sephardic Talmud Torah is similar to those who studied Hebrew at Seattle Talmud Torah. "The teachers I must say were not very good . . . it was largely simply learning to read Hebrew, learning the prayers," said Albert Franco.[60] As late as 1935, two young people, Isaac and Sarah Israel, complained in a letter to the *Progress*, a Seattle Sephardic monthly periodical, that they "received a smattering of Jewish history absolutely lacking in coherence . . . so saturated with myths and miracles that at present I am wondering where the Bible left off and my teacher's imagination started."[61] "The disappoint-ing Jewish education I received as a young man was slow to change," wrote Rabbi Marc D. Angel.[62] On the other hand, Elazar Behar, who thought that the main function of the Sephardic Talmud Torah was to teach one to read Hebrew, recalled that the "method of instruction was good."[63] It was a typical generational response, with the young questioning and the older people accepting.

Another reason for Sephardic Talmud Torah's failure is that during the 1930s, some families enrolled their children in the Seattle Talmud Torah. Hoping to guard against this practice, Marco Franco, president of Sephardic Talmud Torah, asked the Seattle Talmud Torah Board of Directors to cease enrolling Sephardic children in the lower grades. After much discussion, the board voted that "for the best interests of Jewish education in Seattle the Seattle Talmud Torah and the Sephardic Talmud Torah shall co-operate with each other as far as possible, par-ticularly in regard to enrollment and registration."[64] How they did so has not been recorded.

A few years later, in 1939, Ezra Bessaroth's Rabbi Isidore Kahan asked if Sephardic children could study in the Seattle Talmud Torah with his board governing the children's instruction. Though there is no record of a negative vote, minutes from the Seattle Talmud Torah board meeting indicate they most likely rejected Kahan's request.[65] The discussion, however, might be considered the first tentative steps toward combining the Ashkenazic and Sephardic Talmud Torahs.

A graduating event at Spokane's Temple Emanu-El, June 1925. Identified individuals, top row: Henry Kaye (first boy on the left) and Irving Walker (first boy on the right next to teacher Abe Hertzka). Third row: Rabbi Levin (at left) and Mildred Mackoff (second girl from left). Second row: Jeanne Porteguese and Jeanne Seligman (second and third girls). First row: Beverly Soss (Jaffe) (far right). Courtesy of Temple Beth Shalom Archives, Spokane.

Jewish Education in Spokane

In 1899 at Temple Emanu-El, Rabbi Bernard Lurie announced that their twice-a-week Sunday School emphasized a "fundamental distinction of Judaism which lays stress on knowledge rather than belief."[66] Emanuel Schreiber, the temple's first rabbi, organized the religious school in 1892.

Keneseth Israel Synagogue offered Hebrew lessons soon after it organized in 1901. It did not have a principal for a separate program until Rabbi S. Reuben assumed that position in 1909. A second teacher, Rabbi Bernard H. Rosengard, initiated daily classes from 4 to 6 P.M. and Sundays from 10 to noon in 1911. Rosengard expressed a willingness to teach thirty to forty pupils, but the board was dissatisfied with his teaching and did not renew his contract.[67]

Also in 1911, Spokane Jewry incorporated a separate community Hebrew school, The Spokane Free Hebrew School and Educational Alliance, which taught Jewish history, arts, literature, and ethics. Both men and women were admitted, and textbooks were free. In addition, according to an article in *The*

9-8. Leading Shabbat services at Keneseth Israel in 1941 were confirmation class members Sam Zarkin, Don Levin, Jack Duitch, Marvin Rose, and Bud Freedman. Courtesy of Temple Beth Shalom Archives, Spokane.

Advanced students celebrate confirmation at Tacoma's Temple Beth Israel, 1932. From left: Belle Ruth Clayman, Elva Jacobs, Phyllis Friedman, and Annette Friedman. Courtesy of Josephine Kleiner Heiman, Tacoma.

Spokesman-Review of October 13, 1911, "English will be taught together with a study of the history of the United States for the benefit of Hebrews young and old who have not had the opportunity of attending the public schools." The school's directors, including Dr. David Levine, J. Apfel, Abraham Wilkomerson, and Samuel Ofner, proposed that the "school [be] free from any sectarian differences and teach only broad doctrine of Judaism on which all Hebrews can unite."[68] From the wording in the newspaper, it seems as if this liberal approach to Jewish education was for the benefit of immigrants. Since no records remain, it is unknown how long the school lasted.

As mentioned above, Keneseth Israel Synagogue offered Hebrew lessons soon after 1901. Although the first committee authorized to solicit funds for a Hebrew school came back empty-handed, Keneseth Israel eventually managed to begin a free Hebrew School.[69] Samuel Huppin, who came to Spokane from Turisk, Russia, in 1908, served as administrator until 1921.[70] Whether that school had any affiliation with The Spokane Free Hebrew School and Educational Alliance is difficult to know. Several persons, such as J. Apfel and Abraham Wilkomerson, are listed as teachers in both schools. Acknowledging the problems inherent in Jewish education, Rabbi Joseph Krixtein said in 1928 that he would "establish a thoroughly efficient modern Hebrew School."[71]

A grant from the Julius Galland estate in 1929 made it possible for Keneseth Israel Synagogue to set up The Julius Galland Hebrew School in a separate building. Students attended school two hours a day, four days a week, until the 1940s. When the synagogue became Conservative, Hebrew instruction consisted of two or three hours of weekly after-school Hebrew lessons.[72] When Temple Emanu-El and the synagogue joined together in 1966 as the liberal Conservative synagogue Temple Beth Shalom, Sunday and mid-week Hebrew classes continued.

Jewish Education in Tacoma

The 1892 constitution for Temple Beth Israel stated that the congregation should have a school where children could receive instruction in Jewish history, religion, and the Hebrew language.[73] Women from the Lady Judith Montefiore Society promised the new temple that they would "turn over the Sunday School to them."[74] An 1896 listing in the city directory shows that the temple had a twice-weekly German and Hebrew school.[75] In 1921 the temple board requested its rabbi to invite all Tacoma children to a free Hebrew school on Mondays and Thursdays, and a free religious school on Sunday mornings.

Orthodox Jews sent their children to Congregation Talmud Torah's Hebrew School, which from 1909 to 1914 occupied space in a room at the Sampson Hotel. Mr. Aronin and Abe Lavious were the first teachers. When the congregation moved into its own building, the Hebrew School went with it. A separate Hebrew School, directed by Dr. Ivar Spector, emerged sometime during the 1930s. Located at the Talmud Torah Synagogue, the school had its own organization, The Board of Hebrew Education, chaired by S. L. Nudelman. In 1930 there were eight classes of sixty-five students who studied the Bible and Jewish history and customs, and learned to read, speak, and write Hebrew.[76]

While the school did not have an official relationship with the Talmud Torah Synagogue, the synagogue's ladies' auxiliary sponsored events to benefit the school. Students attended holiday services such as Purim at the synagogue. Unfortunately, finding money during the Great Depression proved difficult, and the school folded.[77] Hebrew classes reverted back to the synagogue.

Hebrew Schools in Washington's Smaller Towns

Cities with synagogues, such as Bellingham and Everett, conducted after-school heders where the rabbi taught Hebrew and prepared boys for a Bar Mitzvah. "I went just to heder five days a week," recalled Edward Glazer, who was born in Bellingham and attended Hebrew school about 1915. "At that time, our religious education consisted of having a Bar Mitzvah . . . then, our education was through. . . . No Talmud . . . that's advanced education already."[78]

When the synagogue did not have a rabbi, families had to hope someone else would come forward to instruct their children in Hebrew. "We had one Jewish

Young Bellingham students at Synagogue Beth Israel, ca. 1920. Top row: Leo Friedman, Edie Schafer, Dave Friedman, Sol Shure, Lew Goffee, Sol Glazer, Mike Benolski, unidentified individual, and Joe Benolski. Center row: Mike Zerblatt, unidentified individual, Hymie Cohen, Harry Dubonsky, Leo Perlstein, Meyer Thal, an individual with the last name of Cohen (first name unknown), Eddie Glazer, Sara "Toots" Glazer, Nessie Adrien, Sara Adrien, and Dottie Bonsky. Bottom row: Henry Grieff, Dave Glazer, Sallie Koretz, Arthur Thal, an individual with the last name of Tall (first name unknown), Jack Glazer, an individual with the last name of Cohen (first name unknown), Ben Glazer, and Pete Dubonsky. Far right: Rabbi Cohen; far left: Arthur Thal's father. MSCUA/ UWL, neg. 9384.

man that took time to teach the kids how to become Jews. His name was Moishe Silverstone. . . . He did that for many years," observed William (Billy) Sturman, who came to Everett in 1924.[79]

Learning Hebrew and Jewish religion in a small town without a synagogue or congregation was even more difficult. "I am the only Jew here, and the question of educating my child in Hebrew studies is most acute," Sam Bergman wrote from Snohomish.[80] People either hired a special teacher or journeyed to the closest city that had Hebrew classes. Those in Chehalis and Centralia had the good fortune to attend a Sunday School organized by Dr. Raphael Goldenstein, rabbi of Tacoma's Temple Beth Israel, in 1919.[81] Walla Walla, which had ten Jewish families in 1933, relied on resident Esther Barer to teach the town's Jewish children.[82] She, with help from other women, continued teaching when Congregation Beth Israel opened.

Children in other outlying areas learned by correspondence. In 1927, the Ladies' Auxiliary of Temple De Hirsch, under the leadership of Libbie Goldsby, established a Religious Correspondence School for families who lived in small towns. Students not only received lessons, but parents were reminded of coming holidays and festivals and encouraged to have their sons prepare for a Bar Mitzvah.[83] In 1929, twenty-six students from nine towns studied their Jewish heritage by correspondence. "There are twelve Jewish families and fifteen Jewish boys and girls most of whom have had religious instruction through correspondence," Mrs. S. Shapiro wrote from Yakima in 1933.[84]

Whether sending children to a traditional *heder* where children memorized Hebrew prayers or to a temple correspondence school, pioneer community leaders endeavored to establish a pattern for learning. This diverse approach to learning reflected the conflict over Jewish identity seen all over America. A debate continued between those who believed that Judaism could accommodate to the American environment and those who saw changes as evidence of decline. By participating in or contributing to Jewish education, Washington Jewry influenced the way their children learned about their Jewish heritage. That learning would in turn guide future generations as they struggled to secure funds and commitment to Jewish education.

More Than a Basket of Food

FROM THE 1920S THROUGH WORLD WAR II, PHILANTHROPY by voluntary organizations reflected the changing structure and interests of community members. During an era marked by the Great Depression, Hitler's march over Europe, World War II, and the Holocaust, Washington's Jewish voluntary agencies began offering a variety of social services.

When the effects of the Great Depression began to dominate social policy, smaller groups like Seattle's Infant Aid Society, comprised of women who sewed outfits for poor Jewish babies, disappeared. Those that remained or came on board during this period usually were part of national organizations which increasingly set policy for local chapters or sections. Some of the groups focused on specific problems; the Jewish Consumptive Relief Society, for example, raised money for its hospital in Denver. Other groups had broader agendas that provided a range of services. Jewish Family Service (formerly the Seattle Hebrew Benevolent Society); the National Council of Jewish Women, Seattle Section; and the Caroline Kline Galland Home for the Aged grew so large that they hired professionals to direct some of their activities and sought additional funds from the city of Seattle, the state, and the federal government.

In smaller cities such as Bellingham, people boasted that their forty-five Jewish families supported seven charitable organizations.[1] Yakima, with sixteen Jewish families, installed a B'nai B'rith chapter in 1937. And Bremerton, which had had few Jewish people prior to World War II, when the shipping industry brought in thousands of workers, started a B'nai B'rith chapter with a women's auxiliary; a Bremerton Section, National Council of Jewish Women; and created a Bremerton Hebrew Congregation.[2] In Tacoma, the National Council of Jewish Women and Hadassah set up organizations, and in Spokane, B'nai B'rith lodges and women's auxiliaries continued their community activities.

As groups reorganized and outside events intervened, Washington Jewry wrestled with substantive issues such as whether it was better to provide help for transient Jewish men or ignore their plight, accept government money to fund programs, or decrease services to those in need. They probably wondered if mutual aid, sick benefits, and doctor's services provided by B'nai B'rith and Sons of Israel would really provide sufficient funds in time of need. They must have asked how to balance the social and cultural values of Jewish immigrants with the effort to become Americans. And surely they questioned whether professional social workers would change the agencies' mission and the role of active volunteers.

When May Goldsmith, Jewish Welfare Society's first executive secretary, was dismissed in 1945, "she felt as though we had stabbed her in the back," recalled Florence Flaks, a volunteer. "Who knows better than I these people and their needs," said Goldsmith.[3]

Goldsmith, an experienced agency worker but not a professionally trained social worker, came of age when those who worked with the needy used a case study method "that focused on the problems of individual families and unintentionally blurred the underlying environmental forces they wished to expose."[4] That approach relied on volunteers gathering food, clothing, and money for indigent families rather than providing a broad range of services, some of which would be financed by the government.

By the forties and fifties, those out-of-date ideas had been replaced by an emphasis on a multidisciplinary approach that would improve standards of living, such as better diets and quality of housing. Social workers now had to consider the applicants' social needs as well as their medical needs. And with the government implementing welfare ideas such as social security, a way had to be found to allow agencies like the Caroline Kline Galland Home for the Aged to admit other than destitute persons. If agencies wanted to continue providing services, they needed a trained social worker. A look at how organizations grappled with a myriad of social problems provides a glimpse into the complexity and growth of Washington's Jewish community.

Seattle Hebrew Benevolent Society (Jewish Family Service)

When Seattle established the Community Chest (now United Way) in 1921, the Seattle Hebrew Benevolent Society became one of the first to receive funds. The Society, like so many other volunteer agencies, had recognized the need to deal with problems stemming from poverty, juvenile delinquency, and care of the elderly. So many people needed help in 1925 that the Society's Ways and Means Committee reported, "from month to month our disbursements are from $200 to $300 more than our income."[5] To help administer its enlarged programs, the Society hired May Goldsmith in 1927.

Deciding "benevolent" was an obsolete term and recognizing the switch to professionalism, the Society's board voted in 1929 to change the name to Jewish Welfare Society (JWS) and to "engage generally in social service work upon the broadest principles of humanity."[6] The change of name to Jewish Family and Child Service in 1947 (JFCS), and finally, Jewish Family Service in 1978 (JFS), reflected the role the agency played in working with families.

Board reports during the late 1920s and the Depression years testify that Jewish Welfare Society devoted time and energy providing for men who went from city to city seeking funds. Although some members considered these men worthless, the organization did not condemn them without an investigation. Usually JWS granted emergency relief under guidelines set forth by the National Conference of Social Work. "We [JWS] wish the community to realize that every applicant is received with sympathy . . . if mistakes are made it is preferable to err on the side of mercy."[7] To keep track of the transients, Jewish welfare agencies in Portland, San Francisco, Los Angeles, and Oakland established a check system, which circulated descriptions of those seeking aid between the cities.[8]

During the Great Depression, unemployed people overwhelmed the system. Washington, like the rest of the nation, faced unprecedented relief problems. Moreover, Washington State Governor Roland Hartley saw relief as a moral issue, and rejected any notion of the state's obligation in providing assistance. JWS, with the help of all the other Jewish organizations, cared for many who needed food and shelter, but voluntary help alone could not meet the demands of so many hungry people out of work.

Elected on a platform of promising to fight the Great Depression, Franklin D. Roosevelt set up a host of New Deal federal programs, including the Federal Emergency Relief Administration (FERA), Civil Works Administration (CWA), and the Civilian Conservation Corps (CCC). By 1934, 22.2 percent of America's population received government welfare money.[9] Whether placing men at construction sites or painting murals in public buildings, the federal government intended to provide work for the unemployed.

In 1931, the Jewish Welfare Society noted that "all our transients are sent to the Central Registry for men . . . and single men and unemployed family men are registered for what public works are available, but so many men are out of work, and so few jobs listed that the agencies are taxed to their limit."[10] Commenting on

Roosevelt's relief efforts, a 1934 report stated: "In previous years, the Jewish Welfare Society gave relief and social service to all Jewish people . . . but with the operation of FERA, our work has changed. During the last several months, all Jewish transients have been handled by the Federal Transient Men's Bureau. Also a large number of our single men and women have been transferred to the rolls of the County Relief . . . [which] has been supplemented by us from our reduced funds." [11] FERA additionally granted the agency vouchers, which could be distributed to families and be used to pay for food, clothing and fuel.

While the Depression lasted, JWS continued to complement governmental agencies such as the Works Progress Administration (WPA) and Families with Aid to Dependent Children (ADC). "Federal Aid gives food . . . fuel, some clothing, lodging. Are these all that our Jewish families need? Can you visualize a family of five, mother, father, and three children living on five dollars and sixty cents?" asked May Goldsmith, executive secretary. [12]

When unemployable men and women were sent to the county's public welfare department, many received supplemental help from JWS. "It is only by availing ourselves of all Federal and State relief facilities that we can with our limited income render the best service to the families [ninety-eight families per month] under our supervision and care," the residents' annual report in 1936 stated. That year the agency received $6,000 from the Community Chest. Two years later, the annual report admitted that with the help of welfare departments, JWS would "devote itself more and more to . . . the prevention of family disorder, [and] to the rebuilding of individuals . . . we cannot say, as we formerly said that we are taking care of all the Jewish families in Seattle." [13]

The turmoil in Europe before and during World War II brought new problems and new immigrants to Washington State and led the Jewish Welfare Society to work with more organizations. For example, JWS administered the funds allocated to the Ladies' Montefiore Aid Society and by Seattle's Community Chest. It worked with the Americanization program of the National Council of Jewish Women, Seattle Section, to assist refugees trying to establish citizenship. And in 1941, in partnership with the Jewish Welfare Board, JWS began assisting servicemen. [14]

When World War II ended, the Jewish Welfare Society found itself solving family conflicts, including emotional problems, unemployment, delinquent children, old age care, and assistance to returning Jewish veterans. "The clients come to the office for consultation just as they would go to a doctor's office. The trained social worker is able to work out their problems with them. . . . It is rehabilitation of the person," Goldsmith wrote when she left the agency in 1945. [15]

Disagreement between Eugene Levy, the trustee administering Isaac Cooper's will, and Jewish Family and Child Service's board about how the agency was to administer funds resulted in a lawsuit against JFCS in 1948. Cooper, Levy's brother-in-law and husband of Elizabeth (Lizzie) Cooper, one of the founders of the Ladies' Hebrew Benevolent Society, had bequeathed half of his funds to JFCS (about $40,000 per year in 1948). According to Levy, executive director Ann Kaufman had increased expenses "to build up a big organization to promote herself." Angry about the agency's new directions and upset because his wife, Ruby, had not received a place on the board, Levy sued. After a three-day battle in King County Superior Court, Judge Malcolm Douglas ruled in Levy's favor, deciding that "funds of Isaac Cooper Estate must be used exclusively for providing direct material assistance to the poor and needy, in the form of money, food, clothing and housing and that a semi-annual statement must be rendered to the Trustees."[16]

Much of the controversy centered on the definition of "poor and needy." The board took a broad view. They did not believe families had to be destitute to be eligible for financial aid. On the other hand, Levy maintained the money should be used only "to help people in real need and not to provide a better living standard for people who have a modest income barely sufficient to provide the living essentials."[17]

Considerable correspondence passed between Levy and JFCS concerning the allocation of funds, but Levy never changed his thinking. In fact, because he fervently believed the social service work of JFCS duplicated services performed by Family Society, a Red Feather Agency of the Seattle Community Chest, he ceased his donations to the Community Chest.[18]

Other JFCS members may have considered a "basket of food" sufficient, but institutional and ideological changes continued. By the 1950s, Jewish Family and Child Service, with a staff of twelve, supported a range of humanitarian issues and lobbied for increased welfare support.

Caroline Kline Galland Home for the Aged

In the years before Franklin Roosevelt's Social Security Act of 1935, neither federal nor state governments gave much assistance to the poor or aged. Before the Great Depression devastated the economy, many believed personal weakness caused poverty. On February 16, 1907, when the will of twice-widowed Caroline Kline Galland was made public, Seattle Jewry learned that she had left practically all of her $1,500,000 estate to charity, the bulk of it going to the Caroline Kline Galland Home for the Aged and Feeble Poor. Kline had inherited most of her money from

Caroline Kline Galland. WSJHS, 60.

In 1916, Galland's first home for the Jewish aged (below) accommodated seven persons, who helped with the cooking and cleaning. By 1967 it had grown into a multimillion-dollar, quality-care skilled nursing home. The facility at 7500 Seward Park South in Seattle today is a geriatric nursing home that provides a broad range of services for the elderly regardless of economic circumstances. MSCUA/UWL, 1909.

her first husband, Samuel Kline, who with his partner, Emanuel Rosenberg, had invested in real estate in downtown Seattle.

Nine years later when a home opened at "Wildwood Property" overlooking Lake Washington, it had the distinction of being the only resource in Washington State for older, indigent Jewish people who required help or assistance. Unfortunately, because of delays in settling the will, disposing of real estate to generate funds, and overcoming neighbors' objections to the location of the home in a residential neighborhood, the small building that opened in 1916 for seven residents lacked the space and amenities Caroline Galland had preferred.

It took a favorable decision by the United States Supreme Court in 1929 to order the Seattle Superintendent of Buildings to issue a building permit for a larger facility. Finally, in the midst of the Great Depression, side additions to the existing wooden building made it possible in 1932 to accommodate twenty-five persons (initially called "inmates" and later changed to "guests" in 1923).[19]

Galland's will specified that an advisory board, consisting of the president and the vice-president of Temple De Hirsch, the president and the secretary of the Ladies' Hebrew Benevolent Society (which later became JFS), and a trustee (The Seattle Trust and Savings Bank) should actively manage and supervise the Caroline Kline Galland Home for the Aged. Leo Kohn and Elkan Morgenstern, representing Temple De Hirsh; Esther Levy and Elizabeth (Lizzie) Cooper from the Ladies' Hebrew Benevolent Society; and Isaac Cooper, trustee, made up the first Advisory Committee. The committee (which changed to "board" in 1923) not only ruled on applicants and hired staff, it approved mundane items like the purchase of a toaster or lawn mower. "We did not have a professional social worker . . . so I had to o.k. the bills out there, help plan the menus," noted Viola Gutmann Silver, secretary of Jewish Family Service for ten years.[20] To widen community participation, in the 1940s the Board invited vice-presidents and immediate past presidents of Temple De Hirsch and JFS, and the rabbi of Temple De Hirsch, to attend meetings and take part in the discussions, but not to vote.[21]

In the early years, applicants applied directly to the board, which decided their eligibility. Applications were often rejected if, in the opinion of the Board, family members could assume financial responsibility. The Kline Galland Home did not admit blind and mentally disturbed persons, and if a resident's mental condition or behavior became unacceptable, the board had authority to ask him or her to leave. Everyone had to agree to "abide by all the rules and regulations of said Home, and in all things so conduct myself so as not to interfere with the peace and good order of the institution under penalty of expulsion."[22]

Until the 1940s, those in charge believed they had to furnish only food, shelter, and some medical care. The guests cared for their own rooms and performed other household chores. The Kline Galland Home did not provide special diets for health purposes, physical or occupational therapy, or entertainment, except visits sponsored by Jewish organizations. "Since the time when I was a very young child I can remember Mother [Helen Berkman Blumenthal] going out to visit 'the old people.' She and her friends formed a Volunteer Group which provided a monthly birthday party for the residents of the Home, and a yearly Chanukah Party," recalled Caroline Danz.[23]

After discovering a guest (resident) sewing for profit, the Kline Galland Home in 1936 posted a notice, "Duties of Guests (Residents)," so that residents understood their obligations. King County Hospital (Harborview) provided free medical care for residents who needed hospitalization. If families did not assume responsibility for burial, the Kline Galland Home paid for a funeral.

Whatever assets the applicant owned, no matter how small, had to be transferred to the agency, a policy that continued until 1957. "With our present facilities we must adhere to the policy of admitting only the indigent," stated a board report in 1949.[24] Persons with ample funds were not considered eligible until a new facility, with new rules, opened its doors in 1967 on the same site.

Community concern about the large number of residents being discharged for minor rule violations and the increasing amount of time spent by the board in maintaining direct participation in both admission screening and resident management led the board in 1937 to hire May Goldsmith, executive secretary at the Jewish Welfare Society, to process applicants.[25] Most of her duties included checking the "social background" of the applicants to make certain the client was truly indigent. Goldsmith did not follow applicants after admittance, a practice that Ann Kaufman, a professional social worker and executive director of Jewish Family Service, tried to initiate when she replaced Goldsmith in 1945. Kaufman believed that follow-up was a necessary component of good social work. The lay board, which was probably not familiar with this type of service, declined the request.[26]

In the beginning, a Mrs. Weiss lived on the premises and supervised staff. When she left in 1919, Mr. and Mrs. A. Padeck took charge and remained for sixteen years. Although purchases had to be approved by the board, the Padecks managed daily affairs and kept tabs on the residents. During their tenure, the Kline Galland Home appointed a medical advisor, reaffirmed its practice of providing kosher meals, and invited local rabbis to conduct services. In 1937 the board hired its first Jewish superintendents, Dr. and Mrs. Herman Mayerson. Dr. Mayerson was a chiropodist; Mrs. Mayerson had experience in a Jewish residential center. They assumed management at a joint salary of $225 per month. For the first time, the agency was able to realize the strict preparation of kosher meals. The Mayersons also encouraged socializing and recreational activities. They stayed for ten years.[27]

Between 1930 and 1950, financial problems, an inadequate facility, and difficulty in implementing new services such as occupational therapy plagued the Kline Galland Home, which was still being administered by a lay board. In 1941, the board decided to investigate increasing revenue through public assistance grants, a process they did not resolve until 1957, when thirty of the thirty-five residents paid their way with funds received from the federal Old Age Assistance program.

The dispute about Old Age Assistance grants arose from the wording of Galland's will, which stipulated that the Kline Galland Home could not set a charge for services. Because federally regulated Old Age Assistance grants went directly to qualified residents, in essence the residents were paying for services if they turned grants over to the home. The conflict was resolved when lawyers interpreted Galland's intent to provide "the greatest degree of contentment and happiness" to mean the agency must do more than shelter residents. Since additional services would cost money, Old Age Assistance grants became acceptable.[28]

To foster community awareness about desperate financial situations at the Kline Galland Home and to counter "the mistaken idea that there are unlimited funds," the board in 1948 formed an auxiliary group, "The Friends of the Caroline Kline Galland Home."[29] The Kline Galland Home also applied to the Seattle Jewish Federated Fund for additional money, and in April 1949, reported that the "Fund will be willing to contribute towards the operational expenses of an additional wing to the Home."[30]

In reality, until 1956 Kline Galland Home acted more as a boarding home for the elderly than as a nursing facility. A survey by Kurt G. Hertz, sanctioned by the board in 1955, pointed out specific problems, such as the building not being fireproof, the lack of an elevator, and inadequate refrigeration in the kitchen. The report also clearly stated the new role of nursing homes: "The function of the home is no longer the exclusive care of the well aged but also, and increasingly so, the care of the chronically ill and mentally senile who need nursing home care, intensive medical, social and, at times, psychiatric services."[31]

With the 1956 hiring of Arthur Farber, a graduate of New York University's School of Social Work, the board began the process of making the Kline Galland Home a geriatric nursing home that would provide a broad range of services for those in need regardless of economic circumstances. After being labeled "an antiquated, inadequate facility" by the Washington State Department of Health in

1960, the board initiated a campaign to raise funds for a new building. Successful fund drives first directed by Sol Esfeld replaced the original wooden building with a multimillion-dollar, quality-care, skilled nursing home at 7500 Seward Park South. Instead of live-in matrons, professional administrators aided by registered nurses, social workers, and dietitians managed the home and the care of its residents. In 1976 the Kline Galland Home incorporated as a nonprofit charitable organization with an independent board elected by members of the Jewish community.

Sephardim Unite

Bold wording in *The Jewish Transcript* on March 7, 1930, announced that the Seattle Progressive Fraternity and its Ladies' Auxiliary "has undertaken the tremendous task of creating and establishing one united Community" for Sephardim. It had been a slow process. Differences among the Sephardim had created five societies offering similar services between 1921 and 1935.

In the days before public and social welfare programs, many of these organizations not only provided a place to socialize, they offered assistance to those in need. "The Seattle Progressive Fraternity has been very helpful in adjustments with Sephardic families, and has been generous with donations for increased expenditures at Pesach and High Holidays," noted the 1931 report from the president of the Jewish Welfare Society.[32]

Organized in 1921 the Seattle Progressive Fraternity not only helped those in need, it sponsored educational programs and prepared its members for American citizenship. To that end, each meeting ended with the singing of the "Star Spangled Banner." "It was the most important club in the city," wrote Albert Adatto, an early Seattle Sephardic historian.[33]

On the other hand, David Jacob Almeleh believed the Seattle Progressive Fraternity was "exclusive." He, with the support of Marco Romey, Henry Benezra, Gordon DeLeon, John Calderon, and Joseph Cordova, established Shalom Alehem in the 1930s. Through its newspaper, *Progress*, a monthly periodical, Almeleh and his associates worked to promote a single Sephardic organization. The newspaper did not survive, but the other various fraternities, including the Shalom Aleichem Society, Shalom Aleichem Ladies' Auxiliary, Ladies' Sephardic Association, Seattle Progressive Fraternity, and Ahavat Shalom, did consolidate to form the Sephardic Brotherhood.[34]

The Brotherhood, according to Gordon DeLeon, the first president, expected to take care of all the activities of the community and unite Sephardic congrega-

Abraham Fis, Rev. David Behar, Leon Israel, and Morris Sadis buried worn out prayer shawls, tefillin, and prayer books in a special cemetery concrete vault called the Geniza. WSJHS, *125.*

tions Bikur Holim, Ahavath Ahim, and Ezra Bessaroth. Uniting the congregations failed, but the Brotherhood continued the charitable work begun by the earlier societies and made it possible for the Sephardim to agree to one cemetery. "That Brotherhood cemetery . . . is only in the hands of the Seattle Sephardic Brotherhood today because the Ezra Bessaroth relinquished it to them as part of this new, one Sephardic community in the city of Seattle," recalled Elazar Behar.[35]

Like every religious group, the Sephardim, who in the beginning had used Bikur Cholim cemetery, wanted their own cemetery. In 1917 they purchased 110 burial sites from Bikur Cholim for $750.[36] In 1929, Ahavath Ahim also purchased cemetery plots from Bikur Cholim.[37] Referred to as the "old cemetery," this was the Sephardim burial ground until Ezra Bessaroth, along with Machzikay Hadath Congregation, purchased cemetery ground at 167th Street, east of Aurora Avenue, in 1933. "It was a large parcel of land. . . . The portion retained by the Machzikay Hadath for their cemetery would constitute only about one-fourth of the total site."[38] Two years later, the Sephardic portion came under the jurisdiction of the Sephardic Brotherhood. All of the Sephardic congregations used this cemetery.[39] In 1956, thanks to the generosity of the family of Nessim Alhadeff, the Brotherhood dedicated the Nessim Alhadeff Memorial Chapel.[40]

Besides managing the cemetery, the Brotherhood and Sisterhood also set up a scholarship fund, raised funds for schools in Israel, and provided social functions for the members. "A lot of the work [by the Brotherhood] was done very quietly. I won't use the word secretly, but it was not public. It was not a secret but it was not divulged to anybody so that the families that were receiving charity would not be embarrassed," Behar emphasized.[41] Outside of the synagogues, it remains the largest Sephardic organization in Washington.

B'nai B'rith

During the tumultuous years between the two world wars, both Reform and Orthodox men and women joined B'nai B'rith. In smaller towns, B'nai B'rith was usually the only place Jews had a chance to be with other Jews. Everett Lodge, which had begun in 1914 but dissolved in a few years, started up again in 1925 because Everett was the only city of its size on the West Coast without a Jewish fraternal group.

Whether attending a B'nai B'rith convention hosted by Spokane's Abraham Geiger Lodge in 1928, participating in Brotherhood dinners sponsored by Seattle's Lodge in 1936, or meeting in Kelso to discuss ways of supporting the war effort, men and women eagerly participated in B'nai B'rith. Frequently members journeyed to lodges in other cities to forge links with Jewish people throughout the state. "Every Jew in its district, [Centralia, Chehalis, Toledo, and Olympia] joined Anunoh Lodge," said P. Allen Rickles when he installed Maurice Rubenstein of Centralia as president and Stanley Blumenthal, Jr., the one Jew in Toledo, as warden.[42] The lodge, organized in Olympia in 1930, also had a women's auxiliary. In 1936, Mrs. Al Levinson from Chehalis became its president.

B'nai B'rith introduced young people to volunteer work and to the benefits of shared communities when they created youth groups such as Aleph Zadik Aleph (AZA) and Junior BB Girls. AZA dances were often the place where a spark of romance kindled a marriage. Support for a Jewish summer camp at Long Lake acquainted boys from distressed families with a wilderness experience. Barney Lustig, chairman of the Seattle B'nai B'rith Lodge No. 503 and of the Young Men's Hebrew Association's social service committee, initiated the idea for the B'nai B'rith–Y.M.H.A Summer Camp for Boys and donated five acres of land to the project.[43]

In 1939, Seattle's B'nai B'rith, whose one thousand members represented all factions of the Seattle Jewish community, set up a special committee, Coordination of Jewish Activities, to unite Jewish organizations. Made up of representatives from

AZA, an arm of B'nai B'rith for Jewish youth, carried on its own philanthropic and social activities. Here Tacoma's 1940 AZA members celebrate with a traditional Sweetheart Ball. Jerry Spellman, Bernie Friedman, Leo Lavine (regional B'nai B'rith youth director), 1938 Sweetheart Bluma Novikoff (Goldfarb), and Paul Goldfarb watched as Mary Eastern (Donion), the 1939 Sweetheart, pinned 1940 Sweetheart Josephine Kleiner (Heiman). Courtesy of Josephine Kleiner Heiman, Tacoma.

Bikur Cholim, Temple De Hirsch, Herzl Congregation, Sephardic Bikur Holim, and Ezra Bessaroth, the committee planed "to foster a new era of unity and cooperation between all groups . . . at this critical hour in our people's fate," said Simon Wampold, Jr., B'nai B'rith president.[44] This consolidation of efforts, especially in fund-raising, was one of the positive effects of the Depression.

During World War II men's and women's lodges throughout Washington arduously supported bond drives, helped resettle refugees, and along with all the Jewish organizations, gave assistance to servicemen stationed in their cities. Being so close to Fort Lewis, B'nai B'rith in Tacoma took an active role in welcoming servicemen to the area synagogues and temples.

"Participation in war work is keeping this city's Jewish women busy," said Dorothy Barer in *The Jewish Transcript* of September 7, 1942. The women, members of the Walla Walla B'nai B'rith Auxiliary, knitted and sewed for the Red Cross, helped furnish a day room for soldiers at the local air base, acted as hostesses at the United Service Organization, and assisted the men's group in raising $6,200 at a bond rally. Active members of the women's Walla Walla auxiliary included Maxine Carlisle, Dorothy Barer, Esther Barer, Mrs. Abe (Violet) Epstein, and Mrs. Harry (Eva) Bergman, chair.[45] In 1951 Esther Barer served as president of the Pacific Northwest Conference of B'nai B'rith Women.

In Spokane, Mona Rickles, war savings chairwoman of the Ida Bluen Strauss Auxiliary, spearheaded a drive to sell savings stamps. Rickles, concerned that stores missed the opportunity to sell savings stamps because they allowed their supply to dwindle, began buying stamps and then selling them to the stores. She became so successful that the U.S. Treasury Department heard of her work and named her "Uncle Sam's Errand Girl No. 1." Her calling cards, decorated with a tiny American

Under the chairmanship of Joe Gluck, Seattle's B'nai B'rith raised more than $3,000,000 in U.S. War Bonds, a sum so large that the U.S. government honored the organization by naming a B-17 Flying Fortress the "Seattle B'nai B'rith." MSCUA/UWL, neg. 18962.

flag and the message to "phone Uncle Sam's Errand Girl No. 1 when your supply of War Savings Stamps runs low" were posted in stores throughout Spokane.[46]

Seattle lodges formed the War Service Committee in 1942. Working with the Jewish Welfare Board, they recruited blood plasma donors and provided entertainment and special gifts for servicemen. Under the chairmanship of Joe Gluck, B'nai B'rith Lodge No. 503 raised more than $3 million in U.S. War Bonds, a sum so large that the U.S. government honored them by naming a B-17 Flying Fortress the "Seattle B'nai B'rith." In addition, B'nai B'rith adopted the uss *Farquhar* and promised to accept responsibility for recreational programs for the entire crew.[47]

Gluck was also promotional director for the state of Washington. He, along with Mrs. Max Tobias, executive secretary, supervised the fund raising of eleven Seattle Jewish organizations during World War II. During the Seventh War Loan Bond Drive, clubs and organizations such as Avivah Organization, Bikur Cholim, Seattle B'nai B'rith Lodge No. 503, Sons of Israel, and the Workman's Circle raised $6,547,925.[48]

In 1948, thirty enthusiastic Seattle women organized a separate B'nai B'rith Women's Chapter No. 647. Mrs. Irving Stolzoff was elected temporary chairman, and Shirley (Mrs. Sam) Berch was elected president. Berch had been active with B'nai B'rith's women in Bremerton.[49] Members of the No. 647 chapter, which replaced auxiliaries, raised funds for B'nai B'rith projects, participated in local community affairs, and worked as teaching aids in Seattle public schools. Through their Dolls for Democracy program, the women taught children about other races and cultures.

National Council of Jewish Women

As the Great Depression continued, National Council of Jewish Women membership fell in smaller cities such as Bellingham, Everett, and Spokane. By the 1950s, only Seattle and Tacoma women had active sections.

The Seattle Section's largest program, the funding and management of the Educational Center (Settlement House), moved forward through the Roaring Twenties, the Great Depression, and World War II. With so many refugees coming in after World War I, the mainly volunteer staff had much to do. "It aims to be a civic center through which all the interests of the locality, philanthropic, civic, and religious may flow," wrote Mrs. Emar Goldberg, chairwoman of the Educational Board.[50] In 1922 the Educational Center hired a trained social worker.

As people signed up for drama, music, art, literature, and dancing classes, attended plays and recitals, and waltzed and fox-trotted in spacious ballrooms, instructors had to be found and classes scheduled. Funds from the federal Works Progress Administration (WPA), which paid the salaries of out-of-work actors, artists, and musicians, helped, as did money from the Community Chest (now United Way).

The Educational Center continued the Americanization program, with its emphasis on speaking English and embracing middle-class America, but in the late 1920s the staff recognized the need to preserve the immigrants' culture. With the U.S. government's 1924 laws restricting immigration, the Educational Center now catered to second-generation clients who lacked their parents' rich heritage. To rectify this problem, the Center allowed groups such as the Hazomir Choral Society to present Yiddish folk songs, and the Yiddish Dramatic Society to give plays. No doubt Center members were heeding the message stated in *The Jewish Transcript*: "When Jews suddenly cut themselves loose from the Yiddish and Ladino that they or their parents have spoken they have uprooted themselves from the Jewish past and present."[51]

Another successful project of the Educational Center, the Vocational Scholarship Program, which provided financial aid to students who would otherwise be forced to drop out of high school and go to work, began in 1922. Although the money was a gift from the Educational Center board, not a loan, many recipients voluntarily repaid and kept the fund solvent. Later the Fund was broadened to include college scholarships.

When the Jewish population in the neighborhood represented a minority of persons using the Educational Center, its board, on January 1, 1948, changed the name to Neighborhood House. They also recommended that the Center "aim to involve more of the neighborhood people in the administration and responsibility for the Educational Center program."[52] By 1953, National Council of Jewish Women members no longer dominated the board.

In 1952, working with the University of Washington Department of Nursing and Jewish Family and Child Service, Seattle's National Council of Jewish Women spearheaded the drive to open a nursery school. The money came from the Bonham Galland Fund, established in 1915 and never used, as the will stipulated that the money should "remain intact until it amounts to $50,000."[53] At the school, housed at Temple De Hirsch, preschool-aged children of Jewish immigrants played and learned with American children of all races and religions. Leone (Mrs. Harvard) Kaufman chaired the project, and council members, after receiving twelve hours of training, volunteered to work in the nursery school.[54]

Tacoma women reorganized a Tacoma Section of the National Council of Jewish Women in 1920. It quickly became an active organization. Under the presidency of Jessie Feist, who had the distinction of holding that office four different times, the Tacoma Section solicited funds to furnish apartments and find jobs for Jewish refugee families settling in their community, sponsored Sunday socials for servicemen stationed at Fort Lewis, and partnered in the organization of Tacoma's Community Chest. The Tacoma Section additionally devoted Tuesdays to sewing clothing for the Palestine Relief Association. "Our meeting place looked like a dressmakers' establishment—some cutting, some sewing and some using the machine. . . . We made seventy-two pairs of gray flannel bloomers and forty-seven tam-o-shanters our first year," members wrote in 1935.[55]

The Tacoma Section pioneered work with blind babies, first creating toys and games, and later teaching and typing children's Braille books. Their work blazed the way for blind children to attend public schools.[56]

An extensive USO program begun during World War II, and a day set aside to aid the Red Cross, involved the women in the war effort. The Tacoma Section was later active in promoting progressive state legislation and coordinating its work with other community organizations.[57]

Women's American Organization for Rehabilitation through Training

The creation of the State of Israel prompted Jewish women in Seattle to establish a chapter of Women's American Organization for Rehabilitation through Training (ORT). First organized as the Society for the Promotion of Handicraft, Industry and Agriculture Among Jews, or in Russian, *Obschestvo Remeslenovoi Zemledelcheskovo Trouda*, the members established vocational training for craftsmen moving out of the Pale of Settlement. ORT became an international organization in 1919, and established a Women's American ORT in 1927. Washington joined in 1951.[58]

Helen Schuster presided at the first Washington meeting held in the Crystal Room of the Bon Marche. A month later, the women presented an ORT Workshop Institute to explain how ORT provides teacher training and advanced technical training in its own schools, and grants scholarships for higher education. "We want to help people to help themselves. . . . ORT is the means through which we alleviate their [poor Jews in Israel] low estate and give them the immediate means for a decent standard of living," wrote Frances Rogers, secretary of Seattle ORT."[59]

In the 1960s regular lunch meetings helped preserve membership in the Seattle ORT. A mother-daughter luncheon, with a prize for the largest family gathering, brought in younger women. A monthly bulletin prepared by Elsa Levinson and Rose Collier kept members informed, and card parties and sales of scholarship

Seattle women raised money to support Women's American Organization for Rehabilitation through Training's education and training programs. Left to right: Becky Weinstein, Mrs. Kaplan (national president), Helen Schuster, Rene Solomon, Ruth (Ross) Roseman (chapter president), Shirley Donner, Sally Sondheim, unidentified individual, Sylvia Kaufman, unidentified individual, Mary Ackerman, Sylvia Koss, Mary Lou Walters, and Eeda Walters. MSCUA/UWL, neg. 18789.

cards supported programs. Dinner parties at members' homes became a popular way to add money to the Maintenance Overseas Training Project. For her work in ORT and other Jewish organizations, Levinson received the Woman of the Year Award at the Jewish National Fund Hanukkah dinner on January 3, 1968.[60]

Learning to cope and survive is a vital component of an active community. Clearly, change had come to the Jewish community of Washington. Although the energy and skill of the early organizers remained, taking care of one's own required more than handing out a basket of food. In progressing from merely asking community members to provide funds to actively pursuing fund-raising projects and work with government agencies, Washington Jewish philanthropic organizations, strengthened an already rich heritage.

The Crisis Years

T HE INTERWAR YEARS MARKED THE ASCENDANCY OF Eastern European Jews across America and in Washington State. The Conservative branch of Judaism gained a foothold in Washington State as the children of the Eastern European immigrants sought modes of worship that they perceived were more compatible with the American setting. Responding to a series of crises afflicting the Jews of Europe and Palestine in the late 1920s and throughout the 1930s, which culminated in the Holocaust, Washington's Jewish communities organized to raise funds for the relief of their stricken brethren. These efforts were complicated by clashing ideas about Zionism, the movement to establish a Jewish state in Palestine.

Seattle's Jewish community, like large Jewish communities in European and other American cities, was divided on ethnic, class, religious, and ideological lines. The polarization in Washington State between the early-arriving Jews from German-speaking lands and the Eastern Europeans, whose numbers overwhelmed the Germans, was little different from the experience of other American communities. It was the addition of the large Sephardic component that gave Seattle a unique mix.

In Seattle, the Temple De Hirsch Jews, usually identified as German, dominated many of the important early community organizations by virtue of their longevity in the United States and their economic power. Yet from early in the twentieth century, leaders of the temple, the Eastern Europeans, and the Sephardim worked together to meet Jewish needs, locally and around the world, particularly in emergency situations. The economic success of a number of Jews of Eastern European origin allowed many to challenge the leadership of the temple Jews in Seattle, Tacoma, and Spokane. A small number of Sephardim participated in the wider Seattle Jewish community in the years before World War II, but the philanthropic efforts of the economically secure Sephardim were concentrated on taking care of their own.

The split between secular and religious Jews was not as prominent in Washington as elsewhere because the state lacked a large Jewish proletariat. The socialist-leaning membership of the Workman's Circle consisted mostly of small shop owners and business people. During the Red Scare that swept the United States following World War I, minutes of the Seattle Section, National Council of Jewish Women, reported that:

The Juvenile Court and Secret Service sent representatives to us seeking our aid to counteract and to crush by good influence and constructive work in the proper directions the effect of radical teaching carried on in this neighborhood. The source of this insidious work is a school called the Workman's Circle where children five years and up are taught the principals of bolshevism from text books.[1]

But the Workman's Circle was more of a fraternal organization and a Yiddish cultural society than a radical political group. By the late 1920s, *The Jewish Transcript* featured a weekly column on the activities of the Workman's Circle, which had very active branches in Seattle and Tacoma. Another group of forty, mostly Communists, did manage to spark the ire of the *Transcript* by holding a Yom Kippur banquet in 1932. "Seattle Jewish revolutionists, banded together as a 'society of godless,' attacked religion and made merry of Kol Nidre evening," the paper reported.[2]

Conservative Judaism Comes to Seattle and Tacoma

The rise of the Conservative movement in the United States was symptomatic of the forces of Americanization, assimilation, and acculturation working on immigrant Jews and their children. The movement sought to "conserve" the content of traditional Judaism while at the same time adapting its form to modern life. With little direction from the national organization, this congregation-based effort evolved as the American-born children of the immigrants rationalized their religion with their surroundings. They introduced English in the services, sat women with men, emphasized an orderly ceremony led by a rabbi, and initiated Friday night services. The Conservatives could not accept the rationalist criteria of Reform, but chafed under old-world religious practices. They saw their movement as an evolutionary form of Judaism, and many fully expected Conservatism to replace Orthodoxy in the United States.[3]

A December 1927 editorial in *The Jewish Transcript* played on these themes.[4] The editor, Herman Horowitz, claimed that Seattle was one of the very few large American cities without a Conservative congregation. As a result, about 1,100 unaffiliated yet not indifferent Jews felt at home "neither in temple nor in shul. . . . They are usually American-born or thoroughly Americanized children of orthodox Jewish parents who immigrated here from Eastern Europe." Horowitz surmised that these unaffiliated Jews were uncomfortable with the segregation of the sexes, Hebrew prayers without English translation, and when "the Rov dovens in Yiddish."[5] Horowitz played an active role in the Conservative movement in Seattle and always gave prominent and sympathetic coverage of Conservatism in the *Transcript*. In the years to come, he used the *Transcript* to promote the movement as the branch of Judaism most compatible with tradition and the American scene.

An independent group was organized as The Conservative Congregation of Seattle in 1930 and was chaired by P. Allen Rickles, who had served as president of Bikur Cholim. The group held its first large public meeting in March 1930, announcing plans to hold High Holiday services in rented quarters in the fall. Sol Esfeld, a member of both Herzl Congregation and Temple De Hirsch, outlined decisions already made by the leadership with characteristic wit:

Don't discharge your favorite bootlegger, as no wine will be sold.

Services will be held after dinner on Friday evening and on Saturday morning, as well, of course, on all Jewish holidays with the exception of Christmas.

Men and women will be permitted to sit together since it is hoped that the advent of styles in longer dresses will not distract the attention of the men from the services.

. . . . Since everyone who joins this congregation will be granted long life and happiness, no thought of a cemetery has yet been given. . . .

The issues put to a vote included some surprising entries: Should men wear hats during services? Should there be an organ? Should the services be predominately in Hebrew or in English? Should the men wear *tallitot*? (The outcome of the vote is not available.) The group then elected officers and a board of directors, with P. Allen Rickles as president.[6]

Herman Horowitz trumpeted the new Conservative synagogue in his *Transcript* editorial of April 4, 1930:

[I]t is hoped . . . a conservative congregation will strengthen Jewish life [in Seattle]. The middle group[,] floundering between the orthodox synagogue because it is . . .

too foreign . . . in its entire Hebrew service, and the reform because of its distance from tradition and ritual . . . strikes a happy medium. . . .

No evidence survives that The Conservative Congregation actually held High Holiday services in 1930. With every congregation in the city in bad financial condition at the outset of the Great Depression, Sol Esfeld "almost despaired" of inaugurating the new Conservative enterprise. "There is just one possibility," he suggested, "to amalgamate or take over the Herzl Congregation. . . . Then we would have the community with us instead of against us as we are sure to have if we start a new congregation."[7] The following January, the group advised its friends that Herzl's board agreed to conform to all standards of Conservative worship.[8]

By this time, Herzl Congregation had been moving in the direction of conservatism for more than two years. Founded as an Orthodox congregation in 1906, and known colloquially for many years as the Zionist *shul*, the congregation split in the late 1920s over modernization and financial difficulties arising from construction of its new building at Twentieth Avenue and Spruce Street. Arch traditionalist Rabbi Baruch Shapiro resigned from Herzl's pulpit prior to the 1929 High Holidays, leading his more *frum* (traditional) followers to establish Congregation Machzikay Hadath.[9]

A year later, the congregation voted to seat women with men for the 1930 High Holidays. Herzl hired an English-speaking rabbi to conduct services. Despite these changes, Herzl continued to identify its worship as Orthodox, and the congregation conducted a combined religious school with Bikur Cholim at the new Talmud Torah building.[10] Herzl completed its transformation into a Conservative synagogue in 1932 when the congregation hired Rabbi Philip A. Langh, a graduate of the Conservative movement's Jewish Theological Seminary.

P. Allen Rickles wrote his impressions of Herzl's 1932 High Holiday services in the *Transcript*, contrasting them with Orthodox practice. "I could simply feel that there had been added to the traditional Orthodox services, order and decorum, understanding and dignity."[11] For the thoroughly American Rickles, one of the few Jewish lawyers in Seattle, order and decorum were essential adaptations to Judaism. And *Transcript* editor Horowitz never lost an opportunity to identify Rickles as the "former president of Bikur Cholim" in articles about Herzl.[12]

Rabbi Langh galvanized Herzl and much of Seattle Jewry, and Herzl's Friday night services established a new standard for the city. In Orthodox synagogues, men attended *Kabbalat Shabbat* services at sundown on Friday and returned home for Sabbath dinners with their families. Temple De Hirsch had long held Friday night services, but in the Reform manner. Herzl's after-dinner Sabbath services found a very receptive audience among Seattle's more traditional Jews, as they were conveniently adapted to the American work week.

"The old Herzl [at Twentieth and Spruce] had a seating capacity of somewhere near 1100 or 1200," Charles Jassen remembered. "It was standing room only on Friday nights!"[13] So innovative and popular were the Friday night services that they elicited a response from the Orthodox. "We, as Orthodox Jews, must see to it that every Orthodox Jew in Seattle unites in observing Friday evening at home, with his family," Bikur Cholim's Rabbi Solomon Wohlgelernter said. "Saturday, too, should be devoted to the home."[14] Herzl filled again the following Friday, and more than a hundred people were turned away.[15]

Rabbi Philip A. Langh, a graduate of the Conservative movement's Jewish Theological Seminary, took over as Herzl Synagogue's first Conservative rabbi. He is pictured here with his 1935 Herzl confirmation class. From left: Dorothy Cohen, Helen Kay, Edith Laboff, Rabbi Langh, Gladys Caplan, Margaret Sterling, Shirley Rickles Kleinman, and Elsie Deutsch Weiner. MSCUA/UWL, neg. 1121.

Conservatism recognized a larger role for women; Herzl not only had mixed pews, women were invited to participate in services and called to read the Scriptures. Mayor Bertha Landes spoke from Herzl's pulpit. Rabbi Langh, the *Transcript* reported, "said that in the past, Jewish women were relieved of religious duties because of the labor of home duties, but today if women who are at the sides of their husbands in the market place shall not be entitled to sit by men in the House of God, and not be allowed to come up to the pulpit, these are vile slurs on the dignity of Jewish womanhood." [16]

Herzl's social activities also achieved success in the 1930s, giving a hint of the cohesive force of a Conservative group in the community. The lecture series begun in 1933 attracted a wide audience from the Jewish community. The Herzl Junior Guild offered "any kind of activity you want," Carl Sternoff remembered, including study groups, hiking, baseball, and trips to Mount Rainier every year. During the Depression, with "no money, nothing to do, this out of clear blue sky was a godsend. We had 600 members, all Jewish. We drew from the Temple De Hirsch and the Sephardic congregations. A lot of couples today, met there." [17]

Rabbi Langh also assisted Tacoma's Talmud Torah Congregation in its transformation from Orthodox to Conservative in 1936. Under the leadership of Morris J. Friedman, a five-term president of the synagogue, Talmud Torah hired Jewish Theological Seminary graduate Rabbi Baruch I. Treiger as its first permanent spiritual leader. "We feel we are taking a definite step forward," Friedman said, "in meeting the demand for a modern synagogue service, retaining all the beauty of the traditional Orthodox ritual and at the same time adapting itself to present-day conditions." Rabbi Treiger had a distinguished background; he was formerly head of Portland's Hebrew schools, and had degrees from Reed College and Columbia University. [18]

Despite Herzl's auspicious beginnings as a Conservative congregation, after Rabbi Langh left in 1939, it failed to maintain its momentum. The congregation's financial problems had persisted through the Depression years. Rabbi Langh was followed by a succession of rabbis, two of whom lasted less than a year and none whom lasted longer than five years. [19]

As a result of these events, Herzl failed to attract and hold a large enough portion of Seattle Jewry to provide the vital center for a diverse community. Unlike developments in most other sizable Jewish communities in United States cities, the Conservative movement in Seattle never achieved dominance. The Orthodox Bikur Cholim remained as strong as Herzl. Reform Temple De Hirsch remained the city's largest congregation and considered itself Seattle's Jewish social and communal center into the post–World War II era.

Early Efforts to Coordinate Fund Raising

Seattle Jewry's earliest attempt to create a centralized Jewish philanthropic organization, the Seattle Jewish Fund, was established in 1928 as a clearinghouse to deal with out-of-state fund raisers for Jewish causes. Seattle Jews, like others around the country, were constantly visited by solicitors from around the United States, Palestine, and Europe seeking funds for religious schools and institutions. The Jewish Fund aimed to make fund raising more efficient and to "eliminate the frequent and often vexatious calls by the field secretaries of the various institutions." In its first year, the Fund raised and distributed $16,575 to nonlocal institutions, a respectable amount for the day.[20]

But the Fund was riven with dissent. The fact that Seattle's wealthiest and most established Jews, as pillars of the city's society, gave generously to city-wide philanthropies as well as the Jewish Fund supplied one source of conflict. "[M]any very prominent Jewish women (read: those from Temple De Hirsch) played a large role in soliciting for the Seattle Community Chest (the predecessor to the United Way)," P. Allen Rickles noted in his weekly column in *The Jewish Transcript*. Rickles queried why those same women were not active in soliciting for the Seattle Jewish Fund, which Rabbi Samuel Koch had worked diligently to create. Rickles failed to mention that the bulk of the funds raised by the Seattle Jewish Fund came from the families of those women, that Rabbi Koch was a founder of the Seattle Community Chest, and that the Community Chest provided dollars to Jewish charitable organizations.[21] The different social strata the groups occupied were demonstrated by the fact that the Temple families could afford and desired to give to both secular and Jewish causes, while the Eastern Europeans and Sephardim focused their more modest philanthropy on Jewish needs. The Temple Jews participated in civic philanthropy as a part of the city's elite.

Another conflict arose over the allocation of funds raised. The German Jews claimed the Orthodox failed to cooperate with them by insisting on sending funds to Jewish schools outside Washington State.[22]

Consequently, the Seattle Jewish Fund failed in the summer of 1932. The Eastern Europeans and Sephardim blamed the failure on Temple dominance of the board. The twenty-member directorate of the Seattle Jewish Fund was composed of ten representatives from Temple De Hirsch and ten from the rest of the community, including B'nai B'rith, the two Ashkenazic Orthodox congregations, and the Sephardim.[23] "The rank and file of Jewry was not represented," Eastern European leader Sol Esfeld explained, "and this element is the backbone of all communal work."[24] Centralized fund raising was not revived until 1936 under the name of the Seattle Jewish Federated Fund.

In times of great peril to Jews in Europe or Palestine, the entire Jewish community proved it could work together. In 1929, Alfred Shemanski convened a committee of sixteen prominent Seattle Jewish leaders who pledged to raise $3,500 to relieve Jews in Palestine suffering from Arab rioting. The men, almost exclusively from Temple De Hirsch, raised a good portion of the quota among themselves with $100 to $200 pledges. But the committee turned down a written offer of $1,000 from the absent Julius Lang as too generous for an individual committee member. An additional $1,500 was raised at a mass meeting of eight hundred people at Bikur Cholim synagogue. A week later, *The Jewish Transcript* editorialized that Seattle need not be unduly proud of its effort:

Why this city set for itself a quota far lower than the sums raised by other cities of this size we have not yet found out. It is our opinion that Seattle's most generous donor, who being away from the city, wrote offering to give as much as $1,000 had the correct idea of how much Seattle should give.[25]

The nationwide Allied Jewish Campaign in 1930 aimed to raise $6 million to aid world Jewry. The American Jewish Joint Distribution Committee (JDC or the "Joint"), a non-Zionist organization dominated by wealthy German Jews whose mission was to aid needy Jewish communities "in place," was one component organization. The other was the United Palestine Appeal (UPA), a leading Zionist organization promoting settlement and development in Palestine.[26] The Washington State campaign, again under the leadership of Alfred Shemanski, pledged $45,000 to relieve the hardship of Jews in Poland, Russia, and Palestine and to protest British policy of severely limiting immigration to Palestine. The campaign was endorsed by "both Seattle rabbis," Samuel Koch and Solomon Wohlgelernter.[27]

Sounding the twin themes of urgency and unity, Nathan Eckstein and Sol Esfeld were the principal speakers at the community meeting kicking off the Allied Jewish Campaign. "We all know what the purposes of this campaign are," Eckstein declared.

There is no time to ask questions. There is time now only for action. This state must more than make its quota. Our people are in need of help. They are hungry, sick, unemployed!

The purpose of the campaign, Eckstein continued, was to make Jews everywhere self-sustaining through such programs as training schools and free loans. Esfeld was encouraged by the unified campaign in that "both great hands have joined, Zionist and non-Zionist." On a more solemn note, Esfeld observed that the Great

Depression had eliminated surplus wealth but had not yet greatly affected the standard of living for most people.[28] Forty percent of Washington's quota was pledged within two weeks of the beginning of the campaign.

National organizations kept Washington State's Jewish leaders informed of events in Europe and Palestine, and the correspondence of national leaders conveyed a great sense of urgency as early as 1931. Jonah B. Wise, national chairman of the American Jewish Joint Distribution Committee, wrote to Alfred Shemanski to plead that Washington's 1931 fund-raising campaign for JDC not be postponed to 1932. Such delay, even in a depressed business atmosphere, would set a bad precedent. Furthermore, the need was great in Eastern Europe.[29]

In anticipation of a Zionist rally at Bikur Cholim to protest the British White Paper cutting off Jewish immigration to Palestine, the feisty P. Allen Rickles needled the anti- and non-Zionists during the Allied Jewish Campaign of 1930. "I would love to make up a list of our prominent Seattle leaders who ought to be at such a meeting," Rickles wrote. He questioned whether these leaders had Jewish consciousness "or whether our leaders simply are interested in the prominence of their positions in the business and social world."[30]

Of course Seattle's prominent Jews were concerned with business and social position. And more than a few assimilated into the wider Christian community and were lost to Judaism.[31]

But Rickles's column insulted people such as Nathan and Mina Eckstein and Julius Lang, who never shirked their leadership of Seattle Jewry or their financial support of Jewish causes. Furthermore, several Zionist leaders were members of Temple De Hirsch, including Max and Viola Silver and Emanuel Rosenberg.

The Issue of Zionism

Zionism was a divisive issue in all American cities, and Seattle had a long-lived fling with anti-Zionism, even after 1948. Many of the assimilated German Jewish elite in America opposed the idea of a Jewish state, arguing that Jews no longer constituted a nation but were exclusively a religious community. They feared that Jewish nationalism raised the question of dual loyalty for Jewish citizens of the United States and other nations, thus jeopardizing their hard-earned social and economic status.

Washington had a number of Zionist organizations from early in the twentieth century, but the state's Zionists dispersed into numerous and usually weak groups, as occurred throughout American Zionism. David Levine, a Russian immigrant active in Seattle labor organizations and a future four-term city councilman, was one of the first in Washington to ardently support Zionism.[32]

Under the leadership of Louis Brandeis, the Zionist Organization of America (ZOA) adapted the movement to American progressive ideals and became the most powerful Zionist organization in the world. Brandeis argued that Zionism shared Americans' basic belief in democracy and social justice and that the progressive idea of cultural pluralism meshed with the Zionist goal of self-determination for Jews. He also rejected the belief that Zionism required that all Jews make aliyah (move to Palestine) to counter the charge of dual loyalty.[33] But because a myriad of cultural, religious, and political differences divided the ZOA groups, implementation of a common strategy proved elusive at the national and local levels.

The Tacoma District ZOA was established in 1919, with Reform Rabbi Dr. Raphael Goldenstein of Temple Beth Israel as its first president, but soon disbanded because of indifference. The chapter did not reorganize until 1943. In Spokane, Orthodox Rabbi Joseph Krixtein organized a branch of Young Judea in 1925 to teach students about Zionism, but the ZOA branch was not established until after World War II. Throughout the 1920s, the ZOA's Seattle District constantly faltered and reorganized despite diligent leadership from both the Reform and Orthodox communities. In 1926, for instance, the ZOA national office complained that "Your membership has fallen down from year to year and Seattle is now the only important city in the country without an active Zionist District."[34]

Religious Zionists, mostly from Congregation Bikur Cholim, set up Seattle chapters of Mizrachi and Ladies' Mizrachi in 1916, and were galvanized by a visit from Rabbi Meyer Berlin from the Mizrachi Organization of America. Early leaders included Sam Prottas, Mrs. Benjamin Ordell, Goldie Shucklin, and Jennie Friedman. During Libby Anches's tenure as president, the Ladies' Mizrachi raised funds for Palestine and hosted Zionist speakers. In 1940, under Meta Buttnick's presidency, the Ladies' Mizrachi sponsored Seattle's first kosher banquet at a downtown hotel, the New Washington. The event triggered a spate of negative phone calls from people who considered a public kosher dinner un-American.[35] One observer recalled that most of the male members of Mizrachi were young and middle-class because the older people were not "so anxious to become leaders of an organization that will bring us to Israel. They thought God will bring us, not a human being."[36] Although nationally some Orthodox Jews opposed Zionism, in Washington State Orthodox Jews usually led the groups working and supporting Zionist causes.

Hadassah may have been the most successful Zionist organization in Washington State, with active chapters in several cities. Founded nationally in 1912 by Henrietta Szold to aid Jews settling in Palestine, Hadassah appeared in Seattle

Helen Feinburg and Fortuna Eskenazi behind the counter at Hadassah's Nearly New Shop in Seattle. The shop provided a source of income for the organization's many philanthropic projects. MSCUA/UWL, *neg.* 18966.

in 1923. Three early groups, headed by Esther Lurie, Rose Lurie, and Sonia Witt, merged to form the Seattle chapter in 1927. As more women entered the workplace, Laura Berch started Hadassah's Business and Professional Division in 1938. The organization raised funds for the Child Welfare Fund and Hadassah University Hospital in Palestine with card parties, musical programs, rummage sales, a circulating library, and luncheons. Hadassah also increased members' knowledge of Jewish issues with speakers and discussions.[37] Elsa Levinson, Rena Anches, and Mrs. Jack Kessler served on the board of the Pacific Coast Region of Hadassah in 1944.[38]

In Tacoma, Rabbi Baruch I. Treiger and his wife, Lena, formed a Hadassah Council in 1938, bringing together women from several organizations, including Talmud Torah Synagogue and Temple Beth Israel. The group pledged to save at least one European child.[39] Amelia (Mrs. Norman) Davis was instrumental in transforming the Council into a bona fide Hadassah chapter in 1944. Tacoma Hadassah sent money and clothing to the Jews of Palestine.

A small chapter formed in Bellingham in 1927, with Florence (Mrs. Morrey) Weisfield as president, but disbanded during the Great Depression. It reorganized under the leadership of Rose Thal in 1943.[40] Everett Hadassah began in 1946, meeting at the Montefiore Congregation, with Mrs. Harry Goldberg as first president.[41] The Spokane chapter started in 1936 under the leadership of Marion Huppin and Pauline Kalin. It remains the only women's Jewish organization in the Inland Empire.

The Reform movement in general, and several prominent Washington Reform Jews in particular, embraced Zionism early on, following the lead of Justice Louis Brandeis. Reform's Central Conference of American Rabbis (CCAR) passed a resolution in 1923 supporting the Jewish settlement in Palestine "where progressive ideas could be carried out." By 1937, the CCAR adopted the "Guiding Principles of Reform Judaism," also known as the Columbus Platform, to replace the movement's original nineteenth-century principles, the Pittsburgh Platform. The new canon now spoke of "Judaism [as] the soul of which Israel is the body," in an attempt to rejoin ethnic Jewishness and Judaism. With the new emphasis on the survival of the Jewish people, the Reform movement legitimized the idea of a Jewish homeland and placed itself closer to the consensus in American Jewry.[42]

However, several Reform rabbis, including Temple De Hirsch's influential Samuel Koch, and many influential lay members supported the classical Reform position that Judaism was a religion only, and that Jews did not comprise a nation or a people. In 1943, a group of Reform rabbis created the American Council for Judaism (ACJ) to combat the Zionist position of the CCAR and Zionism in general. The Council stressed the early principles of Reform Judaism, which saw Jews differing from their countrymen in religion only, and opposed the effort to establish a Jewish state in Palestine or anywhere.[43]

ACJ supporters in Seattle and other western cities, especially San Francisco, were well established in both the Jewish and non-Jewish communities. They had achieved wealth and had been integrated into the civic and cultural lives of their cities. What has been suggested about San Francisco members of ACJ is also applicable to Seattle members: "Their opposition to Zionism was motivated, at least in part, by their desire to preserve their standing as patriotic Americans in a western milieu that traditionally had been open to Jews and that remained largely undisfigured by anti-Semitism. Perhaps the Council appealed to elite San Franciscans precisely because the west had given them so much that they feared to lose."[44]

Seattle had a strong chapter of ACJ for several years. Rabbi Koch died before the ACJ was organized, but Morton Schwabacher, scion of one of Washington's most important Jewish families, clothing store owner Alfred Shemanski, lawyer Edward Starin, and furniture store owners Otto Grunbaum and Herbert Schoenfeld provided influential leadership to the small chapter. The group's motivations and positions are revealed in Morton Schwabacher's statement to *The Jewish Transcript* in September 1946. Schwabacher stated that "the clamor for a Jewish national state in Palestine not only jeopardized the hard-won security of Jews in America and throughout the world, but renders a distinct disservice to thousands of refugees and displaced Jews in Europe or Asia." He advocated unrestricted immigration to Palestine together with the establishment of "democratic self-government in that country, in which citizens of all faiths may live together on terms of complete equality." He protested against the use of "'Jewish' flags, 'Jewish' national anthems, and the intrusion of Jewish political nationalism in the American scene."[45] The Seattle chapter of ACJ persisted into the 1950s, long after ACJ founder Rabbi Louis Wolsey called for the Council's dissolution and urged members to "cease attacking a movement which . . . gives our harried people the only possibility of decency, freedom and dignity."[46] Only with the passage of time and the death of its most persistent proponents has Jewish anti-Zionism largely faded away.

The issue of Zionism led to the publication of a second Seattle Jewish newspaper in 1932. According to the paper's president and publisher Roy Rosenthal, *The Jewish Chronicle* was launched because of the perception that *The Jewish Transcript* seemed "so strongly Zionist. . . . It [the *Chronicle*] was not put out as an anti-Zionist paper but [Rabbi Koch] didn't like the other one. It was just too strong for him."[47] The paper was backed by Alfred Shemanski, Nathan Eckstein, Alfred Shyman, Fred Fisher, and Otto Grunbaum, all leaders of Temple De Hirsch. *The Jewish Chronicle* lasted one year. "It had made its point and lost its money," said editor Stella Sameth.[48] The two Jewish papers merged at the close of 1932 at the urging of leaders who saw the rivalry as a threat to community unity.[49]

Reestablishing Centralized Fund Raising

As the Eastern Europeans rose economically, their most successful and community-minded members gradually took over leadership in Jewish organizations. Sol Esfeld provides a good example of this phenomenon in Seattle, rising from selling newspapers on city streets as a young immigrant teenager, graduating from business school, entering the insurance business, and rising to leadership in congregational and Jewish community organizations. In Seattle, Eugene Levy of the Cooper-Levy family accused this new leadership of being nouveau riche and battled the new guard over control of the Jewish Family and Child Service, which was founded by his mother (see chapter 10, "More Than a Basket of Food").

By the mid-1930s, *The Jewish Transcript* was filled with horror stories about the precarious situation of the Jews of Europe. The situation of the Jews in Germany had reached its lowest ebb, Jonah B. Wise of the "Joint" wrote to local leaders such as Sol Esfeld, describing his emergency visit to Germany in 1935.[50]

Jews from Washington cities reorganized to raise money to meet the dire need of their fellow Jews, despite the hardships of the Depression. Budgets for foreign relief gradually rose, as wealthy and poor Jews alike contributed what they could.[51]

Even after centralized fund raising was established in 1936 under the name Seattle Jewish Federated Fund (hereafter also referred to as the Federated Fund or the Federation), the vexatious problem of numerous freelance solicitors for Jewish institutions would not go away. The *shnorrers* (beggers) often were people working territories on commission and representing various institutions. For instance, Sol Esfeld had to deal with a claim by a solicitor for the Ex-Patients' Tubercular Home of Denver that the Colorado institution failed to pay him for funds raised. In response to Esfeld's inquiry, the Ex-Patients' Tubercular Home's secretary stated that the solicitor agreed that "if Seattle becomes federated in 1936, that [he] has no claim for the compensation on the allotment for that year. . . . Furthermore, the object of the federation allotment is to eliminate the cost of collection. . . ."[52] Beneficiary institutions, therefore, also had a stake in federation formation around the nation.

In 1938, Federation president Sol Esfeld appointed a yeshiva committee, including Rabbi Solomon Wohlgelernter, to deal with the large number of Orthodox schools requesting aid. "This one service of our Federation is worthy of your complete support. How would you like to have seventy-five 'mishulochim' call upon you every year for a contribution to their institution."[53] Two years later Esfeld was appointed to a new committee to "discuss with Rabbi Wohlgelernter the possibility of dissuading him from soliciting for private funds in Seattle."[54]

Under the leadership of men such as Sol Esfeld, Alfred Shemanski, and Richard Lang, the Seattle Jewish Federated Fund was put on a firm footing as American Jews sought to cope with the European emergency. "European Jewry is certainly in more desperate circumstances today than at any time in its history," Esfeld stated. He proudly claimed that "We have the highest per capita contribution of any of the larger Federations in America."[55]

Tacoma and Spokane Jews had their own federations. Tacoma's Jewish Fund was established in 1929, also for the purpose of consolidating fund raising by national and international Jewish institutions into a single drive. Under the leadership of Morris Kleiner, Jessie Feist, Lee Lewis, and Herman Jacobs, Tacoma Jews raised and distributed just over $1,000 in the Fund's first year. Ben Slotnick was re-elected to lead Tacoma's Jewish Fund in 1941, along with J. R. Bender and Dr. Lester Baskin. Lena Treiger continued to serve as secretary, while her husband, rabbi of the Conservative Talmud Torah Synagogue, was a board member.[56] The smaller communities looked to Seattle.[57]

Jews in Washington State turned to the national organizations for direction in how best to help the Jews of Europe. The emergency finally induced three leading American Jewish charities to unite their fund-raising efforts. The American Jewish

*Spokane Jewish community's U.S.O. Dance at the B.O.F. (Brotherhood of Friends)
Building during World War II was led by ardent elders. Fourth from right: Ralph Mackoff,
Gladys Soss, Lue Soss, and Rose Soss. Courtesy of Temple Beth Shalom Archives,
Spokane.*

Tacoma men donned chefs' garb to cook up meals for a U.S.O. entertainment event in 1944. From left: Ben Weinsoft, Harry Lorber, Wilbur Meier, Norman Davis, Leon J. Kleiner, Joe Sommer, Morris Kleiner, Bob Warnick, Ben Schwarz, Sam Powell, and Dave Klegman. Courtesy of Josephine Kleiner Heiman, Tacoma.

Joint Distribution Committee, the United Palestine Appeal, and the National Refugee Service combined their efforts for three years, 1939 through 1941, under the United Jewish Appeal for Refugees and Overseas Needs. After 1941, Jews in the Pacific Northwest, like Jews across America, had to deal once again with rivalries between these organizations attempting to confront the terrible events in Europe. "[T]he great majority of Jewish communal leaders deplored the dissolution of the United Jewish Appeal and urged its reconstitution in order that their capacity to raise larger funds might not be dissipated through separate appeals," wrote Abba Hillel Silver and Jonah B. Wise of the United Jewish Appeal to Esfeld and other local leaders. "They declared that the emergency position in which millions of Jews find themselves during this war period requires cooperative action among Jewish leaders in America."[58]

In 1941, Fort Lewis tailor Joseph Rome created the shorty jacket known as the "Ike" jacket for future president Dwight D. Eisenhower, who was then Lt. Co., Chief-of-Staff of the 3rd Division, U.S. Army. A Russian immigrant who arrived in Tacoma in 1913, Rome engaged in tailoring for the Army throughout both World War I and II. The jacket, tight at the waist, with two breast pockets and with back pleats, started an Army fashion worn by millions of GIs all over the world.

—"Fort Tailor Made Ike's Shorty Jacket," *The Tacoma Sunday News Tribune and Ledger,* 26 August 1956

The composition of the Seattle Federated Jewish Fund leadership continued to be top-heavy with Temple De Hirsch people because of their economic and social positions. The organization's 1940 letterhead included several congregational rabbis but only two Sephardim, Charles Alhadeff and Dr. Henry Tarica. The

Reform leaders were not always sensitive to the needs of their more traditional compatriots. When the Seattle Jewish Federated Fund held its first-ever dinner meeting to solicit the largest contributors (those donating at least $100) in 1941, the event was held at Glendale Country Club. Glendale, while a Jewish club, did not keep a kosher kitchen. The Advanced Gifts Group dinner the following year was held at the Talmud Torah and was advertised as "Kosher? Of Course! In fact, it will be kosher enough to suit the strictest adherents of our dietary laws. . . ."[59]

Hortence (Mrs. Lester) Kleinberg, heading the Women's Division of the Seattle Jewish Federated Fund in 1942, pledged that "all the women's contributions [will be used]

Helen Waldbaum and Rose Prottas took to the Seattle streets to sell war stamps. MSCUA/UWL, *neg. 10229.*

to feed child war-sufferers in Europe." Her effective letter personalized the appeal to Jewish women by focusing on the plight of the children.[60]

The Jewish Transcript did an admirable job during the war of keeping the plight of Jews in Europe, at least as far as the press knew of the situation, before its readership. And the paper was filled with patriotic editorials and articles on war bond drives and civil defense. On the home front, the *Transcript* covered the activities of the local Jewish Welfare Board (JWB) and its social and religious programs for Jewish servicemen and women in the area, held under the auspices of the United Service Organization (USO). One headline read: "Dancing Daughters Wanted for Next Soldiers' Party." The JWB maintained an office in Seattle with a paid secretary.[61]

On the issue of the removal of people of Japanese ancestry from the Pacific Coast, *The Jewish Transcript* made only one statement. A February 13, 1942, editorial, "Don't Compromise with Danger," supported the Bellingham American Legion Post's call for removal of all Japanese aliens from the coast. The *Transcript* failed to comment on the internment of all Japanese, both aliens and citizens, in May 1942 under Executive Order 9066. On February 20, 1942, the paper did cover an AZA-sponsored "Youth and Democracy Rally" at Temple De Hirsch's Temple Center, which brought together four hundred youths from African American, Chinese, Filipino, and Japanese groups in Seattle. The *Transcript*'s failure to come to the defense of the Japanese can only be understood in light of the fear felt by inhabitants of the West Coast following Pearl Harbor. The paper was usually hypersensitive to the rights of ethnic and racial minorities.

As the war years wore on, Federated Fund budgets grew with the needs of Jewish refugees. In Seattle, the Federation Board decided to solicit 1944 contributions early "due to larger earnings, restricted buying opportunities, social consciousness stimulated by the war, and tax provisions."[62] The 1944 campaign goal grew to $125,000 to support the needs of nonlocal Jews.

Civic Contributions

Many Jews had important impacts on the wider society during the years between the wars. The contributions of several, Nathan Eckstein for instance, have already been discussed. Others included Harris Warnick of Tacoma, who acted as mentor for troubled young men caught up in the juvenile justice system in Pierce County. Labor leader David Levine served four terms on Seattle's City Council, and Bellingham Park Commissioner Henry Gordon was an unsuccessful candidate for mayor in 1933. Dr. David C. Cowen, a Spokane dentist, began his remarkable career in the Washington State Legislature in 1935, when he was elected to House of Representatives. He served as state senator from 1943 to 1966. When Dr. Cowen, the longest serving legislator in state history, died in 1975, the *Seattle Post-Intelligencer* remembered him as "philanthropist, civic leader, and dean of the Washington State Senate."[63]

One of the least-known examples was Jesse Epstein, a University of Washington law school graduate from Great Falls, Montana. When the National Housing Authority formed in 1937, Epstein approached Seattle Mayor Arthur Langlie with a plan to use New Deal funds to remove slums and develop housing in the city. After writing proposed legislation to create local agencies and selling the project to the legislature, Epstein became the first executive director of the Seattle Housing Authority in 1939. Under his leadership, Yesler Terrace replaced the city's worst slum neighborhood on the southern slope of First Hill. From the beginning, Epstein insisted that Yesler Terrace, and subsequent projects at Rainier Vista, Holly Park, High Point, and Sand Point, be racially integrated, the first such integrated public housing in the country. Jesse Epstein went on to head the region's federal housing agency and was recognized as the father of public housing in the Pacific Northwest.[64]

Despite the sluggish economy of the 1920s in Washington and the real hardships of the Great Depression, the Eastern Europeans, particularly the Americanized children of the immigrants, established an economic foothold. They challenged the community leadership of the established pioneer families from Central Europe and, in many ways, determined the direction the Jewish community would take in religious and secular arenas. A number of these first-generation American-born Jews from Eastern European immigrant Orthodox families turned to Conservative Judaism in Seattle in an effort to modernize and Americanize their religious traditions. In attempts to centralize fund raising in citywide Jewish federated funds, the Eastern European Jews injected their own concerns into the debates on allocation of resources, particularly the issue of Zionism. The era culminated in growing crises for the Jews of Europe and Palestine, World War II, and the catastrophe of the Holocaust, all of which had profound impacts on the local scene in Washington State.[65]

The Fourth Wave of Immigration

W**HEN J. HANS LEHMANN BEGAN HIS SEVENTH**
semester of medical school in Munich in 1933, he found a notice on the
door of his classroom: *Jewish students are allowed to occupy only the last
two rows of seats in this auditorium.* Lehmann turned on his heels and left. He went
to Italy, learned Italian, finished medical school in Perugia, passed his medical ex-
ams, and emigrated to the United States in 1935.[1] Lehmann was among the first of
the Jews who came to America before World War II fleeing Hitler's regime. Hitler's
governance, which started with barring Jewish students from classrooms, dismiss-
ing Jews from civil service, and boycotting all Jewish-owned businesses, escalated
to anti-Semitic rioting, the destruction of synagogues, beatings, and death camps.
Germany's Third Reich under Chancellor Adolph Hitler lasted from January 1933
to April 1945. During these twelve years and four months, six million people were
killed because they were Jewish.[2]

Like many other states throughout the country, Washington gained a wave
of immigrants fleeing Hitler's Germany before World War II and survivors from
Hitler's death camps after the war. Of the approximately 150,000 Jews who came to
the United States, almost a thousand of them settled in and around Seattle.[3]

Many of those who planted new roots in this fourth wave of Jewish immigration to the Pacific Northwest were or became physicians, professors, teachers, rabbis, cantors, musicians, artists, and business and health workers of all kinds. They
helped revitalize Jewish life in the state and added to Washington's cultural and
intellectual life. "The survivors and their children constituted approximately eight
per cent of American Jewry," said historian Edward S. Shapiro, "and their influence on American Jewish life was much greater than their numbers."[4]

Rabbi Richard Rosenthal, for example, was a boy of nine when he saw the

Rabbi Richard Rosenthal became the spiritual leader of Tacoma's Temple Beth El in 1960. His thirty-seven years of service made him the longest-serving rabbi of a single congregation in the Pacific Northwest. Courtesy of Temple Beth El, Tacoma.

Nazi's first sweep of violence against Jews in Germany during Kristallnacht (Night of Broken Glass) in 1938. The night of terror, in which he saw his father beaten beyond recognition, was one reason Rosenthal became a rabbi. The memory sowed the seeds of his interest in fostering community among peoples.[5] Rosenthal arrived in New York as a refugee in 1939 and, as a young rabbi in 1956, moved with his wife of one year to Tacoma to lead his first congregation, Temple Beth Israel. One of his effects in Tacoma was getting two strong-minded Jewish congregations to merge, thus uniting them as one Jewish community. With Rosenthal, Tacoma's Jewish community gained a rabbi whose influence went well beyond Jewish circles. Scholarly and spiritual, with a warm, down-to-earth manner, he served on many boards, including those of the Tacoma Urban League and MultiCare Health System. He taught religion courses at the University of Puget Sound, counseled with ministers in the area, and wrote a monthly column for *The News Tribune*. Described by congregation members as a "mensch," a decent human being, Rosenthal and his wife, Barbara, raised a family of three children.[6]

Like Lehmann, who served as an officer in the United States Army and was one of Germany's Jews who came to Washington State, many refugees joined the U.S. armed forces to fight for their newly adopted country. "Trying to lay a foundation for normal life," they and the survivors who arrived after the war entered actively into the economic, professional, cultural, and religious lives of Seattle, Spokane, Bellingham, Tacoma, and other cities, and became an integral part of their new country.[7] Lehmann, for example, became a highly regarded oncologist, a founder of Seattle's Ballard Hospital in the 1940s, a central figure in the creation of the University of Washington Medical School, a member of the University of Washington Board of Regents, and a lifelong supporter of Seattle's arts organizations. He served on the boards of the Seattle Symphony, the Seattle Repertory Playhouse, and the Cornish School.

Welcoming the New Americans

The Holocaust and the creation of the state of Israel changed not only the lives of the survivors but the way Washington Jewry and all other American Jewish communities saw themselves. No Jew living in America or any other place in the world was left with the same mindset as before.

American Jews, who had been enjoying a growing sense of ease, comfort, and security under improvements in social and economic conditions, found the first news of atrocities against Jews filtering out of Germany impossible to believe. "For once, the Jewish mania for speech was subdued," writer Irving Howe pointed out. What rose instead, all over America, was an outpouring of meetings and manifestos.[8] Established and newly established Jewish organizations in Washington State eased the arrival of Jewish refugees fleeing the Nazi regime and the survivors who continued to arrive for several years after the war ended. In 1936, the Seattle Jewish Federated Fund collected more dollars than they had ever raised before to send to such organizations as the American Jewish Joint Distribution Committee; to Hadassah and Youth Aliyah, to transplant children from ages fourteen to seventeen out of Germany and Poland; to the Hebrew Immigrant Aid Society, to help Jews emigrate from one country to another; and to the Jewish Welfare Board.[9] Even so, emigration was difficult and in many instances impossible. Not many countries were willing to accept Jews seeking refuge. The United States, adhering strictly to the immigration quota system passed in 1924, allowed only 27,000 individuals from Germany to enter each year. Although immigrants had the help of the Hebrew Immigrant Aid Society, the American Jewish Joint Distribution Committee, and the United Service for New Americans, difficulties abounded. For instance, Jews were not allowed to take out any money when they left Germany. To enter the United States, an immigrant needed an affidavit of support signed by an American host guaranteeing against becoming a public charge. Even with an affidavit, problems remained. For example, despite an affidavit from his mother's New York cousin, which arrived immediately following Kristallnacht on November 9, 1938, Ernest Stiefel experienced two years of attempts, disappointments, delays and more delays before he was able to procure an American visa.[10]

The Seattle Section of the National Council of Jewish Women (NCJW) began locating relatives and others who would provide affidavits for German and Polish Jews to come to Washington State. Concerned Seattle Jews such as Sol Esfeld, Sol Levy, and Alex Goldman signed many affidavits. "Some of the most affluent men in the city signed affidavits for 40 to 50 families," recalled NCJW's leader, Florence Flaks. Seattle's NCJW organization began providing funds in 1936 for first citizenship papers for arriving Jewish immigrants. In as many ways as it could, Seattle's NCJW helped Jews leave Germany and aided them when they arrived. Such work was reflected among members of NCJW from the West Coast to the East.[11]

When President Franklin D. Roosevelt issued a blanket affidavit in 1937 permitting children from Germany to enter the United States providing homes could be found for them, Seattle's NCJW surveyed the Seattle area to find suitable homes and offered monthly payments of $20. Although the task was sometimes disheartening, particularly when it involved taking in German children—"We don't feel capable," or "We don't feel up to it," or "It's too much responsibility"—Seattle's NCJW members continued in their efforts. In 1938, twelve-year-old Gerda Katz was the first of two German Jewish refugee children who came to Seattle on this program. She grew up in Florence and Lewis Flaks's home.[12]

Established in 1939 by Seattle's NCJW and the Jewish Welfare Society, the Washington Émigré Bureau coordinated resettlement of refugees, providing funds to disembark, emergency money, housing, help in finding jobs, and orientation to Seattle's milieu. The Bureau's volunteer workers as well as needed funds came from such organizations as Seattle's NCJW, the Jewish Welfare Society, Hebrew Immigrant Aid Society, Seattle Jewish Federated Fund, Temple De Hirsch's Ladies' Auxiliary, Herzl Sisterhood, and Congregation Bikur Cholim.[13] The Bureau's volunteer committee gave special attention to the women and children, many of whom were "sick and tired and worried and befuddled and lost." They lodged the newcomers in the Frye Hotel, paid for by Seattle's NCJW, or in private homes, and helped in other ways, such as providing clothing for the children.[14]

A New Imperative

As the need grew for finding work for émigrés either sent by the National Refugee Service or arriving on their own, Sol Esfeld joined Herman Schocken on the Washington Émigré Bureau's employment committee.[15] When jobs in Seattle could not easily be found, they sent the newcomers to live where work was available. "We had committees go to all sections of the state to talk to Jewish leaders in those communities and ask them to take one or two émigrés," said Esfeld.[16] Wenatchee, with a Jewish community of only five families, took several immigrants; unfortunately, not all of them were happy to be placed in such a small community.[17] Some of the newcomers went to Everett, Spokane, Tacoma, Bellingham, Olympia, and Yakima, with the largest number settling in Seattle. Besides providing housing for the newcomers, said Esfeld, "we had committees actively going to all the groups within the community to find jobs for these people":

Some of them we assisted in establishing small businesses. We made them loans so that they could have a little store for themselves. . . . We established a workshop downtown [Seattle] for those we weren't able to place (collecting used clothing, etc.) and we had about twenty, twenty-five people employed in that capacity."[18]

That Workshop and Sales Room, under the auspices of Seattle's NCJW, was first located in the Security Public Market, and later moved to 1919 First Avenue. It provided a place where men and women could learn a trade and become self-sufficient citizens. "This service saved the community thousands of dollars . . . has kept these people off city and company relief rolls," wrote Joan Koch, daughter-in-law of Temple De Hirsch's Rabbi Samuel Koch.[19] When it was no longer needed as a workshop, it became a thrift shop in 1956, staffed by NCJW volunteers and a few paid workers.[20]

"Though the active work was done by a comparatively small number of men and women, the entire Jewish community furnished the necessary means very liberally to carry out the work," Herman Schocken reported to the National Refugee Service.[21] Washington Émigré Bureau's self-imposed responsibility for immigrants ceased when the newcomers became citizens, or after five years of residence, but the Bureau continued to be available to new citizens in searching for lost members of their families and in assisting them to reunite.[22] (After the war's end, the Bureau ceased providing direct services, leaving that to the professional staff of the Jewish Family and Child Service, with the Bureau handling only the policy-making responsibility.[23])

When the East Coast in 1939 stopped the entry of refugees because of the danger of German submarines, emigrants started coming by way of Asia. Seattle then became one of the largest ports of debarkation, as in World War I, and Jewish refugees arrived daily.[24] "Ours was the first boat of new immigrants to arrive in Seattle via Russia," said Ernest Stiefel, then a youth of nineteen. He arrived in Seattle on the *Hikawa Maru*, a passenger ship of the Japanese line Nippon Yusen Kaisha, which pulled into the Great Northern Dock at Pier 88 in Seattle on August 3, 1940. (Later, during the war, this same *Hikawa Maru* did duty as a Japanese hospital ship, and was thus the only undestroyed Japanese passenger ship.)[25] "Many Seattle Jewish individuals were on hand to greet us," Stiefel recalled." We received an official welcome from the Washington Émigré Bureau. . . . Mrs. Clara Nieder, the professional of the agency, and Miss Marianne Katz (later Weingarten), the newly hired secretary of the agency, were their representatives."[26]

"Sometimes we would have 100 to 200 people," said Florence Flaks.[27] The new arrivals hailed from Polish cities, Vienna, Berlin, Frankfurt, Manheim, Darmstadt, and elsewhere. Not all remained in Seattle. Some had transportation funds to other parts of the country and were anxious to be on their way. Others wanted to stay only long enough to contact relatives and friends elsewhere. Many who planned to stay in Seattle had little idea of where they would live or how they would find work, and it surprised them to find so many Seattle people ready to help. Julius Shafer, Otto Guthman, Rabbi Solomon Wohlgelernter, Herman Schocken, and Frank W. Bishop often waited at the dock to greet incoming ships.[28] Other Jewish citizens waited with cars to help take the arrivals to temporary quarters in the city. Minnie Bernhard, a representative of Temple De Hirsch Sisterhood and Seattle's NCJW recalled:

Mrs. Otto Guthman and I met every boat that came in and Otto Guthman called me "Minnie the Horse" because I used to take the wheelbarrow to help them take their baggage, put them in my car, and take them to the house that we had ready for them. We knew they were coming and before they came we already had a place to take them.[29]

Through one helping agency or another, or through a well-established Jewish resident or family, Jews landing in Seattle in flight from Hitler's regime received aid. For example, aided by the Hebrew Immigrant Aid Society (HIAS), Emilie and Nuchim Steinbrecher arrived in Seattle from Vienna in 1940 with two suitcases and $10, but without their two sons. The year before, their sixteen-year-old son, Erwin, had left Germany for Palestine, admitted as one of the few legal immigrants under the auspices of the Youth Aliyah. At the same time, their ten-year-old son, Kurt, became one of fifty Jewish Viennese children brought to New York and Philadelphia by the American Jewish rescue organization Brit Sholom. There they were cared for until they could be reunited with their parents or placed in foster homes.[30] For eleven days after they arrived in Seattle, the Steinbrechers stayed with Mr. and Mrs. Louis Fine. "They gave us a room and they gave us board and everything we needed . . . even the writing paper and stamps for me," Emilie recalled. Although their older son remained in Palestine, HIAS helped the Steinbrechers bring their younger son to Seattle when he was thirteen years old. Kurt attended Garfield High School, went on to get a pharmacy degree at the University of Washington, and in 1952 went into the Army.[31]

Embracing America

Many of the Jewish immigrants from Germany found immediate friends in the Jewish Club of Washington, formed by a group of early arriving refugees who had banded together to help each other start new lives in America. Founded in the mid-1930s by Dr. Paul Barnass, Dr. Hannah Kostelitz, Walter Lowen, and Werner Grunfeld, the Jewish Club helped other immigrant refugees integrate into the American Jewish community as well as the community at large.[32] Despite their embrace of American culture, all immigrants who arrived in Seattle carrying German passports were officially known as "enemy aliens," subject to an 8 P.M. curfew until they became citizens. Perhaps it was the term "enemy aliens" that led to a rumor which reached all the way to Washington, D.C. Shortly after the United States entered the war, Senator Harry Truman arrived in Seattle to investigate a rumor that the Jewish Club of Washington was made up of a "bunch of spies." Thanks to a hastily formed group led by Herman Schocken and Rabbi Samuel Koch, which met with the senator, Truman returned to Washington, D.C., to denounce the accusation as "a bunch of baloney."[33]

During the war, the Jewish Club of Washington temporarily ceased its informal get-togethers, resuming at war's end under the leadership of Herman Schocken with a wider scope of activities. Its members gave assistance in finding homes and jobs, provided social contact with monthly programs, and gave emotional support to many who had lost family members and friends to Hitler's carnage and were starting a new life.[34]

Membership reached about four hundred; yearly dues began at fifty cents and later rose to one dollar. Committing to an annual project, one year the club members donated a pressing machine to the Hadassah Shop; other years they sent money to needy organizations. They joined the Association of Jews Coming from Europe headquartered in New York, and they sent money every year to help support it. They bought Israel bonds and participated in Holocaust education programs.[35]

In 1945, Schocken of the Washington Émigré Bureau reported: "Our work has helped to settle a goodly number of fine families in our city and state, and these families are becoming a valuable part of our Jewish community."[36] Typical of many of the new families settling in Seattle were Edith Merzbach Lobe and her husband, Ludwig (Lutz) Lobe, emigrants from Berlin. They arrived in Seattle on August 8, 1937, and became active participants in both the Jewish and the civic lives of Seattle. Their activities ranged from a founding membership in Temple Beth Am to Edith Lobe's presidency of The League of Women Voters to Lutz Lobe's chairmanship of the Washington State Hospital Commission.[37]

Edith Lobe gained a University of Washington bachelor's degree in 1942, a master's degree in social work ten years later, and raised two sons. Soft-spoken, competent, and caring, she continually fought against social injustice while maintaining a wry sense of humor. Among volunteer activities, she was president of the Crisis Clinic and the United Community Services. Named "Outstanding Citizen of the Year" in 1970 by the Seattle–King County Municipal League, Edith Lobe became the first non-attorney member of the Washington Bar Association's Disciplinary Board.[38]

A managing partner of the firm Friedman, Lobe and Block, Lutz Lobe was often described as "crusty" and sometimes as "stubborn," "abrasive," and "outspoken." His characterizations by fellow workers, however, also included "caring" and "motivated by a strong sense of honesty and decency." A civic activist, he developed a system for health, welfare, and pension funds that became a national model, and helped found Seattle's first senior center, The Tallmadge Hamilton House.[39]

Henry Eisenhardt's escape from Germany to Seattle in 1939 propelled him to join the U.S. armed forces when war was declared. A native of Berlin, with no close members of the family anywhere in the world to help him leave, Eisenhardt was saved from Nazi terror by the daughter of a former maid in his grandparents' house, who signed the papers needed for his emigration to the United States. Eisenhardt served under General George S. Patton in the infantry and survived Omaha Beach, the Battle of Normandy, the Siegfried Line, and finally the Battle of the Bulge in Luxemburg. He also served in the Office of Strategic Services or OSS. "One of the bittersweet, unforgettable memories," Eisenhardt said, "was the liberation of several concentration camps. I was one of the few Jewish refugees who was a liberator."[40]

In a certain sense, Eisenhardt also helped liberate the minds of many Seattle schoolchildren confined to overcrowded classrooms. He founded the after-school program Chess Mates, in which two thousand children learned to play chess, which helped them to become focused and achieving young citizens. "This is a rare and wonderful program," said Dr. Terry Bergeson, state superintendent of public instruction, "started [in 1989] by an incredible man and continued by a team whom he inspired."[41]

The new lives in Seattle of Doris and Ernest Stiefel provide another example of the positive expression of American adaptation in Herman Schocken's 1945 report. Arriving late in the summer of 1940, Stiefel served in the U.S. Army Air Force for three years, graduated magna cum laude from the University of Washington, and became a certified public accountant. Marriage in 1950 to Doris Pintus, another German refugee, and the births of their three children capped these events. Four years after her marriage, Doris Stiefel became the first female graduate from the University of Washington School of Dentistry. She later received her Master of Science degree and joined the faculty of the University of Washington's School of Dentistry.[42] Ernest Stiefel's activities in community service included becoming president of the Jewish Federation of Greater Seattle, B'nai B'rith Hillel Foundation at the University of Washington, and Congregation Beth Shalom. Along with other activities both in the Jewish and non-Jewish communities, he gave five years of service to *The Jewish Transcript* as treasurer.[43]

Among the refugees in this fourth wave of immigrants to Washington State was Arthur Lagawier, who escaped Holland with his family shortly before the Nazi take-over and settled in Seattle in 1943. A Zionist since his youth, a lover of the Hebrew language, and a Judaic scholar, Lagawier was neither a "Dr." (although everyone addressed him in this manner) nor officially a "rabbi" (he completed Orthodox rabbinical studies in Amsterdam, but declined ordination). People were often surprised to discover that this Judaic scholar, who arbitrated disputes over Jewish law and argued with rabbis over rulings, was not an observant Jew. He called himself an "Orthodox atheist." After her father's death on January 5, 1999, his daughter said that her father believed "that religion with its rituals and prayers is only one aspect of Judaism and not necessarily its most important one. He was convinced that the Jewish concept of God is not that of a personal god who watches over every individual or who answers prayers with miracles but is an abstract term used metaphorically and poetically to delineate a program for life that is ethical, just and compassionate."[44]

Lagawier was a frequent lecturer both in Seattle and in cities he visited while working as a diamond importer and wholesaler, skills he had gained from his father in Holland. He taught classes at Herzl, helped found Seattle's Institute of Jewish Studies, and from 1965 to 1969 was the Institute's education director and teacher.

In November 1946, Klaus Stern and his wife, Paula, were the first married couple to arrive together in Seattle as survivors of the Nazi concentration camps. They came from Bremerhaven to New York on the American troop ship the SS *Marlene*, and then traveled by train through Chicago on to Seattle. Paula was six months' pregnant, although she had claimed to be only three months into her pregnancy in order to be allowed transport.[45]

The Sterns were just starting their newly married life in Berlin when they were deported to a series of concentration camps. Their longest stay was in Auschwitz, the infamous death camp situated in Poland, where the old, the handicapped, and women with children were sent to the gas chambers while the young and healthy were put to labor. The Sterns' nightmarish memories of the more than two years they spent separated in the camp before they were reunited would be as permanent as the blue identification numbers tattooed on their forearms. Their daughter, Marian, was born in Seattle in January 1947, almost at the same time Klaus Stern started work at Langendorf Bakery in shipping and inventory. Recommended by Rabbi Franklin Cohen of Herzl Congregation, Stern worked there for thirty-five and a half years. Eventually Klaus Stern began telling his story of surviving the Holocaust to Seattle and Bremerton high school students, and in Ellensburg to students at Central Washington University.

Local Volunteers Aid in Rescue

Like the Sterns, other survivors who arrived in the United States after the end of World War II were aided by the Hebrew Immigrant Aid Society, the American Jewish Joint Distribution Committee, and the United Service for New Americans. At the same time, American Jews were turning their attention to the survivors who remained still stranded in Europe. In 1947, 180 American volunteers joined a clandestine rescue operation organized by the Haganah Palestine Jewish underground to transport sixty thousand Holocaust survivors to Palestine in sixty ships. Ten of the ships were American, acquired as U.S. war surplus at fire-sale prices. Among the volunteers were three young Seattle Jews: twenty-year-old Sidney Abrams, nineteen-year-old Elihu Bergman, and twenty-five-year-old Bailey Nieder. Asked why they had volunteered, Abrams said, ". . . it was a chance to help fellow Jews." Since Nieder's mother and both Abrams's and Bergman's parents had arrived in earlier immigrations from Europe, Abrams added, "Knowing that we could have been Holocaust victims was an additional incentive. We learned that there were American ships and American volunteers going, and we wanted in on that action."[46]

Because Palestine in 1947 was still under British rule and a prewar policy that limited Jewish immigration to a few hundred a month, the rescue operation, labeled "Aliya Bet" by the Jewish underground, was "illegal immigration." A British air and sea blockade, deployed to prevent any arrivals in Palestine, extended from the Palestine coast through the Mediterranean.

Despite the fact that the three Seattle volunteers could barely tell port from starboard, the shakedown cruise from Miami to New York in March 1947 made sailors of them in one week's time. "They taught us to know that a rope is a line, and a stair is a ladder, and the bathroom is a head."[47] Their ship, of 1902 vintage, was originally built as a gunboat for the U.S. Navy and was called the *Paducah*. At only 190 feet in length, with a 36-foot beam and a weight of 900 gross tons, the ship was small and every bit her age. The Haganah rescue mission with its volunteer crew of thirty would be her last voyage. Designed to carry fewer than 50, the ship was refitted for 1,500 passengers and renamed the *Geula* (Redemption).[48]

As seamen aboard the *Geula*, the three Seattle volunteers helped 1,400 refugees get to Palestine. In the process, they were rammed by British ships, overcome by tear gas, sprayed with DDT, taken to Cyprus (an internment that Nieder managed to escape), and in the case of Bergman, imprisoned in Palestine. The American ships together succeeded in providing transport for 30,000 immigrants. Forty years later, Abrams, Bergman, and Nieder were invited to Israel to commemorate their participation in the historic illegal rescue mission. An assertion of Jewish rights to settle in Palestine, Aliyah Bet was a seminal act in the establishment of the state of Israel.

Making New Lives

Many of the survivors settling in Washington State whose lives had been interrupted precipitously by Hitler's Holocaust found ways to make their existence meaningful for themselves and others. For example, as a sixteen-year-old, Arno Motulsky, a native of Germany, was a passenger on the ship the *St. Louis*, which set out from Germany to Cuba in May 1939 with 930 Jewish refugees aboard. Memorialized in the movie *Voyage of the Damned*, the *St. Louis* was turned away at Havana, made for Miami, and found no sanctuary there either. Forced to sail back to Europe, the ship disembarked its passengers at four different destinations: Belgium, France, England, and Germany.[49] Motulsky landed in Belgium, and spent fifteen months in a concentration camp in France. (Two hundred of the *St. Louis* passengers died in concentration camps.) Emigrating to the United States in 1941, Motulsky met his future wife, Gretel, also a German refugee, at a small college in Chicago. They were married in 1945, moved to Seattle eight years later, and became the parents of two children.[50]

As professor of medicine and genetics and director of the Center for Inherited Diseases at the University of Washington, Motulsky received numerous honors for his research in genetic diseases, including the Martin Luther King, Jr., Medical Achievement Award for his research in sickle cell anemia. For Motulsky, the promise of genetic engineering lay in protecting children from inheriting genetic diseases. He was the only Pacific Northwest physician chosen to be one of eleven members of the Presidential Commission for the Study of Ethical Problems in Medicine. Selected in the 1970s to the Institute of Medicine for his work as a physician and for his medical research, and to the National Academy of Science for outstanding scientific achievement, he became president of the International Congress of Human Genetics in 1986 and received the March of Dimes Birth Defect Foundation award for lifetime achievement in genetics.[51]

While the circumstance of the Holocaust continued to "press deep into the consciousness of Jews" all over America,[52] the pain of the Holocaust remained with the refugees and survivors, even those who found secure and safe lives in America. Like the indelible numbers left on their arms, the memories remained, and those memories often influenced the directions of their lives.

"No longer did I wear a yellow star on my blouse, but I still wore it inside my head," said Noemi Ban, an Auschwitz survivor who made Bellingham her home after first settling in St. Louis, Missouri.[53] Though they could not forget their experiences in the concentration camps of Germany, few survivors wanted to remember. "I had three lives," said Gizel Herskowitz Berman, "one before the war, one during the war, one after the war." Her first life began in Slovakia in 1919 where she was born, and ended after the beginning years of her marriage with Nick Berman, a young dental surgeon. They lived in Uzharod, a small town east of Prague, which was part of Czechoslovakia under Hungarian occupation until 1944. Her second life began in 1944 at Auschwitz. She and her husband survived; more than forty members of her family were exterminated. Her third life began in Seattle in 1945 with Nick and the oncoming birth of a daughter.[54]

Erasing the many past unhappy events from her mind was impossible. Not until many years later did Gizel Berman begin to write down some of the events of her "second life" and begin to talk about them to students in Seattle's high schools. "I taught myself how to forget," she said. Yet the sculpture she designed for the Samuel and Althea Stroum Jewish Community Center of Greater Seattle on Mercer Island as a memorial to the six million Jewish dead featured the first letters of the words, "Thou shalt not forget."[55]

More then thirty-five years passed before Stella DeLeon, one of the hundred Sephardim who survived Auschwitz out of the three thousand Jews sent there from the island of Rhodes, related the horror she had lived through when she was sixteen years old.[56] Hand in hand with the survivors' initial reluctance to talk went the resistance to listen in those who had lived in the towns and cities of Washington State during the war years, more or less unaware of Hitler's atrocities. "Nobody wanted to know," said Paula Stern, when asked by a casual friend in a beauty parlor why she had never talked about her experiences.[57] Not only did people not want to know, many did not believe the accounts even when they heard them. DeLeon said that when the NBC television drama *The Holocaust* was shown to the staff in a Catholic school in Chicago where her daughter was teaching, the general comment was, "That could never happen." Even when DeLeon's daughter told her colleagues that it had happened to her mother, and there was a tattooed number on her mother's arm to prove it, they remained skeptical.

The Telling

Many years passed before the survivors living in Washington State began to realize that what had happened to them and their families had to be told. They were part of a history in danger of being lost. Eva Lassman, a survivor of the Polish death camps of Maidenek and Szarzyco, expanded her life in Spokane with her husband and her three sons. She taught music and the realities of Hitler's regime to Spokane's schoolchildren.[58]

For many years after she arrived in Seattle, Bronka Kohn Serebrin's past was something she never discussed. "I was upset with people denying it happened . . . I was driven to speak," she said. When Germany invaded her native Poland in 1939, her extended family numbered sixty-five. The lives of all but two were lost. Bronka and her sister, Genia, survived slave labor camps, a death march from Germany to Austria, and Mauthausen concentration camp, where they were liberated in May 1945.[59] She spoke to thousands of students throughout the region. She became chairwoman of the Holocaust Education Committee for the Anti-Defamation League of the Pacific Northwest, was profiled in a PBS documentary on the Holocaust, and was interviewed by a film crew from Steven Spielberg's Shoah (Hebrew for Holocaust) Foundation.[60]

In the towns and cities of Washington State, speaking in temples, churches, schools, and community centers, well-established citizens and others who had arrived as Holocaust survivors of the Nazi era transformed memories into tools for teaching. They told tales of beatings and near-starvation, of death marches, slave labor, gas chambers and ovens, rampant dysentery and scarlet fever, of witnessing death and escaping death, and of the loss of mothers and fathers, brothers and sisters.

Survivor Henry Friedman won nationwide recognition for his teachings about the Holocaust. When Friedman was thirteen years old, the Nazis occupied his hometown of Brody in Poland. Until liberated by the Russians in March 1944, Friedman spent eighteen months in hiding with barely enough food to stay alive.

A memorial to the six million Jews who perished in the Holocaust stands near the entrance to the Samuel and Althea Stroum Jewish Community Center of Greater Seattle, Mercer Island. Designed by Gizell Herskowitz Berman and wrought of six Hebrew letters of bronze, the sculpture reaches twelve feet in height. The letters stand for the Old Testament words in Deuteronomy 25:19: "Thou shalt not forget." Courtesy of Washington State Holocaust Education Resource Center.

With his pregnant mother, brother, and a young teacher, he shared a crawl space not large enough to stand in. The death of the infant born to his mother in that confined area was never forgotten. After three years in a displaced person camp in Austria, Friedman arrived in Seattle on November 30, 1949. From 1950 to 1952,

The lighting of the Jerusalem Torch of Freedom heralded the first visit of Abba Eban, Israel's ambassador to the United States, in 1955. Participating in the torch-lighting ceremony at Seattle's Alki Point were (from left): Rabbi Baruch Shapiro, Rabbi Isidore Kahan, Rabbi Solomon Maimon, Rabbi Joseph H. Wagner (holding the torch), Max A. Silver, and Rabbi Garsion Appel. MSCUA/UWL, neg. 17018.

he served in the U.S. Army in Japan and Korea. On his retirement from business, Friedman began his telling of the lessons of the Holocaust throughout Washington State. Under his leadership, an Auschwitz exhibit at the Seattle Center in 1987 was viewed by 26,000 people. In 1989 Friedman founded Surviving Generations of the Holocaust and, in 1991, the Washington State Holocaust Resource Center.[61]

Supporting the New State of Israel

While American Jewish realization of what was happening to their fellow Jews in Germany beginning in the 1930s generally was slow in coming, the response to the creation of the state of Israel on May 14, 1948, was swift and euphoric. "The reaction of most American Jews," wrote Irving Howe, "whether immigrant or native-born, was to show their solidarity with Israel less as a fulfillment of the Zionist or any other idea than as a vibrant historical reality, the place where survivors of the Holocaust and other Jews in flight could make a life for themselves."[62]

Emphasizing the necessity of helping the fledgling state take its first steps, Seattle Jewish Federated Fund campaign chairman Frank Newman, Sr. called upon Seattle Jewry to join with the five million Jews of America to sustain the new state by "giving sacrificially." Fund officers Louis Friedlander, Leo Weisfield, and Sam W. Tarshis asked all contributors to double or triple their contributions "for Israel's sake."[63]

Washington State's other Jewish organizations jumped into intense fund-raising campaigns along with their coreligionists throughout America to ensure the life of the tiny new nation. Fund-raising dinners, lunches, breakfasts, picnics, card parties, and dances overflowed the calendars of Washington's Jews in every town and city where they lived. Gifts of Israel bonds and the planting of trees in Israel took the place of checks and fountain pens for birthdays, Bar Mitzvahs, and graduations.

No one expected the giving to be a one-time effort. America's Jews continued to aid Israel year after year. The great hope is, said Esfeld, "that when peace finally comes there with the Arab nations, Israel will be able to take care of itself and will contribute to the general welfare of the whole world."[64]

The new state of Israel brought "a new consciousness" to Jews living in Washington State, as it did to Jews over all America.[65] The fact that Israel existed provided both sustenance and reinforcement to two thousand years of Jewish life. Helping Israel to continue to exist became a communal activity among American Jews and an ongoing imperative of American Jewish organizations in Seattle and elsewhere.

Postwar Growth

T HE SECOND WORLD WAR HAD AN ENORMOUS IMPACT on Washington State and forever changed the state's economy, population, and the outlook of its citizens. The war transformed Seattle into a major industrial center and added to the population a large number of workers, including Jews from around the United States as well as Holocaust refugees. Boeing, for instance, the largest wartime employer in the area, recruited graduating engineers from around the nation.

By 1960, fewer than half of Seattle's 557,000 residents were native to Washington State.[1] This influx, among other things, led to the breakup of the old Jewish neighborhood in Seattle, an assault on discrimination against Jews and other minorities, the development of a strong Jewish Federation of Greater Seattle, the establishment of a Jewish Community Center, and a new awareness of Jewish concerns at the University of Washington. The postwar era witnessed growing assertiveness of Jews and other minority groups in Washington and throughout the nation.

The Breakup of the Old Jewish Neighborhood

Seattle's Jewish community, like all of American society, was profoundly changed by World War II.[2] The war brought the Great Depression to an abrupt end. War-related industry in Seattle drew migrants from across the nation, putting great stress on housing.[3] The Jewish neighborhood felt the pressure of an overflowing African American community. Newcomers doubled and possibly tripled the pre-war black population of about 3,800, and de facto racial segregation confined those newcomers to the city's Central Area.[4]

250

The African American population continued to grow in the postwar years, as did the Jewish population, both fed by newcomers from other parts of the country. Despite the fact that racially restrictive covenants were struck down by the United States Supreme Court in 1948, blacks continued to face discrimination in housing that effectively confined their fast-growing numbers to the Central Area well into the 1960s. The Jewish neighborhood thus also became the black neighborhood.[5]

Jews, like so many Americans, had experienced rising expectations resulting from the end of the Depression and victory in war. Following the war, the upwardly mobile children of Jewish immigrants, Americanized in public schools and on city streets, moved to the eastern fringes of the old neighborhood or left it altogether for newer, more desirable neighborhoods—Seward Park, Madison Park, Mount Baker, Magnolia, Montlake, and the North End. The growing number of African Americans in their midst was only one reason for the dispersal. Newcomers to Seattle had no attachments to the old neighborhood. Returning servicemen were able to use the GI Bill to purchase homes as well as attend college. Improved economic circumstances allowed families to move to newer housing.

For Orthodox Jews, the move from the old neighborhood was particularly traumatic because it meant leaving the synagogues they had grown up in. The Orthodox lingered the longest, but younger families began to leave in the early 1950s.

After visiting Seattle in early 1948, the Rev. Dr. D. de Sola Pool, president of the Union of Sephardic Congregations, made the following observations to Morris Hanan of Ezra Bessaroth Synagogue:

The rapidly changing character of the neighborhood in which your excellent synagogue buildings are situated and the moving of many of your members to the Lake Washington district and other areas, complete the problems of synagogue and Talmud Torah attendance.

These conditions also put a final veto on your plans to enlarge your synagogue. . . . Once a residential district deteriorates, it very rarely reestablishes itself. You therefore now are in the position of having to consider the long range possibility of setting up a center in some other part of the town where in the near future such a building could truly function as a conveniently located neighborhood community center.[6]

De Sola Pool's letter was prophetic, and Seattle's Jews still living in the Central District, like Jews in so many other inner cities across the nation, continued to migrate to more desirable neighborhoods and suburbs. The process was sometimes painful, as the first to move were perceived as abandoning their synagogues, friends, and family. But eventually, after enough people had moved, the synagogues followed them.

Beginning in the 1950s, a number of Orthodox families relocated to the Seward Park neighborhood, bordering Lake Washington in south Seattle. This was a difficult move, both for the families and the congregations to which they belonged. Central Area synagogues rejected some attempts to form branches in new neighborhoods, and those who remained in the Central Area questioned the loyalty of those moving away. Racial tensions in the inner city in the late 1960s and early 1970s helped spur the relocation.[7]

The migration out of the Central Area took more than two decades to accomplish. The relocation to Seward Park of Ezra Bessaroth in 1958 and of Sephardic Bikur Holim and Bikur Cholim in 1968 removed the last institutional ties to the old neighborhood and concentrated the Orthodox in this south-end neighborhood. A few scattered people remained, mostly elderly. An Orthodox *minyan* (a prayer group of ten men) has persisted in the area, first meeting in the old Temple De Hirsch sanctuary at Fifteenth Avenue and Union Street, and later at the nearby Council House. With a number of younger people moving into the Central Area as it gentrified, the *minyan* grew into a lively congregation affiliated with Bikur Cholim. Meanwhile, the suburban cities of Bellevue and Mercer Island started to attract a large concentration of Jews.

Fighting Discrimination

Until early in the twentieth century, Jewish immigrants to Washington were generally accepted as part of a rapidly expanding, self-consciously frontier society. They acted as leaders in civic activities, helped found social clubs, held political office, and gave to philanthropic causes. Some of the most prominent Jews were thoroughly assimilated into the emerging elite society in Seattle, and many of their children were lost as Jews as they disappeared into the broader American culture.[8]

Discrimination appeared after the turn of the century as social clubs, some of them founded by Jews, began to exclude Jews and other minorities. The Seattle Golf Club, Seattle Tennis Club, Rainier Club, and Washington Athletic Club all had Jewish founders, and all at some point stopped admitting Jews. Restrictive covenants in property deeds prohibited Jews from living in certain neighborhoods, such as Broadmoor and Sand Point Country Club. Asian Americans and African Americans were excluded from more neighborhoods, jobs, and clubs than were the Jews.

The Anti-Defamation League (ADL), the B'nai B'rith's arm to fight discrimination, hired attorney and Seattle native P. Allen Rickles as its first Seattle part-time director in 1940. During and immediately after the war, Rickles supplied the FBI with information on anti-Semitic groups in the state and claimed credit for the arrest of one anti-Semite for sedition, the exclusion of German sympathizers from the coastal area, and the denial of citizenship to former Silver Shirts (Nazi sympathizers). He disseminated literature from the national office to libraries and schools, sponsored such patriotic occasions as "I Am an American Day" and "Buy Something British Day," and delivered speeches to various groups to explain the American Jewish point of view as he saw it. When the wartime federal Office of Price Management raised questions about the pricing of scrap metal, Rickles called a meeting of forty local dealers to ensure that Jews did not violate government regulations and thus tarnish the good name of their people. In addition to handling "innumerable anti-Semitic incidents throughout the State," Rickles worked successfully with the daily press to correct erroneous articles, print favorable editorials, and generally heighten the newspapers' sensitivity to Jewish concerns.[9]

Following the Second World War, those who sacrificed on the battlefield or on the home front felt entitled as never before to share in America's bounty. The African Americans' fight for civil rights is only the best-known example of this phenomenon. In postwar Washington State, and across the nation, Jews became a more visible presence, asserting their rights, attempting to move into neighborhoods that barred "Hebrews" as well as African Americans and Asian Americans, demanding to be employed in jobs formerly denied to them, applying to join exclusive clubs, and working to fight anti-Semitism.

The Seattle chapter of the American Jewish Committee (AJC) formed in 1945, a branch of the organization created in New York in 1906 to safeguard the rights of Jews throughout the world. Max Block spearheaded the local AJC, along with attorney Edward Dobrin, businessman Alfred Shyman, and Henry Kotkins, owner of Skyway Luggage Company. As in the national AJC, membership was by invitation only until 1971.[10] "The AJC is a status group," ADL Director Leonard Schroeter wrote in 1955, perhaps with some bias, "with most of its members also members of Temple De Hirsch. It does not, however, have any program or activity, and has little status in the general community, most of whom have never heard of AJC."[11] However, as the AJC chapter grew and developed, it lost its aura of exclusivity and effectively worked against anti-Semitism in both the social and economic fields.

The Anti-Defamation League and the American Jewish Committee led the fight for civil rights for Jews and other minorities. A few examples of their battles illustrate the methods of these agencies.

Employment

A coalition of Washington's civil rights groups focused on discrimination in employment as its key issue following World War II, as did similar groups in several northern and western states. Local chapters of the ADL and AJC joined with the Urban League, National Association for the Advancement of Colored People, the Civic Unity Committee (a local civil rights agency made up of business, labor, and church leaders), and other organizations to promote fair employment legislation in the state. Local affiliates of national organizations received information from their parent bodies about campaigns in other states. The AJC provided research to back up the need for such a law and information on legislation in New York, Massachusetts, and other states. It also arranged for Henry Spitz, general counsel for the New York Fair Employment Commission, to meet with key Washington State lawmakers. Washington activists credited the Spitz visit with dispelling fears about the functioning of fair employment laws, which enabled the advocates to resist crippling amendments to their proposed legislation.[12] Largely as a result of the work of the coalition, the Washington State Board Against Discrimination in Employment was created by law in 1949. Over the next decade, civil rights groups, including the ADL and AJC, criticized the Board for ineffective and counterproductive policies and administration. The Board did not become a potent force combating discrimination until newly elected Democratic Governor Albert Rosellini appointed strong members in the early 1960s.[13]

In the two decades following World War II, employment discrimination mostly affected Jews in the higher echelons of business, the professions, and industry. Jews made their fortunes by creating their own empires, not by rising through the ranks of established companies. The second-generation scions of successful immigrant entrepreneurs built on the foundations of their parents' enterprise, notably in the fish, produce, scrap metal, and jewelry businesses. A new generation of entrepreneurs prospered in real estate development, the music industry, retail and wholesale merchandising, and numerous other fields. So many of the American-born sons of the immigrants sought careers in the legal, medical, and accounting professions that it became a cliché in Jewish circles. But in the early postwar years, even the best Jewish law school graduates could not find work in Seattle's most prestigious law firms. Those Jewish doctors who set up practice in Seattle after the war were barred from practicing at Swedish and Virginia Mason hospitals until the early 1950s. Several more years passed before Jews rose to the higher ranks of hospital staffs.[14]

In 1968, the AJC discovered that nationally, fewer than one in one hundred top executives were Jews in large industry, banking, and higher education.[15] In 1971, Seattle's two largest banks had a total of ninety-nine officers and forty-one directors. None were Jews.[16] The ADL and AJC played important roles in making the larger society aware of such discrimination and helped lay the groundwork for the gradual change that has taken place since the early 1970s.

Private Clubs

P. Allen Rickles moved on to ADL's San Francisco office in 1949. Rickles was replaced by Stanley Jacobs from the Chicago office. Jacobs set out immediately to make connections around the state, visiting Spokane, Wenatchee, Walla Walla, Yakima, Aberdeen, Everett, Bellingham, Bremerton, and Olympia. The outlying communities complained that they had not been advised of any follow-ups to their reports to ADL or to ADL programs. Jacobs battled with "wealthy and extremely conservative" ADL board members "with whom I cannot see eye to eye. . . . The Jewish community here is accustomed to very subservient and self-effacing Jewish professionals. . . . I am not, and never will be, that kind of guy for I think that my opinions have a right to be heard as much as any millionaire's, and I have not been bashful about stating that I intend to lead opinion and action, and not be a clerk. . . ."[17]

The matter of discrimination at the Washington Athletic Club (WAC) portrays an internal division in the Seattle ADL in 1950 and 1951, one that, according to Jacobs, "occupied perhaps a disproportionate amount of the attention given by our Regional Board members to ADL problems." In 1950, Max A. Silver and Frank Gilman, who were both members of the ADL board and of the WAC, met with the WAC's president and its chairman of the admissions committee to ask about the club's policy vis-à-vis Jews. The WAC had about forty Jewish members; no Jewish applicants, however, not even children of existing members, had been admitted since about 1940. Silver and Gilman, to their shock, received a candid answer to the question. The president admitted frankly to an anti-Semitic policy and told them that it was virtually impossible for a Jew to become a member.[18]

The regional ADL board split on what to do about this blatant discrimination. Those board members who belonged to the WAC, along with some others, felt that Jewish members of the WAC should remain in the club and work from within. P. Allen Rickles strongly backed that faction from his post in San Francisco. Stanley Jacobs, ADL Oregon director David Robinson, and some of the younger members of the ADL regional board believed that "the discrimination in the WAC implies second class citizenship for Jews and therefore we must struggle with this thing in order to preserve our self-respect and affirm our belief in judging individuals on their personal qualifications only."[19]

"This is a new field and there are no easy answers," Oscar Cohen of the ADL national office replied. "The exploratory work which you are doing will be helpful elsewhere." Cohen recommended negotiations, working through prominent and sympathetic Gentile members of the WAC.[20] Herman Edelsberg at the ADL's Washington, D.C., office responded more forcefully, advocating that Jewish members resign from the WAC if the policy did not change. He stated that Max A. Silver should not be on the regional board if he failed to resign.[21]

Stanley Jacobs confided to David Robinson that he was "realistic enough to know that I am going to have one hell of a job on my hands getting anybody to resign, but [if] we could get six good men to take leave of the club with a searing public blast, then I think I would be for it. What have we got to lose, the goodwill of sympathizers who are cowardly, or the enmity of bigots?"[22]

Given the division of the regional board, the ADL took no further action in 1950, and the matter of club discrimination was put off for twenty years. But the internal ADL correspondence reveals two views of the Jewish situation in Seattle in 1950.

On the one hand, P. Allen Rickles, the Seattle native, decried the result of making WAC discrimination a public issue. "[W]hat good has it done the Jewish community of Seattle to have made this the subject of public conversation?" Rickles asked. "If there is anyone who thinks that the dignity and position of the Jew in Seattle has been raised by having the entire community conscious of the fact that the WAC doesn't want any more Jewish members, then I say it is a rather peculiar and warped type of thinking."[23]

Jacobs, the newcomer, on the other hand, believed that the "fine public relations" between Seattle's Jews and Gentiles espoused by Rickles was "a pleasant self-delusion and actually, altho on a smaller scale, Seattle, is prey to all the evils and injustices which afflict Chicago, New York, Detroit and any other town."[24] He was particularly annoyed by a nephew of Rickles, Harry Steiner, "who is a featherbrain and given to loose talk. Steiner last fall told another board member, 'We gotta get this guy [Jacobs] out of Seattle. He's a trouble-maker.' I talked with Steiner in a mild vein . . . and he tried to show me what a paradise Seattle is, 'until Eastern Jews come in and cause trouble.'"[25]

During the next twenty years, the WAC and most other exclusive clubs opened their memberships to Jews and other minorities as overt discrimination lost favor in the eyes of the public. In 1970, the ADL and the AJC joined more than twenty groups in the Coalition Against Discrimination (CAD), organized to combat remaining discrimination by private clubs. CAD's strategy, which proved successful within two years, focused on passing legislation to deny Class H liquor licenses and discounted liquor to private clubs, such as the Elks, Moose, and Eagles, that excluded minorities from membership. Peter Schnurman, AJC's local director and member of CAD's executive board, was quoted in *The Seattle Times* as calling such clubs "the last bastion of formalized bigotry in America." CAD put pressure on exclusionary clubs by sending letters to large business organizations requesting that they not schedule Christmas parties at offending clubs.[26] With the backing of Governor Daniel Evans, the Washington State legislature passed a version of CAD's law in 1972. Discrimination at private clubs ended quickly throughout the state.[27]

Religion in the Public Schools

The issue of religion in the public schools, a long-time concern to the national ADL and AJC, also received much attention in Washington State.

Following his 1953 arrival in Seattle as the new ADL state director, Leonard Schroeter wrote the national office that he was "shocked" by the condition of church-state affairs in Washington and that nothing had been done about it.[28] Over the next two years, Schroeter and two members of his ADL regional board, Rabbi Albert Plotkin of Spokane and Rabbi Richard Rosenthal of Tacoma, focused on the "released time" problem in those two cities. The released time program started in Spokane in 1938. Here the local Council of Churches sponsored the released time programs, distributing cards through the public schools whereby parents could grant permission for their children to be released for periods during school hours for religious instruction off school property.[29]

In Spokane, Schroeter found much opposition to released time among school administrators, board members, and the PTA, but also timidity about challenging the leading advocate of the program at the Council of Churches, a woman of great energy and "vitriolic tongue." By the end of 1953, the Spokane ADL advisory board was ready to take all necessary steps to eradicate released time, including legal action. "This is a complete switch from the attitude the Jewish community took some years ago when a local attorney [Bernard Swerland] . . . attempted to bring an action to test the legality of the released time system. At that time they wanted to run him out of town on a rail."[30]

Sol Rabkin at ADL national headquarters advised Schroeter to enlist Christian opponents of released time to the cause and, Rabkin warned, "under no circumstances should atheistic or left-wing groups be included among those discussing the question with the school board." He also cautioned Schroeter to approach litigation carefully because of a recent adverse decision by the United States Supreme Court, worrying that an unsuccessful lawsuit could start a landslide of hostile state decisions.[31]

Rabbi Plotkin in Spokane and Rabbi Rosenthal in Tacoma worked within the Council of Churches to end released time. Rosenthal cooperated with liberal ministers to end the showing of the film *The King of Kings* to public schoolchildren, off school grounds but during school hours and accompanied by teachers, during the week before Easter. Rabbi Rosenthal engaged in a heated debate before the Tacoma School Board, appeared in a televised panel discussion on church-state issues, and was quoted extensively on the topic in the daily press.[32]

The Washington State Supreme Court upheld the released time program in a 1959 decision, *Perry v. School District No. 1, Spokane, Washington*. The program slowly disappeared in the face of opposition from teachers and liberal Protestant groups as well as Jewish opposition.

During the years 1970 and 1971, the AJC's local director Peter Schnurman met with school superintendents and principals in the Seattle area to explain that Christmas and Easter celebrations in the schools violated the Constitutional doctrine of separation of church and state. He disseminated the AJC's publication "Religion in Public Education" and a calendar of Jewish holidays to the local schools and the state superintendent of education.[33] When a Jewish parent called about a parents' orientation night scheduled for Yom Kippur eve at Nathan Eckstein Middle School, Schnurman called on Alfred Cowles, executive director of the State Human Rights Commission and a member of the school board. Cowles called back within ten minutes to say that the event was rescheduled.[34]

"Because we have taken a positive approach to these problems," Schnurman reported to Sam Rabinove at AJC national headquarters, "rather than just being critical of schools for their insensitivities, I think we have begun a series of relationships . . . that will prove to be of increasing benefits in the future. . . . In any case, we have now moved into the arena of sensitizing school personnel to the needs of Jews in the public school system."[35]

The AJC also supported the Seattle Public Schools 1971 school bussing plan to combat de facto segregation. "Although a mandatory bussing plan is not a completely satisfactory way of achieving [desegregation]," an AJC spokesman told *The Seattle Times*, "we cannot afford to wait another generation or more for substantial changes to occur in housing patterns."[36]

Together with ADL, AJC actively opposed legislative campaigns for prayers in the schools, vouchers, and other attempts to use state tax dollars to fund private education as violations of the separation doctrine.[37] In February 1971, Rabinove warned Schnurman against AJC officially intervening in the legislative fight in Olympia over state aid to private schools. He feared that because of AJC's prominent role in the battle relating to discrimination by private clubs, another lobbying effort could endanger AJC's tax-exempt status. Neil Sandberg, AJC's West Coast regional director, replied to Rabinove that it was "unrealistic and dramatic" to cut off the Seattle AJC's legislative activity for the remainder of the year, it being only February. "Your suggestion will virtually put them out of business in a number of critical areas."[38]

The ADL and AJC engaged in numerous campaigns over the years to combat anti-Semitism and discrimination against other minorities and to promote good-will among various ethnic groups. These agencies played important roles in both the Jewish community and the wider society, helping to move America away from the melting pot ideal and toward a celebration of cultural pluralism.

As American society opened to a greater extent than ever before, Jews, with their high educational achievement, were ideally suited to take advantage of the new opportunities presented by the loosening of restrictions on minority peoples. By the time the Baby Boom generation matured, few restrictions remained for Jews. To solidify their position in America and to better serve the needs of the growing Jewish community, Seattle's central Jewish organization, the Federation, evolved into a sophisticated institution.

The Jewish Federation of Greater Seattle

The history of the Jewish Federation of Greater Seattle is outside the scope of this book. This large and important topic is left for future writers to research and analyze. We offer only a sketchy outline here.

Called the Federated Jewish Fund of Seattle following the Second World War, the organization evolved over several decades to become the Jewish Federation of Greater Seattle, growing from a strictly fund-raising entity dealing mostly with out-of-state agencies into a coordinating umbrella organization for local noncongregational Jewish agencies. Although large portions of the budget continued to be earmarked for the United Jewish Appeal for Refugees and Overseas Needs and many smaller outside agencies, the Federated Jewish Fund of Seattle succeeded in centralizing planning for local lay organizations.

In 1951, Merle Cohn chaired a committee formed to study the need of creating a planning and coordinating body. Louis Weintraub, regional director of the Jewish Welfare Board (a national umbrella organization of community centers originally established to serve Jewish servicemen and women in World War I) attended the initial committee meeting and provided direction and expertise. The committee's report concluded "that there was a definite need . . . for a central community organization . . . with the limitation that there shall be no surrender of autonomy of individual organizations, agencies or individuals to such a central body." As a result, the Jewish Federated Fund became the Federated Jewish Fund and Council of Seattle. The organizing committee recommended three initial concerns for policy planning: recreational needs (Jewish Community Center), Jewish education (resulting in the Levy Report), and care of the aged (Kline Galland Home).[39]

According to one observer, the Federated Jewish Fund and Council of Seattle had made little progress by 1955 and was still principally a fund-raising entity: "The Council is merely a Committee of the Fund, meets irregularly, has no power and little participation," ADL director Leonard Schroeter wrote. "The Board of Directors and Budget Committee of the Federation exercise whatever power exists in the Jewish Community. Real power is relatively decentralized, however. Due to a weak Federated Fund Executive and considerable apathy, the Federation not only does no community planning, it also does a poor job of fund raising." Schroeter claimed that contributions had decreased from $600,000 to $280,000 during the previous seven years, a time of relative prosperity and growing population.[40]

Spokane and Tacoma maintained federated funds to raise money for Jewish causes, but those communities did not employ executive directors or paid personnel. Aside from the United Jewish Appeal, these communities raised only a few thousand dollars for all Jewish needs in the mid-1950s. Smaller communities such as Aberdeen, Bellingham, Bremerton, Centralia-Chehalis, Longview-Kelso, and Walla Walla "theoretically" had federated funds but did little fund-raising.[41]

Leonard Schroeter's 1955 snapshot of Washington State's Jewish communities presented an unflattering picture: "In summary, there is little vitality, direction or planning in Jewish life in the State of Washington." He attributed this sorry state to the lack of professional leadership (few professionals and a low level of competence, including rabbis); lack of adequate education and information; no community center; and a "very inadequate *Jewish Transcript*; serious conflict and social distance in the Seattle community (Ashkenazi-Sephardic, Reform-Orthodox); a lack of attention to maintaining Jewish life in the small cities; and, finally, the newness of the area and its distance from the centers of Jewish life."[42] This last insight helps to explain all of the other causes of the problems of Jewish life in Washington, except for the conflict within Seattle's Jewish community. Seattle had a very small Jewish population compared to other American cities of its size. Schroeter's assessment was undoubtedly a minority and unpopular view of the state of Jewish affairs in Washington. But his outsider's perspective is valuable because he was a Jewish professional with experience working in other American cities.

Jewish Washington did mature in the ensuing decades. Seattle's central fund-raising organization (hereafter referred to as the Federation) reorganized a number of times with different names and hired increasingly sophisticated professional staff. Over the years, the Federation worked with community agencies, consistently focused on caring for the elderly (Kline Galland Home) and the needy (Jewish Family Service), Jewish education, creating and then maintaining a Jewish Community Center, and aid to Israel. A leadership development program was instituted in 1962, an endowment fund was created in 1965, and the Community Relations Council was established in 1966.

The Seattle Jewish Community Center

Among American Jewish communities of comparable size, Seattle was the last to establish a Jewish Community Center (JCC). Prior to World War II, the Educational Center (Settlement House), the Young Men's Hebrew Association, and Temple De Hirsch's Temple Center provided some of the services of a community center: meeting rooms, auditoriums, programs, and social activities. In other cities, the Conservative majority formed the backbone of the community center movement, but Seattle's Conservative movement was relatively weak. During the 1930s, young men such as Herzl Congregation's Harry Ash agitated for a community center like the one they saw in Portland. In Seattle, a 1946 survey by the Jewish Welfare Board that identified a need for a community center met with a cool reception from the Orthodox and Reform establishments. The Orthodox, including the Sephardim, were still largely a geographically cohesive community living close to their synagogues. The old Reform families in Temple De Hirsch feared the dissipation of what they perceived as the Temple's power as a community force. Furthermore, many Reform Jews questioned the appropriateness of a "Jewish" social and recreational institution in secular America.[43]

Early Organization

Despite disinterest and opposition, Norman Davis and his interim Jewish Center Committee kept the idea of a community center alive. Davis, English by birth and a newcomer to the United States in the 1930s, served as the Jewish Community Center's first president, from 1949 to 1955. Davis's statement on the eve of incorporating the Seattle JCC in 1949 expressed the intentions of the vast majority of American Jews to make their Jewish lives in the United States:

[T]he time has come to turn our thoughts to our own communities and in particular to the needs of Jews in Seattle whose life and future is here as Americans. I feel most deeply that if this Jewishness is to have validity, if it is to be something other than an everlasting burden and handicap, we must have the background, the culture and social amenities which a fully equipped Jewish Community Center can provide.[44]

Davis suggested that the Jewish community required an institution outside the synagogue and temple to encourage a positive Jewish identity and unity in Seattle's diverse and increasingly dispersed Jewish community. This vision anticipated the needs of the third-generation Jews, grandchildren of the immigrants whose ties to Judaism were more tenuous than those of their parents.

Aiming to recreate the lost sense of community in a modern setting, the founders of the JCC declared that the center's purpose was "to foster and develop Jewish social affiliations."[45] The only controversy over the initial bylaws concerned the Orthodox representatives' insistence that Jewish laws (specifically *kashruth* and the Sabbath) be observed. This controversy continued for many years, but the Orthodox view has always prevailed.[46]

The Seattle Jewish Community Center hired a director in 1955 and rented meeting rooms the following year on Fourth Avenue between Stewart and Virginia Streets. Membership increased dramatically from 100 to 992 families.

Norman Davis with his son Charles, 1947. The creation of Seattle's Jewish Community Center in 1949 was due in large part to the vision of Norman Davis. He passionately believed in a Jewish center outside the synagogue and temple that would serve to encourage Jewish unity in Seattle's diverse and increasingly dispersed Jewish community. Davis served as the Jewish Community Center's first president. Courtesy of Charles and Jonis Davis.

With the purchase of the Elks Building at Fourth Avenue and Spring Street in 1958, expedited by Norman Davis, Dr. Norman Clein, Harold Poll, and Irving Anches, Seattle's JCC had a home of its own. New programs were generated to take advantage of the space and facilities, which included a gymnasium. Membership climbed to 1100 families in 1959.[47] But facilities were far from adequate.

The 1960 campaign to raise $750,000 to renovate the Elks Building collected only $400,000. Some community leaders felt this was promising, given Seattle's "notorious reputation among American cities of comparable size for the difficulty of obtaining coordinated action among the community and difficulty of raising community funds. . . . Other observers were disappointed . . . They pointed out that the Vancouver, British Columbia, Jewish Community Center had been able to obtain double the Seattle pledges with a significantly smaller Jewish population." Consequently, the JCC lost momentum, and membership declined by almost half in the next two years.[48]

In the face of community disaffection, the JCC undertook a "Basic Facilities Study" in 1963. Prepared by University of Washington Professor of Business Administration Albert Schrieber, the study made a remarkably accurate forecast of population trends in Seattle, projecting a 1985 Greater Seattle of 1.65 million people with a Jewish population of about 21,600. Schrieber predicted that the geographical center of Jewish population would float to the east of the Seattle Tennis Club in the middle of Lake Washington. He noted that the ideal site for a main center, the west shore of Lake Washington, was prohibitively expensive. Seattle's Central Area, Mercer Island, and Bellevue were considered as potential sites. The wide dispersion of Jews, Schrieber noted, made selection of a single site for the JCC a difficult choice. Wherever the main facility was eventually located, Schrieber emphasized, extension programs would be necessary to serve the needs of Jewish youth and seniors throughout the area.[49]

A new regime instituted great changes beginning in 1963. Merle Cohn, JCC president, brought in a new, experienced, and energetic executive director, Leo Okin. Okin, formerly consultant to Jewish Community Centers in the western United States for the Jewish Welfare Board, came to Seattle with very distinct goals in mind. He found the JCC in disarray, housed in an inadequate facility that the community was not proud of, and with an almost nonexistent membership. Furthermore, he discovered a Jewish community more sharply divided on ethnic and denominational grounds than those in other western cities, a relatively weak Jewish Federation, a weak Conservative movement, and a lack of strong leadership. Okin set out to put the JCC on solid financial ground, to create a program that would attract members, and, most importantly, to work for a new facility. His underlying agenda was to develop leaders, from all segments of the community, who had an understanding of the total Jewish community.[50]

The JCC's letterhead throughout the 1960s carried the name "Jewish Community Centers of Seattle" (plural) and featured a map with dots representing a downtown central headquarters and north-end, south-end, and overlake (east of Lake Washington) branches as well as Camp Benbow, the JCC's summer camp. Although this letterhead reflected mostly wishful thinking, it was used until the opening of the Jewish Community Center of Greater Seattle (singular) on Mercer Island in 1969.

The Move to Mercer Island

The decision to locate the Jewish Community Center on Mercer Island was dictated by the price of available land and the predicted population trends of the Jewish community.[51] Merle Cohn and Sam W. Tarshis pushed the decision along by purchasing land near the East Channel bridge and offering it to the JCC board at cost.[52] Professor Schrieber's projections of the migration to suburban Bellevue and Mercer Island were borne out. In retrospect, Mercer Island proved to be the right place to build the main facility, although the JCC acted as a magnet for Jewish families and helped to fulfill those projections. North-end Jews vigorously opposed the move to Mercer Island; the promise of a freeway planned to run through the Arboretum, which would make the commute manageable, assuaged a few of them.[53] But the proposed freeway was a victim of rising neighborhood activism in the 1960s and 1970s and was never built, and the JCC dropped plans for satellite centers as all energy was directed to developing the Mercer Island facility. Ironically, both Professor Schrieber and Dr. Charles Kaplan, president of the JCC from 1965 to 1968, lived in the city's North End.

Because of monetary constraints, the Mercer Island JCC was built in two stages. Stage one, completed in 1970, contained a swimming pool, gymnasium-auditorium, locker rooms, men's health club, nursery school rooms, club rooms, lounges, and offices. The second stage, completed in 1981, expanded athletic facilities and added a women's health club, auditorium, kitchen, and additional nursery school rooms. Designed by Paul Thiry, the physical plant fulfilled Leo Okin's imperative to provide first-rate facilities to attract membership from a largely affluent group.

To pay for the Mercer Island JCC, Greater Seattle's Jews had to break through the accepted ceiling on philanthropy and establish a new level of giving. Previous top gifts of $25,000 were given during the capital campaign for the Kline Galland

Home a few years earlier. Campaign leaders set the new threshold with their own gifts. Martin Rind put together a substantial family pledge in memory of his father, Max Rind, with the assistance of his father's close friends Morris Polack, Morris Gordon, and Abe Fallick. Herb Rosen gave a large gift in thankfulness for surviving a heart attack. Both men came out of nowhere, taking on leadership after playing limited roles in community affairs to that point. Just as Leo Okin had hoped, both men went on to assume leadership positions in the Jewish Federation of Greater Seattle.[54]

Interestingly, Rind and Rosen were Seattle natives, raised in the close-knit Yesler Way–Cherry Street neighborhood. Both men believed Seattle needed a JCC to create a meeting place for Jewish youth now dispersed throughout the city.

From the beginning, the JCC offered a wide range of programs in the new facility, experimenting to determine needs and feasibility. Preschool and daycare attracted young families and evolved into first-rate programs under the leadership of Barbara Daniels. As single-parent and two-working-spouse families became more common, early childhood programs at the JCC filled growing and urgent needs. The Golden Age Club worked out transportation problems and served the great need of seniors from around the area to gather on a regular basis. Adults used athletic facilities, and cultural programs enjoyed mixed success. During the 1973 Yom Kippur War, the JCC held nightly meetings where speakers explained the course of the war and helped unify the community's collective response.

Attracting and serving the needs of teenagers and young adults proved to be the JCC's and the community's most difficult task. "Our youth is disenchanted with us, as are all youth," Herb Rosen observed in his 1971 presidential address to the JCC's annual meeting. "Fortunately, they are intelligent, curious and idealistic. We must expand our efforts to answer their needs and, at the same time, educate their parents. If they do not come to us, we must be prepared to reach out and meet them where they are."

The JCC actively searched for a full-time youth director and was the first JCC to offer drug counseling. In this era of the Vietnam War, the Jewish Federation of Greater Seattle hired a draft counselor who met young men at the JCC and at the University of Washington's Hillel Center.[55]

Financial Crisis

Despite a strong membership, unprecedented levels of fund raising, and an unexpected and substantial bequest by A. Pupko in the late 1970s, a number of circumstances led the JCC to the brink of financial disaster in 1981: the Boeing recession

A philanthropic and business leader, Seattle's Sam Stroum was a prominent member of Seattle's Jewish community, a genius at fund raising for good causes, and an influential force in the civic life of the city. MSCUA/UWL., *neg. 18959.*

of 1969 to 1971; a campaign to fund construction of the second phase of the center that raised only half of its $2 million target;[56] and rising interest rates that reached 20.5 percent in August 1981.

The situation reached its crisis point in December 1981. JCC President Eddie Fisher approached the lender, Seafirst Bank, with the problem, but was offered no relief. In meetings and correspondence, the bank alluded to possible buyers of the facility, thereby putting the JCC on notice that the bank would consider forcing a sale of the building should the JCC default on the loan.[57]

When the bank offered no relief, Fisher went to the community leadership. Simultaneously, the new executive director of the JCC, Barry Hantman, spoke with such people as Martin Rind and Morris Polack about the deepening crisis. As a result of these efforts, a group of leading Jewish citizens gathered to attempt to save the JCC.

After considering a number of options, Sam Stroum stepped forward with a daring strategy in late February 1982. Stroum, Seattle Jewry's leading philanthropist, offered to head the emergency campaign only on his own terms—an all or nothing campaign that $4 million be raised within two and a half months to fully pay off the debt and that all money would be returned if the goal was not reached. Despite some skepticism, the JCC Board of Directors had no choice but to accept his conditions.[58]

The JCC crisis went public with the March 4, 1982 issue of *The Jewish Transcript.* An open letter from the emergency committee outlined the crisis and the proposed course of action, setting the tone for the next two and a half months. "It is a Jewish crisis," the letter challenged, "our crisis, rich and poor, young and old, Reform, Orthodox, Conservative, or 'uncommitted.'" Not only was the JCC building at stake, so was the well-being of the community and the good name of every Jew. Over the next two months, the *Transcript* educated its readers, maintained the crisis atmosphere, and reported on the progress of the campaign.

Restaurateur Billy Schwartz and businessman Robert Miller led the efforts to make good on $2 million in uncollected pledges to the building campaign. JCC board members spoke to community groups. Sam Stroum led the major gifts campaign and sought pledges of $100,000 and up.

Just as the Rind family gift in the 1968–69 JCC campaign had done, Stroum's initial pledge significantly raised the level of donations by Seattle Jewry. In approaching potential major donors, Stroum used an updated list of the top contributions. "I would put that [list] in front of people, and whatever number they had in mind, it disappeared very rapidly," he recalled.[59]

Sam Stroum was a powerful and effective fund raiser. A University of Washington regent and a member of several influential boards, both philanthropic and business, Stroum was Seattle's most visible Jew. A warm and charming man, he set a very impressive example with his own gift. Several people initially rebuffed him, stating the amount they were willing to give. Stormy public meetings were held. Many of the major donors, along with the rank and file, seethed with anger at the predicament of the JCC.

Thirty-nine people gave $3.6 million; the balance of $400,000 came from about eighteen hundred gifts. "There's no question that the major dollars—given the time and the enormous sum of money—had to come from a small core group," Stroum recalled. "But in terms of the long-term approach, everyone had to feel a part of saving the J.C.C. . . . Everyone had to feel a part, even if they gave a dollar."[60] In the end, a generous community paid the bank in full and saved the Jewish Community Center. It is now known as the Samuel and Althea Stroum Jewish Community Center of Greater Seattle.

The north-end satellite of the JCC had to wait. By the mid-1980s, after some abortive earlier efforts, a group led by Mike Saran, Joel Erlitz, and Barbara Droker launched JCC programs in rented facilities. *The Jewish Transcript* printed two letters from north-end JCC board members criticizing the decision to spend money to upgrade the main 90,000-square-foot Mercer Island facility while leaving the North End begging in a rented, 2,500-square-foot basement.[61] Those letters and other efforts precipitated the search for a better facility for the North End. In 1988, the north-end branch of the Jewish Community Center established its own facility in a converted supermarket on Thirty-fifth Avenue Northeast.

Jewish Activities and Studies at the University of Washington

Jewish Students and Hillel

With the demise of the Menorah Society in the 1930s, only two fraternities and two sororities remained as Jewish organizations at the University of Washington. Fraternities Zeta Beta Tau and Sigma Alpha Mu and sororities Alpha Epsilon Phi and Phi Sigma Sigma were affiliates of national organizations formed in response to discrimination against Jewish students by the Greek system across the country. It took money to belong to the Greek houses, but during the Depression most Jewish students lacked the means. Furthermore, until the early 1950s, Sephardim were not asked to join even if they had the means.

At the end of 1940, B'nai B'rith Western District Lodge granted University of Washington students approval to organize a Hillel unit as the Jewish campus organization. The university approved, and a house was rented on Seventeenth Avenue Northeast. Rabbi Arthur Zuckerman, a Reform rabbi and Reconstructionist, served as the first director. He maintained kashruth, observed the Sabbath, and respected the beliefs of the Orthodox and Conservative students. Bob Friedman was elected the first president and led Friday services; Charles Jassen and Saul Krakovsky (the actor Steve Hill) acted as cantors. Hoda Stusser (Greenberg) and Elsie Deutsch (Weiner) decorated the first Hillel sukkah in 1941. Milton Lewis, Jack Duitch, Hilda Mayer, and Edith Cohen (Patashnik) also served as presidents of Hillel during the war years. Other active members included Archie Katz, Reva Ketzlach (Twersky), Max Katz, and David Alhadeff.[62]

All the early Hillel officers and active members were independents rather than fraternity or sorority members. Hillel afforded the independents, most of whom lived with their parents, a place to gather on campus. Hillel activities included Passover lunches, holiday observances and celebrations, and lectures and discussion groups. At the end of the 1942 school year, Hillel presented gifts to men entering the military. During the war, Hillel served as a meeting place for Jewish servicemen and servicewomen in the area.

Following World War II, Hillel sponsored a scholarship program "to rescue gifted students from the displaced persons camps and from other hell-holes in Europe."[63] Tom Lantos, a Hungarian refugee, arrived in 1947 as the initial recipient, the first of six to receive the scholarship. Lantos later served several terms as a distinguished U.S. congressman from California.

Rabbi Arthur Jacobovitz, Hillel director at the University of Washington from 1959 to 1989, challenged the university to recognize the concerns of its Jewish students. Rabbi "J" was instrumental in the creation of the Jewish Studies program at the university. Courtesy of Rabbi Arthur Jacobovitz.

Hillel House moved to its permanent building on Seventeenth Avenue Northeast in 1954. A succession of Hillel directors attempted, with varying degrees of success, to reach the University's Jewish students. Religious and cultural events were not as well attended as programs on Israel and social events in the 1950s. In the early 1960s, Director Rabbi Arthur Jacobovitz reported that 65 percent of the University's Jewish students participated in Hillel programs and that 15 percent were very active. Student involvement at Hillel then decreased until 1967, when Israel's Six Day War sparked renewed Jewish awareness.

Rabbi Jacobovitz's arrival in 1959, the first Orthodox Hillel director west of the Mississippi, shook up the campus community and the wider Jewish community. Rabbi "J" challenged students, the University administration, and Seattle's Jewish establishment as they had not been confronted before, raising Jewish issues that had been ignored. Although he made enemies, Rabbi "J" had enough strong supporters to survive thirty years as director until his retirement.

"In a way this was a difficult appointment for the community," Professor Neal Groman remembered,

i.e. to have an Orthodox rabbi appointed. . . . This was a community that had a large Reform congregation, and it wasn't exactly the appointment you would have proposed in order to establish rapport with students who came from these Reform families. On the other hand, he was very energetic, very devoted to the Jewish cause and to the Jewish community, and an interesting man in his own right. I guess an ardent protagonist is how I would characterize him, and a person who was very strongly devoted to principles, sometimes to the point where he could not accommodate. He had many hard times. . . . I think those of us who were close to Hillel, who were on the board, felt that he represented by far a much more capable and devoted person than we could have hoped to get assigned . . . at a school where the student Jewish population was so limited. There was considerable community antagonism to Rabbi Jacobovitz and in some cases great efforts were made to get him removed from his position. . . .[64]

Rabbi Jacobovitz charged the university administration with insensitivity for holding registration on the first day of classes on Rosh Hashonah or Yom Kippur, for including "A.D." (for *anno domini*, the year of our Lord) on diplomas, and for holding graduation on Saturdays so that Sabbath observers could not attend (a battle he lost).[65] "I don't think the University knew how to deal with Jews, Jewish ideas and Jewish community concepts," Groman stated. "Part of the education of the University was Arthur Jacobovitz's coming here and injecting all those issues into the University . . . I think he educated President Odegaard that there were Jews that were concerned with very specific things."[66] These efforts on behalf of a minority, of course, did not take place in a vacuum. This was the era of black and Hispanic demands for recognition in the university community as well.

Rabbi Jacobovitz brought Israeli and Zionist speakers to campus. When American Nazi George Lincoln Rockwell was invited by a student group to speak at the University in 1964, the Anti-Defamation League and other community groups tried to stop the event. Rabbi Jacobovitz, although hostile in his initial reaction, received a lesson in democracy from two of his board members, attorneys Mel Osran and Murray Guterson. In the end, the rabbi supported Rockwell's right to speak. The event took place, Jewish students packed the audience, and no damage was done by exposing Mr. Rockwell's ideas to the light of day.[67]

A coterie of Jewish students was energized by Rabbi Jacobovitz, particularly in the late 1960s and early 1970s, a time of great campus unrest and momentous events in Israel. The floating "Jewish table" in the HUB cafeteria and "Clark's College" at a nearby restaurant provided Jewish students with a forum for discussing the issues of the day with their energetic and provocative "rebbe" far into the night.[68]

Faculty and Jewish Studies

The expansion of higher education in postwar America, driven first by the GI Bill and later by the coming of age of the Baby Boom generation, afforded Jewish academics their first significant opportunities. A number of Jewish professors came to teach at the University of Washington, and more than a few rose to prominence. Sol Katz arrived on the University of Washington campus in 1936 as a teacher of ancient and Byzantine history. He left, more than fifty years later, as provost emeritus. Katz's skills in leadership posts helped turn the once-small state school into a major research university with national stature. Earl Benditt and Russell Ross, successive chairmen of the Pathology Department, and Arno Motulsky in Human Genetics, won international recognition. Jere Bacharach achieved distinction (History and Near East Studies), as did Melville Jacobs (Anthropology), Abe Keller (Romance Languages), David Bodansky (Physics), Walter Williams (Evans School of Public Affairs), Cyrus Rubin (Gastroenterology), and others too numerous to list.

Although some maintained close connections with the local Jewish community, joining congregations and organizations, many did not. Neal Groman, a professor of microbiology in the newly formed University of Washington School of Medicine and the son of an Orthodox rabbi, recalled, "there was almost no contact . . . between university faculty who were Jewish, and the community at large. In fact, I didn't think in those terms at the time. . . . I think we all wanted to live in this ivory tower and didn't want it invaded by the concerns of the community, particularly the Jewish community. Part of it had to do with career development."[69]

Disaffected from Seattle congregations, some university faculty hired the learned Jewish intellectual Arthur Lagawier to teach their children about their heritage. Neal Groman and Leo Sreebny of the Oral Biology Department joined the board of the Jewish Community Center in the 1950s and attempted to institute a program of Jewish education for religion schoolteachers, adults, and the children of Jews not affiliated with congregations. Arthur Lagawier was hired to teach and advise. However, opposition from the congregational rabbis halted the effort.[70]

Hillel director Rabbi Jacobovitz nurtured the idea of a Jewish Studies program for several years after taking up his post. He worked primarily with Professors Neal Groman and Leo Sreebny, and sometimes with Edward Stern (Physics) and with Howard Kaminsky (History), the only humanities professor involved in the early group. Students also participated.

In the spring of 1969, the rabbi and an ad hoc committee from Hillel challenged the administration with the idea that Jewish Studies was a legitimate field of study, proposing an ambitious program of courses.[71] Dean William Phillips of the College of Arts and Sciences sent copies of Hillel's proposal to the chairs of the appropriate departments for their comments, then encouraged Professor Sreebny to contact the chairs and interested faculty.[72] The university hired a temporary lecturer for a year to teach a Jewish history course in the fall of 1969, but the Hillel committee asked for a permanent, full-time Judaic scholar and an annual survey course on Jewish history. The committee also approached the English Department for an annual course on Jewish literature in translation.[73]

English Professor Edward Alexander responded positively with a list of authors who could be included in such a course and stated that he and Donald Kartiganer, both Jews, could be counted on to teach such a course.[74] In the spring of 1970, following a presentation by students, the Jewish Federation of Greater Seattle granted $3,000 to the university for the purchase of materials to support the Jewish Studies courses.[75]

By early 1971, Groman and other advocates believed that the idea of Jewish Studies had enough of a foothold that it was time to take up the cause within the university structure. Edward Alexander agreed to call a meeting of a small interdisciplinary group of professors to further the program.[76] The Hillel committee was dissolved in May 1971, and a faculty committee formed consisting of Alexander, Kaminsky, Kartiganer, Bacharach, Willis Konick (Russian and Comparative Literature), Rabbi Alan Podet, and Barry Scherr (Slavic Languages).[77] The University of Washington officially established the Jewish Studies program in 1974. Within a few years, the program found a secure and welcome home in the Jackson School of International Studies.

Rabbi Jacobovitz had opposed funding of Jewish Studies by the community at large because he believed that would diminish its legitimacy: if Jewish Studies was a field worthy of academic focus, then it was worthy of being treated like other fields of knowledge. But more practical heads prevailed. Jewish Studies at the University of Washington became an established program with the ability to quickly attract distinguished faculty largely because of the beneficence of Samuel and Althea Stroum. The Stroums endowed a chair in Jewish Studies and funded the annual Stroum Lectures, bringing prominent academics to lecture on Jewish subjects beginning in 1976. Several of the lecture series have been published by the University of Washington Press, including Y. H. Yerushalmi's *Zakhor: Jewish History and Jewish Memory,* Yehuda Bauer's *The Holocaust in Historical Perspective,* Joseph Dan's *Jewish Mysticism and Jewish Ethics,* Samuel C. Heilman's *Portrait of American Jews,* Michael Fishbane's *The Kiss of God,* Paula Hyman's *Gender and Assimilation in Modern Jewish History,* Alan Mintz's *Popular Culture and the Shaping of Holocaust Memory in America,* and Steven Zipperstein's *Imagining*

Russian Jewry. More recently, the Strouns created the Hazel D. Cole Fellowship in Jewish Studies to support postdoctoral and graduate fellows.

By 1980, Jewish organizations had succeeded in raising the consciousness of Jews and non-Jews to issues of Jewish concern in Washington State. The post–World War II era witnessed a new assertiveness of Jews and other minorities who refused to accept the old social and economic limits on their opportunities to share in America's bounty.

The most successful Jewish woman entrepreneur in the state of Washington in the postwar era was Nellie Curtis, also known as Yetta Solomon, among various other names. Past mistress of the world's oldest profession, she retired at age 71 to a beachfront residence in West Seattle purchased from jewel merchant Louis Friedlander in 1941. Curtis ran licensed houses of prostitution in Saskatchewan and British Columbia mining towns before she came to Seattle in the late 1920s. She owned the LaSalle Hotel at 83 Pike Street, an infamous brothel during World War II, and the Curtis Hotel in Aberdeen, reputedly the finest sporting house among that city's dozen establishments.

—"Nellie's Place: The IRS vs. The World's Oldest Profession," *Seattle Post-Intelligencer,* 19 March 1971

Expanding Religious Life

"**A** REMARKABLE RISE IN RELIGIOSITY" CHARACTERIZED postwar America, wrote historian Lucy S. Davidowicz in 1982. After the destruction of millions of Eastern European Jews, "the synagogue became, as it had been through the Jewish millennial past, the prime vehicle of Jewish continuity."[1] The attempts in Germany to annihilate the Jews resulted in the proliferation of Reform, Conservative, and Orthodox synagogues in postwar America. It was the Holocaust and its refugees and survivors, many Jewish historians point out, that revitalized Orthodoxy in the United States.[2]

The expansion of Jewish religious life in the aftermath of World War II occurred in the state of Washington as it did over all America. The grown children and grandchildren of Jewish pioneers, arrivals to the state from other parts of the country after World War II, and the influx of refugees and survivors of Hitler's Germany combined to set new directions in the state's Jewish communities. Young Jewish families began to step away from the patterns and prejudices of their parents' and grandparents' generations. The grandchildren of the pioneer families who had established Reform and the children of the immigrant Orthodox moved nearer to each other—residentially, occupationally, and culturally. The ideologies of Reform and of the developing Conservative movement converged in some important aspects, and both were inundated by new arrivals from both in and out of the country as the economy rapidly expanded.

Reflecting postwar growth and its resultant social changes, the expansion of Jewish religious life in Washington State is covered in this chapter from the first postwar new congregation in 1950 to the first Orthodox Hasidic organization in 1972. Within that time, the old Jewish neighborhood in Seattle's Central District gradually disappeared. Families moved to other parts of the city or to Bellevue and

Mercer Island, and new congregations came into being. The Central District's Conservative synagogue relocated to Mercer Island, and the city's major Orthodox synagogues concentrated in the Seward Park area at the south end of Lake Washington. In the new neighborhood as in the old, the Orthodox continued to preserve their traditional way of life: families kept kosher, people walked to shul, and women sat in the balcony for services. The founding of new congregations in the sprawling Seattle area and beyond occurred simultaneously with changes in Jewish communities outside Seattle. Some Orthodox synagogues in small cities shifted to Conservative practices, some Conservative and Reform congregations in larger cities combined, and smaller temples and synagogues throughout the state merged with larger ones of same orientation.

Richland's Beth Sholom built its house of worship in 1957 and was the first new congregation in the state after World War II. Its Torah, acquired in 1966, was rescued from Poland after the Nazi regime. The member-led services often included a dash of ingenuity, such as the occasional "Chocolate Friday" service "for kids of all ages," in which service was followed by ice-cream sundaes. Courtesy of Rhoda Lewis, Richland.

First Postwar New Congregations

The creation of new temple or synagogue congregations in postwar Washington State began with young Jewish families who for various reasons found the established temple or synagogue unsuited to their needs. And some, like the Jewish newcomers to Richland in the late 1940s, found that their new community had no religious accommodations for Jews.

The first postwar new congregation in the state was established in 1950 in the southeast Washington community of Richland, founded as a modern town in 1943. Just as nineteenth-century Jewish settlers created religious communities, so did the handful of young Jewish couples in Richland. But these settlers were twentieth-century professionals: engineers working for General Electric as part of the Hanford Engineer Works, which produced plutonium for nuclear bombs. Their wives were brides or young mothers. They started Richland's Jewish Congregation Beth Sholom in 1950 with eight families. Among the organizers were the first Jews to settle in Richland. They were Meyer and Tillie Elkins, Walt and Doris Lewis, Milt and Rhoda Lewis, Herb and Kathy Isbin, Harold and Dolly Greenfield, Milt

and Lillian Joffe, Hy and Maxine Radow, and Joe Katz. Despite their small numbers, and without the help of a rabbi, they set up a Sunday school and conducted their own services. They named their congregational newsletter the *Bagel Bugle*, and seven years later, with the congregation enlarged to twelve member families, they built Synagogue Beth Sholom. As they grew, they accumulated five sets of prayer books: Conservative, Orthodox, Reform, Sephardic, and

As Queen Esther in Richland's Beth Sholom 1960 Purim Carnival, seven-year-old Robin Lewis wore the crown her great grandfather, Louis Benson, had made for her grandmother, Minnie Benson Sussman, in Bay City, Michigan, in 1896. Courtesy of Rhoda Lewis, Richland.

*Elected leaders of Temple Beth Am after its creation in 1956. Temple Beth Am was
the first Reform congregation chartered in Seattle since the founding of Temple De
Hirsch in 1899. First row (from left): Bert Aronsberg, Lutz Lobe (president), Belle Ruth
Witkin, Howard Breskin, and Harold Thal. Second row: Bert Robinson, Gerald Cone,
Phil Shainman, Rabbi Joseph Messing (Army major stationed at Fort Lewis), Seymour
Kaplan, and Elmer Klein.* MSCUA/UWL, neg. 14612.

Reconstructionist, and used them all in turn.[3] While the Jewish population of
Richland remained more or less variable, with many Jewish families making their
homes there for only a limited time, Beth Sholom maintained a stable leadership.
Its membership roster grew to include families in Kennewick and Pasco, and also
Benton City, Prosser, Ephrata, and Moses Lake. The congregation remodeled and
enlarged their synagogue building in 1967. Richland's Beth Sholom would remain
unaffiliated until January 1983, when it joined the Conservative movement.[4]

It was a different story for a number of young Jewish families living in Seattle's
North End in the 1950s. In 1956 they created Temple Beth Am, the first Reform

congregation to be chartered in Seattle since the establishment of Temple De Hirsch in 1899. Until the rise of Beth Am, Temple De Hirsch embraced all Reform-minded Jews in the area of Seattle, Bellevue, and Mercer Island.

Beth Am originated with thirteen founding families living in the View Ridge neighborhood northeast of the University of Washington. They came together for a variety of reasons: partly geographical, partly religious practices, partly frustration with the politics of the established congregations. Former members of Temple De Hirsch, Herzl, or unaffiliated, about half had come to Seattle after World War II. An initial request to the board of Temple De Hirsch by two representatives, Gerald Cone and Dorothy Saran, to consider establishing a branch congregation in the northeast section of Seattle was declined since De Hirsch was deep in plans for its own expansion. Residents of the North End then decided to see whether there was enough interest in forming an independent congregation. An advertisement in the *University Herald* inviting anyone interested in forming a Jewish congregation in the North End to a Shabbat service on January 6, 1956, at Hillel House decided the matter. With twenty-five chairs set up for possible respondents, more than one hundred people arrived.

Beth Am affiliated with the Union of American Hebrew Congregations in July of 1956. An executive committee chaired by Belle Ruth Witkin headed the organization in its first steps. Aid to the fledgling congregation came from Temple De Hirsch in the form of the loan of a Torah, a gift of excess prayer books, and the encouragement of Rabbi Raphael L. Levine.[5] The new

Seattle Temple Beth Am's first confirmation class, 1959. From left: Steven Weiss, Robert Kaplan, Howard Lowen, and Risha Bay. Howard Lowen was the new Temple's first Bar Mitzvah. MSCUA/UWL, *neg. 19031.*

congregation sought a religious connection both intellectually stimulating and sensitive to social concerns, and specified a provision unusual for the time. Beth Am's first statement of organization called for equal participation by both men and women in religious services and in the affairs of the congregation.

The charter membership of thirty-four families doubled within two years and continued to grow. From Friday night home gatherings to services held at Hillel House to renting space at a Unitarian Church to the purchase of its own property took Temple Beth Am members nine years. Ludwig (Lutz) Lobe, who fled Germany in 1933, became the congregation's first president. Olga Butler, also a refugee from Germany, became Beth Am's first woman president in 1977.

Beth Am soon became the temple of choice for newcomers to Seattle associated with the University of Washington. Its mix of first generation Americans, émigrés, and arrivals from other parts of the country combined to form a congregation that shared common goals and interests.

During Beth Am's first year, Rabbi (Major) Joseph Messing, a chaplain in the U.S. Army at Fort Lewis, led the congregation. Robert L. Zimmerman, a graduate of the Hebrew Union College, assumed rabbinical duties for nearly a year more, and Rabbi Arthur Oles, from Cincinnati, Ohio, served as spiritual leader for the next four years. Rabbi Norman D. Hirsh followed in 1962. Hirsh's participation in a civil rights protest march in St. Augustine, Florida, in 1964 endeared him to his congregation and set the course for his thirty-three-year tenure with Beth Am.[6]

Expansions and Moves in Seattle

When Seattle's Orthodox synagogues, both Ashkenazic and Sephardic, began to move out of the Central District, Temple De Hirsch, the state's oldest and largest congregation, remained exactly where it was, just outside the heart of the old Jewish neighborhood. It responded to Seattle's postwar growth by enlarging its facilities. Despite the surrounding racial tensions and the flight of a number of its members to other areas, its decision to remain was a carefully thought out and conscious one. On May 24, 1959, De Hirsch began the building of a new sanctuary on its historic location at Fifteenth Avenue and East Pike. Designed by B. Marcus Priteca and Detlie & Peck architects, the impressive round edifice, suggesting a desert dwelling, featured stained-glass windows on two sides and a marble *bimah* (pulpit).[7]

Temple De Hirsch's board may have based its decision to stay not only on the advantages of enlarged facilities but also on the growing reputation of its spiritual leader, Rabbi Raphael L. Levine. A University of Minnesota law school graduate,

Levine gave up law to become a rabbi in the liberal Reform movement, although he had been brought up in a traditional Orthodox home. Following Rabbi Samuel Koch as senior rabbi of Temple De Hirsch, Levine worked in building religious understanding between Jews and Christians throughout the state of Washington and was in the forefront of the movement against racism and anti-Semitism in the Seattle community. For example, he invited Martin Luther King Jr. to speak at Temple De Hirsch when a Seattle church refused to hear King. Levine organized the Western Association of Reform Rabbis, taught at Protestant youth camps, and set up summer camping programs for Jewish youth on the Pacific Coast. He formed Camp Brotherhood near Mount Vernon with Catholic priest Father William Treacy, spoke from Christian church pulpits, and wrote articles and books both on Judaism and on his ideas of interfaith brotherhood.[8]

Designed by B. Marcus Priteca and architects Detlie & Peck, Seattle's Temple De Hirsch was built in 1960. Its impressive round edifice suggested a desert dwelling and featured stained-glass window walls on two sides and a marble bimah. Miriam Suttermeister, WSJHS.

Born in the middle of August 1901, in the Jewish ghetto of Vilna in Lithuania, Rabbi Raphael Levine of Seattle's Temple De Hirsch was the youngest of twelve children. He arrived in the United States at eight years of age full of fears of Russian pogroms and non-Jewish peers who called him "Zhid," "Sheeney," and "Christ-killer." Yet Levine grew up to believing that all men were brothers, and found lifelong friend-ships with a Catholic priest and a Protestant minister. MSCUA/UWL, *neg. 8831.*

A board member of the Rotary Club, United Good Neighbors, Washington Society of Crippled Children, Council for the Aging, and the Seattle Human Rights Commission, Levine led a People to People tour to Iron Curtain countries in 1963 and was instrumental in getting people of all faiths to contribute to a Seattle Brotherhood Forest in the Galilee, Israel.[9] "He was one of the greatest religious leaders the Northwest has ever known, particularly in the ecumenical field," said Father William Treacy. Rev. Bill Cate called Levine "an ambassador of religious brotherhood." And Rev. Oscar Rolander named him "the heart and soul of 'Challenge,'" an ongoing KOMO-TV program of informal religious discussions that featured a Catholic priest, a Protestant minister, and Rabbi Levine.[10]

During Levine's tenure as De Hirsch's rabbi, Jewish life in the area of Seattle and its surroundings changed dramatically. In 1958, a year before the groundbreaking ceremony of De Hirsch's new sanctuary, Sephardic Ezra Bessaroth members, led by Rabbi Isidore Kahan and Rev. David Behar, their spiritual leaders, celebrated the completion of the first half of their new building in Seward Park. Ezra Bessaroth was the first congregation to move out of the old Jewish neighborhood. The move followed forty years on Fifteenth Avenue and East Fir Street in the synagogue built by a handful of immigrants from the island of Rhodes. Designed by Seattle architect Ted LaCourse for the site at Wilson Avenue and Brandon Street, the new synagogue evolved in two phases. The first comprised building an all-purpose hall that would seat three hundred for such events as weddings, Bar and Bat Mitzvah receptions, and larger numbers for plays or meetings, a small chapel, six classrooms, a caretaker's apartment, offices, kitchen, and coatroom. Rabbi William Greenberg, as spiritual head, led the second celebration marking the completed

Speaking Yiddish as well as Ladino, Sephardic Bikur Holim's Rabbi Solomon Maimon easily connected with both the Ashkenazic and Sephardic communities. As a senior rabbi in the American Sephardic world and the first made-in-America Sephardic rabbi, Rabbi Maimon became a consultant to communities all over the country, including those in Detroit, Chicago, Los Angeles, and Houston. Seattle Museum of History and Industry.

sanctuary in 1970. In keeping with the Orthodox tradition, the finished building provided separate seating for women at the rear of the one-level sanctuary space.[11]

With many members already living in the neighborhood of Seward Park, Seattle's Sephardic Bikur Holim, headed by Rabbi Solomon Maimon since 1945, dismissed consideration of renovation of its thirty-five-year-old synagogue at Twentieth Avenue and East Fir Street. Rabbi Maimon was five years old and the youngest of eight children when his Tekirdag family arrived in Seattle and his father, Rabbi Abraham Maimon, became spiritual leader of the Sephardic synagogue. Starting in Seattle's Pacific Elementary School for non-English-speaking immigrant children, Solomon Maimon graduated from Garfield High School, attended Yeshiva University in New York City, and became the first Sephardic Jew

Larry Hamlin and Lea Behar, daughter of Elazar Behar and granddaughter of Rev. David Behar, exchanged marriage vows before the Ark of Seattle's Sephardic Ezra Bessaroth Synagogue, June 13, 1971. The first synagogue to move from the old Jewish neighborhood to the Seward Park area, Ezra Bessaroth was designed by Seattle architect Ted LaCourse. Construction started in 1958 and was completed in 1970. Courtesy of Elazar Behar.

in America to receive a *s'micha* (ordination). Fluent in Yiddish as well as Ladino, the first made-in-America Sephardic rabbi easily bridged the differences between the Sephardic and Ashkenazic communities and was a significant influence in the growth of Hebrew education in Seattle.

In 1959, the congregation sold its building to a Baptist church and purchased property on Fifty-second Avenue South and South Morgan Street, but construction didn't start until 1963. Construction management fell to six members headed by Tom Bensussen. Waiting for their synagogue to be erected, those members living in the Seward Park district formed their own *minyan* and prayed in an old house located on the synagogue's property. "After that house was demolished," reported one, "an old house across Morgan Street from the property was rented and it served as our 'branch' for quite some time. Rabbi Solomon Maimon would send *hazanim* from our old synagogue to conduct services in the 'branch' every weekend." [12]

The new Sephardic Bikur Holim synagogue, designed by architect B. Marcus Priteca with assistance from Ben Stertzer, opened to its members in September 1965 with Rabbi Solomon Maimon presiding. Even though the congregation moved into the synagogue months before the benches ordered for the sanctuary arrived, the members agreed that "Dedication day was one of the most glorious days in the entire history of the Sephardic Bikur Holim Congregation." Special guest Dr. Haham Gaon, chief rabbi of Great Britain, arrived from England for the occasion. Young men who had become Bar Mitzvah during that year carried the *sefarim* (Torahs) from the branch to the new sanctuary accompanied by "fanfare, songs, dancing and great jubilation." In the spirit of tradition, members made gifts of money through symbolic purchases with the funds going to the synagogue. The Funes family bought a "key" to the synagogue in honor of their parents, Jack and Julia Funes; and Ben Mezistrano purchased the honor of the first reading of the Sefer Torah. Located only a few blocks from Ezra Bessaroth, their sister synagogue, Sephardic Bikur Holim Congregation grew so fast in its new location that fund raising for a larger social hall began after little more than a dozen years. [13]

The first Ashkenazic Bikur Cholim members who moved to the Seward Park district in the 1950s met unexpected opposition when they requested help from their parent shul in setting up a branch in their new neighborhood. The old *shul* members at Seventeenth Avenue and Yesler Street, ignoring the changing neighborhood and clinging to the hope that the larger part of their membership would continue to sustain them, gave little encouragement to members who left. Forming a minyan, the transplanted Bikur Cholim members found a temporary home in the facilities of the nearby Kline Galland Home. They named the fledgling stand-

The new Sephardic Bikur Holim synagogue, designed by architect B. Marcus Priteca with assistance from Ben Stertzer, opened in the Seward Park area in 1965. The strikingly simple Ark forms the heart of its sanctuary. Miriam Suttermeister, WSJHS.

in congregation "Yavneh" (the name of a town which became the center of learning after the destruction of the Second Temple in Jerusalem in 70 C.E.). Acquiring
a six-month lease on a house in the neighborhood, they created a formal group
with Charles Jassen as president, Ben Willner as treasurer, and the gratis services of
Rabbi Samuel Graudenz, then principal of the Seattle Hebrew Day School. "What
a labor of love that house became!" wrote Adina Russak. "Every Friday, Shirley
Jassen . . . , Cecilia Willner, Eva Graudenz and I would schlep our cleaning gear
from home; pails, vacuum cleaner, brushes and mops and clean Yavneh on hands
and knees to get it ready for the Sabbath (while I paid a woman to clean my own
home!)"[14]

As more and more Ashkenazic Orthodox Jews from the Central District followed their Sephardic brethren to Seward Park, Yavneh outgrew the rented house.
Once again, Yavneh appealed to their parent *shul* to establish Yavneh as a branch
of Bikur Cholim and for aid in buying a lot for a synagogue, and once again received rejection. Undaunted, they found space for a time in the basement of Ezra
Bessaroth. With the Ashkenazic shul on Yesler steadily losing members as families moved out of the district, Bikur Cholim leaders could not continue to ignore
Yavneh's success. "The inevitable finally happened," said Russak. In 1962, Yavneh
merged with Congregation Bikur Cholim and became known as the Seward Park
Branch of Bikur Cholim.[15]

In a very few years the branch became the location of Bikur Cholim itself.
Lorraine Sidell wrote of the closing of the Central District's Ashkenazic Bikur
Cholim *shul* and its move to the area at the south end of Lake Washington:

In 1970 the synagogue building on Yesler was sold and its last services were held on
Sunday morning, October 30. Louis Katsman blew the Shofar there for the last time,
ending an historic era for the Orthodox community of Seattle. The building became
the home of the Langston Hughes Cultural Art Center for use as a neighborhood facility. . . . Groundbreaking for the new synagogue on South Morgan Street was held on
February 28, 1971.[16]

In November 1971, the Seward Park Branch of Bikur Cholim merged with
Machzikay Hadath, the only Orthodox *shul* remaining in the Central District
neighborhood. Evolved from a coterie of Orthodox Jews who, with their beloved
Rabbi Baruch Shapiro, left Herzl when it turned from Orthodox to Conservative,
Machzikay Hadath was founded in 1930 "to be more strictly Orthodox than any
other congregation in the city." It's name meant "strengtheners, supporters and
promoters." With the death of Rabbi Shapiro on November 13, 1970, and the
growing emigration of members from the changing neighborhood, the synagogue

began to erode. "The rabbi's original *chassidim* (most pious men) were passing away, and when the *chassidim* died, we lost the sense of being a community," said Mannie Schreiber, whose parents, Isador and Amy, were founding members. The old-world rabbi's major beneficiary at his death was his beloved Congregation Machzikay Hadath. In the merger, the eighty-year-old Bikur Cholim changed its name to Congregation Bikur Cholim–Machzikay Hadath. It thus preserved the memory of the congregation whose history was part of the Jewish experience in the Pacific Northwest.[17]

Like the Orthodox synagogues which followed their members to Seward Park, Herzl Conservative Synagogue followed its members to Mercer Island when it left the vanishing Jewish neighborhood in 1967.

Other New Seattle-Area Congregations

In little more than a dozen years after the founding of Temple Beth Am, six new congregations sprang up in Seattle, Bellevue, and Mercer Island. They were Conservative Beth Shalom and Modern Orthodox Emanuel in Seattle's North End, Conservative Ner Tamid and Reform Sinai in Bellevue, Reform B'nai Torah on Mercer Island, and the Chasidic Chabad House in Seattle's University District.

Beth Shalom came out of Herzl's decision in 1967 to relocate from the Central Area to Mercer Island, isolating the congregation's North End Conservative members. With a traditional congregation no longer available to them north of the Seward Park area and west of Lake Washington, four families—Jerome and Dorothy Becker, Norman and Shirley Rosenzweig, Murray and Fran Finkelstein, and Edward and Sylvia Stern—began plans for the establishment of a new congregation conveniently located near where they lived. Other families in the area quickly joined the group and less than a year later, on February 29, 1968, Beth Shalom incorporated as the first Conservative congregation in Seattle's North End.[18]

Without a rabbi, and being a highly participatory community of individuals committed to Judaism and to the congregation, lay members conducted services and did everything else that needed to be done in a young and almost fundless congregation. Intent on hiring a cantor for their first High Holiday observance, they rented and manned a fireworks stand at 185th Street and Aurora Avenue to earn enough to pay the cantor. Despite having to hire non-Jews to keep the stand open on the Saturday before the Fourth of July, the plan was so successful that they repeated the experience the following year.[19]

Moving from rental rooms in the Blessed Sacrament Catholic Church school building to a rented church on Thirty-fifth Avenue Northeast, the growing congregation soon faced the choice of either buying the property or hiring a rabbi. Reasoned Jerome Becker: "We decided that it would be impractical to hire a rabbi if we didn't have a place to hang his hat. So we bought the building first. . . . We were gambling on the fact that we would get enough members to pay for [the] building, which we did."[20]

The building at 6800 Thirty-fifth Avenue Northeast, purchased in 1973, became the congregation's permanent home, and the group functioned without a rabbi for six more years. "We have always been proud of being a 'do it yourself' synagogue," wrote Dorothy Becker, Beth Shalom's first woman president elected in 1977. Reform Beth Am's Olga Butler and Conservative Beth Shalom's Dorothy Becker became the first women to preside over congregations in Seattle. During Becker's presidency, Beth Shalom hired Rabbi Ira Stone, its first permanent rabbi, and effected an important change in its Conservative ritual by encouraging women to participate fully in synagogue practices, including reading the Torah and leading prayer services.[21]

The move of Ashkenazic Bikur Cholim from central Seattle to the far south area of Seward Park in 1968 left Orthodox Jews living in the northeast of Seattle without a place to regularly attend services. Three members of Bikur Cholim, Irwin P. Lawson, Jack Steinberg, and Leon Schlossberg (whose father had been a cantor at Bikur Cholim), founded Modern Orthodox Congregation Emanuel, the first Orthodox congregation in northeast Seattle. "Modern" referred to the mixed seating policy and the minimal use of English in the prayers. Services followed traditional Ashkenazic Orthodox liturgy using Orthodox prayer books. Emanuel was the first Modern Orthodox and the only continuously lay-led congregation in the city.[22]

Emanuel's organizational meeting and its first service were held at Hillel House in March and April 1968. The thirteen families attending rose to twenty-six families by the end of the year. Two years after it began, Congregation Emanuel moved its services from Hillel House to a small building of its own on Northeast Sixty-fifth Street just off Thirty-fifth Avenue Northeast.[23] With only one paid worker to complete the wiring and plumbing to required code, congregational members reconstructed the building. The small synagogue thrived with no official rabbi and a nominal dues structure. Members performed all functions, including the duties of a rabbi, and men and women sat together in the main section of the sanctuary, although a section of separated seating was available as well. "The members take great pride in the do-it-yourself aspect of the synagogue," said

Rosalie Sidell Steinbrecher. The do-it-yourself aspect included the Torah table, the Ark, and the lectern, all from the hands of Schlossberg and his television repair shop employee. (At a later remodeling, these would go to the Seattle Hebrew Day School.) Children of members attended The Seattle Hebrew Academy for religious instruction, Bar and Bat Mitzvahs were conducted by the president of the shul, and wedding ceremonies were performed by a guest rabbi.[24]

Bellevue's Ner Tamid, a Conservative synagogue affiliated with the United Synagogue of America, formed in 1965 mainly to serve the growing number of Jewish families living in the area associated with Boeing. By October 1, 1968, its adult membership reached 280. Led by Rabbi Gilbert Kollin, who acted not only as cantor but occasionally as *shamus* (custodian) and all-around handyman, Ner Tamid's membership waxed and waned in rhythm with Boeing's employment practices. "Let's face it," were the frank words of President M. L. Bovarnick in the *Ner Tamid Hi-Lites*. "On the whole, we are a three-day-a-year congregation with a Hebrew School. We barely make a *minyan* on Shabbat and holidays. . . ." Ner Tamid merged with Herzl Congregation to form Herzl Ner Tamid Conservative Congregation in 1970.[25]

The new Herzl Ner Tamid congregation celebrated ground breaking for a new synagogue on the eastern shore of Mercer Island on June 7, 1970. When the first High Holiday services were held in September 1971, a series of Chagall-inspired stained glass windows created by local glass artist Steven Shahbaghlian in collaboration with Manny Lott, a longtime member, fronted the new synagogue. The theater-style structure seated four hundred and featured a movable *bimah*, which increased the seating capacity to 1,100. James Chiarelli was the architect. The Ark and the Eternal Light were the work of artist Phillip Levine.[26]

In 1961 members of Seattle's Temple De Hirsch living on the east side of Lake Washington founded Bellevue's Temple Sinai. It existed as an independent Reform congregation for almost a decade at 556 124th Avenue Northeast, then merged in 1971 with its parent temple and continued in its Bellevue location as a branch. The merger changed both temples' names to Temple De Hirsch Sinai.[27]

A rift between Associate Rabbi Jacob Singer and the Temple De Hirsch board in 1968 resulted in his severance from the Seattle temple and the creation of a Reform congregation on Mercer Island. Congregation B'nai Torah formed in 1969 under the rabbinical leadership of Jacob Singer and a coterie of loyal followers. The first meeting place was a Presbyterian church on Island Crest Way; the first Ark was a child's toy box which Singer's wife, Raida, had lined with silk; and the first Torah was a small scroll "that a Jew had wrapped around his body escaping Hitler's Europe." Two years later, with a membership of about a hundred families,

B'nai Torah moved its services to Mercer Island's Jewish Community Center, and the congregation began planning a building of its own. Designed by architect David Gray, a friend of the Singer family, the new home of B'nai Torah opened in 1974. Artist Rene Soulard designed and carved the Ark with funding from Samuel and Althea Stroum; member Archie Graber designed and sculpted the Ner Tamid, the ever-burning light.[28]

Three years later, a malicious prank by two seventeen-year-old boys playing with fire almost destroyed the young Temple B'nai Torah. Holding the Torahs he had rescued by rushing into the blaze and carrying them out in his arms, Rabbi Singer declared, "We will rebuild." Both the Ark and the Ner Tamid (eternal light) survived the fire, but not without scars. Mercer Island's large Jewish community rallied to the young congregation's aid, and the rebuilt Temple B'nai Torah, designed by Mervin (Sonny) Gorasht, was dedicated in 1979.[29]

An even greater trial, however, lay in store for B'nai Torah. Rabbi Singer's death from cancer left the congregation bereft until a member of the congregation, David Serkin, stepped forth to help. A cantor before moving to Seattle, Serkin rallied the saddened families, taught the Bar and Bat Mitzvah students, and served as spiritual leader until Rabbi James Mirel was hired from Temple De Hirsch Sinai, where he had been serving as associate rabbi. Under the leadership of Rabbi Mirel and Cantor Serkin, B'nai Torah, which relocated to Bellevue in the late 1990s, would continue to grow and become one of the area's most vital religious institutions.[30]

The arrival of New York's Rabbi Sholom Ber Levitin to Seattle in 1972 to establish a regional office of the Chabad-Lubavitch Chassidic movement testified

Rabbi Sholom Ber Levitin added another dimension to Judaic worship in Seattle after he transferred his household from New York in 1972 and established the first Chassidic Orthodox congregation, Shaarei Tefilah-Lubabvitch, in Washington State. Seattle Museum of History and Industry.

*Rabbi Jacob
Singer and his son,
Adam, rescued
Torahs from the
burning B'nai
Torah Temple on
Mercer Island in
1976. MSCUA/UWL,
neg. 18960.*

to the postwar rise of Orthodoxy in the United States. Levitin established Chabad House in the University District. The Chabad House featured services in Hebrew and English "permeated with warm song and intellectual stimulation" and served as headquarters for the Lubavitch movement in the Pacific Northwest. Rabbi Levitin served as regional rabbi, and his assistant, Rabbi Y. Samuels, was rabbi-in-residence. Levitin established Washington State's first Chassidic Orthodox congregation, Shaarei Tefilah-Lubavitch, in temporary quarters, and it later became the state's first Chassidic synagogue and *mikvah* built in the North End of Seattle.[31]

The Chabad-Lubavitch organization, with which the local Chassidic synagogue (and those in Portland, Los Angeles, and other cities) are affiliated, is active worldwide. Its outreach is a continued presence on college campuses across the country. One of the hallmarks of the Chassidic movement is to go beyond theoretical teachings with the use of story and song to express Jewish heritage and tradition.[32]

With its Chabad House, a *heder*, campus and neighborhood outreach efforts, and its Congregation Shaarei Tefilah-Lubavitch, the Chabad-Lubovitchers added a different dimension to Jewish religious life in Washington State. Men and boys with earlocks, dressed in long black coats and black brimmed hats, walking from their homes to services soon became a familiar sight to both Jews and non-Jews in the View Ridge neighborhood in Seattle's North End. Although the garb, adapted from eighteenth-century Polish nobility, may have seemed somewhat out of place

Tacoma's Temple Beth El was created by the merger of Sinai and Beth Israel. It stands surrounded by green lawns in Tacoma's growing West End at 5975 South Twelfth Street. Pictured here in 1968, the sanctuary was built around the Ark, a fifty-five-foot-high tower on the east wall. Courtesy of Temple Beth El, Tacoma.

to residents in late-twentieth-century Seattle, many enjoyed the addition of this colorful branch of Judaism.

Mergers in Tacoma and Spokane

Postwar changes, newcomers, and the maturing of new generations of Americanized Jewish children affected religious development in cities like Tacoma and Spokane, where the temple and synagogue had maintained their separateness for more than forty years. In both Tacoma and Spokane, the Reform temple combined with the Conservative synagogue.

In Tacoma, the offspring of the founding members of the temple and synagogue grew up aware of the tensions between the two establishments. The merger of Tacoma's two congregations was not an instant or easy step for either Reform Beth Israel or for Conservative Sinai, founded as the Orthodox Talmud Torah Synagogue. Not until the arrival of Rabbi Baruch I. Treiger in 1938 as spiritual leader of the Talmud Torah did the tension between the Reform and the Conservative congregations begin to change.[33]

The change, according to men and women who had been teenagers at the time, had its beginnings in the formation of the Junior League of Talmud Torah. "Rabbi Treiger brought the youth of the entire community together," said Josephine Kleiner Heiman, whose father had long been a respected member of both the temple and the synagogue. "We met every Sunday night in the vestry of the Talmud Torah."[34] "We started out with only nine members," said Rhoda Sussman Lewis, first president of the organization, "and by the end of the year we were up to twenty-five members."[35] The friendships made between the youth of the synagogue and the youth of the temple through the Junior League, as well as the AZA boys' group and B'nai B'rith girls' groups which followed, provided much of the strength for the merger, said Heiman.

When talk of combining the Conservative and Reform congregations began, some of Sinai's original Orthodox members strongly rejected the idea. An attempt to merge the two congregations in the forties failed. When the fifties began, the community was still at a stalemate, and a few elderly members steadfastly refused to accept such a change.

Tacoma's Reform Temple Beth El finally formed in 1960 from the merger of Beth Israel and Sinai under the rabbinical leadership of Rabbi Richard Rosenthal. The handsome new temple stood at 5975 South Twelfth Street surrounded by green grounds and ample parking space, and it had 150 member families when it opened.[36] As one pioneer family member put it, "We have become one family."[37]

Like Tacoma, Spokane's two Jewish congregations also became one institution. In 1966, Reform Temple Emanu-El, formed by the early German Jews, and
Conservative Keneseth Israel Synagogue, established by Orthodox Polish, Russian,
and Ukrainian Jewish immigrants, merged as a liberal Conservative synagogue
affiliated with United Synagogue of America. The friction that had existed in
which the synagogue kids were thought of as "poor cousins" and the temple kids as
"haughty and rich" "really didn't pass," said Betty Meyersberg, "until the merging
of the temple and synagogue." As was true all over the country, Reform congrega-

*The combining of Spokane's Temple Emanu-El and Keneseth Israel Synagogue resulted
in the building of the beautiful house of worship Beth Shalom, at Thirtieth and Perry
in 1968. Shown are the doors of the remodeled Ark. Courtesy of Temple Beth Shalom
Archives, Spokane.*

Spokane's Temple Beth Shalom celebrated its first confirmation ceremony in its new structure May 1969. Girls (from left): Michelle Bartman, Adele Levitch, Kathy Hannes, Wendy Sherman, Debra Hindin, and Barbara Selcer. Boys (from left): Mike Rubens, Ken Tatt, Steve Walker, Phil Avnet, Joel Arick. Rabbi Isaac Celnik is on far left. Courtesy of Temple Beth Shalom Archives, Spokane.

tions had become more traditional (its members began to wear *kepot* and *tallitot* for example), and Conservative congregations became "somewhat more Liberal." [38] Still, there were twenty-one main areas of difference between the two existing congregations concerning religious rituals, interpretation of the Halacha (Jewish law), and many aspects of Jewish conduct, education, and living. All were resolved under the sage guidance of two community leaders, Joe Rosenfield, who had moved to Spokane from Seattle in 1935 as city manager for Evergreen Theaters, and Abe Huppin, president of Keneseth Israel Synagogue and son of one of its founders, Samuel Huppin. [39] "The new congregation will combine many of the practices and teachings of the Conservative and Reform branches of the Jewish faith," announced Hy Nelson, last president of Temple Emanu-El. The combined congregations became Temple Beth Shalom, with recently ordained Rabbi Gilbert Kollin as spiritual leader, and Joe Rosenfield as president.[40]

The razing of the Keneseth Israel Synagogue at Fourth and Adams because it was in the path of the new I-90 east-west freeway, and the sale of Temple Emanu-El's Corinthian-style temple at Eighth and Walnut to Plymouth Congregational Church paved the way for the construction of the combined new synagogue, which opened in May 1968. In the new Temple Beth Shalom at Thirtieth and Perry, elements of both old buildings became essential parts of the new. Emanu-El's stained glass windows formed the doors of the new Ark, and Keneseth Israel's menorahs and sanctuary seats found a place in the new chapel. The new Ark housed the Torah scrolls of both synagogues, and the new library combined the books of the two parent libraries.[41]

As "the only synagogue in town," Temple Beth Shalom became the Jewish community center of the greater Spokane area. The Annual Kosher Dinner (originating with Temple Emanu-El's Sisterhood in 1940) thrived there, members of the Spokane chapter of Hadassah and members of the Jewish Women International (formerly B'nai B'rith Women's Center) met there, and adult education classes and workshops became part of the regular activities.[42]

As in Tacoma and Spokane, Jewish communities throughout the state after World War II felt changes brought on by the stimulation of growing prosperity, liberalizing ideas, and the magic carpet of burgeoning freeways. In some small communities, only a handful of members kept the old shul going as older members began to die and children of founding members moved away to larger cities. New young families who were part of the flow of newcomers to the Northwest rejuvenated many smaller Jewish communities, sometimes causing a change in direction in the religious focus of the established congregations.

Changes in Olympia and Bellingham

In both Olympia and Bellingham, congregations gradually shifted from Orthodox to Conservative and then to Reform. In Everett the congregation went from Orthodox to Conservative, and in Centralia-Chehalis, the Orthodox congregation moved to Reform. In Walla Walla, as in Richland's formative years, the congregation achieved a comfortable compromise for its small but diverse membership by using a variety of prayer books.

Although Olympia's early-arriving German Jews created the state's first Jewish cemetery in 1874, the Eastern European Orthodox Jews arriving around 1900 established Olympia's first Jewish congregation. Beth Hatfiloh, built in 1938 at Eighth Avenue and Jefferson Street, was a realized dream for Russian émigré Jacob Bean and a fitting and permanent home for his treasured Torah scrolls. Through the previous two decades and more, he had personally cared for the Sefer Torahs in his home and carried them to the rented Labor Temple or Eagles Hall for such events as High Holy Day services.[43]

Earl Bean, Jacob Bean's grandson, with the help of Jacob Goldberg, Reuben Cohn, and others, spearheaded the building campaign in 1937. Known for his support of numerous charitable organizations and churches in the Olympia area, Earl often said that Beth Hatfiloh could never have been built without the help of Olympia's Gentile merchants.

Olympia's completed house of worship arose as an amalgamation of both Reform-minded and Orthodox Jews. The elder Bean and Austria-born Orthodox Jacob Goldberg agreed to the reading of prayers in English in the new structure "just so long as you do the whole thing in Hebrew first." Dedicated as Temple Beth Hatfiloh, Rabbi Samuel Koch of Seattle's Temple De Hirsch officiated and its fifteen-voiced choir sang at the services. Appropriately, it seemed to many, Percy and Annie Bean were the first couple to be married in the combined synagogue-temple.[44]

Beth Hatfiloh would not have a rabbi of its own until the 1980s. For a time beginning in 1935, the Jews of Olympia and the Jews of Aberdeen shared the services of Rabbi Albert Wolff, chief rabbi of Dresden who fled Germany and Nazi persecution. However, Rabbi Wolff found his role as rabbi of the two communities, many of whose members were traditional Jews, difficult. Eventually he moved on to a permanent pulpit in an all German-Jewish congregation in Chicago.[45]

During the war years, with Fort Lewis on its doorstep, Olympia's congregation opened its doors to transplanted Jewish soldiers and their families. Temple Beth Hatfiloh provided weekly Sunday dinners for Jewish service people and their families. "Our homes were open to pinochle-playing husbands on a free evening," said Eva Goldberg, "with wives sharing recipes and discussing how to rear their small children and babies."[46]

Olympia's Beth Hatfiloh, although mainly Orthodox in its approach to Judaism until well after World War II, gradually shifted its religious focus to an informal mixture of Conservative and Reform worship. In the seventies, Temple Beth Hatfiloh's lay leader Samuel Schnall's Orthodox background combined with a sensitivity to liberal Judaism helped reconcile the variety of viewpoints among the membership. With no full-time rabbi, Beth Hatfiloh's neighboring rabbis and Jewish leaders often lent a hand. They included Rabbi Raphael L. Levine of

Seattle, Rabbi Joshua Stampfer of Portland, Oregon, Robert and Michael Maslan of Seattle, and others. Rabbi Richard Rosenthal of Temple Beth El in Tacoma came to Olympia every other Tuesday to hold Hebrew classes for the children. He assisted with guidelines for setting up a Hebrew school, conducted special Torah services for the congregation's students, and was available at times of sorrow "to provide . . . comfort, understanding, and the healing effects of compassion." Temple Beth Hatfiloh presented Rabbi Rosenthal with a gift "for all his kindnesses to the Olympia congregation." "His greatest gift," wrote Eva Goldberg, "was undoubtedly the affection of the congregation."[47]

Olympia's Beth Hatfiloh would remain unaffiliated up until the year 2000. Although it joined the Reconstructionist Movement, it continued to encompass Reconstructionist, Reform, and traditional styles in turn. Rabbi Vicki Hollander became the first part-time rabbi for the temple in 1985, and in 1990, Rabbi Marna Sapsowitz became its first full-time rabbi in the temple's fifty-three-year history.

The renovation of Bellingham's Beth Israel synagogue in the early 1960s reflected the congregation's move to a more liberal religious focus as new residents joined. The renovation moved the *bimah* from the center of the sanctuary and removed the *mikvah* in the basement.[48] Orthodox until after World War II, Beth Israel's first change came with the arrival of Cantor Frederick S. Gartner as a part-time tutor for Bellingham's Bar Mitzvah students. Although not officially a rabbi, Gartner eventually assumed other rabbinical duties and led the congregation's shift to a more Conservative mode. "Women were no longer restricted to the balcony during services, and only one member walked out when they were first invited down by Cantor Gartner," noted Bellingham historian Tim Baker. Under Cantor Gartner's leadership, Beth Israel members began a program of informative talks to the mostly Christian Bellingham community, speaking to schools and civic organizations about Judaism, the Holocaust, and Jewish culture. Frances Glazer Garmo, daughter of founder Benjamin David Glazer, talked to a variety of school and community groups. Many years later, she still recalled with a shiver a question asked about Passover matzos in a small town out in the county: "Do you still use blood?" It was a shocking echo of nineteenth-century Czarist Russia where Jews were falsely accused of using Christian blood in making matzos.[49]

Although Bellingham's Beth Israel changed its orientation to become more in line with the Conservative movement, it did not formally affiliate with the United Synagogue of America. Its second change would come in 1987, when Reform Rabbi Michael Oblath became head of the congregation, and Beth Israel affiliated with the Union of American Hebrew Congregations, the Reform movement. However, a few members, uncomfortable with Beth Israel's change of direction, continued to use the more Conservative prayer books and to *daven* (pray) in the style more familiar to them. In 1993, they left to create a new, small congregation, Eytz Chaim, affiliated with the United Synagogue of Conservative Judaism.⁵⁰

Changes in Centralia, Walla Walla, and Everett

Adath Israel, built by twenty-five Jewish families of Centralia and Chehalis from 1930 to 1931 (with a clause in the contract forbidding the contractor from working on Saturdays), changed to Reform in the 1950s and replaced its Orthodox prayer books. A Sunday school organized by Marcia Cohn, a local businesswoman, had been held for some time before the temple was built, alternating between Centralia and Chehalis. The confirmands went to Seattle to receive their certificates with the confirmation class of Temple De Hirsch. With no full-time rabbi, confirmands continued to go to Seattle for ceremonies for some years after Adath Israel was built. Founding member David Robinson led weekly Friday night minyans; guest rabbis conducted High Holy Day services; and enthusiastic members of the women's auxiliary put on Purim festivals, Chanukah parties, and pageants, as well as Sukkoth festivals and Simhath Torah celebrations.⁵¹

Gradually, however, the Jewish community of Centralia/Chehalis dwindled. "People started moving away or dying off," said Harold Schwartz, one of the last remaining members. Children of founding members left Centralia and Chehalis for the bigger cities of Seattle and Portland, and Temple Adath Israel would finally close its doors in 1994.⁵²

Even though Walla Walla in the mid-1800s was the center of three of the first Jewish business operations in Washington Territory, its Jewish community remained so small that a formal congregation was not established until the late 1930s. Built in December 1940, the synagogue, named for a prominent Jewish merchant, was called the Beth Israel Myer Youdovitch Memorial. Its spiritual leader,

> David Robinson, a native of Poland and one of the first Jews to settle in Centralia, served as cantor for members of the Orthodox congregation who gathered together in a rented place to celebrate the holidays. His son Jerry recalled fasting through a Yom Kippur service held at a store over a bakery: "I almost died smelling those freshly made maple bars as I came down the stairs during Yom Kippur services."
>
> — *The Jewish Transcript*, 22 November 1991

Rabbi Franklin Cohn, came with his family to the United States in 1939, escaping Hitler's Germany. Cohn served Walla Walla's Jewish community for two years, subsidizing his income by working as a bookkeeper, and later moved to Seattle's Herzl Congregation. Samuel L. Chernis, for many years a leading figure in the affairs of Walla Walla's small Jewish community, was Beth Israel's first president.

With several military bases in the area, membership in Walla Walla's Beth Israel congregation greatly increased during World War II. Rabbi Lee Levinger, a United Service Organization representative recruited by the Jewish Welfare Board, served servicemen in the area as well as the Jewish community, which included not only Walla Walla but the Pasco-Kennewick area in Washington and the towns of Pendleton and LaGrande in Oregon. Although the congregation used the Reform *Hebrew Union Prayer Book*, men wore *kepot* and *tallitot* (a practice not seen in Reform temples at that time), and at least one grandmother read from her own Orthodox prayer book. "Everything was accepted in this small congregation," said community leader Alan L. Barer.[53] Led by community members and other lay leaders after the war, Beth Israel remained a small but vital Jewish unit in eastern Washington.[54]

Until the late thirties, Everett's community of fifty or sixty families held weekly services at Montefiore Congregation and conducted regular religious classes for the children. The membership of the synagogue began to dwindle as elder members died and many of the young people went away to college. "They didn't come back here," said Moe Michelson, a business leader who served on the city council for sixteen years and whose parents came to Everett from Latvia in 1906. Michelson observed that Everett's Jewish young people began going to Seattle for both synagogue and social activities. "The highway made the change," said Michelson. "It's a half hour to Temple in Seattle . . . or to Herzl."[55]

Although Everett's Montefiore Congregation would continue on into the eighties and move from Orthodox tradition to Conservative, the demise of the dwindling congregation was in sight even before the seventies had passed. The young Jews settling in or around Everett, working at the Boeing installation, did not even enter the doors of the old shul. Quite a few of the new families consisted of one Jewish and one non-Jewish partner. Nevertheless, the still mostly Orthodox members of Montefiore invited the newcomers to become part of their congregation. "We told them, they don't have to be a strong Orthodox," said William (Billy) Sturman, a longtime shul member.

But wanting to raise their children as Jews, and knowing that Orthodox only considered children born of Jewish mothers as Jews, Rennie Karr and his non-Jewish wife, Janet, decided to start a synagogue in Everett that could wholeheartedly welcome people like them and their four young children. As the seventies neared an end, the Karrs and others set about establishing Temple Beth Or, which affiliated with the national Reform organization movement. Formed in 1985, two years after the Reform movement began recognizing children of Jewish fathers as born-Jews, Beth Or became Everett's first new congregation in seventy years. Rabbi Vicki Hollander, Beth Or's part-time rabbi who also served Olympia's Beth Hatfiloh, was the first woman rabbi in Washington State to have a pulpit of her own.[56]

The Significant Seventies

Another great expansion of Jewish religious life in Washington State started in the 1970s and accelerated into the 1990s. In this period, striking changes in Jewish worship caused little if any surprise. In Everett, for example, half the couples of the new Temple Beth Or had only one partner who was Jewish, a reflection of the growing trend of interfaith marriages in Washington State and around the country. Beth Or's appointment of Rabbi Vicki Hollander gave little pause to anyone and was soon followed by other congregations choosing women rabbis. Women reading from the Torah and wearing *kepot* and *tallitot* in Conservative synagogues as well as Reform temples hardly raised an eyebrow. Marriages between Jew and non-Jew had became commonplace, and the founding of a temple or synagogue for a special group of people, or the establishment of a congregation other than the traditional Orthodox, Conservative, or Reform, became unremarkable. Among the newly established congregations in and around Seattle, for instance, would be Tikvah Chadashah, serving gay and lesbian Jews; Reconstructionist North Shore in Bothell; Eitz Or, affiliated with the Jewish Renewal movement; and Bet Alef Meditational, "a synagogue without walls." Along with these were a Chabad-Lubavitch worship center in Bellevue, an Ashkenazic-Sephardic Orthodox congregation on Mercer Island led by a Chassidic rabbi, and Reform or Reform-Conservative combinations on Bainbridge Island and in Bremerton, Aberdeen, Woodinville, Port Townsend, Port Angeles, and Yakima.[57]

Arts in the Postwar Years

ORLD WAR II COMING ON THE HEELS OF THE Depression shortened the roster of Washington Jewish actors, artists, musicians, and writers. After the war, an influx of newcomers who had come to work in the war industry or had been attracted to the beauty and livability of the Pacific Northwest broadened the rolls of talented, professional people and expanded the artistic life of the Jewish community. These new Washington artists as well as native-born residents were helped by a robust economy which emerged in the 1950s after a difficult postwar readjustment; an expanding University of Washington; an increase in commercial art galleries and art festivals, such as the Arts and Crafts Festival sponsored by Brandeis Women in 1961; and a more financially secure Seattle Symphony providing paying jobs. Only in the theater did opportunities diminish, but even here a few Jewish names appear. And, although their numbers remained small, Seattle Jewish writers established national reputations.

Visual Artists

In small and large Washington cities, most Jewish artists exhibiting between 1945 and 1970 came from somewhere else. As in the early years, Washington's Jewish artists did not limit themselves to art with Jewish themes. Like many of their contemporaries, they instead chose to express their art in an independent and personal way. If their art had a Jewish motif, it frequently was designed for a particular religious institution. When congregations constructed or enlarged new facilities they often asked local artists, among them Phillip Levine, Edith Weinstein, Estelle Bensussen, Gizel Herskowitz Berman, Reeva Levine, and Erika

Michael in Seattle, Israel Nudelman in Aberdeen, and Irma Arick in Spokane, to craft special ceremonial pieces.[1] Leo A. Meltzer, an ardent volunteer to Jewish causes, spent a year carving an intricately designed wooden tablet bearing the Ten Commandments for Herzl Synagogue. "It was a Labor of Love," announced *The Jewish Transcript*.[2]

Scottish-born B. Marcus Priteca, in a long and fruitful career that spanned six decades, became exclusive architect for the Pantages Theater circuit and designed several of Seattle's synagogues. The Coliseum Theater in Seattle, the Pantages in Hollywood, and the Pantages in Tacoma were among those that came from his drawing board. His synagogue designs include Congregation Bikur Cholim (now Langston Hughes Cultural Arts Center) at Yesler Way and Seventeenth Avenue, the Educational Center at Eighteenth Avenue and Main Street, Seattle Talmud Torah at Twenty-fifth Avenue and Columbia Street, and Sephardic Bikur Holim at 6500 Fifty-second Avenue South. He was consulting architect for Temple De Hirsch Sinai's new building. "It [Bikur Cholim] was our beautiful and comfortable home for sixty years because Priteca was particularly deft in acoustics and arranging seating to accommodate each person's line of sight. He designed the Holy Ark . . . inspired by those he had seen in synagogues in Europe," reported Carol Sidell Michel.[3]

In contrast to the elegant sculpted metal Ark which he created for Herzl Ner Tamid on Mercer Island, Phillip Levine's informal and charming metal figures inhabit parks, schools, walkways, public buildings, and museums throughout the Northwest. Courtesy of Phillip Levine.

Once settled in the Pacific Northwest, Jewish newcomers found an interested public, Jewish and non-Jewish, and gallery space to exhibit their art. They were serious, professional artists, not Sunday painters. Although many Jewish people purchased their art and *The Jewish Transcript* often announced their shows, the artists did not have the financial backing of Jewish institutions. If they were successful, it was because they were talented, not because they were Jewish.

Phillip Levine, Leon Applebaum, Lisel Salzer, and Manfred Lindenberger were among the Jewish newcomers to the Pacific Northwest. Many of their paintings and sculptures are in museums throughout the country.

Leon Applebaum taught at the Cornish School from 1949 to 1950 and then studied painting in Paris under a Louis Comfort Tiffany grant and a Fulbright scholarship. His work has been shown by such institutions as the Metropolitan Museum, the Museum of Modern Art in New York, and the Tate Gallery in London.[4]

Phillip Levine began his metal sculpting career in 1961, the year he received his Master of Fine Arts degree from the University of Washington. Until then, Levine had been drawing, painting, and creating sculpture from clay. Whether depicting the human figure or a soaring seagull, movement has played a principal role in his sculpture. Levine's sculptures appear in several private collections as well as the permanent collections of the Seattle Art Museum and the Denver Art Museum. His bronze *Dancer with Flat Hat*, located in front of the Henry

Arriving in Seattle in March 1937 as a refugee from Nazi Germany, Manfred Lindenberger became a devotee of Northwest art and artists. A friendship with artist Windsor Utley sparked his interest in landscape painting. He flourished as a "Sunday painter" throughout his professional career of dentistry, and received high recognition as an artist after retirement. Courtesy of Manfred Lindenberger.

Art Gallery on the University of Washington campus, greets students, faculty, and visitors.

Enamel artist Lisel Salzer came to the United States in 1939 and settled in Seattle in 1950. Inspired by the sixteenth-century Limoges *Objets d'art* at the Metropolitan Museum of Art in New York, Salzer achieved an acclaimed international reputation when she revived the long-forgotten Limoges technique for her portraits. She was included among the designer craftspeople showing at the Seattle World's Fair in 1962.[5]

German-born Manfred Lindenberger became acquainted with art in Berlin's art museums. In the 1950s, he received recognition and encouragement from the noted northwest painter Kenneth Callahan. Lindenberger received the Seattle Art Museum's Watercolor Society award in 1970 and the Museum of History and Industry's Puget Sound Group of Northwest Painters award in 1972.

Women Painters of Washington began in 1930 to promote the advancement of women in a male-dominated field. Among its alumnae are Therese Asia, Lorraine Cohn, Eva Goldberg, Reeva Levine, and Edith Weinstein from Seattle, and Elsie Weiner from Grays Harbor. All these successful women studied with noted artists at local art schools such as the Cornish College of the Arts and the University of Washington, and exhibited at numerous galleries and museums throughout Washington, including the Henry Art Gallery and Seattle Art Museum. In Tacoma, Rose Lamken exhibited

The decorative etched brass panel on the lectern of Seattle's Temple Beth Am is one of two brass front pieces created by artist Edith Weinstein in 1965. The theme of the panel pictured above is a menorah abstracted from overlapping Hebrew letters. Courtesy of Edith Weinstein, Bellevue.

at local galleries and taught art history at the University of Puget Sound and Fort Steilacoom Community College.

Two Jewish artists who survived concentration camps of Germany are Gizel Herskowitz Berman and Maria Frank Abrams. Berman survived the nightmare of Auschwitz and came to Washington from Czechoslovakia in 1945. One of her most ambitious sculptures is the Holocaust Memorial at the Samuel and Althea

Artist Maria Frank Abrams designed the imaginative sets and costumes for the opera The Dybbuk, *performed at the Seattle Center in 1963. The setting here portrays Nachman singing in the second act, which takes place in the courtyard of a rich merchant's house. The scene exhibits the elfin touch characteristic of many of Abrams's paintings. Courtesy of Maria Frank Abrams.*

Stroum Jewish Community Center of Greater Seattle on Mercer Island. The six Hebrew figures in the title, *Lo Tishkach*, or "Thou shalt not forget," symbolize the six million dead. The letters in the dark bronze sculpture are "figurative abstractions, simultaneously suggesting limbs and the furnaces that burned them." The sculpture, according to Berman, "expresses my feelings about it. That I can't do with words." She considers herself a "survivor and an artist."[6]

Survivor Maria Frank Abrams came to Seattle in 1948 from Hungary and pursued art at the University of Washington. Asked if her years in a concentration camp affected her work, she replied, "It affected my life very much . . . my life is my work now." Art gave her a reason to live after she learned her family was killed.

There was a woman in the same barrack where I was . . . she was an artist; she talked about her work, about her life in Paris, about her past. It was throughout this period when I felt that I wanted to live after all, and that if I lived I wanted to paint. Later on I was taken from Bergen-Belsen to another concentration camp . . . it was possible for me to get paper and pencil. And I used to draw, and the women came to me and said, 'Oh, you can draw. Well, would you draw the clothes I used to have in such-and-such a time' . . . and they loved it. And I loved it. . . . This desire to become a painter helped me live, and it still does."[7]

In 1952 Abrams won first prize at the Bellevue Art Festival for her watercolor *Impressions through a Bridge*.[8] She also designed sets for Seattle Opera productions, including *La Traviata* and *The Dybbuk*. Some of her work is included in the Seattle Art Museum's permanent collection.

Collectors

Jewish art collectors living in Washington assembled diverse collections, including Native American totem poles, Greek gold coins, Jewish ceremonial objects, African masks, and old master drawings. Some acquired their collections by making a concerted effort to obtain a particular style or artist, while for others, collecting was a way to surround themselves with what they found interesting and beautiful. Although Washington has many private collections held by Jewish people, such as Ernest and Erika Michael's Judaica collection, limited space allows us to only include those who began their collections before 1970 and whose collections have been on public display.

Joanna Eckstein, Anne Gerber, Thelma Lehmann, and Morris Alhadeff grew up in Seattle. Eckstein's, Gerber's, and Alhadeff's collections reflect their interest and knowledge of Pacific Northwest art.

As an active member of the Seattle Art Museum Board of Directors, Joanna Eckstein, daughter of civic leader Nathan Eckstein, contributed to the growth of Washington art. Her close personal friendships with and collections of Pacific Northwest artists Mark Tobey, Morris Graves, and Kenneth Callahan made her "a focal point in the first wave of Seattle's cultural renaissance," reported the *Seattle Weekly*.[9]

Anne Gerber majored in art at the University of Washington. Gerber and her husband, Sidney Gerber, began bringing contemporary art to Washington in 1945 after making their first purchase at the Stieglitz Gallery in New York. Ten years later, on a sailing trip through Alaska's Inside Passage, they realized the important contributions of Native American artists from Alaska and British Columbia. Their collection of Northwest Native American masks, blankets, boxes, and other objects, now in the collection of the Burke Museum on the University of Washington campus, did much to make people aware of a neglected aspect of Washington art.[10] Many of non–Native American paintings from the Gerber collection are in the Seattle Art Museum.

Thelma Lehmann added her vision to Washington's art scene as a painter, art critic, collector, and gallery owner. Her first one-person art exhibition was in 1939 at the Seattle Art Museum. From 1969 to 1982 she owned Gallery Nimba, where she introduced Northwesterners to African art.[11]

Morris Alhadeff's long interest in the arts began during his last year at Garfield High School. He is probably best known for his collection of horse and racing prints, including a gallery of horse sketches by Kenneth Callahan that decorated the clubhouse walls at Longacres racetrack. Alhadeff was a charter member of the Seattle Arts Commission, set up in 1971, and received the mayor's Public Service Award for leadership of the commission.[12]

Seattle was also enriched by collectors who moved to the area. Norman Davis, author, scholar, patron of the arts, and a founder of Seattle's Jewish Community Center, brought his family from England to California in 1937 and later settled in Washington. His collection of Greek coins and Greek, Hellenistic, and Etruscan art, his "pride and joy," are part of the permanent works in the Norman Davis Gallery of the Seattle Art Museum. Davis also served as vice-president of the Seattle Art Museum Board of Directors for sixteen years, and as a board member for more than thirty years. In 1962, for the great sum of a dollar a year, Davis directed the Fine Arts Exhibition at the Seattle 1962 World's Fair. "I organized the personnel who created the exhibition. . . . It was one great thrill of my life," said Davis.[13]

Collector Manfred Selig left Germany in 1940 with his wife and children, just a step ahead of the Nazis. Arriving in Seattle with only a few gold coins in the hollowed-out heels of his shoes, Selig began peddling linens. Twenty-five years later, an inaugural exhibit at the state capitol in Olympia focused on over one hundred paintings from Selig's collection.[14]

Writers

In the middle of the twentieth century, numerous American Jewish fiction writers, including Phillip Roth, Bernard Malamud, Delmore Schwartz, and Saul Bellow, received recognition for their writings. Despite the large number of national Jewish essayists, poets, and dramatists whose words are widely read, few nonacademic Jewish writers from Washington have published books. Moreover, except for editorials in the Jewish newspapers, local Jewish authors did not write about contemporary Jewish issues, such as the condition of Jews in Europe. In 1957, when the first publication of *Who's Who Among Pacific Northwest Authors* came out, only Dr. Ivar Spector, an educator and historian at the University of Washington and formerly a Hebrew teacher in Tacoma, made the list. A supplement published in 1961 included novelist Helen Bornstein Rucker.

Several factors may explain why Washington had so few published Jewish writers. Washington lacked local publishers; the state was located far away from the New York publishing world; Washington's Jewish population was probably too small to provide a cadre of writers; and few Jewish authors had the means to become full-time writers. Since virtually every writer included in this chapter, with the exception of newspaper people, are women, one can speculate that the absence of monetary rewards hindered people from pursuing writing as a career. This is not to say that no one in Washington writes, but only that before 1970, few outside of the universities did so.[15]

Famed Alice B. Toklas, daughter of Ferdinand Toklas, who started the profitable Auerbach, Toklas and Singerman firm in 1875, lived in Seattle from 1890 to 1895 and attended the University of Washington for a short time. Although she eventually pursued her career outside of Seattle, Toklas is the first known Jewish woman writer with ties to Washington State.

Toklas entered the publishing world in the late 1920s to further the literary reputation of her partner, Gertrude Stein. In the 1950s, she started her own writing career, subsequently publishing articles in *The New York Times Book Review* and *The Atlantic Monthly.* At the age of seventy-five she agreed to write a cookbook. "To friends, she modestly said that the book [*The Alice B. Toklas Cookbook*] was undertaken for 'the pennies' only." Harper Row, the publisher, thought it "the only way she would ever be coerced into writing her memoirs . . . it was for her cache of anecdotes that they were most enthusiastic."[16]

Two Jewish authors who made headlines in *The Jewish Transcript* during the 1930s were Babette Plechner Hughes and Johanna Frada Greenberg. Hughes wrote mysteries (*Murder in the Zoo*) and plays (*Mrs. Harper's Bazaar*). Greenberg, a Seattle poet and a member of the National League of American Pen Women, was an active member of the Seattle Poetry Club, founded in September 1922.[17] At the Seattle Poetry Club, Greenberg hosted a program of Hebrew poetry and music. Rabbi Samuel Koch talked about the evolution of Hebrew poetry, and Cantor Solomon Tovbin chanted his version of *The Cry of Rachael*.[18] Besides introducing the general public to Hebrew poetry, this event was remarkable for bringing together a Reform rabbi and an Orthodox cantor.

Helen Bornstein Rucker, daughter and daughter-in-law of pioneer Jewish families, began her professional career as an actress, but after marrying, she turned to writing. In 1946, under the tutelage of George Savage, head of the Advanced Writing program at the University of Washington, she developed the first drafts of her novel *Cargo of Brides*, published in 1956. It was a story of a shipload of single young women brought to early Seattle from New England by Asa Mercer. The book received favorable reviews and remained on the *New York Herald Tribune's* "What America Reads" list for eight weeks. She received mention in the updated 1961 publication of *Who's Who Among Pacific Northwest Authors*.

Molly Cone, born in Tacoma, grew up surrounded by three sisters, a brother, a Yiddish-speaking grandmother who presided over their kosher kitchen, and parents who emigrated from Latvia. Cone's books for children often reflected the well-ordered but sometimes tumultuous household of her childhood years. *Mishmash*, published in 1962, grew into a popular series of seven and was among a number of her novels for young readers. *Who Knows Ten*, published in 1965, was revised and reissued in 1998. This and several of her books of Jewish content continued to be used in Reform and Conservative religious schools in Seattle and throughout the country. Cone has received many national awards and the Washington State Governor's Award for writing three times.

The University of Washington brought Greg Dash, a physicist, and his wife, Joan Dash, already a published writer, to Seattle in 1960. Dash writes both fiction and nonfiction for adults as well as teenagers. Books and articles of Jewish interest include *Summoned to Jerusalem: The Life of Henrietta Szold* (1979) and "Sephardim in Seattle," published in the *National Jewish Monthly* in May 1963.

In 1949 journalist Edwin Guthman, a reporter for *The Seattle Times*, received the Pulitzer Prize for distinguished reporting. His prize-winning articles were based on a series of reports clearing University of Washington Professor Melvin Rader of Communist charges. After serving as Assistant for Public Information at the Justice Department during the Kennedy administration, Guthman edited *The Philadelphia Inquirer* and taught journalism at the University of Southern California. Acknowledging his outstanding career, the University of Washington honored Guthman with a Distinguished Alumnus Award in 1975.

Almost thirty years later, another Seattle native, Mary Ellen (Meg) Greenfield, columnist for *Newsweek* magazine and editorial writer for *The Washington Post*, won the 1978 Pulitzer Prize for political commentary. Known for her "sharp-eyed analysis and wry wit," Greenfield's informed commentary had an "impact on the public perception of six Presidential administrations and scores of policy debates, ranging from affirmative action and abortion rights to the Panama Canal treaties and the Persian Gulf war."[19]

Musicians, Composers, Conductors, and Singers

The music festivals begun in the 1930s by Susie and Maurice Friedman continued to play an important role in the Jewish community both locally and nationally. Amateurs and professionals both had roles in their productions, which always drew large crowds. The Friedmans, who toured Army camps during World War II un-

der the auspices of the Jewish Welfare Board's Music Council, believed it was important to "stimulate interest in Jewish music and elevate the standards of such concerts."[20] They placed a particular emphasis on providing interesting Jewish music programs in community centers and synagogues. Seattle's festivals benefited from their advice and participation.

The 1953 Jewish Musical Festival featured the Hillel Glee Club of forty

Zelma Lachman, cello, Minnie Hurwitz Bergman, piano, and Goldie Jaffe, violin, provided entertainment for Jewish organizations. MSCUA/UWL, *neg. 18965.*

voices directed by Nathan Grossman, a student at the University of Washington. Grossman, a prominent young pianist from Spokane, received many music honors while still in high school, including the prestigious National Guild of Piano Teachers award. Strongly dedicated to Jewish tradition and to his community, Grossman returned to Spokane after college, and for forty-two years directed the choir at Keneseth Israel (now Temple Beth Shalom), and served as musical director for special events such as the musical *Fiddler on the Roof.*

The 1958 Jewish Music Festival presented by the Jewish Music Forum and chaired by Susie Michael Friedman was particularly noteworthy for presenting commissioned works by Samuel E. Goldfarb and pianist Herbert Tannhauser, former musical director at Herzl Congregation. A review of the concert praised Leon Israel for a compelling performance of Ladino folk songs and Sephardic chants, and baritone Isaac Levy's success with contemporary Hebrew art songs. The Friedmans received the Samuel E. Goldfarb Award for Creativeness in Jewish Music at B'nai B'rith Lodge No. 503's Fourth Annual Festival of Jewish Music. The festival also featured songs by Leon Israel and Isaac Levy and a selection of Jewish folksongs arranged by Herbert Tannhauser. Minnie Hurwitz Bergman (violin), Zelma Lachman (cello), Goldie Jaffe (piano), and the Seattle Jewish Music Ensemble also performed at the festival.

Leon Israel, who started singing as a young boy, chanted at almost every congregation in the Seattle area. He was cantorial soloist with Temple De Hirsch for thirty years. Seattle Civic Opera and numerous musical programs staged by local organizations benefited from his performances, and Israel's solos preceded many young Jewish brides' walks down the aisle.[21]

Popular musicians Gina (Virginia) Funes and Arny Robbins were born in Seattle and began their musical careers in the 1960s. Funes played in cocktail lounges, supper rooms, and top nightspots of the Pacific Northwest. Later, as vocalist with Fred Radke's band, Funes sang at private parties and entertained residents at the Kline Galland Home. Robbins, who when not playing the trumpet practiced law, entertained at outdoor concerts, political rallies, and private parties with his traditional jazz band.

The Seattle Symphony Orchestra played its first concert in Christensen's Hall on December 29, 1903. Almost fifty years after the first concert, Jewish conductors Manuel Rosenthal and, later, Milton Katims took up the baton to lead the orchestra. In the ensuing years, numerous Jewish musicians, among them concert master Henry Siegl, cellist Edward Handlin, bassists Noah Golden, Morris (Mori) Simon, and Ronald Simon, violinists Sam Meyer and Ada Golden Ash, flutist Sidney Zeitlin, and oboist Bernard Shapiro have been familiar figures at Seattle

Symphony concerts. Another Golden family member, Joseph Golden, played the French horn with the Seattle Youth Symphony before going off to study at Juilliard in New York. Ronald Simon followed his father, Mori Simon, as personnel manager for the Seattle Symphony. The Simons played bass together for twenty-five years.

Manuel Rosenthal, who came to Seattle in May 1948, had been a distinguished composer and conductor of the French National Radio Orchestra. During his tenure as conductor of the Seattle Symphony, Rosenthal elevated the orchestra's standing in Seattle. Because he had come to America with a woman who was not his wife, problems with immigration authorities in 1951 barred Rosenthal from remaining in the United States.[22] Rosenthal returned to America in 1975 when George Balanchine asked him to conduct the New York City Ballet's *Homage à Ravel*.[23]

Milton Katims replaced Rosenthal as conductor of the Seattle Symphony. Born in Brooklyn of Russian Hungarian parentage, Katims began his musical career as a violist and enjoyed an international reputation as an instrumentalist as well as a conductor.[24] His wife, Virginia, was a concert cellist. In 1954 he conducted a program of great Jewish composers to celebrate the Jewish Tercentary in America. Under Katims's direction, the symphony achieved major status in the United States.

A distinguished conductor, violist, and music advisor, Milton Katims, born in New York in 1909 of Russian Hungarian parents, brought the Seattle Symphony Orchestra to major status. One of his first acts in 1954 as conductor of the Seattle Symphony Orchestra was the introduction of free concerts for all fourth graders. He developed and expanded family and youth concerts, invited world-renowned composers and musicians to appear with the orchestra, and introduced young, gifted artists to Seattle audiences in his twenty-two years as conductor with the symphony. Courtesy of Milton Katims.

Bernice Mossafer Rind, Seattle harpist and composer, won a first scholarship to the New York College of Music when she was eleven. Her composition "Rhapsody in F Minor," composed when she was fourteen and published when she was seventeen, won an international award. Rind swapped her promising musical career for home and family. Courtesy of Bernice Rind.

Harpist composer Bernice Mossafer Rind began composing music when she was eight years old and at age fourteen had her work published. She was the first harpist with the Seattle Youth Symphony, and before her teen years had appeared as soloist with the Los Angeles Symphony. In 1982 the state of Israel awarded her the prestigious Jerusalem Medal for outstanding service to humanity.

Gustave Stern, musical director of the City of Seattle Parks Department, inherited his musical ability from both sides of his family. In Germany, where Stern grew up, both grandfathers were *hazanim*. In 1933, with Hitler in power, orchestras barred him from conducting. To avoid further persecution he went to Holland, then Paris, and finally to New York. Unable to find work, Stern moved west. He arrived in Seattle in 1945 and soon met people associated with the Seattle Civic Opera, an amateur company. In 1949, the Superintendent of Parks asked Stern to "take over the music department." For twenty-three years, using mostly local talent, Stern conducted summer concerts at Volunteer Park, Green Lake Aqua Theater, and Seward Park. "When you walk through Seward Park there is an amphitheater. That's where I did *Aida*," Stern recalled.[25]

Melvyn Poll was among those who gained from Stern's teaching. Poll, a renowned tenor who grew up in Seattle, appeared with opera companies all over the world, including the Israel National Opera between 1972 and 1974. As musical

More than fifteen thousand people attended a concert conducted by Gustave Stern in Volunteer Park in 1950. As musical director of the City of Seattle Parks Department, Stern, who left Hitler's Germany in 1933 and settled in Seattle in 1945, conducted summer concerts at Volunteer Park, Green Lake Aqua Theater, and Seward Park from 1949 to 1972. Courtesy of Michel P. Stern.

director and cantorial soloist at Temple De Hirsch Sinai, Poll produced Hayden's *Creation* and *Judas Maccabaeus.*

Composer and conductor Joan Franks Williams, a graduate of the Manhattan School of Music and the Eastman School of Music, founded New Dimensions in Music, a nonprofit organization, in Seattle in 1962. Using tapes and various electronic devices as part of her music, she offered the newest concepts and techniques of twentieth-century music.[26] "Everyone tells me I have my coat on inside out. I tell them it's supposed to look this way. It's just like the kind of music I write—that's 'inside out' too. Our era has its own excitement, its own philosophies and ideas," said Williams.[27] For eleven years she presented her concerts of new music throughout the Northwest. When her family moved to Israel, she continued working in music for the Israel Broadcasting Authority. The Williams lived in Israel for seventeen years before returning to Seattle. "The Israelis are very curious," she said of her radio listeners. "They don't want to miss out on what's happening, so they're very interested in new music. I found the same climate, incidentally, in Seattle when I was working here."[28]

A one-time cantor, tenor Richard Tucker (second from left) sang roles in many of the world's great opera houses. As soloist at the Opera House at Spokane's World's Fair in 1974, he posed with Temple Beth Shalom's Rabbi Eugene Gottesman, Cantor Leo Matzner, and Gene Huppin. Courtesy of Temple Beth Shalom Archives, Spokane.

Music in Washington's Smaller Cities

Spokane's Jewish community benefited when Leo Matzner arrived in 1952 and became cantor at Keneseth Israel. A former concert artist, Matzner had been imprisoned in Poland by the Nazis. He managed to escape, but was captured by the Russians, who put him in a labor camp in Siberia. While in Russia, a whistle saved his life: "I told them [the Russians] I was an artist. . . . When they learned I had been an artistic whistler, they asked me to demonstrate. . . . So I whistled . . . summoning all my strength." The song he chose was a Russian gypsy song, and when he finished, Matzner recalled, "I was aware of a great change; eyes which had been like those of poisonous snakes now were kindly."[29]

Bellingham violinist Arthur Thal continued his career as a faculty member at the School of Music at Western Washington State College of Education (now Western Washington University) in the 1950s. For many years he was also concertmaster for the local symphony orchestra, which was sponsored by the university and the city of Bellingham. A Sunday school lesson at a local church gives an indication of Thal's status in the community:

A couple of weeks before Christmas, a Sunday school teacher asked her class, "Who was the most famous Jew that ever lived?" Nobody answered, and she was very disappointed, so she asked again. Finally a little girl raised her hand and said, "Could it be Mr. Arthur Thal?"[30]

Another Western Washington University faculty member, Jerome Glass, first played Jewish music in an orchestra organized by an Orthodox rabbi in

Three concert masters in one family: (from left), Arthur Thal, concert master of Bellingham Civic Symphony Orchestra; daughter Mimi Sue, concert mistress of Fairhaven Junior High School Orchestra; and son Lennard, concert master of Bellingham High School Orchestra. Courtesy of Temple Beth Israel Archives, Bellingham.

*Sylvia Glass, Sue Mendelsohn, Coleen Koplowitz, Estelle Greenblatt, Phyllis Levin,
Shirley Adelstein, and Jan Orloff dance the cancan at a 1959 fund-raising event for
Bellingham's Beth Israel Congregation. Courtesy of Temple Beth Israel Archives,
Bellingham.*

Minersville, Pennsylvania. At the age of fifteen he was so intent on pursuing a
musical career he misrepresented his age to get into the musician's union. The
passion continued through World War II, and he pursued a doctorate in music.
He arrived in Bellingham in 1955 after accepting a position as instructor and as
orchestra and band director at Western Washington State College of Education.
He also conducted Bellingham's civic band, and in 1960 he led a string orchestra
sponsored by the Jewish Community Center in Vancouver, British Columbia. In
1968 he became conductor for the Seattle Philharmonic Orchestra, a position he
held until 1979.[31]

As in many cities throughout the state, Bellingham's Jewish community
benefited when the Nazi regime caused Jews to flee their homelands. Cantor
Frederick S. Gartner, spiritual leader at Beth Israel Synagogue in Bellingham from
1951 to 1982, had sung opera in Vienna until Hitler came to power. In 1933 Gartner
went to Palestine, where he sang in the Hebrew Opera. Subsequently he moved to
New York and assumed cantorial duties at a synagogue in Jackson Heights. From

there he went to Vancouver, British Columbia, where the Bellingham congregation heard him sing and hired him first as cantor and then as acting rabbi, although he was never officially ordained.[32]

Theater

An active secular and Yiddish theater disappeared during the postwar years. Instead of presenting plays, organizations sponsored carnivals, cabaret nights, and elegant dinners. In Seattle, the demise of the Seattle Repertory Playhouse, directed by Florence and Burton James, meant actors no longer had a popular theater for performances. The Burtons had had to close the theater after being charged with membership in the Communist Party by Washington State's Un-American Activities Committee, chaired by Rep. Albert Canwell. Canwell's committee ignored normal constitutional protections, such as the right to due process, and had a tendency to believe that anyone who disagreed with their policies was a Communist.

In 1959, seven theater groups from Seattle and the Puget Sound area met to form the League of Community Theaters. It was a first attempt to bring back theatrical productions of high quality. The Center Stagers, based at the Jewish Community Center in Seattle, participated in the league. In a production of Thornton Wilder's *Our Town*, Gerson M. Goldman acted as stage manager and Irving Zimmer directed the players.[33]

But except for plays staged by the Drama Department at the University of Washington, Eugene Keene's Cirque Theater, and small community groups such as the Jewish Community Center's Center Stagers, early postwar theater dwindled in Seattle until the Seattle Repertory Theater opened in 1963. Thereafter, the opening of more professional companies, such as A Contemporary Theater (ACT), Intiman, and Empty Space, brought in more accomplished actors. Seattle now had a choice of good regional theater.

In the three decades beyond 1970, Jewish involvement in the arts would radically change. Temples and synagogues regularly held art shows featuring Jewish artists; the board of the north-end branch of the Samuel and Althea Stroum Jewish Community Center of Greater Seattle established a Pacific Northwest Center for Jewish Arts; Washington State galleries featured paintings and sculpture by Jewish artists; and books written by Jewish authors were reviewed in local and national publications as well as in *The Jewish Transcript*. Similar changes also would occur in Washington's music world with Klezmer music (unknown to most people, even

Jews, before the Mazeltones introduced it in the 1980s) becoming a regular feature at folk music concerts, weddings, and Bar and Bat Mitzvahs; with the Seattle Symphony continuing under the baton of Gerard Schwarz, a Jewish conductor; and with citizens such as Althea and Sam Stroum and Rebecca and Jack Benaroya sitting on the boards of major art institutions.

Epilogue: A Look Beyond the 1970s

T WO DECADES BEFORE THE END OF THE MILLENNIUM, one Seattle rabbi feared that the non-Jewish world in Washington State would eventually overcome the Jewish one. As he put it, "Like everyone else, Jews would rather be skiing." The rabbi stood in a long line of those concerned with Jewish survival in the New World. People have sounded the alarm over the disappearing American Jew since the early nineteenth century. Although the offspring of some of the earliest pioneer families assimilated into the mainstream and disappeared as Jews, descendants of a remarkable number of early settlers survived as Jews and thrived as Americans. At the dawn of the new millennium, Washington's Jews could view their future both as Jews and as Americans with optimism.

The last two decades of the twentieth century, a period not covered by this history, witnessed a flowering of Washington's Jewish communities. By the end of the millennium, these communities maintained an array of professionally operated institutions concerned with both their own interests and those of other minority peoples. For example, in Seattle, a program to eliminate discrimination in social clubs as well as in businesses was so successful that Glendale, a formerly all-Jewish country club, found itself with more Gentile members than Jewish members. Local chapters of national and international organizations carried on the work of fund raising, advocating for civil rights and for Israel, and promoting the education and health of Jews everywhere. Seattle Jews hosted the American Sephardi Federation convention in 1989 and the General Assembly of the Council of Jewish Federations in 1996.

Jewish citizens of Washington State figured not only as generous participants in Jewish institutions and organizations, but also as leaders in local secular charities and Washington-based enterprises, both civic and business. Many families became prominent in both Jewish and non-Jewish communities. A notable example: the Herb Bridge family in Seattle included an admiral in the Naval Reserve, a State Supreme Court justice, a physician, an attorney and business leader, and a rabbi. While the Samuel and Althea Stroum Jewish Community Center of Greater Seattle is an example of Jewish interest in promoting the education and well-being of Seattle-area Jews, the famed Benaroya Symphony Hall, named to honor the major gifts of Jack and Rebecca Benaroya, stands as an example of Jewish participation and contribution to the wider civic good. More than a few Jewish individuals have held distinguished positions on the faculty of the University of Washington and in the legal, medical, and scientific arenas of the state. Jeweler Paul Friedlander founded PONCHO, a major source of support for local arts organizations. Artists such as Gerard Schwartz, conductor of the Seattle Symphony, and entrepreneurs such as Starbuck's Howard Shultz and Costco's creator Jeff Brotman, have helped put Seattle on the world map.

By the 1990s, little trace of the early division between Ashkenazic and Sephardic immigrants remained. While the rate of marriage between Jew and non-Jew continued to soar in Washington State as elsewhere, religion remained central to Jewish life. Notable was the increase in the diversity of religious lifestyles of the Jews of the Evergreen State.

At the beginning of the year 2000, Greater Seattle had seventeen Jewish congregations, demonstrating more diversity than ever. For those who chose to worship in a traditional manner, seven Orthodox congregations provided a range of choices, including two Sephardic, three affiliated with the Chabad-Lubavitch Chassidic movement, and one Modern Orthodox. At the five Reform congregations, following a trend in the Reform movement in general, elements of more traditional worship were increasingly evident, including more use of Hebrew and the wearing of *keppot* (skull caps) and *tallitot* (prayer shawls). Greater Seattle maintained two large and thriving Conservative congregations, but the Conservative remained the smallest branch in contrast to most other U.S. cities. In addition to Orthodox, Reform, and Conservative, Seattle's Jewish community included the progressive Kadima organization, a meditation synagogue, a gay and lesbian congregation, and one that identified with the Jewish Renewal movement.

Around the state, twenty more congregations served Jews in cities and towns. Mostly they were Reform or unaffiliated, although several stemmed from Orthodox roots, and four were Conservative. They ranged from large congregations in Tacoma, Bellingham, and Spokane to *chavurot* (group of friends) in smaller towns, many of which were led by laypeople. For example, the Jewish community of Palouse, serving the communities of Pullman, Washington (home of Washington State University), and Moscow, Idaho (home of the University of Idaho), offered cultural, religious, and social activities for the Jews of the area, including university students. Bet Shira (House of Song) Congregation in the seaport city of Port Townsend described itself as an inclusive Jewish Community of more than a hundred families from the North Olympic Peninsula. On Bainbridge Island and in North Kitsap County, on the west side of Puget Sound, about fifty families made up the nondenominational Chavurat Shir Hayam (Song of the Sea), inspired by the Jewish Renewal movement. The *chavurat* celebrated the full Jewish calendar of holidays and rituals in addition to frequent Shabbat and lifecycle gatherings.

Whereas there was only one before 1980, by the year 2000 Seattle supported six Jewish day schools that variously educated children in the primary, middle school, and high school years. The Samuel and Althea Stroum Jewish Community Center of Greater Seattle, Chabad House, Temple De Hirsch, and The Seattle Hebrew Academy all offered preschools. The Community High School of Jewish Studies met weekly during the school year, as did the religious schools offered by the congregations. Adult Jewish education programs abounded, both within congregations and in the wider community, in addition to the University of Washington's flourishing Jewish Studies program.

For the Orthodox community, The Va'ad HaRabanim of Greater Seattle supervised *kashruth* and provided a *beth din* (religious court for divorces, conversions, and hearing legal disputes). Congregation Bikur Cholim–Machzikay Hadath established an eruv in the Seward Park neighborhood in 1991, a system of fences, poles and wires surrounding the area within which Orthodox Jews were allowed to carry items on the Sabbath.

This history of the building of a vital Jewish community in what was once an outpost on the Jewish map makes a powerful argument for the continued viability of Jews in Washington State and throughout the world. Jews have proved to be a remarkably tenacious people, hanging on to their faith and their traditions for three thousand years while at the same time adapting to the host cultures in which they live. *Family of Strangers* provides another chapter in that continuing story.

NOTES

■ MCUA/ULW Manuscripts, Special Collections,
  University Archives/University of Washington Libraries
■ WSJHS Washington State Jewish Historical Society

Central European Pioneers

1. Howard Muggamin, *The Jewish Americans* (New York and Philadelphia: Chelsea House, 1996), 40.

2. Howard A. Droker, "A Coat of Many Colors: History of Seattle's Jewish Community," *Portage* 4 (spring 1983): 4–9.

3. Olympia's eighth territorial governor was Edward Salomon, elected 1870. The 1901 University of Washington Law School graduate was Bella Weretnikow Rosenbaum. Washington State Jewish legislators were David Levin, Tacoma, elected 1897; Harry Rosenhaupt, Spokane, elected 1889, 1901, and elected senator in 1906, 1910. Jewish mayors were Bailey Gatzert, Seattle, 1875; Mitchell Harris, Olympia, 1910; Max Gerson, Port Townsend, 1908; Israel Katz, Port Townsend, 1915, 1916; Samuel Kriedel, Ellensburg, 1915; Harry Robinson, Elma, 1934.

4. "First Jew in the Pacific Northwest?" *Jewish Western Bulletin*, British Columbia Centenary Issue (June 30, 1958): 6; conversations with Judge Leonard Friedman, Sacramento, Calif., 1997.

5. Ray Ruppert, "The Land Was a Lure for Early Jewish Immigrants," *The Seattle Sunday Times Magazine*, 8 October 1978, pp. 8–9.

6. Judith E. Endelman, *The Jewish Community of Indianapolis* (Bloomington: Indiana University Press, 1984), 67.

7. Ron Manheimer and Caroline Manheimer, "Olympia," *Washington State Jewish Historical Society Newsletter* (hereafter cited as *WSJHS Newsletter*) (September 1983).

8. Murray Morgan, *Puget's Sound: A Narrative of Early Tacoma and the Southern Sound* (Seattle and London: University of Washington Press, 1979), 87.

9. *Olympia (Washington Territory) Pioneer-Democrat*, 2 December 1854 and 7 April 1855.

10. Ibid., 26 September 1856.

11. Muggamin, *The Jewish Americans*, 113.

12. Endelman, *The Jewish Community of Indianapolis*, p. 12, citing Selma Stern-Taeubler, "The Motivation of the German Jewish Emigration to America in the Post-Mendelssohnian Era," in *Essays in American Jewish History* (Cincinnati: American Jewish Archives, 1958), 249–55.

13. Abraham J. Karp, *Haven and Home: A History of the Jews in America* (New York: Schocken Books, 1985), 52.

14. William Cronon, *Nature's Metropolis: Chicago and the Great West* (New York: W. W. Norton & Company, 1991), xv.

15. Leon A. Jick, *The Americanization of the Synagogue 1820–1870* (Hanover, N.H.: Published for Brandeis University Press by the University Press of New England, 1976), xi, 153–56, 173, 185.

16. In an article published in *The Portland (Oregon) American Hebrew News*, 28 May 1897, pp. 5–6.

17. Manheimer and Manheimer, "Olympia."

18. Ibid.

19. Sylvia Wolff Epstein, transcript of interview, Manuscripts, Special Collections, University Archives, University of Washington Libraries (hereafter cited as MSCUA/UWL), Acc. 4787-001.

20. Manheimer and Manheimer, "Olympia."

21. Epstein, interview.

22. Deborah K. Freedman, "Jewish Pioneers of Tacoma," unpublished manuscript, 1998, 44 (with excerpts from Herbert Hunt, *Tacoma, Its History and Its Builders, A Half-Century of History*, 3 vols. [Chicago: S. J. Clarke, 1916]).

23. Ibid., 94.

24. Jefferson County Historical Society, *With Pride in Heritage: A History of Jefferson County, A Symposium* (Port Townsend: Jefferson County Historical Society, 1966), 403–404.

25. Ibid., "Rothschild," 403. See also Pete Simpson, ed., *City of Dreams: A Guide to Port Townsend* (Port Townsend: Bay Press, 1986), 229.

26. Julia Niebuhr Eulenberg, "Jewish Enterprise in the American West: Washington, 1853–1909" (Ph.D. diss., University of Washington, 1996), 163.

27. For information on Katz, see Simpson, *City of Dreams*, 69.

28. Patricia Spaeth, "Port Townsend Jewish History Notes," MSCUA/UWL, Acc. 4064.

29. Oppenheimer Family, Ms. 145, Box 1/3, Eastern Washington State Historical Society, Cheney Cowles Museum; "Marcus Oppenheimer of Marcus, Washington," *Western States Jewish History* 15 (July 1983): 334; Don Taylor, *A Short History, Marcus, Washington, Then and Now*, in Eric Offenbacher papers, MSCUA/UWL, Acc. 3898-2.

30. Eulenberg, "Jewish Enterprise," 63–64.

31. Ibid., 127–28.

32. Ibid., 144.

33. Joanna Eckstein, transcript of interview, MSCUA/UWL, Acc. 460.

34. Eulenberg, "Jewish Enterprise," 195–97, 149–50.

35. Population figure: Morgan, *Puget's Sound*, 272.

36. Meta Buttnick, "This Old House," *WSJHS Newsletter* (July 1987). The November 12, 1905 edition of the *Seattle Post-Intelligencer* lists H. Uhlfelder, J. Brunn, A. J. Brunn, and a Mr. Mitchell as Seattle residents in 1868, and David Magnus, Sam Frauenthal, D. Kaufman, Bailey Gatzert, Jacob Frauenthal, Joseph Frauenthal, Simon Davis, and Jack Davis as Seattle residents in 1869.

37. Eckstein, interview, 209.

38. *Walla Walla Sunday Union Bulletin*, 1 September 1935, p. 6.

39. Eulenberg, "Jewish Enterprise."

40. Clarence Bagley, *History of King County*, vol. 1 (Chicago: S. J. Clarke, 1929), 368.

41. Information on Gatzert is based on the following: James R. Warren, "Gatzert Left Name to Seattle," *Seattle Post-Intelligencer*, 23 May 1982, p. D3; Rev. H. K. Hines, D.D., *History of the State of Washington* (Chicago: The Lewis Publishing Co., 1893), 671–72; Clarence B. Bagley, *History of Seattle from Earliest Settlement to the Present Time* (Chicago: S. J. Clarke, 1916); Raphael H. Levine, "Reflections," *The Seattle Times Magazine*, 13 January 1980, pp. 8–10; and Meta Buttnick, "Bailey Gatzert Commemorative Riverboat Stamp," *WSJHS Newsletter* (winter 1996): 2. The *Bailey Gatzert* paddle-wheel steamboat was featured on a stamp issued by the U.S. Postal Service on August 22, 1996, as one of the five designs of riverboats operating from 1860 through the 1900s within the United States. The *Bailey Gatzert* plied the Columbia River and Puget Sound from 1890 to 1923. At 175 feet and 3 inches long, she sailed between Seattle, Tacoma, and Olympia, and was the first ferry to operate in the Olympic Peninsula region. E. W. Wright, editor of *Lewis & Dryden Marine History of the Pacific Northwest* (New York: Antiquarian Press, 1961), characterized the *Bailey Gatzert* as "One of the finest sternwheel steamers afloat."

42. Eckstein information based on Eckstein, interview; Rabbi Raphael Levine, "Nathan Eckstein: Always a Leader," *The Seattle Sunday Times Magazine*, 1 April 1979, p. 6.

43. David Buerge, *Seattle in the 1880s* (Seattle: The Historical Society of Seattle and King County, 1986), 76.

44. John Friedlander, transcript of interview, MSCUA/UWL, Acc. 2496.

45. Paul Dorpat, "Now & Then," *The Seattle Times Pacific Magazine*, date not identified.

46. Herbert Hunt and Floyd C. Kaylor, *Washington, West of the Cascades*, vol. 2 (Chicago: S. J. Clarke, 1917), 255–61.

47. William C. Speidel, *Sons of the Profits; or, There's No Business Like Grow Business: The Seattle Story, 1851–1903* (Seattle: Nettle Creek Publishing Co., 1967), 257.

48. "Gottstein Here 30 Years Today," *The Seattle Times*, 24 December 1913.

49. "Pioneer Capitalist of Seattle Dies at 70 Years," *The Seattle Times*, 2 June 1917.

50. Temple Beth El, *Centuries to Celebrate* (Tacoma: Temple Beth El, 1992), 6.

51. For information on Gross Brothers, see Freedman, "Jewish Pioneers," 46–54.

52. *Tacoma Sunday Ledger*, 23 March 1890 and 17 January 1892.

53. Ibid.

54. *Tacoma Daily Ledger*, 30 November 1890.

55. Ibid. See also Freedman, "Jewish Pioneers," 105.

56. Freedman, "Jewish Pioneers," 114.

57. For information on Loeb, see ibid., 87.

58. For information on Bachrach, see ibid., 30.

59. Lucille Feist Hurst, transcript of interview, MSCUA/UWL, Acc. 4053; conversation with Lucille Feist Hurst, July 14, 1997.

60. Freedman, "Jewish Pioneers," 41.

61. Ibid., 19. See also "The Club Officers" (featuring Meyer Kaufman), *The Tacoma Daily News*, 13 August 1889, p. 1; "Prominent Tacomans" (featuring Charles Reichenbach), *The Tacoma Sunday Ledger*, 30 November 1890, p. 1; and "The Harmony Ball," *The Tacoma News*, 9 January 1890.

62. Morgan, *Puget's Sound*, 328. See also Roger Sale, *Seattle, Past to Present* (Seattle: University of Washington Press, 1976), population chart on p. 51.

63. Words of Michelle Hubert in Bart Ripp, "Infamous Ship Claimed Titanic Businessman," *The Tacoma News Tribune*, 12 April 2001, p. 1. Hubert added, "The guy went down with the Titanic. You can't get more famous than that."

64. Ibid.

65. "Temple Beth Shalom, Spokane, Washington, General History," J. Wolff papers, MSCUA/UWL, Acc. 1495.

66. N. W. Durham, *History of the City of Spokane and Spokane County, Washington*, vol. 1 (Spokane, Chicago and Philadelphia: S. J. Clarke, 1912), 361.

67. Moses N. Janton, *History of the Jews in Spokane, Washington* (Spokane: Star Printing House, 1926), 3–4.

68. "The City by the Mighty Falls," *Spokane Area Visitors Guide*, undated, p. 9.

69. Ibid. See also *Spokane Daily Chronicle*, 16 July 1964, p. 21.

70. Janton, *History of the Jews in Spokane*, 7.

71. Letter to *The American Israelite*, November 15, 1984, published in *Western States Jewish Historical Quarterly* 2 (April 1979): 309.

72. Janton, *History of the Jews in Spokane*, 3.

73. Joseph Rosenfeld, "Remarks," MSCUA/UWL, Acc. 3987. Over a generation later, during the Great Depression, voters would elect David C. Cowen to the Washington State House, and, eight years later, to the Washington State Senate. Called "Dean of the Legislature" by the *Seattle Post-Intelligencer*, Cowen would serve more than thirty years, the longest of any legislator in the state's history.

74. Eulenberg, "Jewish Enterprise," 18, 50–51, 63.

75. Information on the Kleinbergs based on articles by Meta Buttnick in the *WSJHS Newsletter*, May 1982 and fall 1995; on obituaries of Henry Kleinberg in *The Jewish Transcript*, 22 January 1932, and in the *Seattle Times*, 17 January 1932; on Lena Kleinberg Holzman, transcript of interview, MSCUA/UWL, Acc. 3199; and on materials in the possession of Larry Kleinberg, grandson of Henry Kleinberg.

76. Eulenberg, "Jewish Enterprise," 18.

77. Ibid., 50–51.

78. Ibid., 210–11.

79. *Tacoma Daily Ledger*, 30 November 1890, p. 1.

80. See Thurston County case files 0316/0314 and 0502/0498 in *Frontier Justice, 1853–*

1889: A Guide to Court Records of Washington Territory (Olympia: State of Washington, Office of the Secretary of State, Division of Archives and Record Management, 1987).

81. For information on Levy and shanghaiing, see Simpson, *City of Dreams.* See also Richard H. Dillon, *Shanghaiing Days* (New York: Coward McCann, 1961), 264.

82. For information on Sachs, see Jefferson County Historical Society, *With Pride in Heritage,* 404, and news clipping, "Local 'Faro' Judge Tried by Legislature in 1891," in Spaeth, "Port Townsend Jewish History Notes."

83. "Married," *The Victoria (B.C.) Daily British Colonist,* 28 December 1864, p. 3.

84. Hurst, interview; see also Freedman, "Jewish Pioneers," 41.

85. *Kalama (Washington Territory) Beacon,* 11 January 1873, cited in Eulenberg, "Jewish Enterprise," 56.

86. For the best account of the Yukon gold rush, see Pierre Berton, *The Klondike Fever: The Life and Death of the Last Great Gold Rush* (New York: Alfred A. Knopf, 1958). Berton found that Seattle bought five times as much advertising as any other city (p. 124).

87. *Seattle Post-Intelligencer,* 25 July 1897, p. 1.

88. Sale, *Seattle, Past to Present,* 52–53. Sale argues that Seattle benefited from the gold rush because it had a superior commercial infrastructure.

Eastern European Pioneers

1. Howard Muggamin, *The Jewish Americans* (New York and Philadelphia: Chelsea House, 1996), 14.

2. Irving Howe, *World of Our Fathers* (New York and London: Harcourt Brace Jovanovich, 1976), 26.

3. Gerald Sorin, *A Time for Building: The Third Migration, 1880–1920* (Baltimore: Johns Hopkins University Press, 1992), 12–37.

4. Jack Radinsky, transcript of interview, MSCUA/UWL, Acc. 2407.

5. Howe, *World of Our Fathers,* 5, 26–27.

6. Ibid., 36–37.

7. Esther Rickles King, "Journal," in possession of Evelyn Brickman, San Francisco.

8. Howe, *World of Our Fathers,* 40–41.

9. Sol Esfeld, transcript of interview, MSCUA/UWL, Acc. 2018-3.

10. Howe, *World of Our Fathers,* 43.

11. Ibid., 45; see also *Life,* September 1990.

12. Cindy Muscatel, "Coming to American," *Newsletter* (September 1990).

13. Howe, *World of Our Fathers,* 46.

14. Tobi Faye Kestenberg, "From the Shtetl to Bellingham: The History of New Whatcom's Jewish Community, 1908–1984," MSCUA/UWL, Acc. 3718.

15. Muggamin, *The Jewish Americans,* 44.

16. Howe, *World of Our Fathers,* 47; Ray Ruppert, "The Land Was a Lure for Early Jewish Immigrants," *The Seattle Sunday Times Magazine,* 8 October 1978, p. 9. See also J. Sanford Rikoon, ed., *Rachel Calef's Story: Jewish Homesteaders on the Northern Plains*

(Bloomington: Indiana University Press, 1995).

17. Rickles King, "Journal"; Max Katz, transcript of interview, MSCUA/UWL, Acc. 3247.

18. Howe, *World of Our Fathers*, 31–32; Abram Leon Sachar, *A History of the Jews* (New York: Alfred A. Knopf, 1930), 307.

19. Harry Pruzan, transcript of interview, MSCUA/UWL, Acc. 4001.

20. Conversations with Judge Leonard Friedman, Sacramento, Calif., 1997.

21. "First Jew in the Pacific Northwest?" *Jewish Western Bulletin*, British Columbia Centenary Issue (June 30, 1958): p. 6; Deborah K. Freedman, "Jewish Pioneers of Tacoma," unpublished manuscript, 1998, 44.

22. Lorraine Sussman Braverman, "Frank Sussman and Family," notes and clippings, Lorraine Sussman Braverman papers, Tacoma, 1998.

23. Molly Cone reminiscence.

24. Except where otherwise noted, Bellingham information is from the following articles by Tim Baker published in *The Bellingham Shul Shofar*: "Unofficial History of Beth Israel Synagogue," 15 September 1996; "From Skopishok to Bellingham—Birth of a Community," March 1997; "Beginnings of Beth Israel Synagogue: The Little Shul on the Hill," November 1996, p. 6.

25. William C. Speidel, *Sons of the Profits; or, There's No Business Like Grow Business: The Seattle Story, 1851–1903* (Seattle: Nettle Creek Publishing Co., 1967), 48.

26. Kestenberg, "From the Shtetl to Bellingham."

27. Edward Glazer, transcript of interview, MSCUA/UWL, Acc. 3215.

28. Mary Kosher Brown, transcript of interview, MSCUA/UWL, Acc. 3785.

29. Moe Michelson, transcript of interview, MSCUA/UWL, Acc. 3661.

30. William Rosen, transcript of interview, MSCUA/UWL, Acc. 2284.

31. Rabbi R. H. Levine, "Alfred Shemanski: A Community Giant," a *Seattle Times Magazine*, 6 May 1979; Herbert Lipman, transcript of interview, MSCUA/UWL, Acc. 2301.

32. Statistics from Fred Cordova, Office of News and Information, University of Washington.

33. Henry Ralkowski, transcript of interview, MSCUA/UWL, Acc. 2111.

34. Unless otherwise noted, information on Brenner is based on Itsy and Joe Brenner, transcript of interview, MSCUA/UWL, Acc. 3934-2, and on Doug Margeson, "How Charlie, Itsy and Joe Shaped Bread and Business," *Bellevue Journal-American*, 22 April 1986.

35. Based on clippings from *The Jewish Transcript*, 1926 and 1934, and *The Seattle Times* obituary, 1951, Julius Shafer papers, MSCUA/UWL, Acc. 2830. Shafer's success had a strange effect on reports of his origins. The *Times* obituary reported that he was born in Austria, thus identifying him with the prestigious German Jews, although a 1926 *Jewish Transcript* article stated he was Russian-born.

36. Ben Genauer, transcript of interview, MSCUA/UWL, Acc. 1750.

37. Conversations with Joe Diamond, Seattle.

38. Muriel Weissberg, "Morris Schneider, Pioneer Washington State Merchant," *Western States Jewish History* 25 (July 1992): 308–14.

39. Ibid.

40. Information on settlers in Republic based on Meta Buttnick and Julia Niebuhr Eulenberg, "Jewish Settlement in the Small Towns of Washington State: Republic," WSJHS Newsletter (March 1984) and news clippings from The Spokane Review dated 1907, 1908, and 1914.

41. Charles Pierce Le Warne, Utopias on Puget Sound, 1885–1915 (Seattle: University of Washington Press, 1975), 168–226.

42. Ibid., 198.

43. Ibid. See also Lorraine Sidell, "Home Colony," WSJHS Newsletter (December 1990).

44. Sidell, "Home Colony."

45. Le Warne, Utopias on Puget Sound, 225–26.

46. Henry L. Feingold, A Time for Searching: Entering the Mainstream (Baltimore: The Johns Hopkins University Press, 1992), 129.

Sephardic Pioneers

1. Albert Adatto, "Sephardim and the Seattle Sephardic Community" (Master's thesis, University of Washington, 1939), 183–203. First Sephardi arrival also cited as 1903. See also Lorraine Sidell, "Sephardic Jews of Seattle," Western States Jewish History 24 (April 1992): 201–13. "Tefillin" or phylacteries were two small leather cubes with straps containing religious inscriptions.

2. Adatto, "Sephardim and the Seattle Sephardic Community," 183–203.

3. Ladino or Judeo-Spanish is a Hispanic language written in Hebrew characters. Just as Yiddish is basically German with an admixture of Hebrew and some Slavic words, Ladino is basically medieval Castilian Spanish with an admixture of Hebrew and some Turkish, Greek, Arabic, and other regional languages.

4. Esther Rickles King, "Journal," in possession of Evelyn Brickman, San Francisco.

5. Irving Howe, World of Our Fathers (New York and London: Harcourt Brace Jovanovich, 1976), 57–63. See also Judith E. Endelman, The Jewish Community of Indianapolis (Bloomington: Indiana University Press, 1984), 67.

6. Adatto, "Sephardim and the Seattle Sephardic Community," 192.

7. Ibid., 194–98.

8. Ibid., 196–98.

9. Ibid.

10. Rachel Cohen Israel, transcript of interview, MSCUA/UWL, Acc. 2383.

11. Adatto, "Sephardim and the Seattle Sephardic Community," 65; Sidell, "Sephardic Jews of Seattle," 202.

12. Charles Alhadeff, transcript of interview, MSCUA/UWL, Acc. 3290.

13. Adatto, "Sephardim and the Seattle Sephardic Community," 67.

14. Cynthia H. Wilson, "On Being a Jew in Seattle," The Seattle Weekly, 8 December 1982, 31–37.

15. Marc D. Angel, "The Sephardim of the U.S.: An Exploratory Study," in the American

Jewish Yearbook 1973 (New York: The American Jewish Committee; Philadelphia: The Jewish Publication Society of America, 1973), 85.

16. Adatto, "Sephardim and the Seattle Sephardic Community," 200.

17. Endelman, *The Jewish Community of Indianapolis*, 66. See also Marc D. Angel, "Notes on the Early History of Seattle's Sephardic Community," *Western States Jewish Historical Quarterly* 7 (October 1974): 23. Angel noted that another estimate in 1912 numbered eight hundred. He could not vouch for the reliability of either figure.

18. Adatto, "Sephardim and the Seattle Sephardic Community," 162. See also Angel, "The Sephardim of the U.S.," 87.

19. Adatto, "Sephardim and the Seattle Sephardic Community," 80; Sidell, "Sephardic Jews of Seattle," 203–204.

20. Carey Quan Gelernter, "Landlord Sam," *The Seattle Times*, 13 July 1981, p. A1, and "Samuel Israel, Eccentric and a Loner," *The Seattle Times*, 13 July 1981, p. C1; Richard Seven, "The Collector," *The Seattle Times Magazine*, 11 April 1999, pp. 16–18; and conversation with David Hasson, Samis Foundation, Seattle.

21. Seven, "The Collector."

22. David Behar, "To Be a Sephardic Jew," *The Seattle Times/Post-Intelligencer*, 17 May 1992, p. 18.

23. Adatto, "Sephardim and the Seattle Sephardic Community," 163.

Unity, Division, and Friction

1. Schwabacher family, transcript of interview, MSCUA/UWL, Acc. 2149-3.

2. Ibid.; Esther Borish Friedman, transcript of interview, MSCUA/UWL, Acc. 2273; conversations with Goldie Rickles Cone and her East European immigrant friends. Similar sentiments are cited in Irving Howe, *World of Our Fathers* (New York and London: Harcourt Brace Jovanovich, 1976).

3. Leni Peha LaMarche, transcript of interview, MSCUA/UWL, Acc. 3452.

4. Morris Kleiner, "Memoirs, 1889–1974," MSCUA/UWL, Acc. 2342; Rabbi Richard Rosenthal, transcript of interview, MSCUA/UWL, Acc. 4052.

5. Betty Meyersberg, transcript of interview, Spokane Jewish community, Ms. 151 (OH-812), Eastern Washington State Historical Society, Cheney Cowles Museum.

6. Dina Tanners and Paul Tanners, "Interview with Pearl Duitch Singer and Bob Singer," Ms. 151, Eastern Washington State Historical Society, Cheney Cowles Museum.

7. Marc D. Angel, "The Sephardim of the U.S.: An Exploratory Study," in *American Jewish Year Book* 1973 (New York: The American Jewish Committee; Philadelphia: The Jewish Publication Society of America, 1973), 125.

8. Friedman, interview.

9. Ibid.

10. Marc D. Angel, "A Personal and Scholarly Account: Early Sephardim in Seattle," in *Western States Jewish History*, ed. William M. Kramer (Los Angeles: Isaac Nathan Co., Inc., 1996), 562.

11. Ibid., 562, 573.

12. Charles Alhadeff, transcript of interview, MSCUA/UWL, Acc. 3290.

13. Ibid.

14. Angel, "The Sephardim of the U.S.," 77–138.

15. Albert Adatto, "Sephardim and the Seattle Sephardic Community" (Master's thesis, University of Washington, 1939).

16. *The Jewish Voice*, 3 January 1919. See also Jane A. Avner and Meta Buttnick, "Historic Jewish Seattle: A Tour Guide," Washington State Jewish Historical Society pamphlet, 1995, p. 14.

17. Conversation with Meta Buttnick, 1996.

18. Albert Franco, transcript of interview, MSCUA/UWL, Acc. 2834.

19. Alfred Shemanski to Sol Esfeld, May 22, 1930, Sol Esfeld papers, MSCUA/UWL, Acc. 2018.

20. Adatto "Sephardim and the Seattle Sephardic Community," 19.

First Organizations

1. C. G. Montefiore and H. Loewe, *A Rabbinic Anthology* (New York: Schocken Books, 1974), 412. See also Ewa Morawska, "Assimilation of Nineteenth-Century Jewish Women," in *Jewish Women in America: An Historical Encyclopedia*, ed. Paula E. Hyman and Deborah Dash Moore (New York: Routledge, 1998), 83–90. For how *tzedakah* has been and is part of Jewish belief, see Charlotte Baum, Paula Hyman, and Sonya Michel, *The Jewish Woman in America* (New York: The Dial Press, 1976), and Nathan Glazer, *American Judaism* (Chicago: University of Chicago Press, 1957), 1–12.

2. In 1891, people in both Tacoma and Spokane complained about the men who went from city to city seeking aid. Tacoma's complaint is cited in Temple Beth El, *Centuries to Celebrate* (Tacoma: Temple Beth El, 1992), 5; for Spokane, see unsigned letter to *The American Israelite*, 26 November 1891, p. 3.

3. Paula Hyman, *Gender and Assimilation in Modern Jewish History* (Seattle: University of Washington Press, 1995), 15.

4. See H. H. Ben-Sasson, ed., *A History of the Jewish People* (Cambridge: Harvard University Press, 1976), 834, for a discussion of the ideological changes in Europe.

5. Benevolent societies, both Jewish and non-Jewish, became popular on the East Coast in the early part of the nineteenth century. Jewish groups usually inserted the word "Hebrew" in their organizations. Rebecca Gratz of Philadelphia established the first Female Hebrew Benevolent Society in that city in 1819.

6. Glazer, *American Judaism*, 54–55.

7. *The Olympia Washington Standard*, 1 November 1873.

8. *Articles of Incorporation for the Hebrew Benevolent Society*, vol. 10, p. 367, Deed Records, Thurston County Title Co., Olympia, January 19, 1874.

9. Ibid.

10. "Chronology of the Jewish Cemetery in Olympia," a typewritten, one-page data sheet from the Thurston County History Preservation Office, Olympia.

11. Unless otherwise stated, information about Tacoma's cemetery is from Deborah K. Freedman, comp., "Home of Peace Cemetery Inscriptions," Draft 8, May 1998 (Tacoma: Genfreed Press, 1998).

12. Because the only early records of the cemetery are from newspaper accounts, there is some confusion as to whether the Hebrew Benevolent Association of Tacoma is also the group that organized Tacoma's first temple.

13. Information is from *Tacoma News*, 8 January 1890, 9 January 1891, 16 January 1891, and 14 February 1891, and from *Polk's Tacoma City Directory*. The name disappears from the Polk directory in 1896.

14. Information supplied to Jacqueline Williams from Deborah Freedman, who is conducting detailed studies of Tacoma's early Jewish community.

15. Names of B'nai B'rith lodges and dates of incorporation are from B'nai B'rith International, Washington D.C. The Tacoma lodge is also mentioned in Herbert Hunt, *Tacoma, Its History and Its Builders: A Half-Century of History* (Chicago: S. J. Clarke, 1916), 26. Organizational records are not available.

16. Ben-Sasson, *A History of the Jewish People*, 852.

17. Roy Rosenthal, transcript of interview, MSCUA/UWL, Acc. 2352. There are no records from the Grays Harbor B'nai B'rith. Bellingham and Everett also started a B'nai B'rith lodge in 1914, but there are no records of this lodge.

18. Morris Kleiner, transcript of interview, MSCUA/UWL, Acc. 2392.

19. Tacoma B'nai B'rith minutes, May 14, 1914, B'nai B'rith Lodge No. 741, 1913–1918, MSCUA/UWL, Acc. 5119 - 001.

20. Ibid., December 10, 1914.

21. *Jewish Voice*, 15 February 1918.

22. Tacoma B'nai B'rith minutes, May 23, 1918, B'nai B'rith Lodge No. 741, 1913–1918, MSCUA/UWL, Acc. 5119 - 001.

23. Lady Judith Montefiore Society minutes, May 1, 1890 and November 13, 1891, American Jewish Archives, Microfilm 2236–37. *The Jewish Tribune*, Portland, Oregon, September 25, 1903, and notes on Hoffman family in possession of Deborah Freedman, Tacoma, Washington.

24. There are no surviving written minutes or organizational records from the Tacoma Young Men's Hebrew Association.

25. This is the date listed in the records of B'nai B'rith International in Washington, D.C.

26. *Seattle Daily Post-Intelligencer*, 28 October 1884.

27. Annual report, October 20, 1901, Temple De Hirsch Sinai, Box 1, MSCUA/UWL, Acc. 2370 -4.

28. *Polk's Seattle City Directory* (Seattle: Polk's Seattle Directory Co., 1889–c. 1928) gives names of presidents, but the *Jewish Voice* has only the names of clubs listed. Except for an occasional newspaper item that reports on a dance, there are no records of members or activities.

29. Silver family, transcript of interview, Silver family papers, Box 1, MSCUA/UWL, Acc. 1826.

30. *Jewish Voice*, 28 July 1916 and 17 July 1917.

31. "A Bit of History," B'nai B'rith Seattle Lodge No. 503, Box 1, MSCUA/UWL, Acc. 3589; 3589-2.

32. Organizational materials, Jewish Family and Child Service, Box 6/16, MSCUA/UWL, Acc. 2003.

33. Unless otherwise stated, information is from *Temple Tidings*, 8 January 1917, Temple De Hirsch Sinai, Box 6, MSCUA/UWL, Acc. 2370, 2370-4.

34. In the resolution to merge, formally adopted in April 1925, mention is made of reasons and perhaps disputes that had to be solved, but states, "the records have been lost." Jewish Family and Child Service, Box 6/12, MSCUA/UWL, Acc. 2003.

35. Roy Rosenthal, unpublished, typewritten "History of the Jews of Seattle" (1914), Box 1, MSCUA/UWL, Acc. 2352-2. Meta Buttnick, local Jewish historian, in an unpublished paper says the Hebrew Relief Society was founded in 1904, disbanded sometime later (she gives no date), and formed again in 1932.

36. *Seattle Post-Intelligencer*, 9 January 1916.

37. Abe Hoffman, transcript of interview, MSCUA/UWL, Acc. 2744.

38. *The Jewish Transcript*, 6 May 1924.

39. Viola Gutmann Silver and Max Silver, transcript of interviews, Silver family papers, Box 1, MSCUA/UWL, Acc. 1826, 1826-2; Menorah program, 1917, Elizabeth Stusser papers, MSCUA/UWL, Acc. 2828.

40. Viola Gutmann Silver, interview. There are no records.

41. Ibid.

42. Gordon DeLeon, transcript of interview, MSCUA/UWL, Acc. 3268.

43. Ibid.

44. Albert Adatto, "Sephardim and the Seattle Sephardic Community" (Master's thesis, University of Washington, 1939).

45. *Jewish Voice*, 11 February 1916.

46. Morawska, "Assimilation of Nineteenth-Century Jewish Women," 83.

47. Baum, Hyman, and Michel, *The Jewish Woman in America*, 30.

48. Helen Berkman Blumenthal, transcript of interview, MSCUA/UWL, Acc. 2121, 2121-3; and Carolyn Blumenthal Danz, transcript of interview, MSCUA/UWL, Acc. 3895.

49. See Baum, Hyman, and Michel, *The Jewish Woman in America*, 46–53, for a discussion of the Jewish organization woman.

50. Organizational materials, Jewish Family and Child Service, Box 6/14, MSCUA/UWL, Acc. 2003.

51. Historical materials, Jewish Family and Child Services, Box 1/1, MSCUA/UWL, Acc. 2003. Dramatic programs and dances were popular ways of raising money in the nineteenth and early twentieth centuries.

52. Bernice Degginger Greengard, transcript of interview, MSCUA/UWL, Acc. 2403-2.

53. Anecdotal evidence gives 1895 as the date the Lady Judith Montifiore Aid Society was founded; the *Jewish Voice*, 19 February 1917, the earliest written source, reports 1899. Shucklin seems to have come to Seattle about 1892.

54. Gerald Shucklin, transcript of interview, MSCUA/UWL, Acc. 2331; the *Jewish Voice* of February 9, 1917, reported that Mrs. Dave Taylor and Goldie Shucklin organized the society.

55. Hoffman, interview.

56. *Jewish Voice*, 11 February 1916.

57. Russell Hollander, "Our Brothers' Keepers: The Story of Human Services in Washington, 1853–1932," *Columbia, The Magazine of Northwest History* 3 (spring 1989): 19.

58. Goldie Shucklin Memorial Fund, Jewish Family and Child Service, Box 3, MSCUA/UWL, Acc. 2003-7.

59. Baum, Hyman, and Michel, *The Jewish Woman in America*, 48–49.

60. Faith Rogow, "National Council of Jewish Women," in ibid., 71–72.

61. Copy of original minutes, *Temple Tidings*, May 1925, Temple De Hirsch Sinai, Box 6, MSCUA/UWL, Acc. 2370.

62. William Toll, *The Making of an Ethnic Middle Class: Portland Jewry Over Four Generations* (Albany: State University of New York Press, 1982), 76.

63. Report of Committee of Philanthropy, 1909, National Council of Jewish Women, Seattle Section, Box 1/1, MSCUA/UWL, Acc. 2089-2.

64. Jean Devine, "From Settlement House to Neighborhood House, 1906–76," 5–6, MSCUA/UWL, Acc. 2632, 2632-2.

65. Sarah Efron, transcript of interview, MSCUA/UWL, Acc. 2535.

66. DeLeon, interview.

67. Efron, interview.

68. See Dorothy Bilik, "Settlement Houses," in *Jewish Women in America: An Historical Encyclopedia*, ed. Hyman and Moore, 1231–36.

69. Efron, interview; Hoffman, interview; and Sol Esfeld, transcript of interview, MSCUA/UWL, Acc. 2018-3, are just a few of the sources that gave views about Settlement House days.

70. Devine, "From Settlement House to Neighborhood House, 1906–76," 5–6.

71. Report of Committee of Philanthropy, 1919–20, National Council of Jewish Women, Seattle Section, MSCUA/UWL, Acc. 2089-2.

72. *Jewish Voice*, 18 January 1918.

73. Grace Rubin, speech to Hebrew Ladies' Free Loan Society, October 25, 1965, Hebrew Ladies' Free Loan Society, Box 1, MSCUA/UWL, Acc. 1568. The organization increased the amount of its loans during the Depression. There are no surviving records.

74. Articles of Incorporation, June 1914, Hebrew Education and Free Loan Association, MSCUA/UWL, Acc. 3254.

75. *The Jewish Transcript*, 22 December 1983. As of 2001 the organization is still granting loans, albeit using a more formal request system.

76. Irving Howe, *World of Our Fathers* (New York and London: Harcourt Brace Jovanovich, 1976), 47–50. HIAS today dates its founding from 1881. E-mail to Jacqueline Williams from Morris Ardoin, Director of Communication, HIAS, April 30, 2001.

77. Because of submarine warfare on the Atlantic Coast during the First World War, immigrants entered the United States via the West Coast.

78. "Jewish Immigration Bulletin," December 1917, p. 13, Hebrew Sheltering and Immigrant Aid Society of America, Box 1, MSCUA/UWL, Acc. 3409.

79. *Jewish Voice*, 21 April 1916.

80. Efron, interview.

81. "Jewish Immigration Bulletin," March 1917, p. 15, Hebrew Sheltering and Immigrant Aid Society of America, MSCUA/UWL, Acc. 3409.

82. *Spokane Spokesman-Review,* 8 October 1916.

83. *Jewish Voice,* 31 December 1915.

84. *Spokane Spokesman-Review,* 13 February 1920.

85. Articles of Incorporation, September 1, 1891, Spokane, Washington, American Jewish Archives, Microfilm 2236-37.

86. Congregation Emanu-El minutes, December 18, 1892, American Jewish Archives, Microfilm 2236-37.

87. Dr. David Levine, "History of the Jews in Spokane," *The Reform Advocate,* Emil G. Hirsch, ed., no date but probably 1914.

88. "The Up and the Down of Jewish Activity in Spokane, 1891–1894," *Western States Jewish Quarterly* 5 (July 1979): 308–309.

89. Levine, "History of the Jews in Spokane." On February 5, 1926, *The Jewish Transcript* reported that this and other societies "are now out of existence...as some more modern and progressive ones took their place." Bellingham also had a Ladies' Hebrew Benevolent Society. The name appears in documents found in the cornerstone of the 1925 synagogue. No records remain.

90. B'nai B'rith International records the date for the women's auxiliary as February 24, 1912. There are no board minutes from either the men's or women's groups.

91. *The Jewish Transcript,* 5 February 1926.

92. *Spokane Spokesman-Review,* 10 December 1917.

93. *Jewish Herald, Spokane and Inland Empire,* 26 September 1935, Spokane Jewish Community, Ms. 151, Box 1/33, Eastern Washington State Historical Society, Cheney Cowles Museum. There were only a few issues of this paper.

94. Minutes, Bilou Club, Spokane Jewish Community, Ms. 151, Box 1/38, Eastern Washington State Historical Society, Cheney Cowles Museum.

95. *The Jewish Transcript,* 14 February 1930.

First Congregations

1. *The Olympia Washington Standard,* 23 September 1871.

2. *Tacoma News,* 21 September 1882; N. W. Durham, *History of the City of Spokane and Spokane County, Washington,* vol. 1 (Spokane-Chicago-Philadelphia: S. J. Clarke, 1912), 580; *Seattle Post-Intelligencer,* 6 September 1888.

3. Hasia R. Diner, *A Time For Gathering: The Second Migration, 1820–1880* (Baltimore: Johns Hopkins University Press, 1992), 137.

4. Ibid., 6.

5. Ibid., 16.

6. For a discussion of the Emancipation era and the beginning of Reform Judaism, see ibid., 6–36.

7. Nathan Glazer, *American Judaism,* (Chicago: University of Chicago Press, 1957), 40–42.

8. Articles of Incorporation of Congregation Ohaveth Sholum, Washington State Archives—Puget Sound Branch, Bellevue, Wash.

9. Unless otherwise stated, information about Ohaveth Sholum is from Howard Droker, "Ohaveth Sholum: Seattle's First Congregation," *Western States Jewish History* 17 (October 1984): 26–34.

10. Ewa Morawska, "Assimilation of Nineteenth-Century Jewish Women," in *Jewish Women in America: An Historical Encyclopedia*, ed. Paula E. Hyman and Deborah Dash Moore (New York: Routledge, 1998), 88.

11. Droker suggests that Ohaveth Sholum is patterned after San Francisco's Congregation Emanu-El. Julia Niebuhr Eulenberg, in "Jewish Enterprise in the American West: Washington, 1853–1909" (Ph.D. diss., University of Washington, 1996), p. 370, suggests that it could easily have been patterned after San Francisco's so-called Bush Street Synagogue.

12. Temple minutes reprinted in *Temple Tidings*, February 1925, Temple De Hirsch Sinai, MSCUA/UWL, Acc. 2370, 2370-4.

13. *Seattle Post-Intelligencer*, 12 November 1905.

14. Although Rabbi Joseph's statement could be questioned, as he was not there at the time, it seems unlikely the newspaper could have made up something like Minnich Poland. See also Julius Rickles, transcript of interview, MSCUA/UWL, Acc. 962.

15. Secretary's report, May 30, 1899, and Minutes, May 29, 1899, Temple De Hirsch Sinai, Box 1, MSCUA/UWL, Acc. 2370, 2370-4.

16. *Seattle Post-Intelligencer*, 22 December 1899.

17. Ibid., 10 June 1901.

18. Third Annual Report, October 20, 1901, Temple De Hirsch Sinai, Box 1, MSCUA/UWL, Acc. 2370, 2370-4.

19. Articles of Incorporation, April 12, 1900, Temple De Hirsch Sinai, Box 1, MSCUA/UWL, Acc. 2370, 2370-4.

20. Secretary's report, May 30, 1899, and Minutes, May 29, 1899, Temple De Hirsch, Box 1, MSCUA/UWL, Acc. 2370, 2370-4.

21. Minutes, October 1, 1899, Temple De Hirsch, Box 1, MSCUA/UWL, Acc. 2370, 2370-4.

22. Ibid., August 28.

23. *Temple Tidings*, March 1925, Temple De Hirsch Sinai, Box 6, MSCUA/UWL; *The Jewish Transcript*, 10 May 1929.

24. President's report, October 19, 1899; Seventh Annual Report, November 5, 1905, Temple De Hirsch Sinai, Box 1, MSCUA/UWL, Acc. 2370, 2370-4.

25. See Julia Niebuhr Eulenberg, "Samuel Koch: Seattle's Social Justice Rabbi" (Master's thesis, University of Washington, 1984), for more information about Rabbi Samuel Koch.

26. *Temple Tidings*, June 1910, Temple De Hirsch Sinai, Box 6, MSCUA/UWL, Acc. 2370, 2370-4.

27. Bikur Cholim Fair and Bazaar Program, 1917, Jacob Kaplan papers, Box 1/14, MSCUA/UWL, Acc. 1960, 1960-2–4. A brief history in the Fair and Bazaar Program notes that the first Chevra was called Chevra Anshe Ahmed.

28. Articles of Incorporation, November 17, 1891, B. Myers, M.D., President, Jacob Kaplan papers, Box 1/18, MSCUA/UWL, Acc. 1960, 1960-2-4.

29. Minutes, June 3, 1917, Congregation Bikur Cholim, Box 3/2, MSCUA/UWL, Acc. 2450, 2450-2, 1035, 1779.

30. *Polk's Seattle City Directory* (Seattle: Polk's Seattle Directory Co., 1894–95). Jacob Alpern, who died April 17, 1895, is the first person buried in the cemetery. Eighty acres in the northeast section of the Oak Lake cemetery are first assessed to Chevra Bikur Cholim in 1896. M. S. Whitman's name is listed as the person being assessed, but taxes are paid by the estate of Clara E. Hutton. Washington State Archives—Puget Sound Branch, Bellevue, Wash.

31. Laura C. Daly, "A Change of Worlds: A History of Seattle Cemeteries," *Portage* 5 (winter/spring 1984): 22; Meta R. Buttnick, "Seattle's Jewish Cemeteries," *WSJHS Newsletter*, (summer 1997): 3.

32. Notarized statement from Office of the Secretary of State, June 14, 1900, Congregation Bikur Cholim–Machzikay Hadath, Box 1, MSCUA/UWL, Acc. 2450-5–7, 2450-9–14.

33. Rickles, interview. *Polk's Seattle City Directory*, 1894–95, lists Chevra Bikur Cholim as located in the Hinckley Block from 1894 to 1895; in the Latimer Building from 1895 to 1896; and on Fifth Avenue South in 1898.

34. *Seattle Post-Intelligencer*, 8 September 1896. The paper reported that Abromowitz came from San Francisco, but another story reports he was from Portland. The story also said Abromowitz had been here before.

35. Esther Gross, transcript of interview, MSCUA/UWL, Acc. 2281. The Grozinsky family first shows up in *Polk's Seattle City Directory*, 1892–93. At that time, Zalman is spelled Selman, and the family lives at 713 Third Avenue. In the 1895–96 *Polk's Seattle City Directory*, the home address is 1417 Washington. In 1898, the family is listed under Gross.

36. Roger Sale, *Seattle, Past to Present* (Seattle: University of Washington Press, 1976), 58.

37. Bond, July 11, 1898, and Warranty deed, July 6, 1900, Jacob Kaplan papers, Box 1/18, MSCUA/UWL, Acc. 1960, 1960-2-4.

38. *The Jewish Transcript*, 19 September 1925.

39. *Seattle Post-Intelligencer*, 3 October 1898.

40. See Meta Buttnick, "Congregation Bikur Cholim–Machzikay Hadath of Seattle: The Beginning Years," *Western States Jewish History* 22 (January 1990): 140, note 5, in which Julius Rickles recalled that the overbooking occurred in Christensen's Hall in 1908 and gave this as the reason for building the newer synagogue at Seventeenth and Yesler.

41. Minutes of Bikur Cholim meetings do not begin until 1909. Early histories published as part of an anniversary program, and stories covering these events in *The Jewish Transcript* in 1917 and 1925, do not mention this event.

42. "Golden Jubilee," November 1941, Congregation Bikur Cholim, Box 1/1a, MSCUA/UWL, Acc. 1035, 1779, 2450, 2450-4.

43. Abe Hoffman, transcript of interview, MSCUA/UWL, Acc. 2744.

44. Rickles, interview.

45. Minutes, January 29, 1911, Congregation Bikur Cholim, Box 3, MSCUA/UWL, Acc. 1035, 1779, 2450, 2450-4.

46. Minutes, February 25, 1912, Congregation Bikur Cholim, Box 3/1, MSCUA/UWL, Acc. 1035, 1779, 2450, 2450-4.

47. Articles of Incorporation, 1906, Herzl Conservative Congregation, MSCUA/UWL, Acc. 2884.

48. Sam Prottas, transcript of interview, MSCUA/UWL, Acc. 2216-3.

49. *Seattle Post-Intelligencer*, 23 August 1909, p. 2.

50. *Jewish Voice*, 17 July 1917.

51. Historical material, Herzl Ner Tamid Conservative Congregation (Mercer Island, Wash.), Box 1/8, MSCUA/UWL, Acc. 2102-4.

52. *The Jewish Transcript*, 3 September 1937, and June 28, 1940.

53. Meta Buttnick, "Herzl-Ner Tamid Conservative Congregation of Seattle: the Beginning Years," Part 1, *Western States Jewish History* 15 (April 1993): 248, 250.

54. Albert Adatto, "Sephardim and the Seattle Sephardic Community" (Master's thesis, University of Washington, 1939), 65–66.

55. Marc D. Angel, "Notes on the Early History of Seattle's Sephardic Community," *Western States Jewish Historical Quarterly* 7 (October 1974): 56–58.

56. "The First 70 Years of the Sephardic Bikur Holim Congregation 1914–1984," Sephardic Bikur Holim, MSCUA/UWL, Acc. 2389-5.

57. Isaac Maimon, "History of the Congregation Ahavath Ahim of Seattle, Washington, 1906–1996" (unpublished typewritten manuscript). Because early records are lost, no one knows for certain where members attended services before acquiring a building. Some say people attended Ezra Bessaroth or Sephardic Bikur Holim on Saturday and rented Washington Hall for holiday services.

58. William M. Kramer, "The History of Congregation Ahavath Achim of Portland," *Western States Jewish History* 29 (October 1996): 629.

59. See Angel, "Early History of Seattle's Sephardic Community," 560.

60. *The Jewish Transcript*, 29 January 1932. Hoping a reorganization would strengthen the synagogue, Congregation Ahavath Ahim's remaining members wrote new bylaws, re-incorporated, and hired Rev. Morris L. Scharhon to conduct services. Scharhon held the dwindling membership together until 1944, when Ahavath Ahim closed its doors.

61. "67 Years Preserving Sephardic Tradition," Ezra Bessaroth, MSCUA/UWL, Acc. 2739-2.

62. Elazar Behar, transcript of interview, MSCUA/UWL, Acc. 3209.

63. Gordon DeLeon, transcript of interview, MSCUA/UWL, Acc. 3268.

64. Angel, "Early History of Seattle's Sephardic Community," 569–70. On January 11, 1918, the *Jewish Voice* reported a meeting to discuss possibly merging the two synagogues, but this seems to have created some controversy; in a later issue, the paper emphasized this was just talk and that nothing had been decided.

65. *Spokane Falls Review*, 24 September 1890.

66. Emil G. Hirsch, ed., *The Reform Advocate*, no date, Spokane Jewish Community, Ms. 151, Box 1/2, Eastern Washington State Historical Society, Cheney Cowles Museum; Moses N. Janton, *History of the Jews in Spokane, Washington* (Spokane: Star

Printing House, 1926); J. Wolff, self-published document, MSCUA/UWL, Acc. 1495; and Miscellaneous records, 1890–1930, Congregation Emanu-El (Spokane, Wash.), American Jewish Archives, Microfilm 2236–37.

67. *Polk's Spokane City Directory*, 1892.

68. Miscellaneous records, 1890–1930, Congregation Emanu-El, American Jewish Archives.

69. Letter printed in *Western States Jewish Historical Quarterly* 9 (July 1979): 4. Rabbi Isaac Mayer Wise founded *The American Israelite*.

70. *Spokane Falls Review*, 24 September 1890.

71. Board minutes, June 13, 1919, and Miscellaneous records, 1890–1930, Congregation Emanu-El, American Jewish Archives.

72. "The Jewish Voice of the Island Empire," Spokane, June 22, 1928, Jacob Kaplan papers, Box 1/2, MSCUA/UWL, Acc. 1960, 1960-2-4.

73. Excerpt from address of S. Edelstein, July 5, 1929, Miscellaneous records, 1890–1930, Congregation Emanu-El, American Jewish Archives.

74. "The First Sixty Years of Our Congregation Life," J. Wolff papers, MSCUA/UWL, Acc. 1495.

75. *The Jewish Transcript*, 2 November 1934.

76. Board Minutes, April 19, 1903, Congregation Keneseth Israel, Ms. 74, Eastern Washington State Historical Society, Cheney Cowles Museum.

77. Ibid., October 28, 1906.

78. Ibid., December 25, 1908; January 3, 1909.

79. Ibid., April 2, 1904.

80. Ibid., February 3, 1908.

81. Janton, *The History of the Jews in Spokane, Washington*. In 1957, a Mount Nebo Cemetery Committee assumed the tasks performed by the Helping Hand Society. The committee is now part of Temple Beth Shalom.

82. Board minutes, June 30, 1912, Congregation Keneseth Israel, Ms. 74, Eastern Washington State Historical Society, Cheney Cowles Museum.

83. Constitution and bylaws of the Congregation Keneseth Israel, 1926, Ms. 151, Box 4/34, Spokane Jewish Community, Eastern Washington State Historical Society, Cheney Cowles Museum.

84. Conversation with Nate Grossman, February 12, 1998. Grossman is helping to organize the Spokane Jewish Community archives.

85. Hirsch, *The Reform Advocate*. Ann Roberts, *Spokane County Cemetery Guide* (Orting, Wash.: Heritage Quest Press, 1989), p. 93, states that Ahavath Israel dedicated a cemetery on April 23, 1914, but that rock in the area made it too hard to serve as a cemetery.

86. *Tacoma Daily Ledger*, 14 February 1892.

87. *Tacoma Daily Ledger*, 10 March 1892.

88. *Tacoma Daily Ledger*, 4 December 1892; Temple Beth El, *Centuries to Celebrate*, (Tacoma: Temple Beth El, 1992), counts the Temple Aid Society and the Lady Judith Montefiore Society as being forerunners of the Sisterhood. Sisterhood minutes dated September 10, 1919, report a meeting held in the Tacoma Hotel to form a new Sisterhood

independent of the Lady Judith Montefiore Society. American Jewish Archives, Microfilm 2236–37.

89. *Tacoma Daily Ledger*, 11 September 1893.

90. Minutes of Beth Israel, December 21, 1924 (microfilm), Temple Beth Israel (Tacoma, Wash.), MSCUA/UWL, Acc. 2155. The 1892 Constitution of Congregation Beth Israel stated that the congregation was "to wear their hats during services."

91. B'nai B'rith minutes, June 28, 1917, and April 29, 1919, Temple Beth Israel (Tacoma, Wash.), MSCUA/UWL, Acc. 2155. *Tacoma Daily Ledger*, August 23, 1903.

92. *The Jewish Transcript*, 22 June 1928.

93. "Temple Beth El, *Centuries to Celebrate*, 6, and Congregation Talmud Torah, "Twentieth Anniversary Celebration," program pamphlet.

94. See Quintard Taylor, *The Forging of a Black Community: Seattle's Central District from 1870 through the Civil Rights Era* (Seattle: University of Washington Press, 1994), and David M. Buerge and Junius Rochester, *Roots and Branches* (Seattle: Church Council of Greater Seattle, 1988) for an overall discussion of earlier minority churches.

95. Tim Baker, "Bellingham Celebrates 100 Years of Jewish Life," *The Jewish Transcript*, 6 October 2000.

96. Many traveling rabbis who acted as shohet, mohel, and Hebrew teacher did not have clerical certification. See Jeffrey S. Gurock, *American Jewish Orthodoxy in Historical Perspective* (Hoboken, N.J.: KTAV Publishing House, Inc., 1996).

97. Edward Glazer, transcript of interview, MSCUA/UWL, Acc. 3215.

98. Rules found in old ledger written in Yiddish/Hebrew and translated in 1989 by Rabbi Feuerstein of Congregation Schara Teedeck, Vancouver, B.C. Ledger is in possession of Diane Garmo, Bellingham.

99. Frances Garmo, transcript of interview, MSCUA/UWL, Acc. 2550.

100. Both congregations are listed in the calendar published in the *Jewish Voice*, 1915–19. None of the respondents in the oral history interviews mention House of Israel.

101. William Sturman, transcript of interview, MSCUA/UWL, Acc. 3663; and Moe Michelson, transcript of interview, MSCUA/UWL, Acc. 3661. In some places Silverstone is alleged to have conducted services for fifty years; others say only forty. Synagogue board minutes dated October 29, 1925, show the board agreed to hire a rabbi for a year. A letter dated January 1927 shows agreement reached between a Rabbi L. Merport and the synagogue. The rabbi was also to function as shohet and as a Hebrew instructor for children. However, the next year Mr. Poplack from Bellingham was hired for High Holy Days. Montefiore Congregation (Everett, Wash.), Box 1, MSCUA/UWL, Acc. 3574, 3574-2.

102. Sturman, interview, and Michelson, interview. When interviewed in 1985, Moe Michelson and William (Billy) Sturman lamented that now they could hardly find enough men to form a minyan.

103. Sylvia Wolff Epstein, transcript of interview, MSCUA/UWL, Acc. 4787-001.

104. *Jewish Voice*, 1 October 1915.

105. Epstein, interview.

106. *The Jewish Transcript*, 6 December 1929, 19 April 1929, and 21 February 1930.

107. Jonathan D. Sarna, ed., *The American Experience* (New York: Holmes & Meier, 1997), xiii.

Seattle's Jewish Neighborhood

1. Lawyers had given the name to the area because of their colorful complaints about frequent cable car breakdowns that necessitated steep uphill hikes to the King County Court House, built at Ninth Avenue and Yesler Way in 1890. Irene Miller, *Profanity Hill* (Everett, Wash.: The Working Press, 1979), 10.

2. Lori Cohn, "Residential Patterns of the Jewish Community of the Seattle Area, 1910–1980" (Master's thesis, University of Washington, 1982), 32. Cohn's statistics take into account only affiliated Jews. For population statistics on Seattle as a whole, with special attention to the foreign-born, see Richard C. Berner, *Seattle 1900–1920: From Boomtown, Urban Turbulence, to Restoration* (Seattle: Charles Press, 1991), chapter 7, "The Framework of Life in the City."

3. Meta Buttnick, "Landmarks," *WSJHS Newsletter* (May 1981).

4. Ibid.

5. Benjamin Asia, transcript of interview, MSCUA/UWL, Acc. 4301.

6. See Peter Levine, "The *American Hebrew* Looks at 'Our Crowd': The Jewish Country Club in the 1920s," *American Jewish History* 83 (March 1995): 27–49. Quoted p. 31.

7. Joanna Eckstein, transcript of interview, MSCUA/UWL, Acc. 460.

8. William Staadecker, transcript of interview, MSCUA/UWL, Acc. 3206.

9. Deborah Dash Moore, "The Construction of Community: Jewish Migration and Ethnicity in the United States," in *The Jews of North America*, ed. Moses Rischin, (Detroit: Wayne State University Press, 1987), 107.

10. Max Katz, transcript of interview, MSCUA/UWL, Acc. 3247.

11. Harry Pruzan, "Yesler Way—A Ghetto of the Past," 1932 manuscript, MSCUA/UWL, Acc. 4001.

12. Miller, *Profanity Hill*, is an account of the building of Yesler Terrace.

13. Cohn, "Residential Patterns of the Jewish Community of the Seattle Area," 35. For a history of Seattle's African American community, including housing patterns, and for a good discussion of Seattle's Asian communities, see Quintard Taylor, *The Forging of a Black Community: Seattle's Central District from 1870 through the Civil Rights Era* (Seattle: University of Washington Press, 1994).

14. Moore, "The Construction of Community," 114.

15. Conversation with June Rose Droker, July 25, 1997.

16. Gordon DeLeon, transcript of interview, MSCUA/UWL, Acc. 3268.

17. This description of the Yesler business district is based on research in *Polk's Seattle City Directories* for 1915–25, and on a list of businesses in the Itsy and Joe Brenner papers, MSCUA/UWL, Acc. 3934-2.

18. Pruzan, "Yesler Way," 13.

19. Elazar Behar, transcript of interview, MSCUA/UWL, Acc. 3209.

20. Sol Esfeld, transcript of interview, MSCUA/UWL, Acc. 2018-3.

21. For instance, Harry Russak, a pillar of Bikur Cholim Congregation, often worked on Saturdays until his son Joseph insisted on ending the practice. Joseph Russak, transcript of

interview, MSCUA/UWL, Acc. 2669.

22. Conversation with Herbert Droker, June 1, 1997.

23. Asia, interview.

24. Behar, interview.

25. Ibid.

26. Harry Glickman, "My Brother Louie," unpublished manuscript in possession of Howard Droker, 1997.

27. Clara Gordon Rubin, transcript of interview, MSCUA/UWL, Acc. 3296.

28. Glickman, "My Brother Louie."

29. Katz, interview.

30. Pruzan, "Yesler Way," 13.

31. Ibid., 27.

32. Ibid.

33. Katz, interview.

34. Lorraine Sidell, "Historically Speaking," *WSJHS Newsletter* (March 1990).

35. Emmett Watson, *Digressions of a Native Son* (Seattle: Pacific Institute, 1982), 204.

36. Pruzan, "Yesler Way," 31; Sidell, "Historically Speaking."

37. See Gerald Sorin, *A Time for Building: The Third Migration 1880–1920* (Baltimore: Johns Hopkins University Press, 1992), chapter 5, "Mobility and Community Beyond New York." See also Gerald Nash, *The American West in the Twentieth Century* (Albuquerque: University of New Mexico Press, 1977), on housing patterns in the West. Nash found that all western cities except San Francisco contained low-density neighborhoods (p. 18), giving them a "distinctly rural or small-town aspect," while at the same time being ethnically diverse (p. 77).

38. Henry L. Feingold, *A Time for Searching: Entering the Mainstream* (Baltimore: Johns Hopkins University Press, 1992), 41–42.

Art, Music & Theater in the Early Years

1. Annual Report, Seattle Art Institute, 1929, Seattle Public Library. See also Dodie Trip, *Washington State Art and Artists, 1850–1950* (Olympia: Sherburne Antiques & Fine Art, Inc., 1992), 50.

2. *The Seattle Town Crier*, 16 November 1929, p. 8.

3. *The Jewish Transcript*, 29 November 1929. Maria Sharylen, *Artists of The Pacific Northwest: A Biographical Dictionary, 1600–1970* (Jefferson, N.C.: McFarland Pub., 1993), 54, describes Deutsch as a specialist in Jewish genres.

4. *Temple Tidings*, 10 January 1933, Temple De Hirsch Sinai, Box 6, MSCUA/UWL, Acc. 2370, 2370-4.

5. Minutes, Vocational Scholarship Committee, January 18, 1933, National Council of Jewish Women, Seattle Section, Box 3, MSCUA/UWL, Acc. 2089-29.

6. See Martha Kingsbury, *Celebrating Washington's Art* (Olympia: Centennial Commission, 1989), 5–12, and Patricia Helen Svoboda, "Zoe Dusanne: Seattle Art Dealer from 1950–1964" (Master's thesis, University of Washington, 1980), xii, 59, 63, 117–25, for

names of early galleries in Washington.

7. Marion Brymner Appleton, ed., *Who's Who in Northwest Art* (Seattle: Frank McCaffrey, 1941), 8, 11.

8. Sylvia Allper, transcript of interview, MSCUA/UWL, Acc. 3468.

9. Information about the Ratman series supplied by Martin-Zambito Fine Art Gallery, Seattle.

10. Appleton, *Who's Who in Northwest Art*, and telephone interview between Leo Blashko and Jacqueline Williams, February 1998.

11. Jean Devine, "From Settlement House to Neighborhood House, 1906–76," MSCUA/UWL, Acc. 2632, 2632-2.

12. Appleton, *Who's Who in Northwest Art*, 11.

13. *The Seattle Town Crier*, 5 December 1931, 48–49.

14. A. W. Binder, "The Jewish Music Movement in America," Susan M. Friedman papers, Box 1, MSCUA/UWL, Acc. 2115-2.

15. President's report, October 19, 1899, Temple De Hirsch Sinai, Box 1, MSCUA/UWL, Acc. 2370-2–3, 2370-6–7. The choir began using paid members in 1905.

16. University of Washington *Tyee Yearbook*, 1900.

17. Newspaper clippings, Cooper-Levy Family, Box 23/2, MSCUA/UWL, Acc. 2366, 2366-2.

18. *Seattle Post-Intelligencer*, 1 January 1931.

19. Music scrapbook, newspaper clippings, Seattle Public Library; *Jewish Voice*, 18 February 1916.

20. *Seattle Post-Intelligencer*, 2 March 1913; *The Jewish Transcript*, 18 January 1929, and 31 May 1948; and undated newspaper clippings, Fred Bergman papers, Box 2, MSCUA/UWL, Acc. 2975-005.

21. Story told to Jacqueline Williams by Jean Singer Savan. Jean, who died in 1999, was eighty-nine when she and Williams first met.

22. Devine, "From Settlement House to Neighborhood House, 1906–76."

23. *The Jewish Transcript*, 4 February 1927 and 18 January 1929.

24. Ibid., 5 October 1928.

25. Ibid., 4 May 1928.

26. Ibid.

27. Ibid.

28. Ibid., 27 September 1929.

29. Ibid., 30 September 1927.

30. Undated newspaper clippings, Fred Bergman papers, Box 2, MSCUA/UWL, Acc. 2975-005.

31. Artur Holde, *Jews in Music* (New York: Bloch Publishing Co., 1974), 42. Holde also mentions Milton Katims, Manuel Rosenthal, and Marion Eugenie Bauer.

32. Binder, "The Jewish Music Movement in America."

33. *The Jewish Transcript*, 18 April 1930.

34. Undated newspaper clippings, Samuel Goldfarb, Box 8/3, MSCUA/UWL, Acc. 2784-3.

35. *The Jewish Transcript*, New Year's edition, 10 September 1948.

36. Binder, "The Jewish Music Movement in America."

37. Elazar Behar, transcript of interview, MSCUA/UWL, Acc. 3209.

38. Ibid.

39. Emma Adatto, "A Study of the Linguistic Characteristics of the Seattle Sephardic Folklore" (Master's thesis, University of Washington, 1935).

40. William M. Kramer, "The Beauty of Sephardic Life: Personal Reflections of Seattle's Sam Maimon," *Western States Jewish History* 29 (October 1996): 546.

41. David Romey, "A Study of Spanish Tradition in Isolation as Found in the Romances, Refrains, and Storied Folklore of the Seattle Sephardic Community" (Master's thesis, University of Washington, 1950).

42. Abe Hoffman, transcript of interview, MSCUA/UWL, Acc. 2744.

43. Minutes, May 11, 1924, Congregation Bikur Cholim, Box 3, MSCUA/UWL, Acc. 1035, 1779, 2450, 2450-2.

44. Hugh Fordin, *MGM's Greatest Musicals: The Arthur Freed Unit* (New York: Da Capo Press, 1996). (First published in 1975 under the title *The World of Entertainment! Hollywood's Greatest Musicals*.)

45. *Seattle Post-Intelligencer*, 25 April 1982.

46. Burial records, Temple De Hirsch Sinai, Box 2, MSCUA/UWL, Acc. 2370-2–3, 2370-6–7. Fordin, *MGM's Greatest Musicals: The Arthur Freed Unit*, reports that Freed's father, Max, was in the art business. Seattle Public School records indicate he was a real estate dealer working at the Henry Building. Letter, July 21, 1998, to J. Williams from Student Records, Seattle Public Schools.

47. Letter, July 21, 1998, to J. Williams from Student Records, Seattle Public Schools, and letter, August 3, 1998, to J. Williams from Shelley C. Bronk, archives assistant, Phillips Exeter Academy. Freed only attended Phillips Exeter for one term.

48. *Polk's Seattle City Directory*, vol. 34 (Seattle: Polk's Seattle Directory Co., 1920).

49. Minutes, Vocational Scholarship Committee, 1932, National Council of Jewish Women, Seattle Section, Box 3, MSCUA/UWL, Acc. 2089-29.

50. Ibid.; *Seattle Post-Intelligencer*, 6 November 1949; and Carnegie Hall program, April 10, 1954, in Music Scrapbooks, Seattle Public Library.

51. Symphony program, Alan L. Barer, MSCUA/UWL, Acc. 4408.

52. *The Jewish Transcript*, 24 June 1927.

53. *Spokane Spokesman-Review*, 24 October 1924.

54. Newspaper clipping from Bellingham, 1932, Lucille Karsh, unaccessioned, MSCUA/UWL.

55. *The Jewish Transcript*, 17 March 1933.

56. Holde, *Jews in Music*, 252.

57. Irving Howe, *World of Our Fathers* (New York and London: Harcourt Brace Jovanovich, 1976), 461–63.

58. Henry L. Feingold, *A Time for Searching: Entering the Mainstream* (Baltimore: Johns Hopkins University Press, 1992), 64.

59. See Alissa Schwartz, "Americanization and Cultural Preservation in Seattle's Settlement House: 1906–1936" (Master's thesis, University of Washington, 1998), 20–25.

60. Ibid., 30.

61. *The Jewish Transcript*, 28 October 1927.

62. Ibid., 25 March 1924, 29 May 1925, 18 November 1927, and 31 October 1985.

63. Ibid., 27 May 1924.

64. Ibid., 6 May 1924.

65. *Temple Tidings*, January 1925, Temple De Hirsch Sinai, Box 6, MSCUA/UWL, Acc. 2370, 2370-4.

66. *The Jewish Transcript*, 26 February 1926 and 28 October 1927.

67. Ibid., 15 July 1927.

68. Ibid., 23 March 1928.

69. Ibid., 23 December 1927.

70. *Jewish Voice*, 29 October 1915.

71. Undated newspaper article by Marc D. Angel, Becky Resnick papers, MSCUA/UWL, Acc. 2495.

72. Ibid.

73. *The Jewish Transcript*, 19 September 1924.

74. Ibid., 22 July 1927.

75. Ibid., 17 August 1928.

76. Albert N. Youngman, transcript of interview, MSCUA/UWL, Acc. 3583-4.

77. *The Jewish Transcript*, 15 November 1935.

78. *The Tacoma News Tribune*, 28 September 1960.

79. Ibid., 18 January 1970; *Seattle Post-Intelligencer*, 10 February 1980; and *The Seattle Times*, 9 February 1980.

80. Newspaper clippings, Biography and Theater File, Northwest Room, Tacoma Public Library.

81. *The Tacoma News Tribune*, 28 September 1960 and 28 March 1965.

82. Tax records from 1915 show that the Greater Theater Company, along with mill owner and real estate magnate C. D. Stimson, paid the taxes and purchased the property for the Coliseum Theater at the corner of Fifth Avenue and Pike Street. Tax parcel 197579-0155, Washington State Archives—Puget Sound Branch, Bellevue, Wash.; *Seattle Star*, 11 October 1915; *The Jewish Transcript*, 22 September 1939; *The Seattle Times*, 9 January 1916; and Clarence B. Bagley, *History of Seattle from Earliest Settlement to the Present Time* (Chicago: S. J. Clarke, 1916), 699–700. Even though newspaper stories written after 1950 report that Joseph Gottstein, not Jacob Gottstein, hired the architect and built the Coliseum, none of the early reports or tax records mention Joseph's name.

83. *The Seattle Times*, 25 March 1911 and 10 June 1917.

84. *Puget Sound Business Journal*, 30 March 1987.

85. *Seattle Post-Intelligencer*, 23 October 1912.

86. *The Seattle Times*, 18 September 1914.

87. Ibid., 17 June 1917.

88. Ibid., 1 June 1917.

89. *Seattle Post-Intelligencer*, 12 August 1908.

90. Eugene Clinton Elliott, *A History of Variety-Vaudeville in Seattle* (Seattle: University of Washington Press, 1944), 56; *The Seattle Times*, 17 June 1917.

91. *The Jewish Transcript*, 17 May 1929.

92. *Spokane Spokesman-Review*, 24 February 1935, p. 6.

93. Ibid., 6 August 1940, p. 6, and 8 November 1987. The 1940 newspaper article states that Rosenfield would be managing a chain of theaters in southern California, but in the 1987 interview, Rosenfield does not mention California and says he returned to Seattle as general manager for Sterling Theaters.

An Obligation to Study

1. Oscar I. Janowsky, ed., *The American Jew: A Reappraisal* (Philadelphia: The Jewish Publication Society of America, 1964), 123–25, 129.

2. Nathan H. Winter, *Jewish Education in a Pluralist Society: Samson Benderly and Jewish Education in the United States* (New York: New York University Press, 1966), 27–46.

3. *Polk's Seattle City Directory* (Seattle: Polk's Seattle Directory Co., 1893–94; 1894–95). Julius Rickles indicates that the first Hebrew school was held in Seattle Central on Fifth Avenue and Washington Street in 1893 (Julius Rickles, transcript of interview, MSCUA/UWL, Acc. 962). Hebrew Free Schools were first set up in 1864 in New York by wealthy Jews who wanted to keep poorer Jews from attending schools conducted by Christian missionaries.

4. Certificate of Incorporation, February 9, 1899, Jacob Kaplan papers, Box 1/18, MSCUA/UWL, Acc. 1960-2–4.

5. Ibid., deed to transfer land from Bikur Cholim to Talmud Torah, July 11, 1900.

6. "Seventy-Eight years of Jewish Education in Seattle," Seattle Talmud Torah Hebrew School, Box 1/7, MSCUA/UWL, Acc. 1892, 1892-8.

7. *The Jewish Transcript*, 8 September 1933.

8. Sol Esfeld, transcript of interview, MSCUA/UWL, Acc. 2018-3.

9. Sam and George Prottas, transcript of interview, MSCUA/UWL, Acc. 2216-2.

10. Sarah Efron, transcript of interview, MSCUA/UWL, Acc. 2535.

11. Board Minutes, September 7, 1899, vol. 1, Temple De Hirsch Sinai, Box 1, MSCUA/UWL, Acc. 2370, 2370-4.

12. Fourth annual report by President of Congregation, 1902, Temple De Hirsch Sinai, MSCUA/UWL, Acc. 2370.

13. Tillie DeLeon, transcript of interview, MSCUA/UWL, Acc. 3776.

14. *Jewish Voice*, 24 March 1916. Rabbi Theodore Joseph directed the school at Herzl. There are no records, and the school is not mentioned in later pages of the *Jewish Voice*.

15. 1914 YMHA Souvenir Program, Young Men's Hebrew Association, MSCUA/UWL, Acc. 2104-2.

16. *Seattle Post-Intelligencer*, 13 September 1913.

17. *Jewish Voice*, 24 December 1915.

18. *The Jewish Transcript*, 8 September 1933.

19. Joseph Cohen, tape recorded interview, MSCUA/UWL, Acc. 2116. A similar comment appears in Meta Buttnick, "The Seattle Hebrew Academy 1947–1982," Box 1, MSCUA/UWL, Acc. 1849, 1849-5.

20. Prottas's obituary in *The Jewish Transcript*, 8 April 1924, states that he was first president, but the *Seattle Post-Intelligencer*, 13 September 1913, names S. Mezler as president. The announcement in the program cited in note 15 names H. Ross as President. Sol Prottas was on the Modern Hebrew School Board of Education in 1914.

21. *The Jewish Transcript*, 8 September 1933.

22. Viola Gutmann Silver and Max Silver, transcript of interview, Silver family papers, Box 1, MSCUA/UWL, Acc. 1826.

23. *Seattle Post-Intelligencer*, 13 September 1913; *Jewish Voice*, 24 December 1915.

24. *Jewish Voice*, 12 April 1917.

25. Ibid., 23 November 1913.

26. Board minutes, May 17, 1919, Congregation Bikur Cholim–Machzikay Hadath, Box 1/27, MSCUA/UWL, Acc. 2450-5, 2450-7.

27. Certified copy of minutes, June 17, 1920, Seattle Talmud Torah Hebrew School, Box 1/3, MSCUA/UWL, Acc. 1892-8.

28. *The Jewish Transcript*, 8 September 1933.

29. Ibid., Rosh Hashanah edition, 15 September 1928.

30. Ibid., 18 May 1924.

31. Efron, interview.

32. Henry L. Feingold, *A Time for Searching: Entering the Mainstream* (Baltimore: The Johns Hopkins University Press, 1992), 118–20.

33. Seattle Talmud Torah Program, 1932, Laura Berch papers, Box 1/9, MSCUA/UWL, Acc. 2092-2.

34. *The Jewish Transcript*, 9 March 1928.

35. Ibid., 15 March 1929.

36. Ibid., 11 October 1929.

37. Board Minutes, October 16, 1939, Seattle Talmud Torah Hebrew School, Box 1/3, MSCUA/UWL, Acc. 1892-9.

38. Board Minutes, April 30, 1943, and September 9, 1943, Seattle Talmud Torah Hebrew School, Box 1/4, MSCUA/UWL, Acc. 1892, 1892-8.

39. Joseph Frankel, transcript of interview, MSCUA/UWL, Acc. 2813.

40. Annual report, December 30, 1940, Seattle Talmud Torah Hebrew School, Box 1/3, MSCUA/UWL, Acc. 1892-8.

41. Solomon Maimon, transcript of interview, MSCUA/UWL, Acc. 3024, 3024-2.

42. *The Jewish Transcript*, 9 March 1928.

43. Maimon, interview; *The Seattle Times*, 7 October 1984.

44. "Survey of Jewish Education," Ruth Jacobs Levy papers, MSCUA/UWL, Acc. 3803.

45. Speeches and writings, Samuel Graudenz papers, Box 1/6, MSCUA/UWL, Acc. 3545.

46. Jewish Education Committee Report, August 29, 1952, Ruth Jacobs Levy papers, MSCUA/UWL, Acc. 3803.

47. Letter to Dr. Levy from Edward Starin, August 25, 1952, Ruth Jacobs Levy papers, MSCUA/UWL, Acc. 3803.

48. "Seattle Hebrew School," Jewish Federation of Greater Seattle, Box 10/42, MSCUA/UWL, 3051, 3051-2.

49. Harry Ash, transcript of interview, MSCUA/UWL, Acc. 3520.

50. "Jewish Education Committee," Jewish Education Council, Box 1, MSCUA/UWL, Acc. 3255-6.

51. "The Synagogue Tribune," June 1949, Seattle Hebrew Academy, Box 1, MSCUA/UWL, Acc. 3713-2.

52. "Student Parent Handbook 1979–80: Yeshivat Or Hazafon Overview," Seattle Hebrew Academy, Box 2, MSCUA/UWL, Acc. 3713-2.

53. Gordon DeLeon, transcript of interview, MSCUA/UWL, Acc. 3268.

54. Albert Adatto, "Sephardim and the Seattle Sephardic Community" (Master's thesis, University of Washington, 1939), 92.

55. The *Jewish Voice* June 1916 calendar calls the school an Oriental Jewish Community—Talmud Torah, Harry Tarica, president.

56. Isaac Maimon, "History of the Congregation Ahavath Ahim of Seattle, Washington, 1906–1996" (unpublished typewritten manuscript), p. 22.

57. Maimon, interview.

58. *The Jewish Transcript*, 22 May 1931, 12 September 1932, and 8 September 1933. Formal dedication of the school occurred on June 7, 1932. According to oral interviews conducted by Aviva Ben-Ur, who spent the 1999–2000 academic year at the University of Washington, Levy moved to the Seattle area because of health.

59. *The Jewish Transcript*, 13 December 1935.

60. Albert Franco, transcript of interview, MSCUA/UWL, Acc. 2834.

61. Marc D. Angel, "'Progress'—Seattle's Sephardic Monthly 1934–35," *The American Sephardic*, Journal of the Sephardic Studies Program of Yeshiva University 5, no. 1 (1971): 91–95.

62. Marc D. Angel, "A Personal and Scholarly Account: Early Sephardim in Seattle," in *Western States Jewish History*, ed. William M. Kramer (Los Angeles: Isaac Nathan Co., Inc., 1996), 571.

63. Elazar Behar, transcript of interview, MSCUA/UWL, Acc. 3209.

64. Board Minutes, February 18, 1935, Seattle Talmud Torah Hebrew School, Box 1/3, MSCUA/UWL, Acc. 1892, 1892-8.

65. Ibid., August 14, 1939.

66. *The Spokane Spokesman Review*, 26 February 1899.

67. Board Minutes, April 4, 1909, and September 16, 1912, Congregation Keneseth Israel, Ms. 74, Eastern Washington State Historical Society, Cheney Cowles Museum.

68. The notice in the *Spokane Spokesman-Review*, 13 October 1911, is the only record of this school. It is unclear if the school was for children, adults, or both.

69. Board Minutes, September 16, 1912, Congregation Keneseth Israel, Ms. 74, Eastern Washington State Historical Society, Cheney Cowles Museum.

70. Moses N. Janton, *History of the Jews in Spokane, Washington* (Spokane: Star Printing House, 1926), 11. Janton does not mention the earlier school or Samuel Huppin, who, according to unpublished brief histories of Spokane Jews circa 1970, administered the school until 1921.

71. *The Jewish Transcript*, 1 May 1928.

72. Temple Beth Shalom (Spokane, Wash.), General History, Spokane Jewish

Community, Ms. 151, Box 2/10, Eastern Washington State Historical Society, Cheney Cowles Museum.

73. 1892 Constitution, Congregation Beth Israel, vol. 2, Temple Beth Israel, unaccessioned, MSCUA/UWL.

74. The *Tacoma Daily Ledger*, 10 March 1892. The women had established a Sunday school in 1890 and met in the Harmony House rooms.

75. *Polk's Tacoma City Directory*, 1896.

76. *The Jewish Transcript*, 19 September 1930, Rosh Hashanah edition.

77. Dr. Ivar Spector seems to have been with the Tacoma Hebrew School for one or two years. He wrote a column for *The Jewish Transcript* in 1929 and 1930, but then the column disappears. There are no records.

78. Edward Glazer, transcript of interview, MSCUA/UWL, Acc. 3215.

79. William Sturman, transcript of interview, MSCUA/UWL, Acc. 3663.

80. *The Jewish Transcript*, 8 September 1933.

81. "The Temple Beth Israel Light" (Tacoma, Wash.), December 1919, MSCUA/UWL, Acc. 2155.

82. *The Jewish Transcript*, 8 September 1933.

83. Ibid., 8 February 1929.

84. Ibid., 8 September 1933.

More Than a Basket of Food

1. *The Jewish Transcript*, 30 September 1927.

2. Ibid., 11 June 1937, 15 January 1944, 17 January 1944, and 3 April 1944. For information about Bremerton Hebrew Congregation, see *The Tacoma News Tribune*, 8 November 1953. There are no official records.

3. Florence Flaks, transcript of interview, MSCUA/UWL, Acc. 2519.

4. James T. Patterson, *America's Struggle Against Poverty 1900–1994* (Cambridge, Mass.: Harvard University Press, 1994), 6.

5. Ways and Means Committee Report, October 5, 1925, Jewish Family and Child Service, Box 6/18, MSCUA/UWL, Acc. 2003.

6. Minutes, November 20, 1929, Jewish Family and Child Service, Box 6/19, MSCUA/UWL, Acc. 2003.

7. Annual Report, 1926–27, Jewish Family and Child Service, Box 6/18, MSCUA/UWL, Acc. 2003. Concern about transients is mentioned in several annual reports.

8. Ibid. The annual reports mentions that rules for handling these men were set at the National Conference of Social Work.

9. Patterson, *America's Struggle Against Poverty*, 56–59.

10. Annual Report, 1930–31, Jewish Family and Child Service, Box 6/40, MSCUA/UWL, Acc. 2003.

11. Report (title missing), 1934, Jewish Family and Child Service, Box 6/43, MSCUA/UWL, Acc. 2003.

12 Report of Executive Secretary, October 18, 1933, Jewish Family and Child Service,

Box 6/42, MSCUA/UWL, Acc. 2003.

13. Annual Report, 1936, and Report (title missing), 1938, Jewish Family and Child Service, Box 7/1 and Box 7/3, MSCUA/UWL, Acc. 2003.

14. President's Annual Report, October 20, 1937, Jewish Family and Child Service, Box 7/2, MSCUA/UWL, Acc. 2003.

15. "History of Jewish Family and Child Service," Jewish Family and Child Service, Box 6/20, MSCUA/UWL, Acc. 2003.

16. Eugene Levy to William K. Blethen, March 27, 1950, Cooper-Levy family papers, Box 12/4, MSCUA/UWL, Acc. 2366, 2366-2.

17. Eugene Levy to Mrs. Bernard L. Reiter, January 25, 1949, Cooper-Levy family papers, Box 12/4, MSCUA/UWL, Acc. 2366, 2366-2.

18. Eugene Levy to Michael Dederer, October 31, 1951, Cooper-Levy family papers, Box 12/4, MSCUA/UWL, Acc. 2366, 2366-2.

19. "History of Kline Galland Home," Caroline Kline Galland Home for the Aged, Box 1/1, MSCUA/UWL, Acc. 2288, 2288-2–3. The Home dropped "Aged and Feeble Poor" from its name in 1953.

20. Silver family, transcript of interview, Silver family papers, Box 1, MSCUA/UWL, Acc. 1826.

21. Jane Huntley, "Caroline Kline Galland Home for the Aged" (Master's thesis, University of Washington, 1960), 24–26, Caroline Kline Galland Home for the Aged, Box 1, MSCUA/UWL, Acc. 2288-7.

22. Rules and Regulations, April 1924, Caroline Kline Galland Home for the Aged, Box 1/7, MSCUA/UWL, Acc. 2288, 2288-2–3.

23. Carolyn Blumenthal Danz, transcript of interview, MSCUA/UWL, Acc. 3895.

24. Minutes of Advisory Board, February 8, 1949, Caroline Kline Galland Home for the Aged, Box 2/7, MSCUA/UWL, Acc. 2288, 2288-2–3.

25. Ibid., April 19, 1937, Box 2/1.

26. Huntley, "Caroline Kline Galland Home for the Aged," 56.

27. Ibid., 43–44.

28. Ibid., 31–33.

29. Minutes of Advisory Board, December 1, 1948, Caroline Kline Galland Home for the Aged, Box 2/7, MSCUA/UWL, Acc. 2288, 2288-2–3.

30. Ibid., April 22, 1949.

31. "The Caroline Kline Galland Home: Survey Report," Caroline Kline Galland Home for the Aged, Box 3/11, MSCUA/UWL, Acc. 2288, 2288-2–3.

32. Annual Report of President, 1930–31, Jewish Family and Child Service, Box 6/40, MSCUA/UWL, Acc. 2003.

33. Albert Adatto, "Sephardim and the Seattle Sephardic Community" (Master's thesis, University of Washington, 1939), 99.

34. Marc D. Angel, "'Progress'—Seattle's Sephardic Monthly 1934–35," *The American Sephardic*, Journal of the Sephardic Studies Program of Yeshiva University 5, no. 1 (1971): 534. There are no surviving records.

35. Elazar Behar, transcript of interview, MSCUA/UWL, Acc. 3209.

36. Minutes, July 1, 1917, Congregation Bikur Cholim, Box 3/1, MSCUA/UWL, Acc. 1035,

1779, 2450, 2450-2.

37. Isaac Maimon, "History of the Congregation Ahavath Ahim of Seattle, Washington, 1906–1996" (unpublished typewritten manuscript).

38. Behar, interview.

39. Ibid.

40. *The Jewish Transcript*, 21 May 1956.

41. Behar, interview.

42. *The Jewish Transcript*, 17 January 1936.

43. Ibid., 6 March 1924.

44. Ibid., 13 January 1939.

45. Ibid., 16 November 1942. Both of Walla Walla's men's and women's auxiliaries began in 1936.

46. Ibid., 21 September 1942.

47. "Golden Anniversary Program," B'nai B'rith Seattle Lodge No. 503, MSCUA/UWL, Acc. 3589-2. There are no records from Bellingham and Everett. B'nai B'rith International files indicate that there was also a lodge in Yakima.

48. "Seventh War Loan Report: Jewish Organizations," Sons of Israel, Seattle, MSCUA/UWL, Acc. 2225.

49. *The Jewish Transcript*, 31 May 1948 and 2 June 1948.

50. National Council of Jewish Women, Seattle Section, Box 1/1, MSCUA/UWL, Acc. 2089-29.

51. *The Jewish Transcript*, 23 March 1928.

52. Jean Devine, "From Settlement House to Neighborhood House, 1906–76," MSCUA/UWL, Acc. 2632, 2632-2; National Council of Jewish Women, Seattle Section, Box 6/8, MSCUA/UWL, Acc. 2059-29.

53. Bonham Galland Will, Cooper-Levy family papers, Box 38, MSCUA/UWL, Acc. 2366; 2366-2.

54. Board minutes, August 15, 1951, National Council of Jewish Women, Seattle Section, Box 17/2, MSCUA/UWL, Acc. 2089-29; *The Seattle Times*, 5 October 1952.

55. Temple Beth El, *Centuries to Celebrate* (Tacoma: Temple Beth El, 1992), 17.

56. Ibid.

57. *The Tacoma Sunday News Tribune and Sunday Ledger*, 2 October 1960.

58. Women's American ORT Greater Seattle Area Council, Box 1, MSCUA/UWL, Acc. 2810-2. In 1999 the name was changed to Organization for Educational Resources and Technological Training.

59. ORT Workshop Institute, November 1, 1951, Women's American ORT Greater Seattle Area Council, Box 1, MSCUA/UWL, Acc. 2810-2.

60. *The Jewish Transcript*, 7 December 1967.

The Crisis Years

1. Undated minutes, National Council of Jewish Women, Seattle Section, MSCUA/UWL, Acc. 2089-29.

2. "Seattle Godless Mock Yom Kippur," *The Jewish Transcript*, 21 October 1932, p. 1.

3. See generally Marshall Sklare, *Conservative Judaism: An American Religious Movement* (New York: Schocken Books, 1972), and Henry L. Feingold, *A Time for Searching: Entering the Mainstream* (Baltimore: Johns Hopkins University Press, 1992), 103–106.

4. The *Jewish Voice* was the first Jewish newspaper in Washington, published in Seattle between 1915 and 1919 by Sol Krems. Herman Horowitz founded *The Jewish Transcript* in 1924. With the rise of anti-Semitism, Horowitz felt that "the Jew must organize not for aggression but for self-protection," and in order to do so "must have a means of inter-communication." In addition to covering the news, the paper reported social and organizational activities, items of interest from smaller cities such as Bellingham, Spokane, and Tacoma, and tried to "develop in the younger generation an ardent interest in Judaism, Jewish history and modern Jewish problems." *The Jewish Transcript*, 6 March 1924.

5. "Seattle Needs a Conservative Congregation," *The Jewish Transcript*, 23 December 1927.

6. Typed manuscript on Lipman & Esfeld letterhead, undated but preceding August 1930, Sol Esfeld papers, Box 2-24, MSCUA/UWL, Acc. 2018.

7. Sol Esfeld to Ernest Trattner, November 25, 1930, Sol Esfeld papers, Box 2-24, MSCUA/UWL, Acc. 2018.

8. Conservative Congregation of Seattle form letter, January 14, 1931, Sol Esfeld papers, Box 2-24, MSCUA/UWL, Acc. 2018.

9. "New Congregation Formed in Seattle," *The Jewish Transcript*, 6 September 1929, p. 3.

10. "Registration for New Religious School," *The Jewish Transcript*, 31 October 1930, p. 1.

11. "My Impressions of Seattle's First Conservative Services at Herzl Synagogue," *The Jewish Transcript*, 7 October 1932, p. 7.

12. For instance, in "Herzl Men Form Club," *The Jewish Transcript*, 21 October 1930, p. 1.

13. Charles Jassen, transcript of interview, MSCUA/UWL.

14. "Stay Home on Friday Rabbi Urges," *The Jewish Transcript*, 18 November 1932, p. 1.

15. "Herzl Rites on Friday Draw Crowd of 1100," *The Jewish Transcript*, 2 December 1932, p. 1.

16. "Rabbi Langh Hits Double Standard in House of God," *The Jewish Transcript*, 20 January 1933, p. 1.

17. Carl Sternoff, transcript of interview, June 16, 1974, MSCUA/UWL.

18. *The Jewish Transcript*, 31 July 1936, p. 1.

19. Samuel Penner, a charismatic rabbi who served Herzl from 1948 to 1952, attracted a large following of young married couples starting their postwar families. "In those years the congregation really grew and prospered," Herzl's cantor Joseph Frankel recalled (Joseph Frankel, transcript of interview, MSCUA/UWL, Acc. 2813-1). But Rabbi Penner was removed from his pulpit by the Conservative Movement headquarters in New York, allegedly because he was a conscientious objector during the Korean War. His successor, Rabbi Joseph Wagner, was by all accounts an outstanding leader. But Rabbi Wagner left

for California after a few years in Seattle.

20. "Seattle Jewish Funds Makes Good Record," *The Jewish Transcript*, 29 March 1929, p. 1.

21. The debate over the role of Jews in philanthropy for the wider city versus the Jewish community would continue to resonate. In the mid-1990s, a visiting Stroum lecturer at the University of Washington who questioned the Benaroya family gift of $20 million to the Seattle Symphony Hall campaign would fail to recognize the generous contributions of that family to Jewish causes over the years.

22. "'Revive Fund'—Miller," *The Jewish Transcript*, 2 September 1932.

23. "Jewish Fund End Is Hit by Leaders," *The Jewish Transcript*, 26 August 1932, p. 1.

24. Ibid.

25. "Alfred Shemanski to Head Emergency Palestine Drive," *The Jewish Transcript*, 6 September 1929, p. 6; "Zionist Mass Meeting Raises $1,500 For Palestine Relief," ibid., 13 September 1929, p. 6; and "Setting Quota," ibid., 20 September 1929, p. 4.

26. Feingold, *A Time for Searching*, 164–65.

27. "Jews of This State Will Contribute $45,000 to Allied Jewish Campaign," *The Jewish Transcript*, 31 October 1930, p. 1.

28. "Keep the Faith," *The Jewish Transcript*, 7 November 1930, p. 3.

29. Wise to Shemanski, June 24, 1931, Sol Esfeld papers, Box 4-18, MSCUA/UWL, Acc. 2018.

30. "As I See It," *The Jewish Transcript*, 14 November 1930, p. 4.

31. Richard Lang, for instance, served as president of Temple De Hirsch and of the Seattle Jewish Federated Fund in the early 1940s before resigning those posts and ending all affiliation with Judaism in 1943. Richard Lang, interview with Howard Droker, 1982.

32. *The Jewish Transcript*, 11 August 1926. The article reports that Levine set up the first Zionist organization, but does not name the group or give the year.

33. See Melvin I. Urofsky, "Zionism: An American Experience," in Jonathan D. Sarna, ed., *The American Experience* (New York: Holmes & Meier, 1997), 245–55.

34. Letter from national ZOA to Eimon Weiner, October 8, 1926, Sam Prottas papers, Box 3/5, MSCUA/UWL, Acc. 2216-3.

35. "History of Seattle Chapters of Mizrachi," Mizrachi Women, Box 1, MSCUA/UWL, Acc. 2014.

36. Louis Katzman, transcript of interview, MSCUA/UWL, Acc. 2589-2.

37. Sonia Wachtin, transcript of interview, MSCUA/UWL, Acc. 3139; Laura Berch, transcript of interview, MSCUA/UWL, Acc. 2092-1; "In the Beginning—Seattle Hadassah," *Hadassah Herald*, February 1973, Box 1, MSCUA/UWL, Acc. 2092.

38. *The Jewish Transcript*, 22 May 1944.

39. Ibid., 9 December 1938.

40. *The Bellingham Herald*, 13 October 1980, in Hadassah, Northern Pacific Coast Region, MSCUA/UWL, Acc. 4455.

41. *The Everett Herald*, 27 December 1975.

42. Feingold, *A Time for Searching*, 101.

43. See ibid., 100–103, for a discussion of the beginnings of the American Council for Judaism.

44. Editor's introduction to Fred Rosenbaum, "Zionism versus Anti-Zionism: The State of Israel Comes to San Francisco," in *Jews of the American West*, ed. Moses Rischin and John Livingston, (Detroit: Wayne State University Press, 1991), 118.

45. *The Jewish Transcript*, 23 September 1946.

46. Ibid., 19 July 1948.

47. Roy Rosenthal, transcript of interview, MSCUA/UWL, Acc. 2352.

48. Stella Sameth, transcript of interview, MSCUA/UWL, Acc. 2254.

49. *The Jewish Transcript*, 30 December 1932.

50. Wise to Esfeld, April 2, 1935, Sol Esfeld papers, Box 4-18, MSCUA/UWL, Acc. 2018.

51. In 1938, the Lang family gave $3,000, the Ecksteins $1,000, Leo Kreilsheimer $1,500, Herman Shoenfeld $2,000, Morton and Edna Schwabacher $1,200, and Alfred Shemanski $1,000. The butcher Harry Rose and the jewelry salesman Nathan Sulman each gave $12. Contributions as low as $1 were made. List of Donors, Sol Esfeld papers, Box 8-12, MSCUA/UWL, Acc. 2018.

52. Dr. A. M. Blumberg to Sol Esfeld, July 7, 1937, Sol Esfeld papers, Box 8-7, MSCUA/UWL, Acc. 2018.

53. Bulletin No. 2, Vol. 1, August 1, 1938, Sol Esfeld papers, Box 8-13, MSCUA/UWL, Acc. 2018.

54. Henry Kotkins to Sol Esfeld, May 27, 1940, Sol Esfeld papers, Box 8-1, MSCUA/UWL, Acc. 2018.

55. Typescript of speech, 1938, Sol Esfeld papers, Box 8-17, MSCUA/UWL, Acc. 2018.

56. "Tacoma News Items," *The Jewish Transcript*, 18 April 1941.

57. Henry D. Trieger of Port Angeles wrote Sol Esfeld in 1938 that the Seattle campaign should include all the small towns. Of the ten or twelve Jewish families in Port Angeles, he wrote, "They are a unit, quite distant from Jewish life, and the Jewish people generally." Esfeld replied that the small communities would be contacted after the Seattle campaign ended. Trieger to Esfeld, April 10, 1938; Esfeld to Trieger, April 16, 1938, Sol Esfeld papers, Box 8-7, MSCUA/UWL, Acc. 2018.

58. Form letter dated March 7, 1941, Sol Esfeld papers, Box 4-3, MSCUA/UWL, Acc. 2018.

59. Louis Friedlander to Esfeld, March 3, 1941, and Alfred Shemanski to Friend, April 27, 1942, Sol Esfeld papers, Box 8-2, MSCUA/UWL, Acc. 2018.

60. Kleinberg to Mrs. Sadie Esfeld, May 26, 1942, Sol Esfeld papers, Box 8-3, MSCUA/UWL, Acc. 2018.

61. For instance, see October 3, 1941 and March 20, 1942. *The Jewish Transcript* suspended publication from April 3 to September 7, 1942.

62. Alfred Shyman to Esfeld, December 16, 1943, Sol Esfeld papers, MSCUA/UWL, Acc. 2018.

63. "Spokane Dentist, Dr. Cowen, Dies," *Seattle Post-Intelligencer*, 2 May 1975.

64. See Meta Buttnick, "The Jesse Epstein Story," *WSJHS Newsletter* (winter 1994), and Roger Sale, *Seattle, Past to Present* (Seattle: University of Washington Press, 1976), 163–67. Jessie Epstein interview in Howard Droker's papers, MSCUA/UWL, Acc. 2112.

65. See Feingold, *A Time for Searching*, for a history of American Jews during this period. On the Seattle economy, see Sale, *Seattle, Past to Present*, chapter 5, and Richard

C. Berner, *Seattle, 1921–1940: From Boom to Bust* (Seattle: Charles Press, 1992), chapters 4–10.

The Fourth Wave of Immigration

1. Hans J. Lehmann, transcript of interview, MSCUA/UWL, Acc. 3640; *Seattle Times/Post-Intelligencer*, May 27, 1990, pp. L1, L5; *Seattle Post-Intelligencer*, April 2, 1996, p. B2.

2. The purge to rid Germany of all "undesirables" included the slaughter of Gypsies, homosexuals, and many handicapped. According to the Holocaust Conference, there were five million additional victims (*The Seattle Weekly*, May 4, 1983).

3. William B. Helmreich cites 140,000 as the number of Jews who came to America fleeing Hitler's regime in his book *Against All Odds, Holocaust Survivors and the Successful Lives They Made in America* (New York: Simon & Schuster, 1992). The number is listed at "Approx. 150,000" from the 1930s to 1945 in the report "Seattle's Jewish Community—An Historical Perspective Leadership Training Institute," March 19, 1995. Howard Muggamin also cites 150,000 as the number in *The Jewish Americans*, p. 45. Number of settlers who came to Seattle is cited in a report to the National Refugee Service, N.Y., from Herman Schocken, January 9, 1945, in Sol Esfeld, interview and papers, MSCUA/UWL, Acc. 2018, 2018-3.

4. Edward S. Shapiro, *A Time for Healing, American Jewry Since World War II* (Baltimore: The John Hopkins University Press, 1992), 215.

5. Rabbi Richard Rosenthal, transcript of interview, MSCUA/UWL, Acc. 4052.

6. Ibid., and see *The Tacoma News Tribune*, 4 March 1999, p. A7, and 6 March 1999, p. B6.

7. Herman Schocken report, Sol Esfeld papers, Box 4/8, MSCUA/UWL, Acc. 2018.

8. Irving Howe, *World of Our Fathers* (New York and London: Harcourt Brace Jovanovich, 1976), 626.

9. *The Jewish Transcript*, 24 April 1936.

10. Ernest Stiefel, transcript of interview, Box 2, MSCUA/UWL, Acc. 3410-7.

11. Florence Flaks, transcript of interview, MSCUA/UWL, Acc. 2519; "Timeline 1936–1953," National Council of Jewish Women, Seattle Section, Box 9/1, MSCUA/UWL, Acc. 2089-29.

12. Flaks, interview. Gerda married Peter Frumkin, and they had three children. The Flaks helped Gerda's brother and her parents get to South America. Gerda later brought her parents to Seattle.

13. "Timeline, 1936–1953," National Council of Jewish Women, Seattle Section, Box 9/1, MSCUA/UWL, Acc. 2089-29.

14. Flaks, interview; Minnie Bernhard, transcript of interview, MSCUA/UWL, Acc. 2055.

15. Washington Émigré Bureau letter of June 3, 1940, from Herman Schocken to Sol Esfeld, Sol Esfeld papers, MSCUA/UWL, Acc. 2018.

16. Esfeld, interview.

17. See exchange of letters between the Bureau's Frank W. Bishop and Wenatchee's

A. L. Roth and Nathan I. Neubauer, 1940, Nathan I. Neubauer papers, MSCUA/UWL, Acc. 3138.

18. Esfeld, interview.

19. *The Jewish Transcript*, 18 December 1950.

20. "Timeline, 1936–1953," National Council of Jewish Women, Seattle Section, Box 9/1, MSCUA/UWL, Acc. 2089-29.

21. Sol Esfeld papers, Box 4/8, MSCUA/UWL, Acc. 2018.

22. Esfeld, interview.

23. *The Jewish Transcript*, 14 October 1955.

24. "Timeline, 1936–1953," National Council of Jewish Women, Seattle Section, Box 9/1, MSCUA/UWL, Acc. 2089-29.

25. Stiefel, interview.

26. Ibid.

27. Flaks, interview.

28. *The Jewish Transcript*, 13 September 1940, p. 1.

29. Bernhard, interview.

30. Emilie Steinbrecher, transcript of interview, MSCUA/UWL, Acc. 1957.

31. Ibid.

32. *The Jewish Transcript*, 14 October 1955.

33. Ibid. This story is reported to have been told by William Katz at the Jewish Club's 25th anniversary.

34. Klaus Stern, transcript of interview, MSCUA/UWL, Acc. 3693, 3693-2.

35. Ibid.

36. Sol Esfeld papers, January 9, 1945, MSCUA/UWL, Acc. 2018.

37. Articles in *Seattle Post-Intelligencer* of 23 April 1971, p. 8; 11 September 1975, p. A12; 14 July 1981, p. 16; and 27 January 1993, p. E1; and in *The Seattle Times*, 30 January 1993, p. A7; and 6 July 1986, p. 4.

38. *The Seattle Times*, 30 January 1993.

39. Ibid., 6 July 1986.

40. Henry Eisenhardt, "Outline of My History," personal paper, and conversation with Molly Cone, April 1999.

41. Letter from Dr. Terry Bergeson, State Superintendent of Public Instruction, Olympia, December 18, 1998, in possession of Henry Eisenhardt.

42. Stiefel, interview.

43. Ibid.

44. Arthur Lagawier, transcript of interview, MSCUA/UWL, Acc. 22671-1–6; for quote from daughter Edith Lagawier Bloomfield, see Donna Gordon Blankenship, "Scholar's Passing Noted by Family, Followers," *The Jewish Transcript*, 12 February 1999, p. 28.

45. Stern, interview; *The Jewish Transcript*, 31 May 1948.

46. Aryah Dean Cohen, "Seattle Trio Recalls Aliya Bet Operation," *The Jewish Transcript*, 17 September 1987; Elihu Bergman, "A Post World War II Rescue Misson—The American Role in Illegal Immigration to Palestine," adaptation from a presentation at the U. S. Holocaust Memorial Museum, April 7, 1994; and conversations with Abrams, Bergman, and Neider.

47. Cohen, "Seattle Trio Recalls Aliya Bet Operation."

48. Ship's description from Capt. Rudolph W. Patzert, *Running the Palestine Blockade: The Last Voyage of the Paducah* (Annapolis: Naval Institute Press, 1994).

49. The saga of the *St. Louis* is described in Doris Kearns Goodwin, *No Ordinary Time* (New York: Simon and Schuster, 1994), 102.

50. Motulsky conversation with Molly Cone, April 1999.

51. *Seattle Post-Intelligencer,* 17 January 1982, p. A9.

52. Howe, *World of Our Fathers,* 628.

53. "Noemi's Story" by Noemi Ban and Ray Simmers-Wolpow, copyright 1996, in collection of the Washington State Holocaust Resource Center, Seattle.

54. Gizel Berman, transcript of interview, MSCUA/UWL, Acc. 2993.

55. *Seattle Post-Intelligencer,* 17 December 1980.

56. Stella DeLeon, transcript of interview, MSCUA/UWL, Acc. 1271, 3406.

57. Stern, interview; *The Jewish Transcript,* 12 May 1957.

58. Eva Lassman summary from the Washington State Holocaust Education Resource Center, Seattle.

59. Susan Phinney, "A Survivor's Duty," *Seattle Post-Intelligencer,* 10 February 1997, p. C1.

60. Ibid.

61. *The Seattle Times,* 7 April 1992, p. C1; Henry Friedman summary from the Washington State Holocaust Education Resource Center, Seattle.

62. Howe, *World of Our Fathers,* 628.

63. *The Jewish Transcript,* 24 May 1948.

64. Esfeld, interview.

65. Ibid.

Postwar Growth

1. Richard Lingeman, *Don't You Know There's a War On?* (New York: Putnam, 1970), 323–29; *Eighteenth Decennial Census of the United States: Census of Population: 1960,* vol. 1, Part 49 (Washington D.C.: Government Printing Office, 1963), 198.

2. At the beginning of the Second World War, Seattle's population numbered 399,500, of which about 10,300, 2.6 percent, were affiliated Jews. Seattle's percentage of Jews remained steady over the next four decades. While the city had spread its population both north and south, 85 percent of Seattle's Jews remained heavily concentrated in central Seattle through 1945. One census tract, bordered by Yesler on the south, Marion to the north, and by 15th and 23rd Avenues, was 41 percent Jewish in 1940. By 1963, Seattle's Jewish population had grown to 13,600, mostly from migration from around the United States and Canada, and had scattered to Seward Park, Madison Park, Mount Baker, Magnolia, and the North End. By 1980, Seward Park and suburban Mercer Island contained the heaviest concentrations of the over 19,000 Jews in King County. Lori Cohn (Safir), "Residential Patterns of the Jewish Community of the Seattle Area, 1910–1980," (Master's thesis, University of Washington, 1982), 35, 38, 41.

3. From April 1940 to November 1943, thirty-five states had a net civilian population loss, and the largest gainers were California, Washington, and Oregon, in that order. See Howard A. Droker, "Seattle Race Relations during the Second World War," in *Experiences in a Promised Land: Essays in Pacific Northwest History*, ed. G. Thomas Edwards and Carlos A. Schwantes, (Seattle: University of Washington Press, 1986), 367.

4. Ibid., 353–56. See also Quintard Taylor, *The Forging of a Black Community: Seattle's Central District from 1870 through the Civil Rights Era* (Seattle: University of Washington Press, 1994), chapter 6. The one exception to de facto segregation was in the Seattle Housing Authority's projects at Yesler Terrace, Rainier Vista, Holly Park, and Sand Point. The SHA was led by Jesse Epstein, a Montana-born Jewish lawyer.

5. The African American population grew from 3,789 in 1940, to 15,666 in 1950, 26,901 in 1960, and 37,868 in 1970. In 1950, 69 percent of Seattle's African Americans lived within ten of the city's 118 census tracts in the center of the city; by 1960, 78 percent lived in the same ten tracts. Howard A. Droker, "The Seattle Civic Unity Committee and the Civil Rights Movement, 1944–1964" (Ph.D. diss., University of Washington, 1974), 145–46.

6. Rev. Dr. D. de Sola Pool to Morris Hanan, March 22, 1948, Morris Hanan papers, MSCUA/UWL, Acc. 1827-1.

7. The growing assertiveness of the African American population along with incidents of vandalism against Jewish institutions and businesses in the Central Area made the neighborhood increasingly uncomfortable for Jews.

8. For instance, a Schwabacher daughter married a Bornstein, they changed their name to Boren (coincidentally the name of one of Seattle's founding families), and became Episcopalian. Emilie Schwabacher, transcript of interview, MSCUA/UWL, Acc. 3403-1. The most striking instance of assimilation came later, when Richard Lang, who had served as president of Temple De Hirsch and of the Federated Jewish Fund, left the faith in 1943.

9. Annual Reports of the Washington State Director, 1940, 1942, 1943, 1947, Anti-Defamation League papers, Folder 15, Box 7b, MSCUA/UWL, Acc. 2045.

10. "Greater Seattle Chapter, The American Jewish Committee 1945–1995," commemorative booklet, 1995.

11. 1955 Report on Washington State, Anti-Defamation League papers, Folder 16, Box 7b, MSCUA/UWL, Acc. 2045.

12. Droker, "The Seattle Civic Unity Committee," 103–104.

13. Ibid., chapters 4 and 5.

14. Based on conversations with several doctors and lawyers who requested anonymity.

15. Edwin Kiester, Jr., "The Case of the Missing Executive," American Jewish Committee pamphlet, 1968, American Jewish Committee papers, Folder "Executive Suite Discrimination 1971," Box 2, MSCUA/UWL, Acc. 2788.

16. Samuel Freedman to Peter Schnurman, August 25, 1971. Schnurman filled out the questionnaires attached to the letter. American Jewish Committee papers, Folder "Executive Suite Discrimination 1971," Box 2, MSCUA/UWL, Acc. 2788.

17. Stanley Jacobs to Oscar Cohen (National Anti-Defamation League), January 14, 1951, "Discrimination—Clubs—Washington Athletic Club, Seattle, 1949, 1950, 1951," Anti-Defamation League papers, Box 2, MSCUA/UWL, Acc. 2045.

18. Stanley Jacobs to Oscar Cohen, November 6, 1950, Anti-Defamation League papers, MSCUA/UWL, Acc. 2045.

19. Ibid.

20. Cohen to Jacobs, November 10, 1950, Anti-Defamation League papers, MSCUA/UWL, Acc. 2045.

21. Edelsberg to Oscar Cohen, November 17, 1950, Anti-Defamation League papers, MSCUA/UWL, Acc. 2045.

22. Jacobs to Robinson, December 4, 1950, Anti-Defamation League papers, MSCUA/UWL, Acc. 2045.

23. Rickles to Jacobs, December 6, 1950, Anti-Defamation League papers, MSCUA/UWL, Acc. 2045.

24. Jacobs to Robinson, December 4, 1950, Anti-Defamation League papers, MSCUA/UWL, Acc. 2045.

25. Jacobs to Oscar Cohen, January 8, 1951, Anti-Defamation League papers, MSCUA/UWL, Acc. 2045.

26. Coalition Against Discrimination to Washington Mutual Bank, November 12, 1970, American Jewish Committee papers, Folder "Coalition Against Discrimination 1970," Box 1, MSCUA/UWL, Acc. 2045.

27. State Senators George Fleming and George Scott introduced Coalition Against Discrimination's proposed legislation in February 1971. Senate Bill No. 461, February 9, 1971. At the end of the year, Governor Daniel Evans ordered state employees and agencies not to use exclusionary clubs for official business, and he called a special session of the legislature in early 1972 to pass the law. Governor Evans enjoyed wide support from the state's newspapers. "Showdown on the Clubs," editorial in *Bremerton Sun*, 26 November 1971; "Make Them Pay," editorial in *Pullman Daily Evergreen*, 23 November 1971; and "Evans and Clubs," editorial in *Seattle Post-Intelligencer*, 23 November 1971.

28. Schroeter to Oscar Cohen, May 4, 1953, Anti-Defamation League papers, Folder "Public Schools—Church-State Issues—Released Time—Washington State—1953, 1954, 1955, 1959," Box 2, MSCUA/UWL, Acc. 2045.

29. Henry Feingold found that released time started on the East Coast in 1923 and that Jews, particularly Orthodox Jews, participated in the program. Henry L. Feingold, *A Time for Searching: Entering the Mainstream* (Baltimore: The Johns Hopkins University Press, 1992), 121–22.

30. Schroeter to Sol Rabkin, November 23, 1953, Anti-Defamation League papers, Folder "Public Schools—Church-State Issues—Released Time—Washington State—1953, 1954, 1955, 1959," Box 2, MSCUA/UWL, Acc. 2045.

31. Rabkin to Schroeter, November 27, 1953, Anti-Defamation League papers, MSCUA/UWL, Acc. 2045.

32. Clipping from *The Tacoma News Tribune*, 6 November 1953, Anti-Defamation League papers, MSCUA/UWL, Acc. 2045.

33. Schnurman to State Superintendent of Education, November 30, 1971; Schnurman to Mercer Island School Superintendent, December 17, 1971; Schnurman to Seattle School Superintendent, December 17, 1971; Schnurman and Seymour Kaplan, Anti-Defamation League Executive Director, to Seattle School Superintendent, December

29, 1971 (sending calendar of Jewish holidays); all in American Jewish Committee papers, Folder "Church-State 1971," MSCUA/UWL, Acc. 2788.

34. Schnurman to Alfred Cowles, September 27, 1971; Schurman to Neil Sandberg, November 27, 1971, American Jewish Committee papers, MSCUA/UWL, Acc. 2788.

35. Schnurman to Rabinove, December 15, 1971, American Jewish Committee papers, MSCUA/UWL, Acc. 2788.

36. *The Seattle Times*, 22 January 1971.

37. Joint Statement of the American Jewish Committee, Anti-Defamation League, and Community Relations Department of the Jewish Federated Fund, American Jewish Committee papers, Folder "Church-State 1971," Box 1, MSCUA/UWL, Acc. 2788.

38. Rabinove to Schnurman, February 16 and 22, 1971; Sandberg to Rabinove, February 19, 1971, American Jewish Committee papers, MSCUA/UWL, Acc. 2788.

39. "Report of the Committee on Community Council," Jewish Federation Records, Box 1–8, MSCUA/UWL, Acc. 3051, 3051-2.

40. 1955 Report, Anti-Defamation League papers, Folder 16, Box 7b, MSCUA/UWL, Acc. 2045.

41. Ibid.

42. Ibid.

43. Albert Franco, transcript of interview, MSCUA/UWL, Acc. 2834; Harry Ash, transcript of interview, MSCUA/UWL, Acc. 3520.

44. Davis to Melville Monheimer, March 27, 1949, Jewish Federation Records, MSCUA/UWL, Acc. 3051.

45. Articles of Incorporation, Seattle Jewish Community Center, July 6, 1949, Jewish Federation Records, MSCUA/UWL, Acc. 3051.

46. Herbert Rosen, transcript of interview, MSCUA/UWL, Acc. 3506-1.

47. Albert Schrieber, University of Washington Professor of Business Administration, "Basic Facility Study," 1963, Jewish Federation Records, MSCUA/UWL, Acc. 3051.

48. Ibid.

49. Ibid.

50. Leo Okin, transcript of interview, MSCUA/UWL, Acc. 3529-1. After fifteen years as executive director, Okin left the Jewish Community Center as a very controversial figure. He has great supporters and bitter enemies. But all agree that Okin was most responsible for developing much of the leadership of the Jewish community in the 1970s, 1980s, and 1990s. Interviews with Robert Miller, Herbert Rosen, and Martin Rind, MSCUA/UWL, Acc. 3513-1, 3506-1, 3603-1.

51. "Report of the Program and Facility Needs Committee," February 17, 1965, Jewish Federation Records, MSCUA/UWL, Acc. 3051.

52. Merle Cohn, conversation with Howard Droker, November 19, 1998.

53. Charles Kaplan, transcript of interview, MSCUA/UWL, Acc. 3425-1.

54. Okin, interview.

55. Herb Rosen speech, May 16, 1971, Jewish Federation Records, MSCUA/UWL, Acc. 3051.

56. The most generous philanthropists failed to make the size of gifts that were required for the campaign to succeed. Some felt the addition was unnecessary; others believed it

was not feasible at the time because they doubted the community's willingness to pay for it. Most of the big givers had moved up from the Jewish Community Center Board to the Jewish Federation Board and, therefore, had a different, perhaps wider perspective than the younger activists on the Jewish Community Center Board.

57. Eddie Fisher, transcript of interview, MSCUA/UWL, Acc. 3505-1.

58. Stroum took on the leadership role despite pressure from Seafirst, on whose board he sat, not to become personally involved. In addition, he was the general chairman of the 1982 United Way campaign.

59. Samuel Stroum, transcript of interview, MSCUA/UWL, Acc. 3519-1.

60. Ibid.

61. Letters to the editor from Adina Angle, Frank Lippman, Paula Schwimmer, and Amy Stephson, *The Jewish Transcript*, 30 June 1988, p. 4, and letter to the editor from Albert Feldman, *The Jewish Transcript*, 21 July 1988, p. 5.

62. The early history of Hillel is based on Reva Twersky's three-part series, "History of Hillel at the University of Washington," in *WSJHS Newsletter* (June, August, and October, 1992).

63. *Hillel Collegian*, 1947, Hillel records, MSCUA/UWL, Acc. 2338-2.

64. Neal Groman, transcript of interview, p. 16, MSCUA/UWL, Acc. 3418.

65. Arthur Jacobovitz, transcript of interview, MSCUA/UWL, Acc. 3786.

66 Groman, interview, p. 18.

67. Jacobovitz, interview.

68. Ibid.

69. Groman, interview, pp. 4, 5.

70. Ibid., pp. 8–12.

71. Jacobovitz et al. to Dr. William L. Phillips, Associate Dean of Arts and Sciences, March 31, 1969, Neal Groman papers, MSCUA/UWL, Acc. 3418-002.

72. Phillips to Jacobovitz, May 2, 1969; Phillips to various department heads, June 17, 1969, Neal Groman papers, MSCUA/UWL, Acc. 3418-002.

73. Minutes of Judaic Studies Steering Committee, November 10, 1969, Neal Groman papers, MSCUA/UWL, Acc. 3418-002.

74. Alexander to Groman, November 12, 1969, Neal Groman papers, MSCUA/UWL, Acc. 3418-002.

75. Draft of a letter to Albert Franco, Chair of Community Relations Division, Jewish Federation of Greater Seattle, Spring 1970; Groman outline, September 2, 1982; Neal Groman papers, MSCUA/UWL, Acc. 3418-002.

76. Groman, notes of meeting with Kaminsky and Alexander, February 16, 1971, Neal Groman papers, MSCUA/UWL, Acc. 3418-002.

77. Groman, notes of May 17, 1971, meeting at Hillel, Neal Groman papers, MSCUA/UWL, Acc. 3418-002.

Expanding Religious Life

1. Lucy S. Davidowicz, *On Equal Terms: Jews in America, 1881–1981* (New York: Holt, Rinehart, and Winston, 1982).

2. Edward S. Shapiro, *A Time for Healing, American Jewry Since World War II* (Baltimore: The John Hopkins University Press, 1992), 189; Henry L. Feingold, *A Time for Searching: Entering the Mainstream* (Baltimore: The Johns Hopkins University Press, 1992).

3. Meyer Elkins with updates by Julia Eulenberg and Rhoda Lewis, "Richland, Washington: 1950–1985," WSJHS *Newsletter* (February 1985): 1–9; conversations of Molly Cone and Jackie Williams with Rhoda Lewis, Richland, Wash., 1998; *The Jewish Transcript*, 24 February 1958, p. 7.

4. Molly Cone conversation with Rhoda Lewis, 1998.

5. Temple Beth Am, "Preliminary Time Line, 1955–1982," created from existing scrapbooks by Beth Am staff; conversations with founding members Jeannette Schrieber, Morrie Shurman, and Gerald Cone, 1998 and 1999; Minutes, March 20, April 17, and May 1, 1956, Temple De Hirsch Sinai, Box 3, MSCUA/UWL, Acc. 2370, 2370-4.

6. Temple Beth Am, "Preliminary Time Line, 1955–1982."

7. *The Jewish Transcript*, 14 November 1960, p. 1.

8. Raphael Levine, transcript of interview, 1970, MSCUA/UWL, Acc. 2016, 2532-6; Ray Ruppert, "Unity and Diversity," *The Seattle Times Magazine*, 21 November 1976, p. 8; John Wolcott, "The Work of God's 'Healer' Continues," *The Progress*, 19 September 1985, p. 8; Lorraine Sidell, "Rabbi Levine's Papers Make Fascinating Reading," *The Jewish Transcript*, 25 September 1986, p. 13A.

9. Ruppert, "Unity and Diversity," p. 8.

10. Don Duncan, "'All Faiths' Cleric Succumbs," *The Seattle Times*, 4 November 1985, p. A1.

11. "Guide," Congregation Ezra Bessaroth, MSCUA/UWL, Acc. 2739-4; *The Jewish Transcript*, 2 September 1957 and 28 July 1958.

12. "History of Sephardic Bikur Holim," MSCUA/UWL, Acc. 2389-5.

13. Ibid.

14. Adina Russak, "History of Yavneh," WSJHS *Newsletter*, Part 1 (winter 1996), and Part 2 (spring 1997); Lorraine Sidell, "Bikur Cholim Machzikay Hadath," WSJHS *Newsletter*, Part 2 (November 1991).

15. Russak, "History of Yavneh," Part 2. See also *The Jewish Transcript*, 3 December 1962, p. 1.

16. Sidell, "Bikur Cholim Machzikay Hadath," Part 2.

17. Ibid.

18. Jane A. Avner, "The History of Congregation Beth Shalom," WSJHS *Newsletter*, summer 1993; Jerome Becker, transcript of interview, MSCUA/UWL, Acc. 3210, 3210-2.

19. Avner, "The History of Congregation Beth Shalom."

20. Becker, interview.

21. Avner, "The History of Congregation Beth Shalom."

22. Rosalie Sidell Steinbrecher, "The History of Emanuel Congregation," WSJHS *Newsletter* (fall 1993).

23. Ibid.

24. Ibid.; conversation with Rosalie Sidell Steinbrecher, April 1999.

25. Becker, interview; *Ner Tamid Hi-Lites*, 1 November 1968; *The Jewish Transcript*, 6 December 1965.

26. Conversations with Sid Weiner and Manny Lott, Mercer Island, Wash. Two doorplates designed by Phillip Levine for Ner Tamid were transferred to the Mercer Island synagogue in the Herzl and Ner Tamid merger.

27. Temple De Hirsch Sinai Fact Sheet, Special Collections and University Archive Inventory Folder, MSCUA/UWL, Acc. 2370; *The Jewish Transcript*, 27 April 1959 and 24 November 1960.

28. Marta Hurwitz, "The History of Temple B'Nai Torah," *WSJHS Newsletter* (spring 1994); Raida Singer, transcript of interview, MSCUA/UWL, Acc. 3819.

29. Hurwitz, "The History of Temple B'Nai Torah."

30. Ibid.

31. "The Jewish Experience in Washington State, A Chronology, 1853–1995" (Seattle: Washington State Jewish Historical Society, 1998); "Guide to Jewish Washington, 1995–1996," a booklet published by *The Jewish Transcript*, 1996.

32. America's Chabad-Lubavitch organization is one of several sects that grew out of the original Chassidic movement founded in the eighteenth century by a charismatic rabbi known as the Ba'al Shem Tov (Master of the Good Name of God). Rabbi Menachem Mendel Schneersohn of New York pioneered the Chabad-Lubavitch movement in America in the latter half of the twentieth century so successfully that many Lubavitcher members looked upon him as the true Messiah.

33. Rabbi Richard Rosenthal, transcript of interview, MSCUA/UWL, Acc. 4052.

34. Conversation with Josephine Kleiner Heiman, Tacoma, June 1999.

35. Conversation with Rhoda Lewis, Richland, Wash., June 1999.

36. Temple Beth El, *Centuries to Celebrate* (Tacoma: Temple Beth El, 1992).

37. Rosenthal, interview.

38. Betty Meyersberg, transcript of interview, Spokane Jewish community, Ms. 151 (OH-812), Eastern Washington State Historical Society, Cheney Cowles Museum.

39. C. E. Huppin papers, MSCUA/UWL, Acc. 3640. See also David M. Buerge and Junius Rochester, *Roots and Branches* (Seattle: Church Council of Greater Seattle, 1988), 232.

40. Ibid. See also *Spokane Daily Chronicle*, 29 March 1966.

41. C. E. Huppin papers, MSCUA/UWL, Acc. 3640.

42. Ibid.

43. This and the following text on Olympia is from Ron Manheimer and Carol Manheimer, "Olympia," *WSJHS Newsletter* (September 1983), and Eva Goldberg, "A History of Temple Beth Hatfiloh" (expanded and revised by Lois Roselle and Daniel Roselle in 1995), Eva Goldberg papers, MSCUA/UWL, Acc. 3777-2-3.

44. Manheimer and Manheimer, "Olympia"; Goldberg, "A History of Temple Beth Hatfiloh," Eva Goldberg papers, MSCUA/UWL, Acc. 3777-2-3.

45. Ibid.

46. Goldberg, "A History of Temple Beth Hatfiloh," Eva Goldberg papers, MSCUA/UWL, Acc. 3777-2-3.

47. Ibid.

48. Tim Baker, "Unofficial History of Beth Israel Synagogue," *The Bellingham Shul Shofar*, September 1996.

49. Ibid. The question posed to Garmo refers to the czarist myth, commonly called "the blood libel."

50. Ibid.

51. Craig Degginger, "Dwindling Congregation Will Force the Sale of Jewish Synagogue," *The Jewish Transcript*, 22 November 1991. See also Adath Israel papers, MSCUA/UWL, Acc. 3165.

52. Schwartz quote from Degginger, "Dwindling Congregation Will Force the Sale of Jewish Synagogue."

53. Alan L. Barer papers, MSCUA/UWL, Acc. 4408. See also Benjamin Rigberg, *Walla Walla: Judaism in a Rural Setting* (Los Angeles: Western States Jewish History Association, 2001), 69.

54. Alan L. Barer papers, MSCUA/UWL, Acc. 4408.

55. Moe Michelson, transcript of interview, MSCUA/UWL, Acc. 3661; William Sturman, transcript of interview, MSCUA/UWL, Acc. 3663.

56. Carey Quan Gelernter, "This Growing Cluster of Liberal Jews Welcomes Interfaith Couples," *Seattle Post-Intelligencer*, 8 December 1985.

57. Donna Gordon Blakenship, ed., "Guide to Jewish Washington, 1999–2000" published by *The Jewish Transcript*.

Arts in the Postwar Years

1. Phillip Levine created the Eternal Light in Temple Beth Am's original building, doorplates for Congregation Ner Tamid, and the Torah Ark for Herzl Ner Tamid on Mercer Island; Edith Weinstein, brass plates for Temple Beth Am's Torah Tables; Estelle Bensussen, Ark panels for Sephardic Bikur Holim at Twentieth Avenue and East Fir Street; Gizel Berman, Holocaust Memorial at Jewish Community Center; Erika Michael, design for needlepoint tapestry, Temple Beth Am; Israel Nudelman, Torah Ark for Congregation Beth Israel in Aberdeen; Irma Arick, decorative hanging for Temple Beth Shalom in Spokane; and Kalee Kirschenbaum, cover drawing for Temple Beth El's publication *Centuries to Celebrate*.

2. *The Jewish Transcript*, 23 November 1934.

3. *WSJHS Newsletter* (May 1989). For more information about Priteca, see Jeffrey Karl Ochsner, ed., *Shaping Seattle Architecture* (Seattle: University of Washington Press, 1994), 180–86; and Dean Arthur Tarrach, "Alexander Pantages: The Seattle Pantages and His Vaudeville Circuit" (Master's thesis, University of Washington, 1973), 68–71.

4. Anne G. Todd, "Applebaum Captures Seascape," *The Seattle Times*, 15 January 1961.

5. University of Washington Archives of Northwest Art, MSCUA/UWL, Acc. 2897-2.

6. Regina Hackett, "A Memorial Uses Beauty to Remind Us of Holocaust," *Seattle Post-Intelligencer*, 4 May 1985; University of Washington Archives of Northwest Art, MSCUA/UWL, Acc. 2897-2.

7. Maria Frank Abrams, transcript of interview, MSCUA/UWL, Acc. 2556-2.

8. *The Jewish Transcript*, 18 August 1952.

9. Meade Emory, "Joanna Eckstein, A Feared and Revered Arts Patron," *The Seattle Weekly*, November 12, 1983.

10. Anne Gerber, transcript of interview, MSCUA/UWL, Acc. 3620.

11. Thelma Lehman, transcript of interview, MSCUA/UWL, Acc. 2554-2.

12. Charles Alhadeff, transcript of interview, MSCUA/UWL, Acc. 3290.

13. Norman Davis, "Doings and Writings," Box 1, MSCUA/UWL, Acc. 2661-7–8.

14. Manfred Selig, summary of taped interview (portion about art collecting cannot be heard), MSCUA/UWL, Acc. 3134.

15. We do not have the space to report the many books written by faculty members at all the universities in Washington State, and we have therefore decided to limit this section to nonacademic writing.

16. Information about Alice B. Toklas is from Linda Simon, *The Biography of Alice B. Toklas* (New York: Doubleday & Company, Inc., 1977).

17. *The Jewish Transcript*, 22 November 1935, 29 January 1932, and 18 November 1932.

18. Program, Seattle Poetry Club, May 26, 1927, Fred Bergman papers, Box 2, MSCUA/UWL, Acc. 2975-005.

19. Felicity Barringer, "Meg Greenfield, Shaper of *Washington Post* Editorial Page," *New York Times*, 14 May 1999, p. A23.

20. Susie M. Friedman, "Writings of Susie Friedman," MSCUA/UWL, Acc. 2115-2.

21. Newspaper clippings, Leon Israel papers, nonaccessioned, MSCUA/UWL.

22. Esther W. Campbell, *Bagpipes in the Woodwind Section: A History of the Seattle Symphony Orchestra and Its Women's Association* (Seattle: Seattle Symphony Women's Association, 1978), 76.

23. R. M. Campbell, "French Conductor Returns to the Town that Ousted Him," *The Seattle Times*, 20 September 1985, p. 3.

24. Campbell, *Bagpipes in the Woodwind Section*, 89.

25. Gustave Stern, transcript of interview, MSCUA/UWL, Acc. 3053.

26. New Dimensions in Music, Box 1, MSCUA/UWL, Acc. 1544-3.

27. Melinda Bargree, "Mideast Meets West through New Sounds," *The Seattle Times*, 29 September 1984, p. C6.

28. Ibid.

29. *Spokane Spokesman-Review*, 1960, and undated newspaper clippings to Jacqueline Williams from Nate Grossman, Spokane.

30. Interview with Rose Thal, widow of Arthur Thal, and son, Rabbi Lennard Thal, son of Arthur Thal, by Tim Baker, Bellingham, Wash., May 26, 1998.

31. E-mail correspondence with Jacqueline Williams from Tim Baker, May 21 and June 25, 1998. Baker interviewed Glass in Bellingham, Wash.

32. *Bellingham Herald*, 15 December 1979; *Vancouver (B.C.) Jewish Western Bulletin*, 20 April 1951, Passover edition.

33. *The Jewish Transcript*, 13 July 1959 and 17 August 1959.

INDEX

Photos are indicated with bold type. Caption information is indicated with "c," notes with "n," and information in the shaded boxes with "sb."